P9-BZO-010

889258

Tyler
is
gay

yes i agree

Terry Fox Secondary School		
NAME	DIV.	YEAR
		1998
Matt Alexander		

Hi

Canada Revisited

A Social and Political History of Canada to 1911

PENNEY CLARK &
ROBERTA McKAY

兒,
I LOVE YOU
4EVER BEBE
JAY愛你

Arnold Publishing Ltd.

Copyright © 1992 Arnold Publishing Ltd.

ALL RIGHTS RESERVED
No part of this book may be reproduced or transmitted in any form or by any means without permission in writing from the publisher. Reproducing passages by electrostatic, photographic, or mechanical means, including mimeographing and photocopying, recording, or by any information storage and retrieval system, is an infringement of copyright law. This applies to classroom usage as well.

Arnold Publishing Ltd.
Suite 101, 10301–104 Street
Edmonton, Alberta, Canada, T5J 1B9
TEL: (403) 426-2998
1-800-563-2665
FAX: (403) 426-4607

Authors: Penney Clark and Roberta McKay

Canadian Cataloguing in Publication Data
Clark, Penney I., 1950–
Canada Revisited

Includes index.
ISBN 0-919913-32-6

1. Canada—History—Juvenile Literature.
2. Canada—Social conditions—Juvenile Literature.
I. McKay, Roberta, 1951–
II. Title.
FC172.M234 1992 971 C91–091547–4
F1008.2.M234 1992

Project Team
Developmental Editor: Phyllis A. Arnold
Editors: Kathleen Vanderlinden, Tim Heath
Validation: Dr. David Mills, Department of History,
   University of Alberta
Design, Illustrations & Cover: Jill Murrin
Chapter Overview Illustrations: Shelah Ruth
Cartography: Wendy Johnson
Index: Kathy Garnsworthy
Photo Research: Kathleen Vanderlinden
Production Director: Jill Murrin
Production: Pauline Herms, Jill Murrin, Michael Burgess
Proofreaders: Barbara Demers, Carole Howrish

Manufacturers: Quality Color Press Inc., Colour Images
   Graphics Inc.

Printed and bound in Canada
Second Printing: 1993
28 000 copies in print

Additional Writings
The following people have contributed to this textbook:

Phyllis Arnold: An Inquiry Model, **p. viii, ix**; The Plains People, **p. 9-10**; the Iroquois, **p. 11-13**; Working with Information, **p. 16, 56, 86**; Building Thinking Strategies, **p. 17, 39, 87**; Exploration and Mercantilism Chart, **p. 23**; Colonization, **p. 26-27**; The Establishment of the Royal Colony: 1663 and Royal Government, **p. 44-45**; Royal Government Chart, **p. 47**; Louisbourg, **p. 64-65**; A Decision-Making Model, **p. 67**; An Exercise in Decision-Making, **p. 67, 72, 81, 121, 181, 187, 219, 220**; An Exercise in Critical Thinking, **p. 75-77, 81, 85, 247**; An Exercise in Problem Solving, **p. 79, 110, 113**; An Exercise in Creative Thinking, **p. 226**; Alternatives Open to the British, **p. 80**; The Proclamation of 1763, **p. 82**; The Quebec Act, 1774, **p. 84**; The Native People, **p. 113**; Government Structure, **p. 120**; Government Chart, **p. 141, 153**; Simulation, A New Home, **p. 144-147, 156**; Definition Review, **p. 162**; The Act of Union, 1841, **p. 164**; Responsible Government, **p. 166**; The Gold Rush, **p. 224-225**; Indian Act, 1876, **p. 238**; Seven Treaties, **p. 246**.

Phyllis Arnold and Elaine Chalus: Key Definitions, **p. xi**, Section I Story, **p. 2-3**; Chapter 1 copy for **p. 6-8**; Section II Story, **p. 40-41**; Colbert, **p. 46**.

Phyllis Arnold and Kathleen Vanderlinden: Cultural Groups in Canada, **p. 203**; Turn-of the Century Immigrants, **p. 263-265**.

Brenda Bellingham: The Last Spike, **p. 242-243**.

Dr. David Mills: Overviews, **p. 4, 18-19, 42-43, 58-59, 90, 100, 132-133, 160-161, 178-179, 206-207, 234-235**.

Tim Heath: Margeurite d'Youville, **p. 57**.

Nancy Sellars Marcotte: Choices to Make! New France–1672, **p. 52-53**, Montcalm and Wolfe, **p. 74**, Patriots and Tories, **p. 101**; Life in the Province of Canada, **p. 167**, After the Rebellions, **p. 168-171**; Education and Ryerson, **p. 172**; Glossary, **p. 274-277**.

Nancy Sellars Marcotte and Kathleen Vanderlinden: captions for photographs, illustrations, and maps.

The following is referred to throughout this book:

Ordinary People in Alberta's Past, by Nancy Sellars Marcotte, **ISBN 0-919913-28-8**, published by Arnold Publishing Ltd.

Table of Contents

Acknowledgements

We would particularly like to express our gratitude to our publisher, Phyllis A. Arnold, who has provided us with support, advice, and a friendship through the many years it has taken this project to come to fruition.

We would like to extend our thanks as well to the talented members of the editiorial, design, and production team at Arnold Publishing. Their creativity and resourcefulness were greatly appreciated.

Finally, our thanks go to our husbands, without whom we would not have seen the humour in the often frustrating and always demanding task of writing a textbook.

Penney Clark
Roberta McKay
March 1992

Dedicated to Hugh Clark

Consultants

HISTORICAL CONSULTANT
Dr. David Mills
Department of History
University of Alberta
Edmonton, Alberta

EDUCATIONAL CONSULTANTS
Elaine Chalus
Department of History
University of Alberta
Edmonton, Alberta

Bill Larkin
The Board of Education
For the Borough of East York
Toronto, Ontario

Ken Osborne
Faculty of Education
The University of Manitoba
Winnipeg, Manitoba

Validators

FIELD VALIDATORS
George Adams
History Department Head
Notre Dame Secondary School
Brampton, Ontario

Angelo Bolotta
Coordinator of Social Sciences
Metropolitan Separate Schools of Toronto
Toronto, Ontario

Tony Burley
Coordinator of Instruction
Red Deer Public School District #104
Red Deer, Alberta

Dr. Bryan Connors
Supervisor, Consultant Services
Edmonton Public Schools
Edmonton, Alberta

Elspeth Deir
Instructor, Faculty of Education
Queen's University
Kingston, Ontario

John Johnston
Vice Principal
Central Junior High School
Red Deer Public School District #104
Red Deer, Alberta

Dr. Barry Gough
Wilfrid Laurier University
Waterloo, Ontario
(Chapters 1 to 3)
Native Validation

FIELD TESTING
Olga Curtis
Teacher
(1992: Grade 8-4, 8-5, 8-7)
Vernon Barford Junior High School
Edmonton, Alberta

Terry Gerling
Teacher
(1992: Grade 8-1, 8-3, and 8-6)
Vernon Barford Junior High School
Edmonton, Alberta

Pat Shields
Teacher
(1992: Grade 8-2 and 8-8)
Vernon Barford Junior High School
Edmonton, Alberta

To the Student

Focus of the Text

Canada Revisited has been developed to trace Canada's history from the time of the First People as they lived prior to European exploration through the years to the first part of the twentieth century. Wherever possible the information is arranged chronologically—in the order in which the events happened. Each chapter is organized around one or more of four key ideas: power, co-operation, decision-making, and conflict.

We have made Canada's history interesting and relevant to you. Our past contains many exciting events and fascinating individuals. The focus of *Canada Revisited* is on the development of government in Canada and how it affected the lives of the people who lived during each particular era. It is a social, political, and economic history of Canada.

In a few years you will be voting. You will, through your work and daily life, be influenced by government policies. Fortunately you live in a country where you can directly influence the government and make this a better place in which to live.

To make a particular period of history personally meaningful to you and to give you the feeling of "revisiting Canadian history," photo essays, works of art, original stories, and excerpts from historical documents have been utilized. You will be drawn into historical situations through role play, simulations, debates, critical-thinking exercises, and decision-making exercises. These techniques to have you "revisit" Canadian historical eras are usually found prior to discussion of major political changes. In this way you can become actively involved in an event, often making predictions of outcomes. Then, through reading of the textual materials, you will find out what actually happened.

Explanation of Terms

In the first chapter of *Canada Revisited,* you will learn that there were many groups of people with quite different lifestyles living in Canada before Europeans came. These people have been called Native people. The term Native includes all aboriginal peoples (Indians, Inuit, Metis) in Canada. In this book, Native peoples may also be called First People, or First Nations. The term Indian refers to status and non-status Indians. People whose ancestors came from Europe have been identified throughout *Canada Revisited* as Europeans, Caucasians, or non-Natives.

The term *Canadien* (spelled with an *e*) refers to French-speaking people in the colony of Quebec and in British North America up until 1867. After 1867 and the creation of Canada, the term *Canadien* has been replaced with the term French-speaking.

At different times in Canada's history many parts of the country have had different names. For example, Cape Breton Island was previously known as Île Royale. Most of the country north and west of the Great Lakes was known as the North-West Territories until 1905. The name and its spelling varied with time, but to avoid confusion, we have consistently used the spelling North-West Territories. (Remember that the Northwest Territories of Canada as they exist today include the most northern part of the former North-West Territories.)

In Conclusion: We have included in *Canada Revisited* features and activities that are enjoyed by people with very different learning styles, so you should find activities in *Canada Revisited* that match your interests. Good luck, have fun, and enjoy your study of Canadian history.

An Inquiry Model for Carrying Out Research

At various locations throughout this textbook you will be asked to solve problems and/or issues. To make your research easier, follow the seven-step inquiry model below, or use one of the models presented later in the textbook. You may decide to design and use your own inquiry model.

Step One: Focusing on the issue or problem to research.

Make a list of questions about the issue or problem. Make your topic narrow enough that it's manageable. Issues involve controversy. Problems ask: who, what, when, where, why or how.

Step Two: Organizing and planning your research.

Decide on the Steps to follow in organizing your information. This plan of action may be in point form or chart form. It may be a time line, a list, or a graphic organizer. For issues: list possible alternatives from which you will later have to choose. Decide on possible sub-topics to study.

Step Three: Locating the information you'll need for your research.

Decide on what type of information you'll need and where you'll find it. Some places information will be found are: textbooks, reference books, graphs, tables, charts, maps, data bases, by interviewing people, or by doing surveys.

Step Four: Recording the information that is related to your research topic.

By following the procedures outlined in Step 2, gather and record the information that is related to your research topic. Do not record information that is off the topic and that doesn't relate to the issue or problem. To record the information you may take notes, make webs, mind maps, or charts, draw pictures or diagrams.

Step Five: Evaluating the information you collected.

Go through all the information you have collected. Organize and summarize and then decide: Do you have enough information to solve the issue or problem? Or, do you have to do more research?

Step Six: Concluding the issue or problem you researched.

Read through your research materials. Make connections, look for relationships, form conclusions. For issues, examine the alternatives you listed in the organizer step (Step 2). Study each alternative. List some consequences for each alternative. Categorize the consequences as positive or negative. Rank order each alternative from most desirable to least desirable. For problems, check to see that you have actually solved it and that your conclusions make sense.

Step Seven: Applying and communicating your conclusions to others.

Assess your plan of action. Make predictions. Check to see whether your conclusions can be applied to other situations. Explain to others your research procedures and findings through a written or oral report using drawings or charts.

An Inquiry Model for Carrying Out Research

1. Focusing on the issue or the problem to research
2. Organizing and planning your research
3. Locating the information you'll need for your research
4. Recording the information that is related to your research topic
5. Evaluating the information you collected
6. Concluding the issue or problem you researched
7. Applying and Communicating your conclusions to others

Key Definitions

Icons

Power, Co-operation, Decision-Making, and Conflict

Throughout *Canada Revisited,* four main concepts will be emphasized. They are power, co-operation, decision-making, and conflict. These concepts will be repeated throughout the textbook. Icons indicate their presence, even if they are not mentioned in a particular paragraph. The use of the icon will help you to identify which of these concepts is the main focus of the material you are reading.

Power

Power

The icon used for power shows a bull. The bull was chosen since it is an international icon for power. Power is:

- commanding people's obedience with or without their agreement
- deciding who gets what
- giving or refusing to give rewards
- using superior strength and authority

There is another way to look at power. People give you power because they trust you to use it well. They believe that you will use the power that they gave you to make life better or easier, or that you will use it to benefit society in general.

Co-operation

Co-operation

The icon used in this textbook for co-operation shows a hand, meaning to shake hands as a symbol of co-operation. Co-operation is:

- working with other people to achieve a common goal
- sharing thoughts and then building upon these ideas
- using the strengths of different individuals to complement each other
- trusting each other
- implying that the team matters, as well as the individual
- agreeing that not everyone gets the same thing or does the same thing

Decision-Making

Decision-making

The icon for decision-making shows someone thinking or making a decision. Decision-making is:

- finding a solution for a problem and/or issue that involves a choice and a decision for action

Conflict

Conflict

The icon for conflict shows a rope tied into a knot. Conflict is:

- a struggle between conflicting forces
- a clash between individuals, groups, or societies holding opposing ideas, interests, or ways of life
- a battle or a war
- a tense situation

Conflict is natural since people often disagree. It can lead to open protest or rebellion. Canada has experienced both in the course of its history. More recently, however, groups of individuals holding conflicting ideas about political or social issues (such as Native rights to self-government or anti-smoking laws) have joined together to form lobby groups. These groups try to persuade the voters and the law-makers to favour their specific side of a controversial issue.

Icon—pictorial representation

Section I
Early Development and Colonization
to 1670

Hi! I'm Jim. Last spring my sister Heather, my mom and dad, and I had a really difficult time working out our vacation plans. We couldn't seem to arrive at a decision. Mom has only two weeks off, in July, from her position on the band council. She wanted to divide the time between camping and visiting our grandparents on their reserve in northern British Columbia. Luckily, Dad has the summer off because he is a teacher. As long as he could spend July at his summer course at the university, he was happy to do whatever the rest of us wanted on our holidays. Heather wanted to go to the mountains and take a rock-climbing course at Mount Yamnuska. She didn't really want to go to the reserve. I just wanted to go backpacking in the mountains and use my new camera.

Now, don't get me wrong. The four of us are a relatively close family. We all camp and hike. So you see, our problem wasn't that we didn't share each other's interests; it was just that we had different

plans for the holidays. Mom pointed out to us that it was normal for each of us to prefer different things, but that we should try to work out some sort of compromise. She explained that if we each gave up a part of what we wanted, then perhaps we could reach an agreement, a compromise she called it, that would make everyone happy.

We sat in the backyard the next evening and tried to arrive at a compromise. Heather's rock-climbing course was a week long. I wanted to hike the Skyline Trail, but that takes a week and it's not a good idea to do it alone. If we were to visit our grandparents and camp on the way to their reserve and back, it would also take over a week. If we were to do every-

thing that we wanted it would take longer than Mom's holidays. It wasn't long before we were talking all at once, and no one seemed to be arriving at any compromise. We all seemed to be stubbornly trying to defend our positions.

We decided to take a vote to figure out what to do. We decided that the majority would win. Mom voted for visiting her parents. Heather voted for rock climbing, and I voted for backpacking. Dad didn't vote because he would be happy with any of our choices. So much for voting! We were no further ahead.

It was at this point that Grandfather Cardinal came over. He's an elder on the reserve and knows much about the old ways. He suggested that we try using a Native consensus model to help us arrive at a decision. He explained that consensus means general agreement and had been used by the Native people for thousands of years in making decisions that would make everyone happy.

Grandfather suggested that we should look at the issue again, but this time we should try following four steps. First, each of us should tell our true feelings and our personal reasons for why we want to spend our holidays the way we do. We shouldn't hold anything back, he said, nor criticize each other. We should all listen very carefully to what the other person is saying. Then he suggested that we should keep talking, and talking, and talking until we all understand and until we can see the issue from the other person's point of view.

Secondly, we should each identify the main issues and the concerns we have. We should be careful not to stubbornly defend or take a definite position, but we should instead be looking at the issues.

Thirdly, we should look at our original options again and then we should consider new options.

Finally, we should try coming up with a solution that is acceptable to everyone involved. If just one person is slightly unhappy, then we should continue talking and go through the steps again. Grandfather said we should keep going through the consensus model, even if it takes us days to arrive at an agreement. In the end, everyone should be totally content with the solution.

We followed the wise advice of Grandfather Cardinal. We debated all of the options for hours. We talked about our feelings and our reasons for wanting our holiday plans to come first. Gradually we began to look at the holiday from the other person's point of view. We really began to see how the other person felt. All of us began to understand that, if we each got our own way,

then the other person might lose out and would be unhappy. I realized how selfish I was being when I heard Heather speak of mountain climbing. She had such a dreamy look in her eyes that I understood how important her plans were to her. It wasn't until Mom talked that I realized she hadn't seen her parents for over two years. I knew we had to visit the reserve. I looked at Heather; her expression told me that she too felt as I did.

Following Grandfather Cardinal's suggestions had made us look at the issue. How could we best plan our holiday so that everyone was happy without each of us standing firm, as we had done when we voted? We decided that we wanted to spend the holiday as a family. All of us would try to work around each other's plans. We discussed our original options and looked at what new ones were available to us. It wasn't long before we had arrived at a consensus that was acceptable to everyone. Grandfather Cardinal certainly knew what he was talking about! ■

Questions to Talk About

Discuss the following questions by referring to the story you have just read. Keep them in mind while you read the following chapter. At the end of the chapter you will be asked to answer these questions on the basis of the information you have gained from your reading.

1. Who makes the decisions in decision-making by consensus?
2. Why is it important to arrive at a consensus that is acceptable to everyone involved?
3. Why is it important to look at an issue from the other person's point of view?
4. Why is it important to identify the main issues and concerns, rather than being stubborn or taking a definite position on the issue?
5. Would decision-making by consensus become more or less difficult if the number of people involved in the decision were increased?
6. In your opinion which are better: decisions by general agreement (consensus) or decisions by one individual?

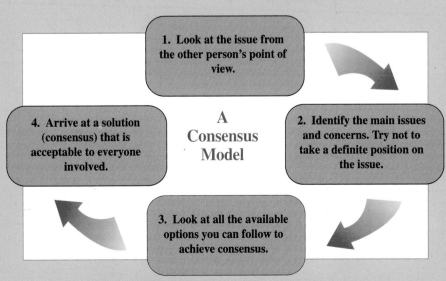

A Consensus Model

1. Look at the issue from the other person's point of view.

2. Identify the main issues and concerns. Try not to take a definite position on the issue.

3. Look at all the available options you can follow to achieve consensus.

4. Arrive at a solution (consensus) that is acceptable to everyone involved.

Chapter 1
The First People
(up to the 1400s)

O v e r v i e w
Use this Overview to predict the events of this chapter.

Theory
Approximately 32 000–36 000 years ago and again 20 000–28 000 years ago, ice-age hunting peoples, following herds of animals, travelled from Siberia across the Beringia land bridge into North America.

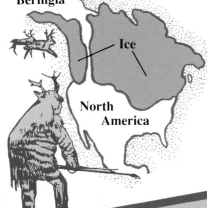

Beringia

Ice

North America

Theory
Through the centuries elders have passed on legends telling how the First People were created in North America by the Creator and have always lived here.

Some Other Theories
- The First People are really Polynesians who came to America in huge outrigger canoes.
- The First People are descendants of a Chinese Buddhist monk spreading the word of Buddha.
- The First People came to North America as the only survivors of the legendary island of Atlantis.

Different cultures developed throughout North America, depending on the resources available in a particular environment.

1400s
Time of Dekanahwideh, the great peacemaker: Founder of the Iroquois Confederacy, with decision-making done by consensus after long discussions.

Chapter 1 Focus

This book uses four concepts—power, co-operation, decision-making, and conflict—to organize the ideas of Canada's social and political history. This chapter is about the **Native** peoples of Canada. Native origins, ways of life, and methods of decision-making are examined here. The concepts of power and conflict are minor themes of this chapter. The concepts of co-operation and decision-making are the focus of Chapter 1.

| Power | Co-operation | Decision-making | Conflict |

Overview/Prediction Chart

Examine the overview found on the previous page. The Native peoples have lived in North America for over 20 000* years; Europeans have been permanent residents for only the last 500 years. Since the First Nations did not leave written documents as records of their history, this overview includes few specific dates, events, or individuals. Yet, Native **cultures** were complex and varied. Knowledge and history were passed from generation to generation orally. Stories and legends formed the basis of this oral tradition.

In pairs or small groups, use the Overview and what you already know about Native cultures to predict answers to the questions in the Prediction Chart. Put your predictions in the "My Predictions" column. Once you have finished the chapter, complete the "What I Found Out" column to help you review and summarize. Your teacher will provide you with a full-sized working copy of the Prediction Chart.

Prediction Chart—What Do You Think?		
Questions	My Predictions (fill out now)	What I Found Out (fill out at end of chapter)
1. What might be the major events?		
2. Who might be some of the important people or groups?		
3. Who might hold power?		
4. What conflicts might occur?		
5. How might the conflicts be resolved?		
6. How might decisions be made?		
7. What might be some examples of co-operation?		
8. Questions you have.		

SAMPLE ONLY

Native Peoples respected and lived in harmony with nature.

Native—includes all aboriginal peoples (Indians, Inuit, Metis) in Canada. In this book, Native peoples may also be called First People, or First Nations. Native peoples means more than one Native group is involved.

*This date is highly controversial and subject to change. It may be as high as 80 000 years or as low as 5000 years.
Culture—the way of life of specific groups of people

Origins

Who were the First People? How did they get to the Americas? Many possible explanations or theories have been advanced to clear up this mystery.

The Beringia theory suggests that ocean levels dropped about 65 to 138 metres during the ice age that occurred in the last million years. This lower water level exposed large masses of land and created a continent-sized land bridge joining Siberia and North America. Scientists have named this land bridge Beringia.

Some scientists and scholars believe that nomadic Asian people began to follow animals across Beringia and down the central ice-free corridor to pastures in North America. These Beringian pioneers could later have spread across the continent to become the ancestors of the Native peoples.

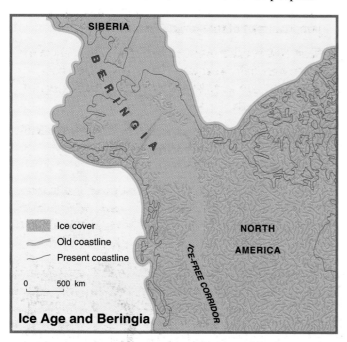

Ice cover
Old coastline
Present coastline

0   500 km

Ice Age and Beringia

Many Native people do not agree with the scientists who advance the Beringia theory. Many **traditional** Native people believe that the First People were created in North America by the Creator. The elders pass Native history from one generation to another through their stories. The first woman and the Trickster—identified as the Old Man in the following legend—figure prominently in this Native version of the creation of the world.

On the great waste of waters created by Manitou,* Old Man was sitting. Nearby was the first woman, whom Manitou had just finished making. They were trying to decide what substance Manitou used to hold up the water.

"I will send down one of these creatures to find out," declared the woman.

First of all she sent one of the fishes, but it soon forgot

why it had been sent, and swam off in another direction. Then the woman sent an otter, but being a timid animal, it lost its courage and sank to the bottom. Next, the woman allowed the boastful wolf to try, because he was a conceited fellow, and was always telling the other animals what to do. Before he got wholly immersed in the cold water, his boastfulness was gone and he was glad to cling to the side of the boat. Last of all the woman sent the muskrat. The muskrat stayed below water for so long a time that the others gave him up for dead. At last his round wet head reappeared and in his forepaw he clutched the sticky brown substance which lay below all the waters. It was mud.

When the woman rolled it about in her hands, it grew larger. Presently it grew so large that she could not hold it, so she cast it into the water. It quickly spread over a wide area and formed an island.

The island was empty until the woman got tired of the troublesome and quarrelsome wolf. She scolded him roundly and flung him onto the island. He ran up and down in the soft mud, and wherever he went his tracks made deep lines. When he stopped to paw the ground, he made a hole that filled with water. These were the beginnings of the rivers and lakes.

Traditional—believers of the old ways: the old customs and traditions

*The First People do not all use the same name for their Creator. There were many names for the Creator or Great Spirit, including Manitou and Ihtsipaitapiiyo'pa.

This legend has been adapted from: Mabel Burkholder, *Before White Man Came* (Toronto: McClelland & Stewart, 1923) 289–93.

Ways of Life

Heterogeneous Cultures

The Native cultures were heterogeneous or dissimilar. Native peoples lived in all of Canada's different regions and were well adapted to their environments. Some groups lived in different areas at different times of the year. Groups that settled near the oceans became fishers. Other groups made use of the good agricultural land and became farmers. Over the course of thousands of years, complex and distinct cultures developed. The First People were made up of different nations with different ways of life. These people are often referred to as the First Nations.

Nation

A nation is a group of people who:
- live in a certain area
- generally speak the same language
- have the same way of life
- have the same system of decision-making (government)
- are usually made up of a number of tribes or groups that are the same.

Homogeneous Cultures

While it is dangerous to overgeneralize and think that all of the First Nations were the same (homogeneous), the First People did share some characteristics:

- Native cultures were complex and varied. Traditions, customs, and history were handed down orally from the elders to the children. Elders were highly respected because of their important role in society.

- Native spiritual beliefs centred on living in harmony with nature. Spiritual beliefs touched every facet of ordinary life. The physical and spiritual worlds were considered to be inseparable. Hunters and gatherers respected nature. Dreams and visions formed a very important part of the spiritual beliefs.

- Most Native cultures emphasized the well-being of the group over individual gain. Thus, sharing and co-operation were more important than accumulating personal wealth.

- Wealth generally meant good health, good friends, and well-being for the First People. It was not always measured by possessions.

- Native cultures were based on a family unit and kinship. Some tribes were matrilineal: they traced their relationships through their mothers. Other tribes were patrilineal: they traced their relationships through their fathers.

Jules by Carl Fontaine. This painting shows a man of Cree and Ojibwa descent.

Tribes

There were over 50 separate tribes in Canada before the arrival of the Europeans. The following chart divides the First People into seven groups and lists the tribes found in each.

You will notice that some of the tribal names are words from Native languages, and others are from English or French. We have tried to use the word that each group uses in referring to itself. Because some names are still changing, you may find that this book has not always caught up with current use.

First People

Algonkian Nations	Northern Hunters	Northwest Coast	Iroquoian Nations	Plains	Plateau	Arctic
• Ojibwa/ Chippewa	• Chipewyan	• Coast Salish	• Mohawk	• Blackfoot (Siksika)	• Interior Salish	• Inuit
• Algonquin	• Beaver	• Nootka	• Oneida	• Blood	• Kootenay	
• Cree	• Slave	• Bella Coola	• Onondaga	• Sarcee	• Chilcotin	
• Montagnais	• Yellowknife	• Tlinkit	• Cayuga	• Plains Cree	• Carrier	
• Naskapi	• Dogrib	• Kwakiutl	• Seneca	• Assiniboine	• Tsetsaut	
• Erie	• Hare	• Haida	• Tuscarora	• Sioux	• Tahltan	
• Malecite	• Sekani	• Tsimshian	• Huron	• Gros Ventre (Atsina)	• Tagish	
• Micmac	• Tutchone		• Tobacco/Petun	• Piegan	• Nicola– Similkameen	
• Beothuk	• Kutchin		• Neutral	• Shuswap		
	• Kaska					

Boundaries did not exist for the First People and groups ranged widely in order to obtain enough food. For centuries the various First People had been trading with each other to obtain the goods they desired. These trading patterns were very complex and often involved travelling long distances over well-known waterways.

The boundaries on the following map indicate the tribes' general territorial areas.

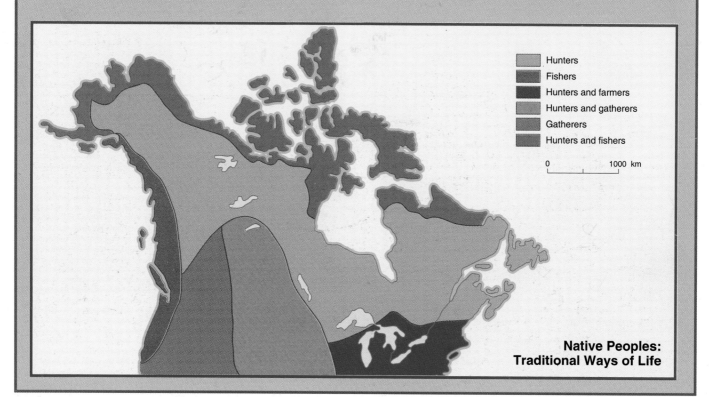

Native Peoples: Traditional Ways of Life

The Plains People

Environment and Resources

The Plains people were hunters and gatherers. Food was plentiful on the plains. Buffalo (bison), deer, elk, and antelope roamed in abundance. Wild berries and plants completed the diet.

Winters on the plains were long and very cold. During the winter the people lived in small family groups in sheltered river valleys or in the foothills of the Rocky Mountains. When spring came, they moved out onto the plains, where they were joined by other groups. The summers were hot but short. Late in the summer a large buffalo hunt was held. Often as many as 1000 people gathered together for such a special event.

Technology

Wood, stone, bone, and animal hides were used to supply the needs of the people of the Plains.

Economic Needs

Food

The Plains people were hunters. The buffalo provided them with most of the raw materials they needed. Study the diagram and note how well they made use of the animal. Hunting buffalo was the men's most important role as the well-being of the group depended on their skill. The largest hunt took place in the late summer or early fall. Strict ceremonies and a carefully chosen police force enforced the regulations. Hunting alone was forbidden for fear that the herd might stampede and leave the tribes without food for the winter. People who broke this rule were severely punished.

In Plains societies, the women's main role was to prepare food, make clothing, build and care for the home, and look after the children. Most of the food preparation revolved around the buffalo hunt. As soon as the men had killed the animals, the women started to skin and butcher the carcasses. The meat was shared among the entire band. Most of the meat was made into jerky or pemmican. Pemmican was a combination of powdered dried buffalo meat and saskatoon berries or chokecherries, all mixed together with melted buffalo fat. Pemmican was very nutritious. One kilogram was thought to be the equivalent of four kilograms of meat.

Shelter

The tipi was the main form of shelter for the Plains tribes. Tipis could be moved to different places as the seasons changed. Each family normally had its own tipi. The tipis were the property of the women.

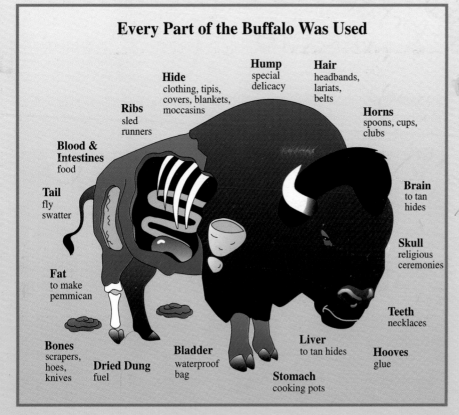

Every Part of the Buffalo Was Used

Hide clothing, tipis, covers, blankets, moccasins

Ribs sled runners

Hump special delicacy

Hair headbands, lariats, belts

Horns spoons, cups, clubs

Blood & Intestines food

Tail fly swatter

Brain to tan hides

Skull religious ceremonies

Fat to make pemmican

Teeth necklaces

Bones scrapers, hoes, knives

Dried Dung fuel

Bladder waterproof bag

Stomach cooking pots

Liver to tan hides

Hooves glue

Political Needs

During the winter, the Plains people lived in small political groups called bands. These groups were either gens or clans. In a gens, membership in the band is patrilineal, or inherited through the father. Clans are found in matrilineal societies. In either case, each band contained about ten **extended families.** The majority of the Plains bands were patrilineal.

Each Plains tribe was governed by a tribal council consisting of both men and women. Group decisions were reached by consensus after the opinions of the adults had been heard. This often took much discussion, debate, and persuasion.

When it was necessary, a Plains tribe would choose a chief. This man was usually brave, generous, a good speaker, a wise decision-maker, and a good hunter. His role was to advise, not to order. He could maintain his power only if the people trusted him and were willing to follow him. The position of chief ended when the special situation requiring a chief had passed.

Bands met in the late spring or early summer for the Sun Dance and again in the late summer for the annual buffalo hunt. Up to 1000 people would attend these events.

Social Needs

The Plains people viewed life as a cycle of events from birth to death. Children were very important because they were the ones who continued the culture. They spent a large part of their time with their grandparents and the band elders. The elders were highly respected for their knowledge of the band's history, customs, and traditions. Long winter evenings were devoted to the telling and retelling of stories from the past. Most of the stories used spirit hero characters (animal, human, and superhuman) to teach a lesson. They showed the children how problems were solved and which values were important.

Spiritual Needs

The Plains tribes believed strongly in the importance of sharing and generosity. Their survival depended on group co-operation. As a result, they did not believe in private ownership of land. The land had been made by the Creator or Great Spirit for all to use. It could not be bought or sold, for it was not theirs individually.

The Plains tribes honoured the Great Spirit. They believed that everything on earth was sacred and was to be respected. They believed that rocks, trees, lakes, rivers, animals, and people had all been given spirits and special roles by the Great Spirit. The hunters and trappers thanked the animals for giving up their lives to provide the people with food, clothing, and shelter. Women thanked the plants they used in the same way.

Sweetgrass

The Plains people believed that one of the Great Spirit's most important gifts was sweetgrass. Sweetgrass grows wild on the plains. It was picked and tobacco was buried in its place as a thanks offering to Mother Earth. Once picked, the sweetgrass was braided into three strands like hair. One strand symbolized the mind, another the body, and the third, the spirit. Each was considered necessary to make a good human being. When all three were woven together, it was possible to see how mind, body, and spirit became one.

Sweetgrass appeared as a symbol of kindness in the stories told by the elders. They taught children to follow the sweetgrass road of kindness and goodness.

Sweetgrass also played an important part in all spiritual ceremonies. The Plains tribes burnt sweetgrass as an incense for purification when they prayed to the Great Spirit. They believed that the smoke from the sweetgrass rose above the earth and alerted the Great Spirit to the fact that the people needed a blessing.

The Circle

The Circle was sacred to the Plains people. They believed that the Circle was the perfect shape. It was perfectly balanced, all parts had the same strength, and it had no beginning and no end. It appears over and over again in their artwork and tools. Objects such as the tipi, the shield, the sacred drum, and many beadwork designs reflect the importance of the Circle. The Plains people perceived that many things in their lives were based on the Circle: the cycle of the day, the four great winds, the phases of the moon, the seasons, and the cycle of life and death.

Extended Family—includes cousins, aunts, uncles, grandparents, and great-grandparents, not just parents and brothers and sisters

The Iroquoi

Environment and Resources

The Iroquois lived near the Great Lakes and the St. Lawrence River on forest-covered rolling hills that were dotted with lakes. The land was very fertile and grew good crops. The forests housed many animals. Summers were long and hot. Winters were often cold. This area was able to provide enough food for a large population.

Technology

The Iroquois used the materials available in their environment—wood, stone, bone, and animal skins—to make the tools and weapons that they needed.

Economic Needs

The Iroquois were farmers who lived in villages of 20 to 350 families. The villages had to be moved to new locations approximately every 12 years, for the crops robbed the soil of **nutrients** and would no longer grow. New villages were located on high ground close to a good water supply. The land would be cleared by the men with stone-bladed axes. Shrubs and stumps were burnt. When the land was cleared, the women used their digging

Nutrient—food for plants or animals; minerals in the soil that provide food and nourishment for plants

sticks to loosen the soil, and then made holes with their stone-tipped hoes. They put fish into the holes for fertilizer, said a prayer, and then added the seeds.

Almost all of the agricultural work was done by women. The Iroquois men recognized the women's contributions to the group by acknowledging their status to be equal with men.

Food

Agriculture provided the Iroquois with 70 percent of their food. Their main crops were maize (corn), beans, and squash. These were so important to the Iroquois diet that they were called "the three sisters." Late in the summer the women also picked berries, wild plants, onions, nuts, pumpkins, cabbages, and sunflowers to add to their winter food supply. Tobacco was grown and harvested in the fall. Maple syrup and sugar were made in late winter. Iroquois men contributed to the food stores by hunting and fishing.

Women did the cooking. Clay cooking pots were hung over the fire or food was wrapped in leaves and placed in the ashes to cook. Since there was normally plenty of food, large groups of people were able to live together and find plenty of food nearby.

Shelter

Iroquois villages were made up of 30 to 75 lodges each. The lodges were called longhouses, as they were long enough for several related families.

Trade

Since the Iroquois women were good farmers, they often had extra food to use in trade. The men often became traders. Corn was the main trade product. The Algonkian were their chief trading partners. They traded furs and game for corn. These trading patterns were firmly established long before the Europeans arrived in North America.

Transportation

Before the arrival of horses, the Iroquois developed other means of transportation such as canoes and snowshoes.

Social Needs

The Iroquois social system reflected the importance of women. The society was matrilineal. Kin relationships were traced through the mother, not the father. Thus, at birth, children became part of their mother's clan. A clan was made up of the female leader, her sisters, their children, and their daughters' children, as well as their husbands. The women chose the leader of the clan from amongst themselves. The leader was highly respected by all of the members of the clan.

Families were very important to the Iroquois. When a man reached the age of marriage, his mother selected his bride and obtained permission from the woman's mother. After marriage, the man became a member of his wife's clan and went to live with her parents.

Iroquois society designated specific roles for men and women. Men did not do women's work, and women did not do men's work.

Storytelling and Games

Stories were used to pass history, spiritual beliefs, values, traditions, and customs from one generation to the next. The elders were the chief storytellers and were highly respected for their wisdom and knowledge. This oral tradition allowed children to learn what was important. Children also learned by watching and helping others.

The Iroquois enjoyed games, especially guessing and gambling games. Racing, archery, double-ball, and snowsnake were also popular. The game of lacrosse—ancestor of modern hockey—was invented by the Iroquois.

Political Needs

The Nation

Iroquois society was based around the fireside, which was made up of a mother and her children. The firesides were part of a larger group of matrilineally related families known as a *kawhatsira*. The *kawhatsira* was part of a clan, and the clan formed part of a tribe. The tribe formed part of a nation.

Each village in the tribe held council meetings to settle its own problems. Men and women took part in this decision-making process. Decisions that affected the entire tribe, however, had to be decided on by a council of the clans' *sachems* or representatives. The female clan leader or matron chose a man to act as *sachem*. He was chosen for his wisdom and ability as a hunter and fighter. It was his job to speak for the clan and follow their instructions at the larger council meetings and in the Iroquois Peace League. If either the matron or the clan was not pleased with his work, he could be replaced at any time. This ensured that the *sachems* respected their clan's wishes.

Sachem—the appointed representative of an individual clan

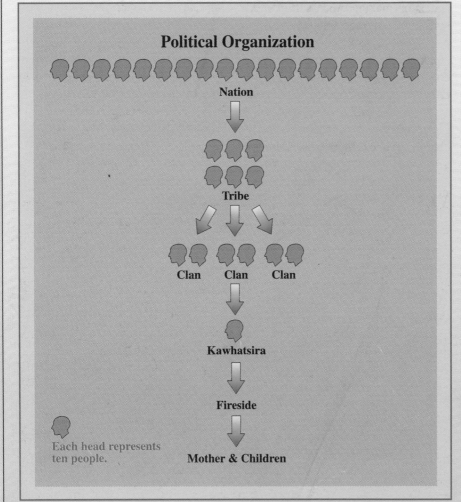

Political Organization

Nation

Tribe

Clan   Clan   Clan

Kawhatsira

Fireside

Mother & Children

Each head represents ten people.

The Iroquois Confederacy

(The League of Five Nations)

The Iroquois Confederacy dates from the 1400s. Dekanahwideh, whose name means "heavenly messenger," founded the Iroquois Confederacy at this time. He was said to have been destined to bring peace and power to his people. Dekanahwideh created an alliance, called the League of Five Nations, that brought peace to the Mohawk, Oneida, Onondaga, Cayuga, and Seneca. The Tuscarora joined the League much later, in the 1700s, at which time the league was called the Confederacy of Six Nations.

The Five Nations' territories formed a symbolic longhouse to reinforce the kinship ties among the groups. Thus, the Confederacy was a spiritual as well as a political organization. The Confederacy Council was made up of 49 *sachems*. It met once a year in the fall around the real and symbolic central fire of the Onondaga Nation.

Each nation had only one vote. Council decisions had to be unanimous. Consensus had to be reached not only among the sachems of each nation, but also among the Five Nations. This method of decision-making was fair for each nation but very time-consuming.

Each tribe had its own local form of government, which made decisions affecting individual villages. The tribes were also part of the larger governing body of the Confederacy.

The Iroquois emphasized decision-making by consensus. Once the group reached consensus, the chief respected the group's decision and had to follow it. This type of democracy allowed everyone to participate in the decision-making process. It worked efficiently, though slowly.

The consensus method of decision-making places the power to make decisions squarely in the hands of the people. In order for a decision to be made, each member of the tribe had to be in agreement. Decisions could not be made unless there was unanimous

agreement. Achieving this unanimity required time, tact, and diplomacy, as decisions were reached only after long discussions and debates. All the adults had a say. The Iroquois men respected women's equal status and power in decision-making. Having so many people involved in the decision-making process made it very time-consuming.

Peace was the most important aspect of the Confederacy, which was based on democratic principles. In the Confederacy, decisions were made by consensus after long discussions and debates.

Dekanahwideh brought unity to his people and is still remembered and honoured today.

Spiritual Needs

Spirituality was part of everyday life for the Iroquois. Corn was believed to be the holy gift of the Creator, or Manitou. Manitou was consulted through prayers at all feasts and ceremonies.

When making decisions, the *sachems* of the League of Five Nations continued discussing until consensus was reached.

Northwest Coast People

Environment and Resources

Northwest Coast people lived along the western coast of the North American continent between what is now northern British Columbia and the American states of Washington and Oregon. This area is composed of many islands and deep, narrow coastal inlets. The climate is mild and rainy. Trees and other plants are plentiful.

Technology

The Northwest Coast people developed sophisticated tools using the materials available to them. For instance, they made **adzes** and chisels from stone, knives from bone or beaver teeth, and sandpaper from shark skin.

Economic Needs

Food

The Northwest Coast people had a much more abundant food supply than did other Native groups. They obtained most of their food from the sea, which was full of fish such as salmon, cod, and halibut; mammals such as whales, seals, porpoises, sea otters, and sea lions; and shellfish such as clams, mussels, and crabs. Edible seaweed was also available.

For meat, these people hunted deer and other land animals. The land also provided fern roots, berries, and the inner bark of hemlock and other trees.

The men's main role was hunting, fishing, and gathering the food; the women's main role was preparing the food.

Clothing

The mild, rainy climate and the materials available determined the clothing worn. People usually went barefoot; in the summer, men wore very little clothing. Cedar bark was the material most often used to make clothes. Goat or dog hair was sometimes made into garments. Cone-shaped hats with wide brims were often worn to keep off the rain.

Shelter

A typical village might contain 30 houses strung along the beach. While most houses were large enough to shelter several families, a chief's house could be as much as 18 metres wide and 32 metres or more long. The houses were made of cedar planks. Inside, the space was divided into individual family areas by planks or woven mats of cedar bark. Each family usually had its own fire for cooking and warmth. A raised wooden platform for sleeping and for storage of family possessions extended around the walls of the house. The Northwest Coast people were able to accumulate far more furniture and possessions than other Native groups because they had permanent villages.

Trade

Trade flourished among Coastal tribes. Dugout canoes were an efficient mode of transportation and made it easy for food, raw materials, and other objects of various kinds to be traded up and down the coast.

Social Needs

The Northwest Coast people had an elaborate **caste system** ranging from aristocrats, who were chiefs, at the top, through nobles and commoners, to slaves. **Rank**, other than that of slave, was based on inheritance, marriage, and wealth acquired in one's lifetime. Slaves could not change their status. They could marry only other slaves and were not allowed personal possessions.

The most important way of sharing good fortune and establishing rank in society was to give a successful potlatch. This was a giant gathering, often lasting for days, where people from other villages were invited to feast, tell stories, dance, and receive gifts. Guests were seated according to rank. The number and quality of the gifts they received also depended on their rank. Gifts consisted of items such as food, utensils, tools, canoes, and slaves. The host sometimes chose to destroy valuable items as

---

Adze—tool similar to an axe, used for shaping wood
Caste System—social system with distinct classes based on differences of birth, rank, position, or wealth
Rank—position based on importance

well as give them away—an impressive gesture. The amount of wealth that the giver of the potlatch gave away and destroyed established his importance. These "gifts" were more like loans because each person who received gifts was expected to host his own potlatch in turn and give away gifts that were even more valuable than those received. If he did not do so, he would suffer a serious loss of prestige.

Spiritual Needs

The Native people of the west coast believed in the existence of one supreme being and lesser spirits. One group, the Haida, believed in a spirit whose name meant the "Power of the Shining Heavens," but this being had no contact with humans. It was the force from which lesser spirits derived their powers. They were the ones who could affect peoples' lives.

There were many **taboos** that had to be observed in order not to offend the many spirits who were everywhere. These included such rituals as placing the first salmon caught from the year's run on an altar facing upstream, cooking it, and giving each person a taste. The bones were then returned to the stream to ensure that the salmon came again next year.

The shaman was a man or woman who was viewed as having special powers for healing and for interpreting of omens. The shaman's advice was sought before engaging in any important activities.

Many of the Coastal tribes developed very sophisticated art forms. Carvers created elaborate ceremonial face masks, canoe prows, wooden chests, and bowls. However, the totem pole is their most famous creation. These were made from the trunks of cedar trees. The poles often stood at the front of a house and depicted the history of the families living in the house.

Political Needs

Kinship ties based on clan and lineage were very important to the Northwest Coast tribes, just as they were to the Plains tribes and the Iroquois. Among the Northwest Coast people, relatives, or people of one lineage, lived together in one house. A village could contain one or more lineages. The northern Coastal tribes were matrilineal; the southern Coastal groups patrilineal; the central coastal groups included some of each. Neighbouring villages were not linked together in a tribal organization, although they would join together in times of need, such as war.

Totem poles were carved by the Native people of the Northwest coast from the huge trees that grew near the Pacific Ocean.

Taboo — custom or tradition that sets things apart as sacred, unclean, or cursed

Review

Summarizing the Chapter

- There are many theories to explain the presence of the First People in North America. None of the theories have yet been proven. Many historians and **anthropologists** believe that the First People may have arrived in North America during the most recent ice age via a land bridge known as Beringia. Many traditional Native people believe the First People were created in North America by the Creator.

- The First People developed cultures appropriate for their environments and the natural resources available to them. The Iroquois used the rich soil to become farmers; the Plains people used the buffalo to supply their needs; the Northwest Coast people used products from the sea to satisfy their needs.

- Native cultures were not all the same. It is not a good idea to overgeneralize about the First People as they were often as different as nations are today. Some cultures were matrilineal while others were patrilineal. In matrilineal cultures, such as the Iroquois, women had higher status in society than men.

- Spirituality was part of everyday Native life. It was reflected in the burning of sweetgrass, the Circle shape of the tipi, the ceremony of the buffalo hunt, and the growth of corn, to name a few examples.

- Conservation and living in harmony with nature were essential elements of the Native way of life.

- Decisions were made by consensus after long discussions and debates. Chiefs and *sachems* were chosen by their bands and could act only as representatives. They had no power of their own.

- Until recently, historians have thought that the First People did not have horses until the 1700s. Recently, some historians have become convinced that the First People had horses earlier than this.

Note: the preceding summary has been written in the past tense as the generalizations refer to the historical period under study. Many Native people today, though, believe in and follow the beliefs and values described above.

Anthropologist— one who studies the origins, development, and culture or way of life of humankind

Checking Predictions

1. At the beginning of this chapter you made some predictions based on the Overview and what you already knew. Now use what you learned from reading the chapter to fill in the third column of the Prediction Chart that you began earlier.
2. Refer to the "Questions to Talk About" on page 3. Discuss the questions based on what you have learned about the First People. Record major ideas in your notes.

Working with Information

Mind Mapping

Mind mapping is an alternative method of organizing information. Mind maps work very much like clusters, only they place each idea on a separate line. Each word or idea must be joined by a line to at least one other word or idea. Coloured sketches are used to represent words or ideas since colour helps us remember. Examine the sample mind map on homogeneous cultures found below. Work with a partner and make a mind map that shows the relationships among the following:

(a) origins of First People
(b) heterogeneous cultures
(c) decision-making among First People
(d) co-operation among First People
(e) nation

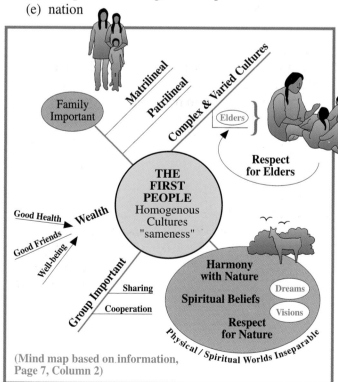

(Mind map based on information, Page 7, Column 2)

Building Thinking Strategies

Decision-Making Review

1. In your own words write down the steps involved in the consensus model presented on pages 2 and 3. Draw a diagram to illustrate your notes.
2. Start a separate section in your binder specifically for decision-making models. Enter all new models in this section. Some you may develop, others may be given to you by your teacher, and yet others you may obtain from your classmates. Try to write them down in a clear, understandable way. Use them to help you solve your problems both in and out of school.

Communicating Ideas

Reading

1. Read "Tlachi" by Eldon Yellowhorn, "Swan-kloo-wass" by Rosa Bell, "Buffalo Hunt" by Eldon Yellowhorn, "Kaksekochin" by Laura Okemaw, and "Katsitsiéntha" by Chief Jacob Thomas in the book *Ordinary People in Canada's Past* by Nancy Sellars Marcotte, published by Arnold Publishing Ltd., Edmonton.
2. Read "Dekanawida, The Great Peacemaker" in the book *Great Canadian Lives*: *Portraits in Heroism to 1867* by Karen Ford, Janet MacLean, and Barry Wanbrough, published by Nelson Canada, Scarborough.

Writing

1. Refer to the map of Native People found on page 8. Research one of the groups that was not studied in depth. Write a three- to five-page "Focus On" the group, using the format employed in the text as your guide. Be sure to use a variety of library and research materials.

Speaking

1. You are a travel agent trying to persuade two clients to take a trip to the Arctic to visit a traditional Inuit village. Prepare a two- to three-minute speech about the trip and the Inuit that would entice them into going. You may present your speech orally in front of the class or on tape.

Listening

1. Invite a Native speaker to speak to the class about Native cultures in modern Canada.

Creating

1. Create a collage that visually illustrates the decision-making process outlined at the start of this section. Use bright illustrations to make the work appealing and understandable. Put your collage up on display.
2. Prepare a bulletin board display of nation, using the visual definition in this chapter.
3. Research the techniques and symbols used by Northwest Coast people in their art. Use some of these techniques and symbols to create a model or drawing such as a mask, a totem pole, or a carved wooden storage chest.

Canada Revisited

This child is in the traditional clothing of the Plains people, ready to take part in a school powwow.

Chapter 2
European Exploration
(up to 1670)

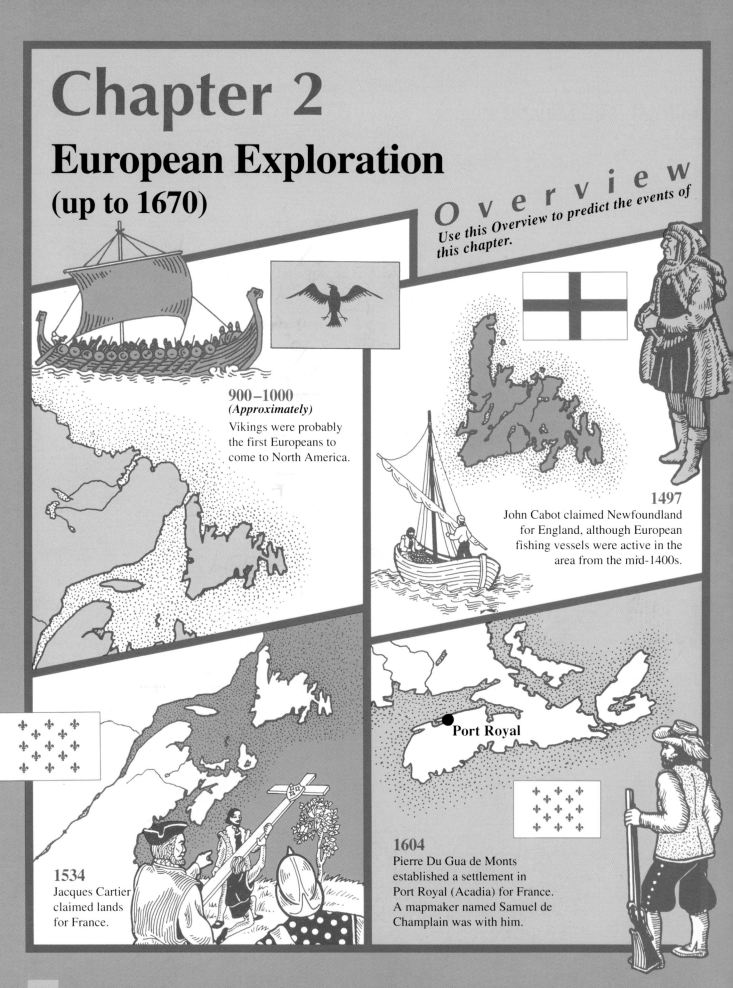

O v e r v i e w
Use this Overview to predict the events of this chapter.

900–1000
(Approximately)
Vikings were probably the first Europeans to come to North America.

1497
John Cabot claimed Newfoundland for England, although European fishing vessels were active in the area from the mid-1400s.

Port Royal

1534
Jacques Cartier claimed lands for France.

1604
Pierre Du Gua de Monts established a settlement in Port Royal (Acadia) for France. A mapmaker named Samuel de Champlain was with him.

1607
The English established a colony, Jamestown, in Virginia. Other colonies along the east coast of North America followed.

Jamestown

American Colonies

1608
Champlain founded the colony of Quebec (New France) and had a habitation built. Settlers arrived in Acadia.

Quebec

New France became a source of inexpensive raw materials and a market for goods manufactured in France.

Port Royal

Acadia

1649
Weakening of the Huron Nation

1670
The Hudson's Bay Company, an English fur-trading company, obtained exclusive trading rights in Rupert's Land.

Chapter 2 Focus

Chapter 1 examined some of the early history of the Native peoples. Chapter 2 is about the European exploration of Canada. The terms *exploration* and *discovery*, in this book, refer only to Europeans. Although what is now Canada was new to the European explorers, the Native people had already discovered and explored the land. The concepts of power, co-operation, decision-making, and conflict underlie the events of this chapter. The concept of power is the special focus of Chapter 2.

Power   Co-operation   Decision-making   Conflict

Overview/Prediction Chart

The Overview found on the previous pages highlights some of the events that occurred in Canada's early development from the first European contact to 1670. In pairs or small groups, use the Overview and what you already know to predict answers to the questions in the Prediction Chart. Put your predictions in the "My Predictions" column. Once you have finished the chapter, complete the "What I Found Out" column to help you review and summarize. Your teacher will provide you with a full-sized working copy of the Prediction Chart.

Prediction Chart—What Do You Think?		
Questions	**My Predictions** (fill out now)	**What I Found Out** (fill out at end of chapter)
1. What might be the major events?		
2. Who might be some of the important people or groups?	SAMPLE	
3. Who might hold power?		
4.		

Exploration
Exploration Today

Space! When we think of exploration today, we think of the exploration of space. The Space Age began on October 4, 1957, when the former Soviet Union launched Sputnik 1, the first artificial satellite to circle the earth. This was also the beginning of the Space Race between the Soviet Union and the United States. Some feared that because the Soviet Union had put the first satellite into space, they would have an important military advantage in using guided missiles in warfare. Many people believed that the United States should race with the Soviet Union to gain power in space.

After 1957, both the United States and the Soviet Union continued to explore space. The Soviet Union sent the first man into space in 1961 and in 1969 the United States landed men on the moon. These men planted America's flag on the moon's surface. The race for knowledge and power has continued with the building of space stations, the space shuttle program, the examination and analysis of materials found on the moon's surface, and the race to explore the other planets and beyond.

Early Europeans set forth on voyages across the Atlantic Ocean for a variety of reasons. Think about space exploration today. Why do people set forth on voyages into space? Some reasons for exploration are: challenge, discovery, competition among countries, power, control, adventure, and wealth. Did the early Europeans cross the Atlantic Ocean for some of the same reasons?

Questions to Talk About

As a class discuss the following questions. Keep these questions in mind as you read this chapter on the early development of Canada. At the end of the chapter, you will be asked to talk about these questions again, based on what you learn in the chapter about the early development of Canada.

1. Why do you think it would be important which country reached newly discovered areas first?
2. Why do you think claiming newly discovered areas would be important?
3. Why do you think setting up permanent settlements in new areas would be important?
4. Why do you think explorers would bring back samples of materials from newly discovered areas?
5. What similarities do you see between space exploration and early European exploration of other lands?

Early European Exploration

Dates	Early Exploration by	Reasons for Exploration
AD500 – AD700	Irish Monks including St. Brendan	Celtic legends told of Atlantic crossings in search of "The Land of Promise."
AD995 – AD1000	The Vikings—Bjarni Herjulfsson, Leif Eriksson	Norse sagas spoke of Herjulfsson reaching the coast of a new land when he was blown off course sailing from Iceland to Greenland. A few years later, Leif Eriksson explored the new land he called Vinland. This was in what we now call North America. The Vikings made some attempts at settlement but did not settle permanently.
1400s	European Fishermen	Voyages were made to rich fishing grounds of the Atlantic by the Portuguese, Spanish, French, Basque, and English.
1492, 1493 1498, 1502	Spanish—Christopher Columbus	The Italian sea captain was sent by Spain to find a short route leading to the riches of the Far East (China) by sailing west. He landed on islands in the West Indies and explored the Caribbean and South American Coast.
1497, 1498	English—John Cabot (Giovanni Caboto)	The Italian explorer John Cabot was sent by Henry VII, King of England, to look for a short route to the Far East. Cabot was granted a **charter** to conquer and occupy new lands and to have a **monopoly** on trade. Voyages reached Newfoundland, establishing English claim.
Early 1500s	English, French, Portuguese, and Spanish Fishermen	Reports from Cabot's voyages of the waters full of fish brought many Europeans to fish near Newfoundland. Some stayed over the winter in order to maintain fish-drying posts. Great profits were made from fishing.
1524	French—Giovanni da Verrazano	Francis I, King of France, commissioned an Italian sea captain to find the short route to the Far East. His maps do not show a sea route to the Far East but do show a solid land mass (America). He travelled up the Eastern coast of North America from Florida to Cape Breton Island.
1534	French—Jacques Cartier, first voyage	Cartier was commissioned by Francis I, King of France, to sail to the New Found Lands in search of a short route to the Far East. He reached the Gulf of St. Lawence and raised on the Gaspé Peninsula a cross that said "Long live the King of France." Cartier established political relations with the Iroquois and took two of their chiefs back to France to learn French so they could tell about their country.
1535	French—Jacques Cartier, second voyage	The Iroquois that Cartier brought back to France with him told the King of vast riches in the Kingdom of Saguenay. Francis I sent Cartier to explore farther up the St. Lawrence for this wealth. He reached as far as present-day Montreal. He and his crew spent the winter in the New Found Land.
1541–43	French—Jacques Cartier, third voyage	Francis I sent Cartier to the St. Lawrence to establish a permanent French settlement. The settlement failed.
Late 1500s	European Fishermen	Increasing numbers of people came to fish in the waters off Newfoundland and in the Gulf of St. Lawrence. Some began to trade for furs with the Native peoples.
1581	French Merchants	French merchants began to organize voyages up the St. Lawrence, specifically for trading in furs.

Charter—written permission given by someone in authority

Monopoly—a right granted for one person or group to control buying and selling

Reasons for Exploration

 From 1095, for the next 300 years, European countries were involved in a series of Holy Wars called the Crusades. During the Crusades, Christians from all over Europe went to the lands of the Eastern Mediterranean to drive out the non-Christians. These wars brought Europeans into direct contact with Eastern ideas, customs, knowledge, and products for the first time. The Crusaders came to appreciate luxuries such as silks and spices from India and China, and when they returned home they wanted to have these items. European countries began to search for short and cheap routes to the riches of the Far East (India and China), and these voyages led to the exploration of lands unfamilar to them. Power struggles occurred amongst the rival European countries for control of these territories.

In addition to the search for Eastern riches, there was a second reason for the increase in European exploration. From 1450 to 1600 there was an "age of exploration" in Europe. This was part of the historical Renaissance period, when there was renewed interest in all areas of knowledge. New ideas, combined with improved methods of building sailing ships, allowed mariners to sail more safely on longer voyages of exploration. But these voyages were still risky and cost a great deal of money. Ships could be gone for long periods of time and there was no guarantee that they would return at all or return with profitable cargo. As a result, voyages of exploration depended on European kings and queens for financial backing. Fortunately, European monarchs were not only eager to find out more about the world, but also wanted to gain power and the riches of the Far East. They hired mariners to search for a water route to the Far East. Portugal and Spain were the first European countries to try to get to the Far East by going west across the Atlantic; they were followed by England and France.

Exploration
Seeking new lands and new routes to old lands.

World Exploration and Mercantilism

 Early European exploration and colonization of areas such as North America, South America, Africa, and India were based on a desire for profit. This was part of a trading theory, very popular in Europe, called mercantilism.

Mercantilism
An economic theory that calls for a country to accumulate wealth in gold and silver. This was done, in part, by developing colonies as sources of raw materials and markets for finished goods.

During the 1500s and 1600s many European countries wanted to be powerful. One way for a country to be powerful was to have wealth in the form of gold and silver. Countries became wealthy by selling finished goods to other nations. The largest profit was made by countries who spent the least on raw materials and sold the finished goods for as much as possible. Colonies became very important to the practice of mercantilism as places for European countries to obtain raw materials and to sell finished goods.

The theory of mercantilism was a major reason behind European exploration and colonization of the world. The kings and queens of Europe encouraged overseas exploration and establishment of colonies for trade. Before colonies could be established, lands unknown to the Europeans had to be explored.

For Your Notebook
1. Define mercantilism in your own words and include a simple sketch beside your definition.
2. Explain how early voyages of exploration were inspired by a belief in mercantilism.
3. Read the chart on page 23. Use the chart to help you write a paragraph to describe exploration and mercantilism.

Exploration and Mercantilism

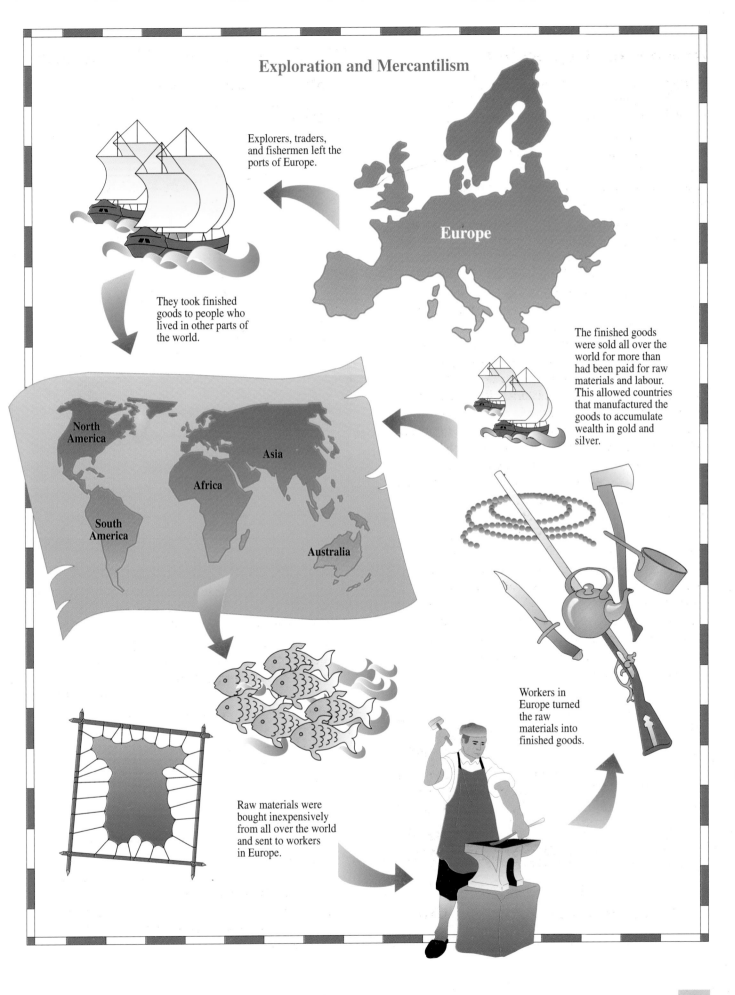

Explorers, traders, and fishermen left the ports of Europe.

Europe

They took finished goods to people who lived in other parts of the world.

The finished goods were sold all over the world for more than had been paid for raw materials and labour. This allowed countries that manufactured the goods to accumulate wealth in gold and silver.

North America

Asia

Africa

South America

Australia

Workers in Europe turned the raw materials into finished goods.

Raw materials were bought inexpensively from all over the world and sent to workers in Europe.

23

Native and European Interaction

Early European explorers such as John Cabot and Jacques Cartier met Native peoples who were already familiar with Europeans. This may have resulted from early contact with the Vikings, but it was more likely the result of contacts made with Spanish, Portuguese, Basque, French, and English people who came to fish on the Grand Banks of Newfoundland every summer. These people dried and salted their catch on land prior to taking it back to sell in Europe. They associated and traded with the local tribes, who lived near the ocean during the summer. The first merchants came to the New World for fish; the rapidly expanding fur market kept them there.

Items from Native culture are exchanged for items from European culture.

Acculturation

When two cultures meet, they affect each other. The two cultures may borrow ideas from each other, or one culture may have a stronger influence on the other. Anthropologists call this process **cultural exchange,** when two cultures meet over a period of time, acculturation.

An Exchange of Technology

The early contacts between Europeans and Native peoples in the New World could be viewed as an exchange of **technology**. The Native peoples taught the early Europeans survival skills such as hunting, trapping, snow-shoeing, and canoeing. They also provided the Europeans with remedies for illnesses such as **scurvy**. Native peoples often provided Europeans with fresh food. In exchange, the Europeans supplied the Native peoples with goods such as tools, weapons, and cooking utensils.

In these exchanges, each group gave something of which they had more than they needed at that time. In return, they received something that they lacked either the technology or the raw materials to make for themselves.

Ethnocentrism

The Native peoples encountered by the early Europeans had different cultural **values**. Since the Native peoples lived differently from the Europeans, different things were important to them. The spiritual beliefs, political organization, and technology were very different from those of the Europeans. This was one reason the Europeans and the Native peoples found it difficult to interpret and understand each other.

When two very different cultures meet there is often misunderstanding. People who have lived in one culture all their lives sometimes believe that their culture is the best because they are used to it and it meets their needs. Anthropologists call this belief, that one's culture is the best, ethnocentrism.

For Your Notebook

1. Re-read the section "An Exchange of Technology." In your opinion did the items traded result in a fair exchange? Did one side gain more than the other? Discuss from the point of view of an early European explorer and from the point of view of a Native person.

Cultural exchange — objects or ideas passed from one culture to another
Technology — the knowledge and application of developments in science, manufacturing, business, and the arts

Scurvy — disease caused by lack of vitamin C
Value — a long-established idea on which one's life is modelled

Read this imaginary conversation between a Frenchman and an Iroquois. Each is attempting to explain his culture. Start by reading what the Frenchman says.

Then read the Iroquois reply directly across the page. Then read what the Frenchman says next. You could try reading with different voices to create a better dialogue.

Frenchman	**Iroquois**
In France, our society is organized by a class system based on power and status. The class into which you are born determines your power and status. Many of us think it is very important to acquire power and wealth.	Our society is organized around a belief that all are born equal. Power and wealth mean different things to us than they do to you.
Our system of land ownership only allows certain classes to own land.	We believe that we are the Keepers of Mother Earth; the land is not ours to buy, sell, or claim.
Permanent buildings and cities are part of our way of life in France. The most powerful people have the largest and most expensive buildings.	Some of our people have permanent homes, but they are unlike yours. Many of us move with the seasons and animals, so our homes are portable.
We have a state and a government headed by a ruler. We call our ruler a king. Our ruler and advisors make all of the governmental decisions for all of the people.	We have non-state societies. This means that the power is not in the hands of one group or one person. As a result, we hold group meetings to discuss important topics and make decisions. Our leaders may try to persuade us, but they do not have the power to make the final decision. Decisions are based on the wishes of the people. Arriving at a consensus is important.
Business and industry are important in France. We have merchants who buy and sell goods. Through trade we accumulate wealth.	We produce enough to meet our needs and share with our kin. We also trade with other tribes. Gift-giving is an important part of trading. Accumulating possessions is not important to us.
It is important for us to explore and conquer new lands to acquire raw materials and markets for our manufactured goods.	We believe that there is plenty of land for all. We do not need to take over new land to gain power and wealth.
Our laws are written down. We also have a legal system with courts, judges, and jails.	Our laws are not written down. We have no need for courts, jails, or judges because wrongs are dealt with by families or individuals.
Most of us are Christians. We build churches in which we worship our God.	Spirituality is central to our lives, but we do not have special buildings in which to worship. We believe in a Creator.

Colonization

Claiming Lands

As lands in the Americas were explored, European rulers claimed ownership over them. This was usually done by planting a huge cross and/or flag of the explorer's home country into the earth of the land being claimed. This claim was recognized by other European countries.

By claiming these lands the European rulers believed they also had the right to control all the trade in the area. This was known as a monopoly. Their control also extended beyond the land and its resources, and included its people. In the Americas, the Europeans claimed the land and extended their control over the people, even though the Native peoples had been living there for thousands of years.

Jacques Cartier

Jacques Cartier was a French mariner who was commissioned by the king of France to search for a short route to the Far East. He reached the Gulf of St. Lawrence in 1534 and placed a cross on the Gaspé Peninsula that read "Long live the King of France," thus claiming French control in North America. Cartier made a second voyage to North America in 1535 and sailed as far west as present-day Montreal. He returned again in 1541 to establish a permanent French settlement as part of France's colonization process. The settlement failed. Cartier was treated with kindness and hospitality by the Native people he met upon arrival in the New World.

Discovery of Canada, by J.D. Kelly. Cartier is shown bartering with the Native people. Percé Rock is in the background. To claim the land for France, Cartier had a huge cross erected on the Gaspé Peninsula.

Settling and Controlling Lands

 To control the newly claimed lands, colonization was essential. Colonization involves one country (historically called the mother country) bringing another separate region under its direct control. This was often accomplished by establishing permanent settlements in the new region. These new settlements were expected to develop the region's resources and supply the European country with inexpensive raw materials or products. Colonies were also expected to provide a market for manufactured products. The raw materials were shipped to the European country to be manufactured and then were shipped back to the colony to be sold at a much higher price. Thus colonies were an important part of the European trading theory of mercantilism.

The French and the English were impressed with the Spanish success at colonization in Central and South America. They too longed to become wealthy and thus began to colonize the area of North America they had claimed.

Early colonization attempts were slowed by the fact that, unlike the Spanish colonies, North America did not immediately yield precious metals and jewels. The first prosperous industry in North America was the fishing industry. Later the fur trade became an important industry. Although these two industries supplied important raw materials, they did not necessarily require permanent settlements. The prospering fishing industry and developing fur trade in North America made many Europeans recognize that these lands were a source of potential wealth.

In European societies, wealth and power were tied to the ownership of land. Since only the aristocrats or nobility could own land, it became a mark of social status. Many settlers moved to the new colonies because land was plentiful and inexpensive. As landowners, the settlers gained status. The colonists believed so strongly in their right to hold their own land (private property) and in the agricultural way of life that these two beliefs became an important basis of Canadian society.

For Your Notebook
1. Why would colonization be essential to maintaining authority over newly claimed lands?

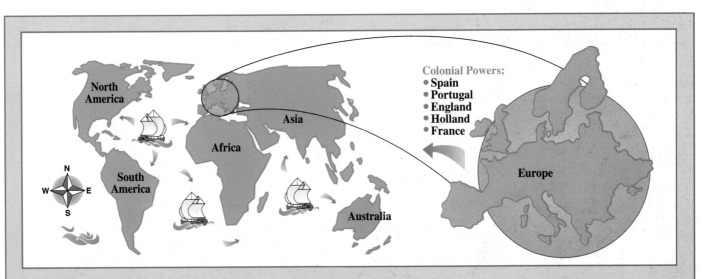

Colonization

Settling and controlling other lands

Places That Were Colonized:
- had lands that Europeans needed to explore before they could establish colonies
- provided raw materials and cheap labour needed to produce raw materials and get them to ports from where they could be shipped to Europe
- bought finished goods manufactured in the European countries

Countries in Europe:
- established numerous colonies in North America, Africa, Asia, and Australia
- had direct influence over the running of the colonies and decided on the types of government for them
- believed that the colonies should be patterned after the mother country
- manufactured finished goods from raw materials

French Colonization

 Prior to the 1660s, France had done very little colonization when compared with other European nations. France had been too busy with European wars to concentrate on colonization. Also, the French mercantile economy was directed by the state (the French government) with the leadership provided by the king and his ministers. Since the money that funded colonization and expansion came from the aristocracy and the Roman Catholic Church, developments were slow and cautious.

The French government granted trading monopolies to trading companies that promised to invest a portion of their profits in colonization. But these merchants were not interested in colonization. Thus, few settlers immigrated to New France before the French government took over the colony in the 1660s.

Rule by Trading Companies

Trading companies controlled and managed the French fur trade in North America. These companies played an important role in mercantilism. The traders were the merchants who obtained the raw materials (furs) from the Native peoples, and shipped them to France to be processed and sold for higher prices. They also sold or traded European manufactured goods with the Native tribes.

That part of North America known as New France was not colonized until the early 1600s because France had been too involved in European wars to concentrate on North America. During a lull between wars, the French king realized that colonies were necessary to protect the riches of the fur trade from other European powers. Mercantilism would not work without colonies. Between 1603 and 1645, the French state granted trading monopolies to individuals and companies. Each of these was supposed to help in the colonization of New France.

Pierre Du Gua de Monts

Settlement At Port Royal

In 1603, Pierre Du Gua de Monts was granted a monopoly on the fur trade in Canada. His goal was to protect his land from illegal fur traders by establishing a permanent settlement near the mouth of the St. Lawrence River. In 1604, de Monts and his mapmaker-manager, Samuel de Champlain, established a French settlement on Ste. Croix Island in Acadia. This settlement was moved to Port Royal in 1605. Unfortunately, Port Royal was poorly located. The settlement did not keep other French fur traders from establishing trading posts and trading for furs.

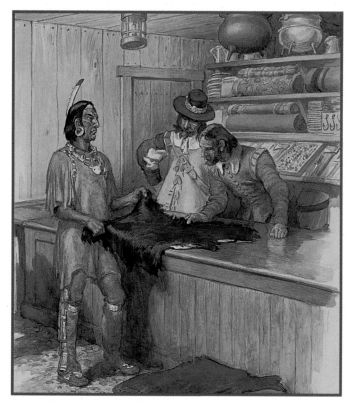

In the Trading Room. A Native person has brought furs to the French at a trading post to trade for European goods.

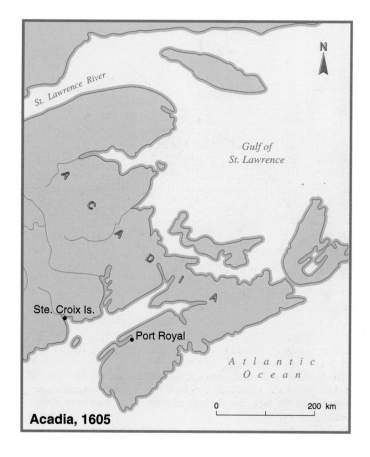

Acadia, 1605

Champlain at Quebec

In 1608, Champlain convinced de Monts to let him try to establish a settlement in the St. Lawrence valley, where there was better access to the Native peoples and the furs. Champlain went to New France as the leader of the 1608 expedition and established a habitation at Quebec. The habitation was built like a miniature European fortress. Champlain formed **alliances** with the Huron against the Iroquois in hopes of expanding the fur trade.

After 1608, the fur trade in New France grew rapidly in the hands of the trading companies. The population of New France, however, did not grow. The trading companies were interested in profits, not in settlement. Champlain realized that control of New France depended on expanding the French population. The English and Dutch were competing with the French for land and furs.* Champlain continued to seek political and financial support from France. Several company structures were tried over the years to encourage the settlement necessary to maintain control of New France and the fur trade.

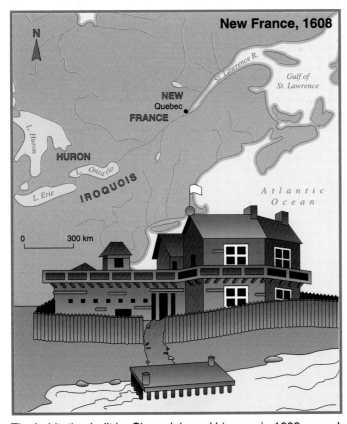

The habitation built by Champlain and his men in 1608 served as both living and working space.

Alliance — union formed between nations or groups of people based on an agreement that benefits both groups
*The English and French were not the only European powers active in the New World; the Dutch also were involved in mercantile and colonial activity here. See the map on page 31 for the extent of the Dutch territory.
Habitant — farmer in New France, and later in Quebec

Samuel de Champlain (1567–1635)

Samuel de Champlain was called the "Father of New France" because of the efforts he made to establish permanent settlements there. The settlements he helped to found included Ste. Croix Island, Port Royal, and Quebec City.

Champlain believed that it was part of his duty to bring Christianity to the First People. This caused him to act sometimes as a missionary for the Roman Catholic Church.

Champlain was a navigator and mapmaker by trade, and some of his maps are accurate even by today's standards.

Hélène Boullée (1598–1654)

Born and raised in Paris, Hélène Boullée married Samuel de Champlain when she was 12 and he was 40. She moved to New France with him in 1620, when she was 22, and stayed there until 1624. Then she returned to France and entered a convent, where she remained for the rest of her life.

Company of 100 Associates

In 1627 the French government granted the Company of 100 Associates a monopoly on the fur trade in New France. In return, the Company was supposed to bring 4000 French Catholics to settle in New France over the next 15 years. The Company allowed the settlers to trade for furs directly with the Native peoples if they sold the furs only to the Company. By 1663, due to the war in Europe between England and France, the Company of 100 Associates had gone out of business.

Company of Habitants

In 1645 the Company of 100 Associates allowed the Company of Habitants to take over the monopoly on the fur trade in New France. The Company asked the **habitants** to cover the costs of administering the colony and settlements. Control of the fur trade was left in the hands of officials appointed by France.

The Fur Trade and the Native Peoples

The settlement of New France was essential for control of the fur trade. The fur trade helped France remain wealthy and powerful. A fashion trend in Europe made furs very popular. Felt hats (made from beaver pelts) were considered a status symbol. The tremendous demand for beaver meant that fur merchants could make large profits.

Numerous Native tribes lived in the territory claimed by France. The Algonkian people lived in the eastern woodlands (*see* map, page 8). They included such people as the Algonquin, Ottawa, Micmac, and Montagnais. Also living in the eastern woodlands were the Huron people—a farming group.

Long before Europeans came to North America, the Huron had established an efficient trading network among the various tribes. Champlain, and later other Frenchmen, established alliances with the Huron and became part of this long-established trading system. Furs were traded for manu-factured European goods, which were in turn traded for furs from tribes in the interior. Thus, furs from the interior finally reached the French through the Huron go-betweens.

The Iroquois tribes and the Huron had few disputes with each other before the arrival of Europeans and the fur trade. Competition for furs and alliances with different European powers strained relations between the two groups and made them enemies. Alliances with the local Native tribes were essential for the Europeans. The Native peoples supplied the Europeans with furs, food, and canoes; acted as guides and interpreters; and often saved their lives. Champlain formed alliances with the Algonquin and the Huron because they were a large group of established traders.

When Champlain allied with the Huron to invade the territory of their Iroquois enemies, a political alliance was formed. The French and Huron sided together against the English, Dutch, and Iroquois. The French needed the Huron to be their military allies to help fight the Iroquois, if the situation arose, as long as the English and French were enemies.

C-11013, National Archives of Canada, Ottawa.

The Fur Fair. In the early days of the fur trade, the Native peoples came to Montreal each summer to trade their furs. The French and the Native peoples provided goods and services that were relatively equal in value to each other's needs.

The *Coureurs de bois*
("runners of the woods")

 One of the reasons the Native peoples were essential to the fur trade was because they brought furs from the interior regions to the French trading posts of Quebec, Trois Rivères, and Montreal. The French could also obtain furs by going into the interior regions themselves. During times of hostilities, the safer method was to have the Native peoples bring furs to the French, but high profits could be made by Frenchmen who were willing to venture into the interior rivers and lakes and bring back beaver pelts themselves. During peaceful times, more and more young men of New France were attracted to the high profits and adventure in the fur trade.

These energetic and daring adventurers became expert canoeists and shrewd businessmen. They were known as *coureurs de bois* or "runners of the woods."

Native trading between bands was customarily done through family contacts. To become part of this family trading system, the French left young men to live with a band during the winter. These young men adapted easily to the Native way of living, often married Native women and became part of their bands. Friendships and trust were thus established between the Native bands and the French traders.

These family ties were useful in future trading sessions. Soon the French had set up elaborate trading alliances with numerous Algonquin and Huron tribes. Later the French used these trading alliances to establish political alliances against the English.

The *coureurs de bois* expanded the fur trade and explored farther and farther into the interior of the country. They did a great deal to extend French control (power) over an increasingly large amount of inland territory.

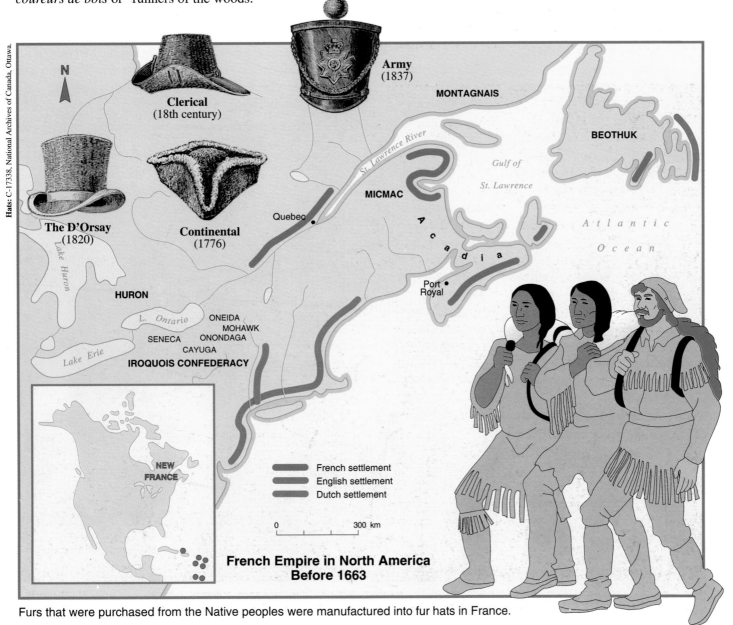

Furs that were purchased from the Native peoples were manufactured into fur hats in France.

The Catholic Church
(Prior to 1663)

Champlain believed that it was partly his responsibility to spread the Roman Catholic religion in New France. As a result, he encouraged the Jesuits—a group of Catholic missionary priests—to come to North America to convert the Native peoples to Christianity. The French king and his ministers believed that New France would be a stronger colony if everyone were Roman Catholic. In 1627, Cardinal Richelieu, a powerful church and state leader, declared that only Catholics could **emigrate** from France to New France.

While the trading companies controlled New France, the main **institution** in the colony was the Roman Catholic Church. The Church concerned itself with the religious life of the colony as well as establishing schools and hospitals. The Jesuits played a leading role in these developments.

The Jesuits

The Jesuits, who first arrived in New France in 1625, were called the "Black Robes" by the Native peoples. They established a college for the sons of settlers at Quebec in 1635, and established hospitals and convents by bringing groups of nuns to New France.

The Jesuits built permanent mission churches and schools for the Huron in Huronia between 1639 and 1649. Huronia is the name of the entire area where the Huron people lived. The Jesuit headquarters were located in the mission of Ste. Marie in Huronia. This mission contained a chapel, a hospital, a bakery, a carpentry shop, and a blacksmith shop. The Jesuits at this mission also planted crops and imported livestock from France. The mission of Ste. Marie in Huronia has been reconstructed. Refer to page 33 for photographic views.

The Jesuits had considerable political influence in New France. Beginning in 1647, the Superior of the Jesuits was one of the three main members of the Superior Council, which administered the colony. François Laval, a Jesuit, was appointed the first Bishop of New France in 1659.

The Jesuits left written records of early life in New France in the *Jesuit Relations*, annual reports that they sent home to Paris.

Montreal

In 1642, Paul de Maisonneuve, backed by the Notre-Dame Society of Montreal, founded a Catholic settlement which became the modern-day city of Montreal.

Emigrate—leave one's own country or region to settle in another
Institution—organization or society established for some public or social purpose. Examples include the church, the family, and educational systems.

Women Who Came to New France for God and Church

The Jesuit priests were not the only people who came to New France to spread the Roman Catholic faith. Other religious men and women also came to establish religious settlements. Many religious women, including the Ursuline Nuns, named after Saint Ursula, came to New France. These women made important contributions to the early settlement in New France:

- Marie Guyart, or Marie de l'Incarnation, came to Quebec in 1639 with other Ursuline Nuns. The nuns founded a convent and school for girls. Marie's letters home to France are important descriptions of life in New France.

- Jeanne Mance came to Montreal in 1642. She established a hospital there and spent more than 30 years nursing the sick and wounded.

- Marie de la Peltrie was a rich French woman who went to Quebec in 1639 and helped found the Ursuline convent and school. In 1642, she went to Montreal and helped Paul de Maisonneuve establish a Catholic settlement there.

Stamp reproduced courtesy of Canada Post Corporation.

Marguerite Bourgeoys (1620–1700)

Marguerite Bourgeoys arrived in New France in 1653. She set up a school and cared for the poor and the sick. When young French women started to arrive in the colony, she gave them a home and helped them to find suitable husbands.

Huronia

Huronia was the name given to the entire area where the Huron people lived. Between 1639 and 1649, the Jesuits built permanent mission churches and schools in Huronia.

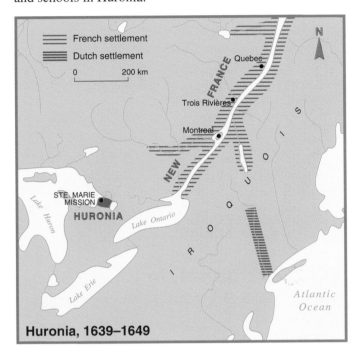

Huronia, 1639–1649

The Huron people were farmers and traders. Their alliance with the French had brought them new materials and technology, but it had also brought them into contact with many European diseases, especially smallpox and measles. From 1634 to 1640, more than 12 000 Huron—nearly half the population—died of these diseases.

The disease problem was compounded by hostilities between the Huron and the Iroquois. In the late 1640s, the Iroquois attacked the fur **brigades** of the French and the Huron. The Iroquois traded with the Dutch, who supplied them with guns. The French did not supply their allies, the Huron, with many guns because the laws in New France forbade it. The French supplied guns only to those Huron who had converted to Catholicism. Consequently, the Huron, who were already weakened by disease, were at a double disadvantage compared to the Iroquois.

In 1648–1649, the Iroquois began attacking and destroying Huron settlements. By 1649, only the mission at Ste. Marie was left. The Jesuits and the remaining Huron decided to retreat and burned the mission themselves before the Iroquois arrived. Finally, in March 1649, 1000 Iroquois warriors descended on Huronia. The combination of disease, death, and war completely destroyed Huronia. The remaining Huron—numbering

Brigade—group of canoes, carts, or dogsleds carrying trade goods and supplies to and from inland posts

approximately 500—retreated, only to starve during the following winter.

The French were left without Native trading partners. The French tried to find another tribe that would take over the role of the Huron. In the end, they had to venture out into the continent themselves to obtain furs. This move led to the expansion of the French fur trading empire.

After 1650, the Catholic Church turned much of its attention to the needs of the French people in the settlement.

Different Points of View

Historians debate the reasons behind the Iroquois attacks on Huronia. Some historians believe that the Iroquois attacked because they wanted to control the fur trade. Others say that the Iroquois were uninterested in the fur trade, since they did not step in as traders for the French. This group believes that the Iroquois simply wanted to destroy the Huron. Still others argue that it was the fatal European diseases that led to the weakening of the Huron nation.

Canada Revisited

The chapel has been reconstructed at Ste. Marie Among the Hurons.

This is a palisade around the reconstructed Huronia mission.

Acadia

The Importance of Acadia

Quebec, Montreal, and Trois Rivières were important settlements in New France because they were profitable fur trading centres. The fur trade was the main source of wealth for France.

Acadia was also a French colony.* The earliest French settlement attempts took place in Acadia. De Monts and Champlain settled at Ste. Croix and Port Royal before moving to the richer fur areas along the St. Lawrence. French settlement in Acadia continued around the Bay of Fundy.

Struggle for Control

  Although Acadia was not important to the French as a major supplier of furs, its location made it crucial. The English and the French were competing for the rich fish and fur resources in the region. Control of Acadia gave a nation power in North America. It is no wonder that the French and the English, who were competing with each other for power in the New World, also fought for possession of the colony of Acadia.

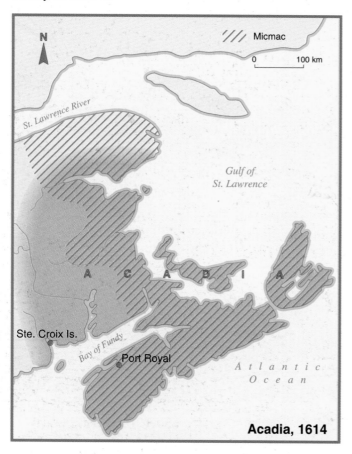

Acadia, 1614

*Acadia included present day Nova Scotia, Prince Edward Island, and parts of New Brunswick and Quebec.

A brief examination of Acadian history between 1614 and 1655 illustrates the struggle for control or power.

- 1614—Because the English feared that the French planned to expand south into the English colonies, they burned Port Royal. Only a handful of French settlers remained. No new settlers arrived until 1623.
- 1621—The English attempted to establish a Scottish settlement in Acadia. It failed after a few years.
- 1632—Acadia was officially returned to the French as part of a peace settlement of a European war between France and England.
- 1654—The English attacked Port Royal again and captured all French settlements around the Bay of Fundy. The English retained control over the southern part of Acadia, while the French controlled northern Acadia.
- 1655—The Treaty of Westminster returned French forts in Acadia to the French.

Acadian Way of Life

It was not until the 1630s that the first women and families settled in Acadia and large houses such as this were built.

Inside, the whitewashed walls provided a pleasing and warm atmosphere, as did the huge fireplace. Furniture was homemade, as was the clothing the people wore. Since families were large, usually with about nine children, there were always lots of helpers, both indoors and in the fields.

French settlers managed to establish homes and farms in spite of the conflict between the French and the English. Since the land was fertile, farming became the basis of the Acadian way of life. In Acadia there were trees to provide lumber for the building of homes, furniture, barns, mills, and boats. Any leftover crops could be traded for manufactured goods such as woven fabrics, tools, and molasses.

Top Right: *Trading.* Very few French ships came to Acadia to trade, so the Acadians traded with people from the Thirteen Colonies—wheat and furs for manufactured goods.

Below: #6663, National Gallery of Canada.

Above: *Repairing a Dyke.* The Acadians reclaimed low, marshy lands from the sea. Dykes were built of earth covered with sod. The dykes held back the water so the fields could be dried out and used for farming.

Right: *Acadians Cutting Saltmarsh Hay.* Each Acadian family had a vegetable garden, fruit orchards, fields of wheat, hay, and livestock. Hay was cut and dried to feed livestock during the winter.

Above: The Micmac lived in Acadia for centuries before the Acadians settled in this area. This painting, titled *Micmac Indians,* shows use of the local environment.

British Colonization

The American Colonies

In the early 1600s, England began to establish colonies in the area now known as the northeastern United States. The English mercantile system differed from France's because the English merchants, not the state, directed the economy. English individuals or groups who applied to the king or queen for charters were interested in profit. The charters allowed them to create settlements in the hope of increasing their profits. The merchants became wealthy and the state became more powerful. This approach allowed the state to remain free of responsibility for the new settlements. It also provided the state with a new source of revenue from taxes, which could be placed on any of the colony's exports.

The first successful English colony was established at Jamestown in 1607. A trading company, the Virginia Company of London, sponsored the colony. The company

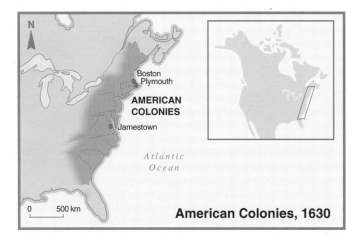

American Colonies, 1630

Below: This is a group of singing townfolk at the reconstructed Plymouth Colony.

This young man at the reconstructed colony of Plymouth is bringing in hay to provide food and bedding for his animals.

had originally expected the settlers to copy the Spanish and find gold and silver to make themselves and the company rich. This did not happen and the settlers nearly starved to death. Only the development of tobacco as a cash crop saved the colony and made it a financial success.

Other English colonies were begun along the east coast of North America. Plymouth Colony was established in 1620 by a group of people who wished to find religious freedom in North America. This colony grew quickly and became prosperous. In 1630, the colony of Boston was established.

The English settlements quickly developed into 13 separate colonies that stretched southward down the Atlantic Coast of North America. These settlements became known as the Thirteen Colonies. They were settled by the English, Irish, Scottish, German, and Dutch. By 1770, the population of the Thirteen Colonies stood at approximately 2 100 000. Fishing, farming, and fur trading were the most profitable industries in the colonies.

The Hudson's Bay Company

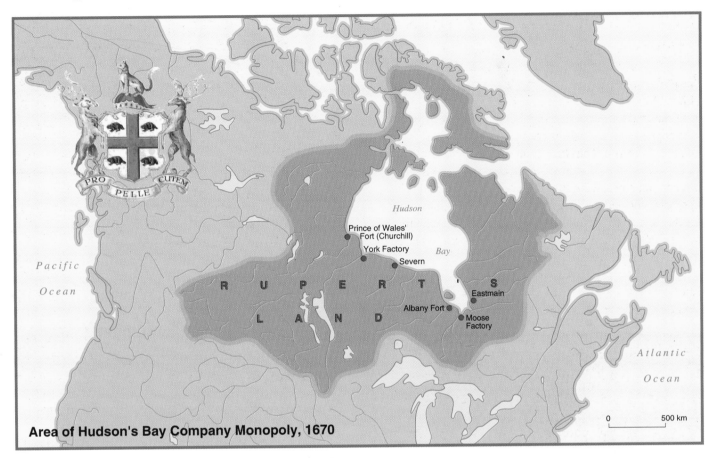

Area of Hudson's Bay Company Monopoly, 1670

Like the French, the English were very interested in gaining wealth from the fur trade in North America. The Hudson's Bay Company proved to be the most lasting of all of the fur trading institutions. Surprisingly enough, considering French and English rivalry and conflict, the Hudson's Bay Company was formed on the advice of two French fur traders, Pierre-Esprit Radisson and Chouart des Groseilliers. These two had tried to persuade the French that the best way to develop the fur trade was to set up trading posts on Hudson Bay. This way, all of the Native peoples whose river systems fed into the Bay could bring in their furs by canoe. The French were not interested—in fact, the French governor fined Radisson and Groseilliers for illegal fur trading—so they presented their idea to the English. The English saw this as a way to increase their power and influence in North America, and to make profits from the fur trade.

The Hudson's Bay Company was formed by a group of English investors. These men persuaded King Charles II of England that huge profits could be made by developing the fur trade in the northern part of North America. They asked for a charter and exclusive trading rights on a large tract of land, which would be controlled by the Company.

The king agreed, and on May 2, 1670, he granted a charter to "The Governor and Company of Adventurers Trading Into Hudson's Bay." The charter was granted in the name of Prince Rupert, the king's cousin. As a result, the Hudson's Bay Company land became known as Rupert's Land. The charter gave the investors a monopoly over the trade in all the territory whose rivers drained into Hudson Bay.

Although the Europeans acted as if the land were uninhabited, there were many tribes who made their homes in Rupert's Land. The Company did not talk to the Native peoples about taking over their lands, or consider how this might affect them.

The Hudson's Bay Company forts were erected at the mouths of the main rivers flowing into Hudson Bay. Native peoples acting as go-betweens brought furs by canoe to the forts for trading. These furs were exchanged for European goods and were in turn traded for more furs from the Native peoples. The Company was dependent on the Native peoples for their interior trade.

Through the fur trade both the Native peoples and Europeans got goods that they could not produce themselves.

Review

Summarizing the Chapter

- This chapter focused on the early development of Canada by the Europeans. As a result of the Holy Wars, called the Crusades, the Europeans wanted items like silk and spices. European countries began searching for routes to the Far East (India and China) to obtain these goods and to find out more about the world. These voyages led to the European exploration of lands in the Americas.

- Accumulating gold and silver was important for European countries to have power and resulted in a trading theory called mercantilism. Mercantilism meant getting raw materials cheaply and selling the finished goods for as much as possible. The theory of mercantilism was a major reason for European exploration and colonization.

- As lands in the Americas were explored by the Europeans, as part of their mercantile policies, the European kings and queens claimed ownership and control of them. They were then able to settle and control these lands through colonization. Usually, the Native peoples who had lived on these lands for thousands of years were not consulted nor considered.

- Both the French and English established colonies in North America. The French settled along the St. Lawrence, where the fur trade was the major occupation, and in Acadia, where farming was the major occupation. Although the St. Lawrence was more important to the fur trade, Acadia was important for its location. The English settled in the Thirteen Colonies and established their fur trade around Hudson Bay.

- The coming of the Europeans to North America resulted in changes to both cultures. The help and contributions that were offered by Native peoples made the Europeans' survival easier. The Native peoples played a major role in both the French and English fur trade. The Iroquois had alliances with the English and the Huron with the French.

- The Roman Catholic Church was the major institution in New France concerning itself with religious life as well as establishing schools and hospitals.

Checking Predictions

1. At the beginning of this chapter, you made some predictions based on the Overview and what you already knew. Now use what you have learned from reading the chapter to fill in the third column of the Prediction Chart that you began earlier.

2. Refer to the "Questions to Talk About" on page 20. Discuss the questions based on what you have learned about the European exploration of North America.

Working with Information

1. This chapter focused on the struggle for power that took place during the early development of Canada. The major aspects of this struggle for power are outlined below. As you review each of these topics, think about what each meant to the French, the English, and the Native peoples. Draw up a chart to show the relationships among the major aspects below:

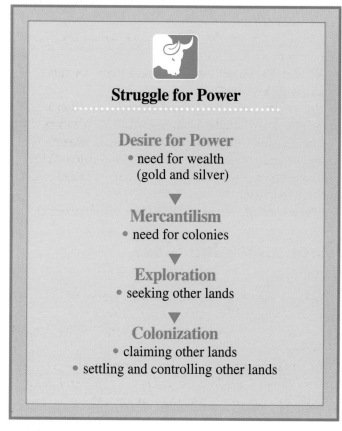

Struggle for Power

Desire for Power
- need for wealth (gold and silver)

▼

Mercantilism
- need for colonies

▼

Exploration
- seeking other lands

▼

Colonization
- claiming other lands
- settling and controlling other lands

2. Go through the Overview for this chapter again. Identify each frame as mercantilism, exploration, and/or colonization. Some may fit into more than one category.

3. Review all of the different examples of power found in this chapter. Work with a partner to draw a mind map that organizes all of these examples on one sheet of paper. Show how this struggle for power affected the exploration and colonization of the land. Use simple line drawings and at least three different colours. A sample mind map is shown on page 16.

Building Thinking Strategies

Conceptualizing

Colonization is a major concept in this chapter. Conceptualizing is a way of interpreting and organizing material by the general ideas and thoughts contained in the information. Working in triads, and using large chart paper to record your work, follow the procedure outlined below.

1. Write down the name of the concept, for example, colonization.
2. Give examples of colonization studied in this chapter.
3. Brainstorm to decide what the examples have in common. Write these on the chart paper. Look for patterns, links, and connections. These are called the key attributes.
4. Classify or group things that are the same (that share common characteristics).
5. What image comes into your mind when you think about colonization?
6. Brainstorm and list additional examples of colonization. Select your examples from historical colonization, colonization today, and possible future colonization.
7. Think again about the concept of colonization. What image comes into your mind now? Share these images with your triad.
8. Make a mobile of your triad's ideas of colonization.

Communicating Ideas

Reading

1. You may wish to read the following stories from Nancy Sellars Marcotte's book, *Ordinary People in Canada's Past*: "Ashooging and Bjarni," "Wiskijek and Henri."
2. You may wish to read the story "Acadian Pioneers" from *Great Canadian Lives: Portraits in Heroism to 1867* by Ford, MacLean and Wansbrough.
3. Read about one of the following people in the book *Great Canadian Lives: Portraits in Heroism to 1867* by Ford, MacLean, and Wansbrough: Chief Donnacona, Marguerite de Roberval, Matthieu da Costa, Chief Membertou, Marie and Louis Hebert, Etienne Brûlé, Paul de Maisonneuve, or Marie de la Tour. Would you have liked to have been this person? Why or why not? Share your findings with a friend.

Writing

1. You have become a *coureur de bois* in New France. Write a letter to a friend of yours in France that explains why you left your farm to take part in such a risky life.
2. Which person from this chapter would you like to have met? Explain why you find that person interesting.

Listening

1. You are a talk show host in a program called *Canada Revisited*. Your guests are a French fur trader, an English fur trader, and a Native person. You must discover how each guest views the struggle for power over the New World. Present your show to the class. After the class has listened to the discussion, have them choose which group they would support. Discuss their choices.

Creating

1. Draw a picture or make a model of either (a) an Acadian home, or (b) the habitation at Port Royal, or (c) the habitation at Quebec.
2. On large chart paper, prepare visual definitions for mercantilism, exploration, and colonization.
3. Pretend you are an actor in Lescarbot's *Theater of Neptune* at Port Royal, or a member in the Order of Good Cheer, Canada's first social club. Perform for your class. You'll have to do research to find out about these first.

Canada Revisited

321 years later, Bay quits fur trade
The Canadian Press, Toronto (January 1991)

Hudson's Bay Co., the retail empire founded on the fur trade, has decided to stop selling furs.

The company which received its charter almost 321 years ago will start liquidating its inventory of furs in February, said Barry Agnew, vice-president of sales and promotion on Wednesday.

"It is ironic to a certain degree that the company is getting out of the business that made it a business," said Agnew.

The decision was denounced by the Fur Council of Canada as a betrayal of its "Canadian heritage."

Section II

Colonial Government 1663–1774

I used to play hockey for Coach John Earnest. Note the fact that I said "used to." Coach Earnest had a reputation as a really good coach and I was thrilled when I finally made his team. What I didn't realize was that hockey with Earnest was hockey under a dictatorship. Let me give you an example.

We were playing in a big tournament in Winnipeg last winter. We'd won our first game easily, but just squeaked through the second one. A third win was essential if we wanted to stay on the winning side of the draw.

Coach Earnest stomped into the steamy dressing room while we were showering. "Team meeting in five minutes," he barked.

The game had been pretty rough, but we were pleased with the way we'd played. Most of the guys were planning to go out and celebrate the win. We were still talking about where to go and what to do as we towelled our hair and congregated around the coach.

"Okay, you guys, you managed to squeak a win out of that game. Tomorrow night we're playing here at 8:00 PM against the home town team. It's going to be a really tough one but I want to see you win by at least a three-goal margin. That means that you'll all be in bed and asleep by 11:00 PM tonight. Breakfast will be at 6:15 tomorrow morning—sharp! At 7:00 AM, we're going to get together in my room and go over the video of tonight's game. Then we're going back to the arena to watch the Regina–Medicine Hat game because we'll be playing one of those two teams. After lunch we've got ice time from 2:00 till 3:00 PM. That'll give you time to grab an hour's rest and some supper before we play." He turned to walk away.

"Coach, I have a suggestion," said Dave, one of our defensemen. "A bunch of us were planning to go out for a while tonight—nothing major, just to catch a show or something—but there's no way we can go and be back in bed by 11:00. If we all ordered pizza for lunch tomorrow, we could watch the video then and we'd even be awake enough to see what we did wrong. On top of that, we saw Regina and Medicine Hat play on Thursday, so it wouldn't really be a problem if we only saw part of their game."

Coach turned slowly to glare at Dave. "Who's the coach here—you or me? I know what you guys need, and that's what you're going to get! Now, get back to your rooms immediately and get to bed! Anyone who breaks curfew will be fined and automatically suspended from the team."

The dressing room went silent. Coach glowered at us, turned, and walked out. ■

Questions to Talk About

Discuss the following questions by referring to the story you have just read. Keep the questions in mind while you read the rest of the chapter. See if there are similarities between how the colonial government was organized and how the hockey team was organized. At the end of the chapter you will be asked to review these questions in light of what you have learned about colonial government.

1. Who made the decisions?
2. How were decisions made?
3. Why did the decision-makers make the decisions they did?
4. What role did ordinary people play in this system of decision-making?
5. Who did the decision-makers take advice from?
6. How can this system of decision-making be effective?
7. What do you see as the advantages/disadvantages of this system of decision-making?

For Your Notebook

Look back at the decision-making model used in the story on pages 2 and 3. In triads design a decision-making model based on the decisions the coach made for the hockey team in this story. Draw an icon to represent this system of decision-making.

Chapter 3 Focus

Chapter 2 covered the period of European exploration in Canada up to 1670. Chapter 3 is about life in New France from 1663 to 1774. The concepts of power, co-operation, decision-making, and conflict underlie the events of this chapter.

The concepts of power and decision-making are the focus of Chapter 3.

Power

Co-operation

Decision-Making

Conflict

Overview/Prediction Chart

Examine the Overview found on the next two pages. In pairs or small groups, use this Overview and what you already know about New France to predict answers to the questions in the Prediction Chart. Put your predictions in the "My Predictions" column. Once you have finished the chapter, complete the "What I Found Out" column to help you review and summarize. Your teacher will provide you with a full-sized working copy of the Prediction Chart.

Prediction Chart—What Do You Think?		
Questions	**My Predictions** (fill out now)	**What I Found Out** (fill out at end of chapter)
1. What might be the major events?		
2. Who might be some of the important people or groups?	SAMPLE	
3. Who might hold power?		
4.		

Chapter 3

New France: A Royal Government
(1663–1760)

Overview
Use this Overview to predict the events of this chapter.

Quebec

1663
Establishment of the Royal Colony. New France was then run completely by King Louis XIV of France and his appointed officials.

1665
Appointment of Jean Talon as intendant. New France was used as a source of raw materials and as a market for goods manufactured in France.

1672
Count Frontenac appointed as Governor General—recalled 1682 and reappointed in 1689.

1674
Laval made Bishop of Quebec.

Seigneurial System

The distribution of the land as seigneuries divided the land into long, narrow strips that stretched back from the rivers.

1701

Peace treaty concluded with the Iroquois; extent of the French empire in North America is shown on the map.

Rupert's Land

Quebec

Thirteen Colonies

The Roman Catholic Church played an important part in the royal colony of New France.

King Louis XIV ruled New France through his appointed officials. The people had little say in governmental policies.

The Establishment of the Royal Colony: 1663

A number of key events happened just prior to 1663 that caused France to establish a Royal Colony in New France. In 1657, control over the fur trade returned to the Company of 100 Associates. The Company of Habitants was in debt and could not meet the colony's expenses. By 1658, increased Iroquois attacks threatened to destroy the colony. The Iroquois did succeed in blocking the fur trade and destroying New France's trading allies, the Huron. Neither the trading companies nor the Roman Catholic Church could deal with the Iroquois. New France sent an appeal for help to France in 1661.

over the colony, making it a Royal Colony. This meant that New France would be governed directly by the king, just as if it were another province in France. The trading companies would become businesses in the colony.

Absolute Monarchy

King Louis XIV was an absolute monarch. Absolute monarchs have unlimited power over their people. Absolute rulers believe they have the right to rule given to them by God. The ruler was supposed to govern his subjects fairly—that was part of his responsibility. Under this system of government, the monarch has control over his subjects, although power is spread throughout the various levels of government. The people have no role or influence in government affairs, although absolute monarchs usually appoint advisory councils that actually run the government. While these groups may give advice to the monarch, he may not follow their advice.

King Louis XIV of France was not the only absolute monarch in Europe. Many of the countries of Europe at this time, including Spain and Portugal, were governed by absolute monarchs.

C-5400, National Archives of Canada, Ottawa (detail).

King Louis XIV of France made New France into a Royal Colony.

King Louis XIV

New France's appeal came when King Louis XIV had time to become interested in the fate of the colony. He was between European wars and very eager to increase France's power and wealth by sponsoring wealthy mercantilistic colonies. In 1663, he took control of New France away from the trading companies and assumed direct control

Absolute Monarchy
Leaders have unlimited power over their people. This power is not restricted by a set of rules (a constitution), or by parliament, or by groups (like an aristocracy).

Royal Government

 The study of government is very complex. To make this study easier, we will look at three areas of absolute rule: (1) government participation, (2) decision-making powers, and (3) majority rule. Examples are given for New France.

Characteristics of an Absolute Monarch

1. **In an absolute monarchy only the people selected by the ruler are allowed to participate in the government.**

- In France and New France King Louis XIV was an absolute monarch.
- Only those people selected by King Louis XIV were allowed to participate in government affairs. These people are shown on the chart on page 47 as the king's advisors. They had some influence on the king but he did not have to listen to them.

2. **In an absolute monarchy one person, the king, has the power to make decisions.**

- Absolute monarchs believed that their power was inherited from their ancestors.
- Absolute monarchs believed they were responsible for the well-being of their subjects.
- Absolute monarchs decide what is best for the people. They may or may not find out what the people want. They may or may not put the people's wishes into effect.

- The power to make decisions about New France was held by King Louis XIV.
- This does not mean that King Louis XIV of France made all the decisions. He appointed advisors, who made up the government of France, to make the decisions for him. If King Louis was unhappy with the decisions his council of advisors made, then he appointed new advisors who would make the kind of decisions he wanted.
- The advisors in the French government passed on the king's decisions to the government in New France. The government in New France was made up of the governor, intendant, bishop, and Sovereign Council. If the government of New France did not follow the decisions made by the king's advisors (and the king), then they were recalled to France and were not allowed to keep their jobs.
- In theory the people as a whole had no role or influence in the decision-making process.
- In practice, because the distance from France to New France was so great, messages took up to a year to travel back and forth. This allowed the people of New France greater autonomy (greater freedom to make their own political decisions).

3. **Majority rule does not exist in an absolute monarchy. Minority rule and one person rule exist in an absolute monarchy.**

- The government of New France was made up of appointed officials in France and in New France. Minority rule existed in New France. The majority of the people did not have a say in the government.

Meeting of the Sovereign Council, by Charles Huot. Headed by the governor, intendant, and bishop, the Sovereign Council included officials in the government of New France who were appointed to carry out decisions made by the king and his advisors in France.

Photo: Kedl

Colbert

C-9628, National Archives of Canada, Ottawa.

Jean-Baptiste Colbert was Chief Official of New France, a colony he never visited.

King Louis XIV appointed Jean-Baptiste Colbert to be in charge of France's economy. Colbert's ideas were used to govern the provinces in France and the French colonies around the world. Colbert wanted to use France's colonies to help make France more powerful. Colbert was very interested in mercantilism, whereby the colonies became a source of inexpensive raw materials and a market for goods manufactured by the mother country.

In New France

When New France became a French province in 1663

- A Sovereign Council was appointed to carry out orders from the king and his government.

Below: Over 1000 king's daughters came from France to New France to marry the single men there.

- Population growth was encouraged in New France. Government grants were given to families of over 10 children. Royal wedding dowries were awarded to couples who married early (under 20 for men, under 16 for women). A dowry is money or property that a woman brings with her into marriage. Fathers were fined for having single children of marriageable age.
- Four thousand French settlers immigrated at government expense between 1666 and 1676. One-third were retiring soldiers. Over 1000 were single women who hoped to marry in the New World (the *filles du roi,* or the "king's girls" or "king's daughters").
- The seigneurial system continued. The seigneurs became high status land settlement agents.
- Militia companies formed in 1669 involved all men aged 16 to 60. The *capitaine de milice,* or militia captain, was an habitant, not a nobleman. A militia is part of an army made up of citizens who are not regular soldiers but who undergo training for emergency duty or national defense.
- Farming, shipbuilding, brewing, fishing, and tanning received government financing. The industries did not become profitable and were a drain on the finances of the French government.
- The French Carignan-Salières regiment conducted a military campaign against the Iroquois in 1666. They burned Iroquois villages and farms. This caused a famine, which led to a truce and 20 years of peace.

C-10688, National Archives of Canada, Ottawa.

C.W. JEFFERYS

Colonial Government in New France

  King Louis XIV was far too busy extending and protecting French interests in Europe to be able to devote all of his attention to New France. Under Colbert's guidance, the old system of rule by trading companies was replaced by an absolute monarchy appointed by the king. The king relied on officials or ministers to do most of the government's work.

He created a Sovereign Council of officials in New France. This council was to carry out orders from the king and his government in France. The people who settled in New France did not have any power over the king or the Sovereign Council. They could not change any decisions made by the ruler. Communication with New France was limited, however, by its distance from France and also by the fact that bad weather made it inaccessible for six or seven months of the year. This meant that the local officials in New France often had far more power over the colony than the French government. The senior members of the Sovereign Council were the governor, intendant, and bishop. When New France had a good governor and intendant (the king's representatives in the colony), the colony had good government. In the early days of the Royal Colony, members of the legal profession were barred from entering New France. As a result, legal decisions were made on the basis of common sense.

The people of New France had little role or influence in the government of the colony, but this did not make them any different from people in European countries. Women were completely excluded from the governing process in New France as well as in all European countries. Occasionally the intendant, who was in charge of justice, finance, and administration, called meetings of prominent local officials to discuss economic policies for the colony. These discussions did not, however, always result in the intendant taking the officials' advice.

The Royal Government in New France was both inexpensive and efficient. It remained intact until the British substituted their system of government in 1763.

Exploring Further

1. Use the information in Chapter 3, especially that on pages 44–49, to prepare a game on New France and on Royal Government. The game should be entirely your own creation. It may be a board game, card game, role play game, or computer game.

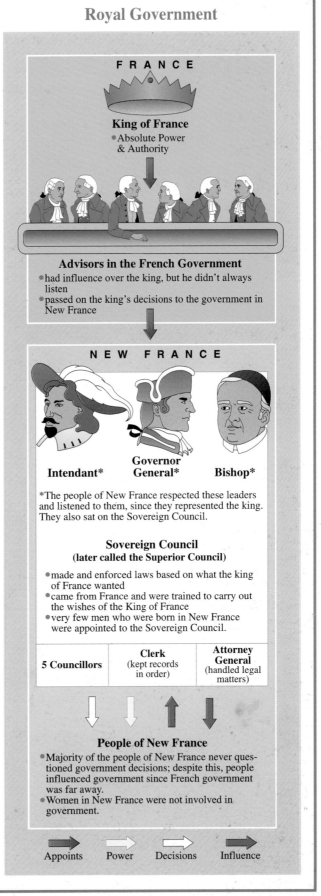

The government of New France is an example of absolute rule.

Important Officials in the Government of New France

The Governor General

- represented the king in New France
- served as a **figurehead,** a living symbol of the king's authority
- was the highest ranking official in New France
- was appointed from the **nobility**
- was chosen from among military officers
- acted as master of New France in the king's name and thus was responsible for military planning, relations with the Native peoples, and ensuring that the other officials did their jobs.

Comte de Frontenac (1622–1698)

Louis de Buade, Comte de Frontenac, was appointed governor of New France in 1672. He was a successful military governor, but because he quarrelled with the intendant and bishop he was recalled to France in 1682.

Frontenac returned to New France in 1689 to create peace by suppressing the Iroquois and to attack English settlements and finally expand France's fur trade. He remained there until his death in 1698.

Frontenac's major concern was the expansion of New France's fur trade.

The Bishop

- represented the Roman Catholic Church in New France
- ruled over parish priests and nuns of New France in the king's name
- was in charge of the missionaries, churches, hospitals, and schools
- was often a member of the French nobility appointed by the king
- reported to the king on colonial activities and ensured harmony among his parishes.

François de Laval (1623–1708)

François de Laval, a Jesuit priest, arrived in Quebec in 1659. He was appointed the first Bishop of Quebec in 1674. Laval, who directed the spiritual life of New France for 29 years, was very active in attempting to Christianize the Native people.

As a leading member of the Sovereign Council, Laval had strong political influence. He organized the **parish** system of New France. The **seminary** that Laval founded at Quebec became Laval University in 1852.

Figurehead—person who is the head of a country in name or title only but has no real power or responsibility. (In New France, the governor was officially a figurehead, but in actual fact he had a lot of power.)

Nobility—a person with special rank and authority by virtue of birth or title. Dukes, counts, earls, and marquises are examples of nobility.

Parish—district that is the responsibility of a particular church

Seminary—special school for the training of priests

The Intendant

- acted as master of New France in the king's name
- informed the king of colonial activities and ensured harmony among the people
- was appointed from the nobility
- supervised the day-to-day running of the colony, law and order, and matters relating to finance (money).

Jean Talon (1625–1694)

Jean Talon was the first intendant of New France. During his term, from 1665 to 1668, he conducted a **census** of the population.

Talon attempted to change the colony from a fur-trade foundation to an agricultural and industrial foundation, but found that this could not be accomplished without a larger population.

Talon arranged for settlers to come to New France, including over 1000 women known as the *filles du roi* ("king's girls" or "king's daughters"). He encouraged further population growth through marriage grants and baby bonuses (money given to a couple when they married and when they had children).

Talon tried to diversify (expand and vary) the economy by introducing new crops such as flax and hops, starting a shipyard and lumber industry, and encouraging mining.*

Developing Industries

Canada's First Shipyard. Intendant Jean Talon tried to make New France less dependent on supplies from France by establishing industries such as shipbuilding, brewing, and shoemaking. This picture shows Talon studying plans at the shipyard at Quebec in 1672.

Canada's First Trade Treaty. The Comte de Frontenac met with Iroquois chiefs at Cataraqui (Kingston), 1673. Frontenac encouraged friendships with the Native peoples, exploration, and military campaigns, all to strengthen New France's most important industry, the fur trade.

Census—an official count of the people of a country or district to find out the number of people living there
*Flax was grown to make a cloth known as linen. Hops are an essential ingredient in making beer.

The Seigneurial System

Structure of the Seigneuries

New France grew along the banks of the St. Lawrence River. Since the river formed the main transportation route, every habitant wanted land along the rivers of New France. For this reason, seigneuries were divided into long narrow strips of land. Each had a section of river front and extended back into uncleared bush away from the river. As the land was passed through the generations, the strips were subdivided. Only when the land along the St. Lawrence was completely used did the colony start a new row of seigneuries behind the first ones. These long, narrow strips of land are still visible along the St. Lawrence River today.

Since the king owned all of the land in New France, he granted the use of the land to people who became seigneurs. The seigneurs then divided the land into smaller lots and brought in settlers called habitants to farm it. Both the seigneurs and the habitants had specific duties. Their land could be taken away if the duties were not performed.

Duties of the Seigneur

- Subdivide the seigneury into 32-hectare parcels and grant land to the habitants.
- Build a house and flour mill on the seigneury.
- Contribute to the construction of a church.
- Report to the intendant information about the population of the seigneury, the amount of land under cultivation, and the dues paid.

Duties of the Habitant

- Pay taxes or dues to the seigneur (cens et rentes).
- Build a house and farm the land.
- Perform unpaid labour for the seigneur a few days each year (corvée).
- Give a percentage of his produce (fish, crops, animals) to the seigneur annually.

#6275, National Gallery of Canada, Ottawa.

A View of the Château Richer, painted by Thomas Davies in 1787, shows houses, barns, sheds, crops, eel traps, fields of wheat and peas, and livestock typical of New France.

Women and the Seigneuries

Unlike legal systems found in many other European countries, including England, the French system of justice allowed women to hold seigneurial land. Women in New France were encouraged to marry by the age of 16. This meant that they often inherited land when their husbands died. Some women took charge of their inherited land; others kept it only until a son was old enough to farm it. Other women, such as Madeleine d'Allonne, held their own seigneuries.

> ### Madeleine d'Allonne (1646–1718)
> Madeleine d'Allonne was one of the first women in New France to take charge of a large seigneury. She cleared the land, built a house and barn, and raised her own crops. She also spoke out in support of the rights of settlers.

Compared to France

The French officials who governed New France attempted to fashion the new colony after the mother country. Many old French institutions became part of the way of life in New France. These institutions were adapted so that they suited life in the New World. Consequently, New France appeared to be structured by old-fashioned institutions, but in reality, often only the names were the same. Pages 50 to 55 examine two institutions in New France: the seigneurial system and the Church. You have already studied a third institution— government.

The seigneurial system was an example of how a traditional French institution changed radically in New France. In France, peasants obtained farmland through the seigneurial system. This was a modified version of a medieval European method of distributing land (called feudalism). Across Europe in the Middle Ages, peasants were granted land by their lords in return for military service, a portion of their produce, or the performance of other unpaid duties. This system was still in effect in France when New France became a Royal Colony.

The seigneurial system varied in purpose between France and New France. In France, the seigneurial system worked to the seigneurs' advantage, as it provided them with great profits and cheap labour. In New France, it benefited the habitant as well as the seigneur. Being a seigneur in New France meant status, but not necessarily wealth. The habitants benefited through increased independence, land, and wealth.

Corvée — unpaid labour performed by the habitants for the seigneur, usually for only a few days of the year

Every autumn the women of New France melted animal fat and beeswax to make candles for the long, dark winters. They dipped strings into this melted mixture over and over again, allowing each layer to harden.

Other significant factors modified the seigneurial system in New France. The seigneur's traditional role as a military commander was taken over by a habitant called the captain of the militia. Also, the new seigneuries were not as wealthy as those in France; seigneurs were often little wealthier than successful habitants. Many of the seigneurs were more interested in the status of their position than in living on their seigneuries or fulfilling their obligations. The position of seigneur actually became that of a high-status land agent.

The habitants gained increased independence and wealth under this new system. Land was plentiful, so habitants were frequently allowed to cultivate as much as their families could farm. Taxes—if they were paid at all—were low, and habitants often kept all of their produce to feed their families. The St. Lawrence River made roads a secondary form of transportation, so habitants did not lose their most valuable farming time performing *corvée*. In addition to these factors, the fur trade presented habitants with another source of income and freedom.

Obtaining Farmland

The French were usually on friendly terms with the Native peoples. The men often married Native women and either continued with the lifestyle of a fur trader, or they decided to become farmers. When seigneurial land was no longer available, new seigneuries were started. Many of the Native people had moved away from the St. Lawrence River to work in the fur trade.

Choices to Make! New France—1672

by Nancy Sellars Marcotte

How odd it was to feel so safe when she was so far away from anything she had ever known! Geneviève had lived through so many uncertainties in her life. She had always been the one who didn't quite belong.

Geneviève was an orphan. She had been raised in the home of her aunt and uncle. They had treated her kindly, but they had six children of their own, all younger than Geneviève. It was difficult for a shoemaker to support six children, even in Paris, where the cobblestones wore shoes out so quickly.

Geneviève had always known that she would have to make her own way in life. Her uncle would not be able to provide any dowry at all. With no money or household goods to bring into a marriage, she was unlikely to find a husband. She was very glad, when she was 12, to find a position in the kitchen of a nobleman's house on the outskirts of Paris. The cleaning and scrubbing that she had to do was very difficult, but she always had enough food.

But the nobleman and his wife were elderly, and the other servants sometimes whispered that perhaps soon they would not need so many servants. The women were particularly worried about where to go if they no longer had jobs in the nobleman's household.

It was another household servant, Françoise, who told Geneviève that the king wanted young women to go to New France. At first Geneviève had laughed. She knew, of course, that young men sometimes went to New France. Some of them went to trade for furs from the Native people. Others, she understood, were farmers. And some were soldiers. But Geneviève did not have a clear idea of where New France was, or how anyone went there.

Françoise's stories began to seem more and more unbelievable. Because the two girls were well-mannered, they could become King's Daughters. Geneviève had not believed this at all until Françoise had explained that they would not be invited to go and live at the palace. It was just that the king wanted many French families living in New France. What he had now were many single men. In fact, Françoise said, there were 15 French men for every French woman in New France. The king would provide dowries for young women who were willing to go and live in New France and marry these young men.

Geneviève had never travelled farther than the outskirts of Paris, but somehow, just a few months after her 14th birthday, she found herself beside Françoise in a wagon jolting toward the seacoast. Then she was aboard a wooden sailing ship and France was just a distant memory behind her.

After six long weeks they were at Quebec. From the ship Geneviève stared at the walled city on the low land near the river. High above on the cliffs was a magnificent stone château.

The month was June, and Geneviève did not think she had ever felt such heat. As the girls clambered from the ship into the rowboat that was to take them to shore, her attention was divided amongst Quebec, the strange little insects that were nipping at her wrists and neck, and the jostling group of men who stood at the shore watching the girls.

Geneviève was a little frightened. Since she had travelled so far, she wanted to be sure that she did not end up in a life that would cause her unhappiness. She soon learned that the nuns who looked after the King's Daughters were as much concerned with the girls' happiness as with providing brides for the young men of New France.

Françoise, always so sure of her decisions, was married within the month. Her husband was a widower, 11 years older than Françoise, whose wife had died of fever the winter before. He was a shipbuilder with a fine house in Quebec. Françoise came back often to see Geneviève, to tell her about the two stepchildren that she was helping her husband to raise. Already Françoise was enthusiastic about the seminary that Bishop Laval had started in Quebec. "If one of my sons chooses to become a priest, he can train right here at Quebec," she told Geneviève. "He can study Greek and Latin and French and mathematics. And do you remember when we thought that all the men of New France were fur traders or farmers or soldiers? Well, my sons can be

Intendant Talon Visiting the Habitants. Jean Talon sometimes visited the habitants in their homes in order to see for himself what life was like for people living on the seigneuries.

apprentices and learn how to be shipbuilders or shoemakers or brewers as well!"

Geneviève was also eager to hear the stories told by King's Daughters who had passed through the convent a few years earlier. One of them, a lovely red-haired young woman named Anne, was just two years older than Geneviève, but already she and her husband had three young children. They lived on a seigneury a short distance west of Quebec.

"Our life is very good," she told Geneviève. "Our farm is long and narrow, but my husband has built our house near the river. Every winter, when the farming is not busy, he builds a little more furniture. We have a fine bed with curtains around it. Our baby sleeps in a cradle beside the bed, and the two older children sleep in the loft above."

Anne told Geneviève about life on a habitant farm. "We spin our own wool from our sheep. Then we weave or knit clothes for our families.

For families with over 10 children, there is a special allowance, but we must pay a fine if we have daughters over 16 who are not married. And any men over 18 who are not married must pay a special tax, and they may lose their hunting and fishing licences."

Anne was proudest of the day that Intendant Jean Talon had made a visit to her home. "He has already made a census of the population to see how many there are of us in New France. Occasionally he comes around to visit our homes. When he stopped at our house, he said that the bread I bake in the seigneur's oven is as fine as any he has tasted, either in France or New France."

As the summer passed, Geneviève met several young men. She knew that each of them was looking for a wife. Geneviève knew that the nuns hoped that she would choose one of the young men to marry, as nearly every other King's Daughter had done, but she did not feel ready to

make that decision. The nuns allowed her to help with the teaching of the young French and Huron girls who came to them to learn a little reading and writing and arithmetic, as well as skills that they would need when they had families to raise. As she helped the younger girls, Geneviève was an eager pupil herself. She knew that it was up to the women of New France to learn how to read and write, as so many of the men did not.

She also spent time helping the nuns look after the sick and injured who came to their hospital. The first time that Geneviève had to cut one of her patients to let some of his blood out, she felt very sick. However, the nuns thought that this cured many infections and fevers, so she carefully learned the skill.

Summer turned to an autumn of vibrantly coloured trees. Then came winter, with a cold that Geneviève could not have imagined. It was too cold for the pupils to come to school in the winter, but Geneviève was kept busier than ever helping the nuns tend to the sick. When spring came round again, Geneviève realized she was no longer a new-comer to New France. Soon she would be helping the next year's King's Daughters with advice about the ways of New France.

"I must decide soon whether I will marry one of these habitants and raise a family of my own, or whether I will remain with the nuns and help the people of New France," she thought. "But that is why I came to New France—so I could make choices, and not just live the life that circumstances would thrust upon me." ∎

Apprentice — a person who works with a skilled craftsperson in order to learn that craft

The Church in New France

#16648, National Gallery of Canada, Ottawa.

Harvest Festival. The success of crops was vital to the habitants of New France.

The Roman Catholic Church played a very important part in the Royal Colony of New France. Nearly all of the people in New France were Roman Catholic because Cardinal Richelieu and the King of France had passed a law that only Roman Catholics could go to New France.

The role of the Church changed when New France became a Royal Colony. Under the trading companies, the Church had been chiefly concerned with missionary work among the Native peoples. After the campaign against the Iroquois, the number of settlers increased and more priests were needed for the people on the seigneuries and in the towns. Education, hospitals, and charity also became Church business. In today's world, few institutions would attempt to deal with so many different responsibilities. Bishop Laval met these needs by bringing in more French priests and starting a seminary at Quebec in 1663.

The seminary trained boys born in New France for the priesthood.

The Church held a very influential position in the government of the Royal Colony. The bishop was one of the three most important members of the Sovereign Council. This meant that Church opinions were taken into consideration whenever decisions about the colony were being made.

The Church's power in New France was limited by the growing independence of the population. When the Church tried to tithe, or tax, farm goods as heavily as it did in France, the seigneurs and habitants refused to pay more than one twenty-sixth of their yearly produce. This sharply limited the Church's income in New France.

In the Towns

The three main towns of New France—Quebec, Montreal, and Trois Rivières—were along the St. Lawrence River. They relied on the river for transportation.

Quebec, the oldest of the three towns, was the military centre of New France. The governor of New France lived in the Château St. Louis on the cliffs of the Upper Town, and crafts people and merchants lived in the Lower Town.

Montreal was started in 1642 as a mission to the Huron and Algonquin. By the 1660s it was the centre of the fur trade. Trois Rivières was known for birchbark canoes.

The three main towns each had a church. The church in Quebec was a stone cathedral with an organ and bells. The bishop or another high-ranking priest conducted the mass.

On the Seigneuries

One of the seigneur's duties was to provide his habitants with a church. These churches were usually small wooden or stone buildings. Each area, or parish, was also supposed to have its own priest. Often there were not enough priests, so one priest would have to travel from parish to parish.

The priests performed many services for the people:

- spiritual service—celebrated mass, heard confessions, baptized babies, performed marriages and funerals
- legal service—drew up wills, recorded business transactions, drew up marriage contracts
- government service—registered births and deaths, acted as government officials, relayed government announcements
- personal service—provided the latest news and gossip from other parishes

For the habitants, the church was the centre of religious life and much of their social life. The priests provided community leadership and tried to see that the teachings and wishes of the Roman Catholic Church were followed.

Role in Education

The Church was the only source of education in the Royal Colony. It taught children the Roman Catholic religion, to read and write Latin and French, and to do arithmetic. Many children, especially boys, did not get any schooling at all. In Quebec, Bishop Laval's seminary trained those boys who were planning to enter the priesthood. Boys who were not intending to become priests often remained illiterate because they were needed to work on the farms. The shortage of priests also made it difficult to provide boys with schooling. Girls often received a better education than their brothers.

The Ursuline nuns established schools for young Native and French girls at Quebec and Trois Rivières. In Montreal, a nun named Marguerite Bourgeoys started the same type of school for girls. Some nuns travelled to the seigneuries to teach the children. In 1676, a boarding school was set up for the daughters of rich merchants and colonists.

In most European countries at this time, women were poorly educated, if they were educated at all. European visitors to New France were often very surprised to find that the women of New France were more educated than their husbands.

C-10520, National Archives of Canada, Ottawa.

First Ursuline Nuns With Children. In 1640, most children in New France were taught by their parents. These Native children, who were taught by the Ursuline nuns, probably had lessons in the Roman Catholic religion, French, and basic mathematics.

Role in Health Care

The Church was the only institution in New France that cared for the sick, the elderly, orphans, and people with disabilities. This type of care usually became the work of the nuns. These women worked very hard in very difficult conditions to ease suffering and help the habitants. The Ursuline nuns established the colony's first hospital in Quebec in 1639. In 1659, they established a hospital in Montreal.

Exploring Further

1. Make a list of all the services provided by the Church in New France. Beside each service, list the government agency that is responsible for that service today.
2. It is 1675. A European pamphlet has just stated that the institutions in New France (the seigneurial system and the Church) are medieval and out-of-date. As an official member of the Sovereign Council, you have been selected to reply to this in a letter.

Review

Summarizing the Chapter

- New France became a Royal Colony, under the direct control of Louis XIV of France, in 1663.

- King Louis XIV was an absolute monarch both in France and in New France. He held all of the political power.

- Colbert, although he had never visited New France, ran the colony as the King's Chief Official. The colony provided a source of inexpensive raw materials and a market for goods manufactured in France.

- There were three major French institutions in New France: the Royal Government, the seigneurial system, and the Church. These institutions, although they came from the mother country, France, were adapted to suit the unique way of life in New France.

- The three most important French officials in New France were the governor general, the bishop, and the intendant.

- The coming of the Europeans to North America affected Native cultures, but not all Native cultures were affected in the same way. European cultures were also affected by the Native cultures.

Checking Predictions

1. At the beginning of this chapter you made some predictions based on the Overview and what you already knew. Now use what you learned from reading the chapter to fill in the third column of the Prediction Chart that you began earlier.

2. Refer to the "Questions to Talk About" on page 41. Discuss the questions based on what you have learned about colonial government in New France. Record the important ideas in your notebook.

Working with Information

1. Here are some main ideas from this chapter:

- Royal Colony
- absolute monarchy
- characteristics of an absolute monarchy
- colonial government
- seigneurial system
- the Church

Use a web to make a permanent record to show the relationships among the main ideas. You may want to add supporting ideas to your web. Explain your web to a classmate.

2. Review all the different examples of power and decision-making found in the chapter. Work with a partner to draw a mind map that organizes all of these examples on one sheet of paper. Show how the desire for power and the methods of decision-making affected the Royal Colony of New France. Use simple line drawings and at least three colours. A sample mind map is shown on page 16. Share your mind map with others in the class.

3. Which person from this chapter would you have liked to meet? Explain why.

4. Prepare a visual definition of absolute monarchy.

Building Thinking Strategies

Comparing

1. Comparing involves seeing the similarities (what is the same) between two or more items or events. Refer to questions 1 to 7 on page 41. Compare the decision-making model you created on page 41 in "For Your Notebook" with the model on page 47 of government in New France. Working in groups of two, divide a piece of chart paper into two headings:

Coach's model	New France Model
1.	
2.	
3.	
4.	
5.	
6.	

SAMPLE

Using the seven questions on page 41, write down the answers for each model. Use a coloured pen to mark which answers are the same on both sides.

2. Working with a partner, write out the steps one uses in comparing. Share your ideas with another group. As a class, write up the procedures involved in comparing.

3. In paragraph form, compare the duties of a seigneur and a habitant. Use what you learned about how to compare when writing your paragraph.

Communicating Ideas

Reading

1. You may wish to read "Sophie Quesnel" by Suzanne Martel in *Ordinary People in Canada's Past* by Nancy Sellars Marcotte.
2. Read to find out some more about Madeleine d'Allonne, who owned her own seigneury.
3. Read to find out about the French Carignan-Salières regiment.
4. Read about one of the following people in the book *Great Canadian Lives: Portraits in Heroism to 1867* by Ford, MacLean, and Wansbrough: Madeleine d'Allonne, Robert de La Salle, Madeleine de Verchères, or Kateri Tekakwitha. Would you have liked to have been this person? Why or why not? Share your findings with a friend.

Writing

1. Write a story from the point of view of a "king's daughter" as she sails for New France. Tell about your hopes for your new life.
2. Write a dialogue between an habitant in New France and a peasant in France, showing the difference in their lives on seigneuries.

Listening

1. Prepare the story on pages 52 and 53 for oral reading to your class.

Speaking

1. You are King Louis XIV. Prepare a speech to give to your classmates defending your right to rule.
2. You and three other classmates have become a poor French family that is considering moving to New France. The mother wishes to go, but not everyone else is convinced. Role play the parts of the different family members. Arrive at a conclusion. Will everyone be content? Practise your dialogue and present it to another group or the class.

Viewing

1. Find pictures, drawings, and diagrams of seigneuries. Prepare a collage for your classroom.

Creating

1. With several other people create a collage that visually illustrates the decision-making process outlined in this chapter. Use bright illustrations (from the coach story and from New France) to make your work appealing and understandable. Put your collage up for display.
2. Design a brochure showing all the services provided by the Church in New France.
3. Dress up as the three most important officials in New France and role-play a discussion where you explain who you are and what you do. Prepare this for presentation to your classmates.

Canada Revisited

Marguerite d'Youville (1701–1771)

Born at Varennes, Quebec, d'Youville is the first person born in Canada to be named a saint by the Roman Catholic Church. For over 100 years attempts to have d'Youville canonized have drawn attention to her miraculous healing powers and prophetic gifts. In December 1990, Pope John Paul II proclaimed Marguerite d'Youville a saint.

In 1737 d'Youville and four other women dedicated themselves to charity and the service of the poor. This group, known as the Sisters of Charity or the Grey Nuns, was put in charge of the bankrupt Hospital General of Quebec. They successfully reorganized the hospital into a home for the elderly, orphans, and homeless women. Today over 13 000 women have become Grey Nuns, the order of which d'Youville is the recognized founder.

Chapter 4
Struggle for Control
(1670–1774)

O v e r v i e w

Use this Overview to predict the events of this chapter.

1755
The French and British struggled to control the western fur territories.

1755
Deportation of the Acadians by the British soldiers.

The French and British fought to control the Atlantic and the colony of Quebec.

French General Montcalm

British General Wolfe

Quebec

Montreal

Louisbourg

1756
Seven Years' War formally declared.

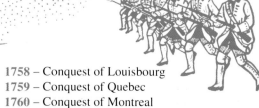

1758 – Conquest of Louisbourg
1759 – Conquest of Quebec
1760 – Conquest of Montreal

Treaty of Paris

- British
- Spanish
- Russian
- French fishing rights
- French

1763
British military rule ended French rule in Quebec. Treaty of Paris (a peace treaty) concluded the Seven Years' War.

1774
Britain decided on a policy of keeping Quebec both French and British.

1763
A British Royal Proclamation created original province of Quebec. Britain decided to assimilate the French into the British Empire.

Chapter 4 Focus

Chapter 3 dealt with New France's early history and the role of France as a colonial power. Chapter 4 is about the conflict that occurred between France and Britain as they tried to gain control of the area now known as Canada. The events of this struggle are described up until 1774. **Biculturalism**, which developed in Canada as a result of French-English co-operation, will also be introduced. Decision-making and conflict are the focus of Chapter 4.

Power

Co-operation

Decision-making

Conflict

Overview/Prediction Chart

Examine the Overview found on the previous pages. In pairs or small groups use the Overview and what you already know about the conflict between the French and British to predict answers to the questions in the Prediction Chart. Once you have finished the chapter, complete the "What I Found Out" column to help you review and summarize. Your teacher will provide you with a full-sized working copy of the Prediction Chart.

Prediction Chart—What Do You Think?		
Questions	My Predictions (fill out now)	What I Found Out (fill out at end of chapter)
1. What might be the major events?		
2. Who might be some of the important people or groups?	SAMPLE	
3. Who might hold power?		
4.		

Below: The British and French struggled to control two major areas: the fur country and the Atlantic Coast.

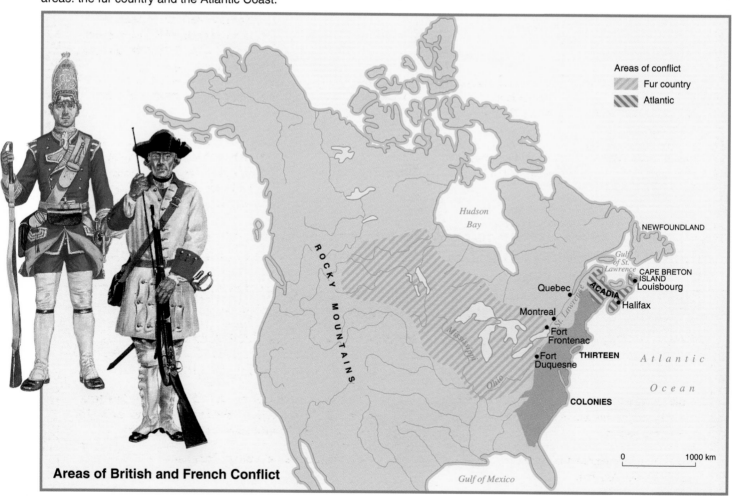

Areas of conflict
- Fur country
- Atlantic

Areas of British and French Conflict

Bicultural—having two cultures existing side by side in the same country or province

Continuing Conflict between Britain and France

Britain and France had long been at war with one another in Europe. These wars, over land, power, and wealth, eventually spread to North America. When treaties to end the European wars were struck, the effects were felt in North America. Land held by either the French or British changed hands as a result of the treaties. The first chart shows the results of the major wars between Britain and France and the resulting land possessions. The second chart outlines the organization of material in this chapter. Refer to it throughout the chapter to aid your learning.

The Wars between Britain and France

In Europe	In North America	Peace Treaty	Results in North America
War of the League of Augsburg (1688–97)	King William's War (1689–97)	Peace of Ryswick (1697)	• brief end to British-French hostilities
War of the Spanish Succession (1702–13)	Queen Anne's War (1701–13)	Treaty of Utrecht (1713)	• French surrendered forts in territories of Hudson's Bay Co. • French gave up claims to Newfoundland and Acadia • Iroquois declared British subjects • islands of the Gulf of St. Lawrence remained French
War of the Austrian Succession (1740–48)	King George's War (1744–48)	Treaty of Aix-la-Chapelle (1748)	• returned Louisbourg to French
Seven Years' War (1756–63)	French and Indian Wars (1754–63)	Treaty of Paris (1763)	• all French land possessions in North America except the tiny islands of St. Pierre and Miquelon off coast of Newfoundland became British

British–French Conflict in North America

There were two main struggles in the attempts of Britain and France to control North America:

Area	Reason for Conflict
• the struggle to control the fur country (west to the Rocky Mountains and in the Ohio Valley). *See* map page 60.	• British desire to control the fur trade and to gain farmland • French desire to control the fur trade and to prevent British expansion into the western part of North America
• the struggle to control the Atlantic (Louisbourg, Halifax, and Acadia). *See* map page 60.	• rich fishing areas and strategic location

The Struggle to Control the Fur Country

Differences between French and British Fur Trade

With the establishment of the Hudson's Bay Company in 1670, the British developed a fur trading system that competed with the French for the wealth of the fur trade. Although both the British and French depended on the Native peoples to supply the furs, the British fur trade was different from the French in two major ways. While the French, under the direction of their Native guides, were exploring farther and farther inland searching for new fur territory, the British waited for the Native people to bring furs to their forts around Hudson Bay.

The second major difference between the British and French fur trade was that the Hudson's Bay Company was formed by a group of merchants who put their money together to share the risks and the profits. They were only interested in profits from the fur trade and had little interest in colonization. The French fur trade was controlled by the government, and colonization was important to New France. This was why they developed the seigneuries and sent colonists to New France, and protected the fur trade whenever possible.

Cultural Exchange

Only a small percentage of Canada's Native peoples ever had any direct contact with the Europeans. In spite of this, European products, such as metal weapons, pots, and pans, were available in areas where no Europeans had ever been. In just a few generations the lifestyle of the Native peoples began to change. The Native peoples lost the skills that were required to make their own weapons and utensils. They began to rely almost entirely on the trade goods of the Europeans. Many hunting bands gave up their **migratory** lifestyles of hunting large game and formed new, small family groups where they hunted and tanned small animal skins for their pelts. These pelts were then traded to other Native peoples acting as go-betweens, or to Europeans for European goods, such as guns, ammunition, food, clothing, and metal pots and pans. The lifestyles of the farming peoples, like the Iroquois, were also affected.

The key to French and British success lay in the help they received from Native men and women.*

Migratory — moving from place to place, usually according to the season. Many hunting bands travelled within their own territory in a circular fashion with seasonal homes within this area.
*For more information on Native and European interaction, *see* page 24.

Animal pelts obtained by the Native peoples were traded for European trade goods, such as guns, metal goods, and clothing.

France Protects the Fur Trade

The French did two things to try to protect the fur trade that was so important to their control in North America. They took military action against the British and expanded inland.

Military Action Against the British

Armed clashes occurred between the two sides from 1679 to 1713, but neither the British nor the French were able to take complete control of the Hudson Bay area. In 1713, the Treaty of Utrecht ended the European war between the French and British and made all of the Hudson Bay posts British property. The French were no longer allowed to enter the fur territory through Hudson Bay. They had to travel overland from Montreal via the St. Lawrence River and the Great Lakes.

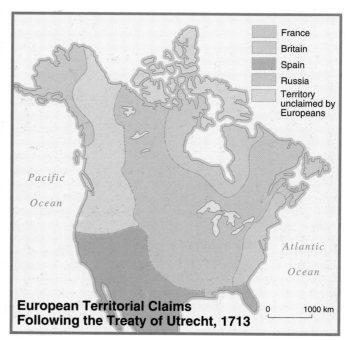

France
Britain
Spain
Russia
Territory unclaimed by Europeans

Pacific Ocean

Atlantic Ocean

European Territorial Claims Following the Treaty of Utrecht, 1713

0   1000 km

Expansion Inland

In the late 1600s, under the direction of Governor Frontenac, New France had expanded south into the Ohio and Mississippi valleys so that it stretched over a vast area from the Gulf of St. Lawrence down to the Gulf of Mexico.

Hoping to stop the Native people from taking their furs to the British trading forts near Hudson Bay, the French sent Pierre La Vérendrye to establish French trading forts inland, closer to the Native people. During the 1730s and early 1740s, La Vérendrye established many French fur trading posts and expanded French control north and west. The Native people began taking their fur pelts to the inland French forts rather than travelling the long distance to Hudson Bay. The British fur trade began to suffer.

Years earlier, the Hudson's Bay Company had sent an explorer, Henry Kelsey, to the interior. Kelsey's journey, which lasted from 1690 to 1692, took him to present-day Saskatchewan and possibly to Alberta. However, Kelsey had not been successful in persuading the Native people to bring their furs to the posts on Hudson Bay.

In 1754 the Hudson's Bay Company sent another trader, Anthony Henday, to the interior. Henday spent the winter of 1754–55 with the Blackfoot in present-day Alberta. However, he also failed to persuade the Plains people to

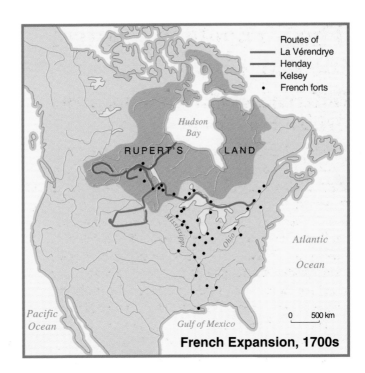

Routes of
— La Vérendrye
— Henday
— Kelsey
• French forts

French Expansion, 1700s

0   500 km

travel to the Hudson's Bay Company forts on Hudson Bay. Henday recommended that the Hudson's Bay Company build trading forts inland, but this did not occur until 1774.

Kelsey hunting buffalo with the Assiniboine. Kelsey was the first European to see large herds of buffalo grazing on the Prairies.

Confederation Life Gallery of Canadian History.

The Struggle to Control the Atlantic

In addition to their attempts to control the fur trade, Britain and France also struggled to control the Atlantic coast of North America.

Louisbourg

The struggle to control the Atlantic coast was concentrated on the French colonies of Île Royale (Cape Breton Island) and Acadia. Île Royale was important because Louisbourg, the centre of French power, was located there.

When France and Britain signed the Treaty of Utrecht in 1713, France lost Acadia and the colony of Newfoundland. (*See* map page 62.) Newfoundland had been an extremely important fishery as it was located close to the Grand Banks, an excellent fishing area. The French were left with Île St. Jean (Prince Edward Island), St. Pierre and Miquelon, and Île Royale. The French carried out their fishing operations from these islands for a time, but since fishing was such a profitable business, they decided they needed a much larger fishing base in the New World. An area known today as Cape Breton Island was selected. It was here that construction began on Louisbourg in 1720.

Louisbourg was much more than a fishing station. The French needed a military and naval base from which they could control the Gulf of St. Lawrence and guard the approaches to New France. The fortress, which was built on a natural harbour, was not only impressive, but also thought to be impossible to break into. Besides a fortress, Louisbourg was also an important royal capital, a naval base, and a thriving centre of commerce.

Although Louisbourg was reputed to be strong, it was poorly constructed and was surrounded by hills from which an enemy could attack. Despite its flaws, the British saw Louisbourg as a threat to their control in North America. The colonists in New England demanded protection from the French and the Native peoples, so the British constructed the fortress of Halifax in 1749.

Louisbourg remained an important French fortress from 1719 until 1760. Twice within this time—1745 and 1758—it was captured by the British. In the attack of 1745, William Pepperell led 4000 New Englanders from Boston. They approached Louisbourg from land and were able to capture the fortress in 46 days. Although the fortress was returned to the French in 1748 through the Treaty of Aix-la-Chapelle, the British now knew that Louisbourg could be conquered.

Above: The fleur-de-lis marked the buildings of King Louis XIV and King Louis XV.

Louisbourg was one of the major military fortresses in the New World. The military citadel dominated the town from on top of the largest hill. This citadel housed a garrison of several hundred soldiers, a prison, and a chapel.

The photographs on pages 64 and 65 show the reconstructed Louisbourg. Louisbourg was one of the busiest seaports in the New World. Ships from the French navy and merchant ships (private trading vessels) from France made frequent trips to and from Louisbourg. Merchant ships from Quebec, New England, the West Indies, and England arrived at Louisbourg on a yearly basis to unload their cargoes of building materials, hardware, fishing supplies, clothing, food, and passengers. These same ships then picked up cargoes of dried and salted fish for delivery to the markets of Europe. In the harbour area were many inns, taverns, and shops.

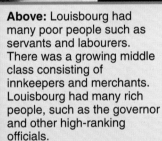

Above: Louisbourg had many poor people such as servants and labourers. There was a growing middle class consisting of innkeepers and merchants. Louisbourg had many rich people, such as the governor and other high-ranking officials.

Left: The majority of the population in the town consisted of young, single men. They worked in the fishing industry or were soldiers from the garrison.

Above: An occasional Micmac could be seen in the town visiting from the interior of the island on which Louisbourg was built.

Right: Fishing was a major industry at Louisbourg as it was located close to the Grand Banks—the waters in North America visited by hundreds of European fishing ships each year. The fish were dried on wooden racks.

The British Build Halifax

Just as the British and French took action to counteract the other's control of the fur trade, each took action to control the Atlantic region. The French built Louisbourg in 1720 and the British began building the fortress of Halifax in 1749. The fortress, built on a harbour, was designed to provide protection from Native and French raids for the British colonists in New England. Halifax became a powerful British base.

Halifax was built differently from Louisbourg. It was a townsite surrounded by five stockades rather than a fortified stone city like Louisbourg. A stockade is a fort or a camp defended by a wall of strong upright posts. Halifax did not need to be a stone fort because it was located at the end of a narrow sea passage that could be easily defended.

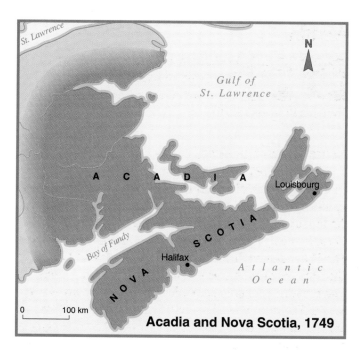

Acadia and Nova Scotia, 1749

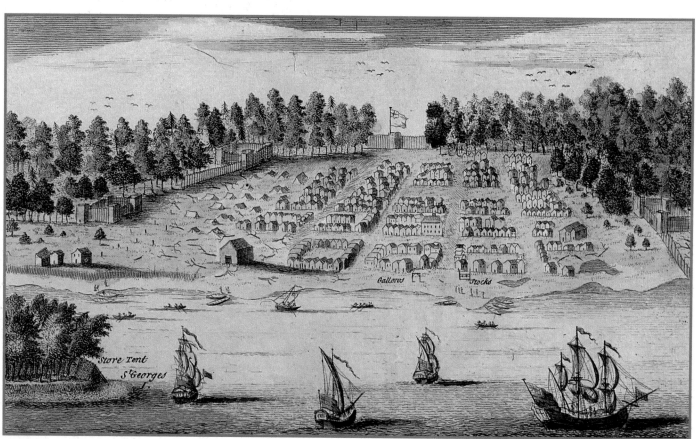

The British began to build the fortress at Halifax in 1749. This view of Halifax shows the stockade, which provided ample protection. The harbour was located at the end of a narrow sea passage, which provided good protection.

Acadia

  In addition to wanting to control the fortress of Louisbourg, the British wanted to take over and control the French colony of Acadia.

Acadia Becomes British

Wars between Britain and France in Europe had effects on the colonies in North America. France and Britain were again at war in Europe from 1701 to 1713. In North America, the French and British continued to fight for control and in 1710, Port Royal was captured by the British once again. The European war ended in 1713. By the Treaty of Utrecht, Britain was given ownership of Rupert's Land, Newfoundland, and most of what is now known as Nova Scotia. The rest of Acadia, including Île Royale, remained under French control. (Please *refer* to the chart on page 61 and the map on page 62.)

Oath of Allegiance

Although the French Acadians had a year to leave after the Treaty of Utrecht, many had chosen to remain neutral, not fighting for France or Britain. They refused to take an unqualified oath of allegiance to the British Crown. Such an oath would have meant that they would fight for the British against all others, including the French.

By the 1750s it seemed that there would be another war between France and Britain in Europe, which would have effects in North America. The French Acadians were seen as a threat to the British in Nova Scotia. Governor Lawrence decided that the Acadians must pledge their loyalty to Britain. Again they refused, as they had done for 42 years. Governor Lawrence had to make a decision. What was to be done with the Acadians? You will be required to revisit Canadian history and become involved in an important decision. Read and follow the exercise on the right.

A Decision-Making Model
• • • • • • •

1. Identify an issue.
2. Identify possible alternatives.
3. Devise a plan for research.
4. Gather, organize, and interpret information.
5. Using collected information, evaluate the alternatives.
6. Make a decision. Plan or take action on the decision (if feasible and desirable).
7. Evaluate the process, the decision, and the action.

An Exercise in Decision-Making

During the 1740s, the French had tried to recapture parts of Acadia. Nearby Louisbourg had been returned to the French. The British wanted to be sure that the French-speaking Acadians would not help France recapture all of Acadia. Read the imaginary comments below.

Acadian

We've refused to take an oath of allegiance to Britain for over 40 years. Nothing ever happened to us before for refusing. Why should it be different this time?

British Governor Lawrence

France and Britain will soon be at war in Europe. That will mean more French–British conflict in the North American colonies. The Acadians must take an oath of allegiance to Britain so we can be sure they will fight for us and not help the French. If they don't take the oath, they must suffer the consequences.

Making the Decision

In small groups decide what Governor Lawrence should do with the Acadians. Follow the decision-making model shown to the left.

The Deportation of the Acadians

The British were concerned about the number of French settlers in Acadia compared to the number of British settlers there. The Acadians were asked again to take an oath of allegiance to the British or they would be **deported**. They refused to take the oath, and in 1755 the British began to deport them from their lands and put them aboard British ships. They were taken to the Thirteen Colonies and to Louisiana. Their homes were burnt and all of their property and land was **confiscated** by the British. Some people were sent back to France and some escaped to Cape Breton Island. Many died in the deportation. Many families were separated and never saw each other again. Some of the Acadians did return many years later. The major deportation of the Acadians happened in 1755, but continued until 1762. It is estimated that as many as 11 000 Acadians were deported during this time.

The Deportation of the Acadians from the Isle of St. Jean, by Lewis Parker, shows the Acadians being forced from their homes.

For Your Notebook

1. Were Governor Lawrence's orders to deport the Acadians too harsh? Why do you think he made the decisions he did?
2. Read the poem "Evangeline" by Longfellow. You may need to ask your librarian for help to locate the poem. As you read, imagine how Evangeline and her family and friends must have felt as they were separated from their homes and loved ones.
3. The Acadians were not prepared for the consequences of their refusal to take an oath of allegiance to the British. Do you think they would still have refused if they had known that Governor Lawrence planned deportation? Discuss in a group.
4. Today there is a large Acadian population in New Brunswick and in Louisiana (the Cajuns). How do you think this came about?

Deport—force people away from their homes or a country by government order
Confiscate—property taken away by someone in authority, usually by a government

The Final Struggle for Control of North America

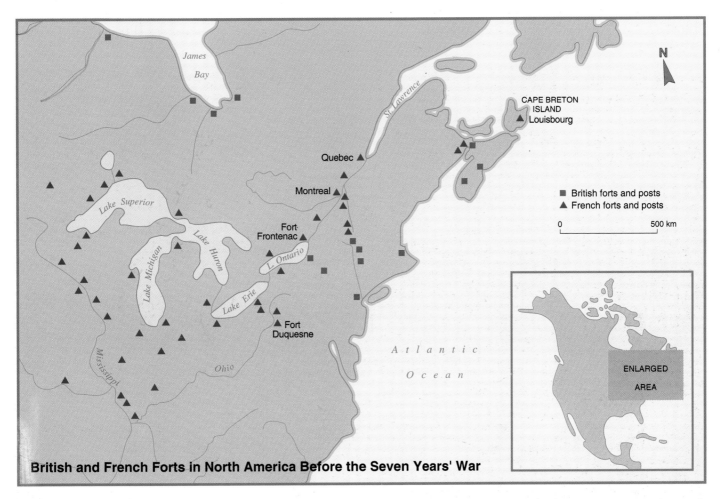

British and French Forts in North America Before the Seven Years' War

We have seen that there was a continuing struggle for control in the New World between Britain and France. The chart at the beginning of the chapter summarizes this conflict. These struggles caused the two nations to go to war in Europe. The Treaty of Utrecht in 1713 gave Newfoundland, Hudson Bay, and most of Acadia to the British. The French reacted by building the fortress of Louisbourg on Cape Breton Island and the Acadians refused to take an oath of allegiance to Britain. When the deportation of the Acadians occurred in 1755, it was clear that France and Britain would soon be at war again in Europe and that conflict between the two empires would increase in North America. One year later, in 1756, the Seven Years' War broke out in Europe between France and Britain. This war had an enormous effect on the history of North America.

The French and the English used different strategies in their struggle to control North America. The French kept most of their soldiers in Europe. Their plan was to use a small number of soldiers to fight the many British in North America. They believed that if fewer French soldiers in North America could keep a large number of British occupied, then the larger French forces in Europe could defeat the British there.

The British were determined to defeat the French in North America. They sent seven or eight times more men than the French did to North America. They planned to attack the French on three fronts: Louisbourg, the Ohio Valley, and Quebec. (*See* above map.) The British knew that it was important to control the St. Lawrence River because this was the route that French supply ships used to reach Quebec and Montreal. Control of the St. Lawrence depended on the control of Louisbourg.

For Your Notebook

1. Use the map above to decide what effect the British strategy would have on the French colonies of Louisbourg, Acadia, and Quebec.

War in North America: A Three-Pronged Attack

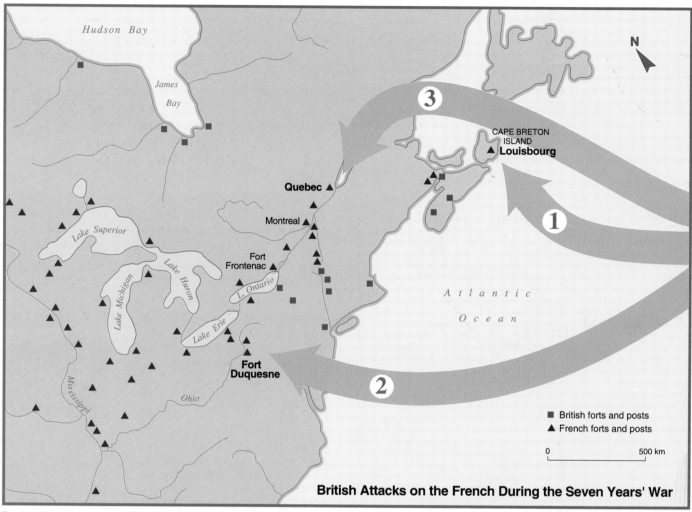

British Attacks on the French During the Seven Years' War

During the Seven Years' War, the British attacked the French in three areas: Louisbourg (1758), the Ohio Valley (1758), and Quebec (1759).

1. The Capture of Louisbourg

The British needed to capture Louisbourg in order to gain control of the entrance to the St. Lawrence River. If successful, they could sail down the river to attack Quebec.

In June of 1758, the British attacked Louisbourg. Imagine the surprise of the French inside the fortress when they saw 200 British ships in the harbour outside their fortification. The battles did not last very long. After fighting for almost 60 days, the British landed on the high ground overlooking Louisbourg and bombarded the fortress. By the time the French surrendered, Louisbourg had been almost completely destroyed by the British.

2. The Capture of the Ohio Valley

The French had many fur forts in the Ohio Valley. British control was necessary to reduce French influence in the large area of the Ohio Valley.

Prior to the fall of Louisbourg, the French had been successful in defending the Ohio Valley. This situation changed quickly with the fall of Louisbourg in July of 1758. In August, Fort Frontenac, a French fort in the Ohio Valley, was captured by the British, followed in November by Fort Duquesne. With the French driven back toward Quebec by the British and with Louisbourg captured, the British now were free to travel up the St. Lawrence to the heart of New France—Quebec.

3. The Capture of Quebec

Quebec was the centre of French power in North America. British capture of the colony of Quebec would mean the end of French control in North America. The British, under the command of General James Wolfe, waited until the spring of 1759 to attack Quebec. Over the summer the British fleet sailed up the St. Lawrence and bombarded the city of Quebec from the water, while the British troops tried to land on the Beauport shore. Wolfe tried for almost three months to capture Quebec without much success. He finally decided to attack from upriver to cut off the source of Quebec's supplies.

Today there is a park on the Plains of Abraham, the site of the 1759 battle between the French and the British.

The British Attack

British Captain John Knox described the first part of the attack on Quebec City in his journal as follows.

Eyewitness Account
Thursday, September 13, 1759.

Before daybreak this morning, we made a descent upon the north shore, about half a quarter of a mile to the eastward of Sillery; and the light troops were fortunately, by the rapidity of the current, carried lower down, between us and Cape Diamond. We had in this debarkation thirty flat-bottomed boats, containing about sixteen hundred men. This was a great surprise to the enemy, who, from the natural strength of the place, did not suspect, and consequently were not prepared against, so bold an attempt. The chain of centries, which they had

posted along the summit of the heights, galled us a little, and picked off several men, and some officers before our light infantry got up to dislodge them. This grand enterprise was conducted and executed with great good order and discretion; as fast as we landed, the boats put off for re-inforcements, and the troops formed with much regularity. The General, with Brigadiers Monckton and Murray, was ashore with the first division. We lost no time here, but clambered up one of the steepest precipices that can be conceived, being almost a perpendicular, and of an incredible height. As soon as we gained the summit all was quiet, and not a shot was heard, owing to the excellent conduct of the light infantry under Colonel Howe. It was by this time clear daylight. Here we formed again, the river and the south country in our rear, our right extending to the town, our left to Sillery, and halted a few minutes. . . . We then faced to the right, and marched toward the town by files till we came to the Plains of Abraham; an even piece of ground which Mr. Wolfe had made choice of, while we stood forming upon the hill.

Weather showery: about six o'clock the enemy first made their appearance upon the heights between us and the town; whereupon we halted and wheeled to the right, thereby forming the line of battle. . . .

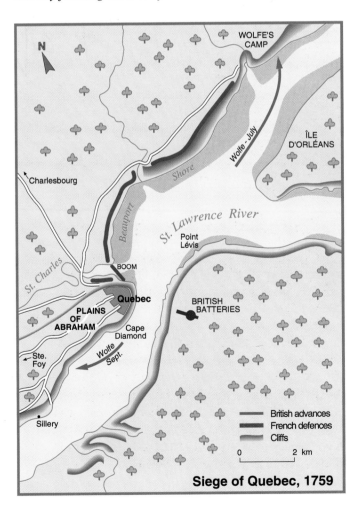

Siege of Quebec, 1759

The French React

In the early morning of September 13, 1759, Montcalm, the leader of the French forces in Quebec, received word that the British army, by a surprise plan, had landed its troops over a poorly defended cliff upstream from Quebec City at Anse aux Foulons. Wolfe's soldiers were waiting on the Plains of Abraham, three kilometres from Quebec City.

The French forces under the command of the Marquis de Montcalm were not all gathered in one place. A portion of the army was 16 kilometres away on the Beauport shore, where it was expected that the British would attack. Montcalm had to decide:

- Should he keep his army in the fortified town of Quebec and wait for the British to attack?
- Should he send word to the rest of his army to attack the British from behind?
- Should he attack immediately, with the men he had, on the Plains of Abraham?

The Battle on the Plains of Abraham

Montcalm took his men and went to meet the British on the open fields of the Plains of Abraham. The French troops were at a disadvantage because they were used to fighting in the forest, not open fields. They made a disorganized charge on the British, who waited until they were near and then fired on them, causing the French ranks to break and retreat in disorder. In less than an hour the battle was over. Both Wolfe and Montcalm died from wounds received in the fighting. Quebec had been taken by the British.

British Captain Knox's Eyewitness Account of the Battle Continues:

The enemy had now likewise formed the line of battle, and got some cannon to play on us, with round and canister shot; but what galled us most was a body of Indians and other marksmen they had concealed in the corn opposite to the front of our right wing, and a coppice that stood opposite to our centre, inclining toward our left. But Colonel Hale, by Brigadier Monckton's orders, advanced some platoons alternately, from the forty-seventh regiment, which after a few rounds obliged these skulkers to retire. We were now ordered to lie down, and remained some time in this position. About eight o'clock we had two pieces of short brass six-pounders playing on the enemy, which threw them into some confusion, and obliged them to alter their disposition; and Montcalm formed them into three large columns. About nine the two armies moved a little nearer each other. The light cavalry made a faint attempt upon our parties at the battery of Sillery, but were soon beat off; and Monsieur de Bougainville, with his troops from Cape Rouge, came
down to attack the flank of our second line, hoping to penetrate there. But by a masterly disposition of Brigadier Townshend, they were forced to desist; and the third battalion of Royal Americans was then detached to the first ground we had formed on after we gained the heights, to preserve the communication with the beach and our boats. About ten o'clock the enemy began to advance briskly in three columns, with loud shouts and recovered arms, two of them inclining to the left of our army, and the third towards our right, firing obliquely at the two extremities of our line, from the distance of one hundred and thirty, — until they came within forty yards; which our troops withstood with the greatest intrepidity and firmness, still reserving their fire and paying the strictest obedience to their officers. This uncommon steadiness, together with the havoc which the grape-shot from our field-pieces made among them, threw them into some disorder, and was most critically maintained by a well-timed, regular, and heavy discharge of our small arms, such as they could no longer oppose. Hereupon they gave way, and fled with precipitation, so that, by the time the cloud of smoke was vanished our men were again loaded and, profiting by the advantage we had over them, pursued them almost to the gates of the town and the bridge over the little river, redoubling our fire with great eagerness, making many Officers and men prisoners . . . .*

Our joy at this success is inexpressibly damped by the loss we sustained of one of the greatest heroes which this or any other age can boast of— GENERAL JAMES WOLFE, who received his mortal wound, as he was exerting himself at the head of the grenadiers . . . .

The Officers who are prisoners say, that Quebec will surrender in a few days: some deserters, who came out to us in the evening, agree in that opinion, and inform us, that the Sieur de Montcalm is dying, in great agony, of a wound he received today in their retreat . . . .

An Exercise in Decison-Making

1. Why do you think Montcalm made the decision he did?
2. What decision would you have made if you were Montcalm? Use one of the decision-making models from this textbook, or design one of your own, to help you arrive at a decision.

A View of the Taking of Quebec, September 13, 1759—Quebec falls to the British. This painting shows a view of the day's events as though they were all happening at once, but really the events took place from late at night until the following morning.

Montreal

After the British took Quebec, the French army and officials retreated to Montreal. The British occupied Quebec over the winter. The French made an attempt to drive the British from Quebec in the spring of 1760. They marched from Montreal to Quebec and were able to force the British to retreat behind the town's walls. The outcome of the struggle for Quebec now depended on whether the first ship through the St. Lawrence that spring brought British or French reinforcements. The first ship to come was British and the French retreated to Montreal again.

In September 1760 the British troops marched to Montreal, burning crops along the St. Lawrence River as they advanced. The French governor, Vaudreuil, realizing future resistance attempts were futile, agreed to peace and surrendered to the British troops. Chevalier de Lévis, the commander of the French army, rather than surrendering the French flags to the enemy, ordered that they be burned. British control in North America was finally achieved.

Surrender of Montreal. On September 8, 1760, Governor General Pierre de Rigaud de Vaudreuil de Cavagnial surrendered Montreal to the British commander, Jeffrey Amherst.

C-27665, National Archives of Canada, Ottawa (detail).

Louis-Joseph, Marquis de Montcalm (1712–1759)

Louis-Joseph de Montcalm was born in France near Nimes. He joined the French army at the age of nine and was a captain at age 17. He won distinction in the War of the Austrian Succession.

By 1756 Montcalm had retired and was living with his wife and children in the south of France when he was asked to go and lead the French forces in Quebec. He did not want to go, but went anyway because he thought it was his duty.

Montcalm quarrelled with Pierre de Rigaud de Vaudreuil, the governor of Quebec. Montcalm thought Vaudreuil could not be a good military leader because he was born in New France and had no experience of European warfare. Actually Montcalm was not experienced in the **guerrilla warfare** that was successful in New France. Montcalm's strategy of withdrawing troops from the interior to defend Quebec was not successful.

On September 13, 1759, Montcalm was surprised to find the British soldiers lined up on the Plains of Abraham. He could have avoided the battle—the British would have to withdraw soon because winter was coming. Both British and French had 4500 soldiers, but the British had forced the French into fighting in the well-organized European style of warfare, so the British won.

Montcalm was **fatally** wounded at the Battle of the Plains of Abraham. There is a highly romanticized painting that shows him dying on the battlefield. Actually he died the next morning in Quebec.

General James Wolfe (1727–1759)

James Wolfe was born in the County of Kent in England. He was not a strong child, but he was determined to be a soldier like his father. He chose a lifetime career in the British army, joining at age 13. He served in Europe and Scotland.

Wolfe came to North America during the Seven Years' War. He served under Lord Amherst in the assault on Louisbourg. He led front line troops who helped the British capture that fort in 1758. After the capture of Louisbourg, Wolfe returned to England, but was selected to command the expedition against Quebec.

Wolfe and his men spent most of the summer of 1759 camped on the St. Lawrence River near Quebec, looking for a way to take the city. The British soldiers were not used to the hot Canadian summer, and many of them became very ill. Wolfe quarrelled with his officers and allowed his men to burn the farms of French militia.

Wolfe's men won the Battle of the Plains of Abraham because they were well disciplined, and they were able to fight on an open field rather than in the guerrilla style preferred by French militia. However, Wolfe was very unpopular. There is a highly romanticized painting of his death. Some officers who were there refused to be in the painting; others who were not there paid to be included.

Guerrilla warfare—fighting in small bands, making sudden attacks and ambushes on the enemy
Fatally—to death

An Exercise in Critical Thinking

Points of View

What was to happen to the people of New France and Acadia? Although the French had been defeated by the British in North America, until the European war between the two countries was settled, the future of New France was undecided.

In this part of the chapter you will be asked to do some critical thinking and to look at issues from several points of view. Critical thinkers realize that there is always more than one position to take on an issue.

This activity should take approximately three class periods. To help you understand the various points of view that existed in New France after the British gained control over the French territory, you will be asked to engage in a group role play activity that ends with a brief writing assignment.

Period One

Your teacher will divide your class into five groups. Use the following as a guide: Native people—five students; Seigneurs—five students; French Clergy—five students; Habitants—eight students; British Merchants— three students. Role play cards follow. Imagine you are one of the people described on the cards. Carry out the instructions on your role play card.

1. Native People

You have gathered together to decide on your future now that the British have defeated the French. You live in the lands to the west of the Thirteen Colonies. Every week more and more British colonists are moving across the Appalachian Mountains onto the lands where you farm and hunt. Use a consensus model (refer to page 3) to decide what you wish to tell the British governor about this situation.

2. Seigneurs

You are members of the seigneury in Quebec. Several of your group are part of the government's Sovereign Council. You have gathered together to discuss recent events in the colony. You are very concerned about what will happen to you now that the British have won the war. Will you be deported from your lands by the British, just as the Acadians were? What will happen to your government? There are approximately 60 000 of you to be ruled by less than 1000 British. What problems will result from this? You have heard that the British will not allow any Roman Catholics to participate in government affairs! Some of your habitants have had problems because British laws and customs are different from French laws and customs. Discuss the situation with your fellow seigneurs and make plans as to what you should do. What alternatives are open to you and your habitants? Discuss the consequences of each alternative. When you have arrived at a decision, outline your plans in a letter to the bishop of Quebec. Ask him if the clergy wishes to join you in your plans.

3. French Clergy

As members of the Roman Catholic clergy, you have gathered together to discuss the future of the French in Quebec now that the British have won the war. The habitants are very concerned and you have instructed the local priests to tell them during Church services that they should obey their new masters. You are concerned with *La Survivance* (cultural survival) and that the British will not allow your people to keep their Roman Catholic religion and French language. You have heard that the British will not support your efforts to collect one twenty-sixth of the grain the habitants grow. You need this tax to help you look after the sick and needy, to educate the children, and to continue your work in Christianizing the Native people. Discuss these issues and make plans as to what you should do. What alternatives are open to you and your people? Discuss the consequence of each alternative. When you have arrived at a decision, outline your plans in a letter to the bishop of Quebec.

4. Habitants

You have gathered together along with some of your fellow habitants to discuss your future. You are very concerned about what will happen to you now that the British have won the war. Will you be deported from your lands by the British, just as the Acadians were? There are approximately 60 000 French to be ruled by less than 1000 British. The local priest has encouraged you to obey your new masters, as have your local seigneurs, but you have many concerns. You have heard that the British system of holding land surveys lots in squares rather than in long narrow strips like the seigneurial system you are used to. You fear you will lose your land and your homes. You have heard that you will have to pay more rent, more taxes, and will not be able to use the local wheat mill. Rumours are everywhere! Discuss the situation with your group and make plans as to what you should do. What alternatives are open to you? Discuss the consequences of each alternative. When you have arrived at a decision, outline your plans in a letter to your local priest.

La Survivance — refers to the French concern for preserving distinctive cultural ideas about their own Roman Catholic religion, French language, and French civil laws

5. British Merchants

You are part of a small group of British merchants who moved into Quebec in 1761 from the Thirteen Colonies (after the Seven Years' War). Customs and traditions certainly are different here. The 60 000 people all speak French, and all are Roman Catholics living under a different system of government and laws than you are used to. Even their system of holding land is strange to you. You had anticipated that large numbers of British merchants would move north to Quebec from the Thirteen Colonies but this has not happened. There are only about 1000 of you here, but you realize that with the help of the British government you hold a very dominant and influential position. Perhaps if you **petition** the British government it will be possible to have an elected **assembly** in the Quebec government, just as you did in the Thirteen Colonies. You could dominate this assembly, and in turn the colony, especially if you are able to exclude all Roman Catholics from participating. As far as you are concerned the British won the war and should use their victory to good advantage. Discuss the situation and make plans as to what you should do. What alternatives are open to you? Discuss the consequences of each alternative. When you have arrived at a decision, outline your plans in a letter to the British government.

Periods Two and Three

1. Each group is to read the letter they have written out loud to the class. The Native group is to explain what they wish to do. After each group has finished, answer the following questions:

   (a) What is the speaker saying? **Paraphrase** the main points in your notebook or use a web or mind map to record the main ideas.
   (b) Record emotionally charged words that tell how the speaker feels.
   (c) What position is the speaker taking?
   (d) What values do you think are important to each speaker?

2. Critical thinkers realize there is more than one point of view on every issue. As a class, list as many alternatives as you can think of that the British had in dealing with the French and the Native peoples. List these alternatives on large chart paper for reference as you study the rest of this chapter. Which alternative do you think the British will turn to first?

Alternatives Open to the British

1	
2	
3	SAMPLE
4	

Petition — a formal request to a government or authority by a group of people, asking for a specific action
Assembly — at this time an elected group that made laws. The Assembly had little power as the governor or his council could veto its decisions.
Paraphrase — to express the meaning of a book, a passage, or a set of words in different words

British Military Rule

C-361, National Archives of Canada, Ottawa.

British Military Rule is established in Quebec.

In North America, the war between Britain and France ended when the British captured Montreal in September 1760. However, the Seven Years' War continued in Europe and other parts of the world until 1763. Until the war was over and a peace treaty signed, the *Canadiens* continued to hope that New France would be returned to France.

Between 1760 and 1763, the British army in New France set up a temporary government. This is known as the period of British Military Rule. British military governors were appointed at Quebec, Montreal, and Trois Rivières. Supreme authority was in the hands of the British commander-in-chief, General Amherst, in New York. Some of the French officials returned to France, but most of the colonists stayed. The British Military Rule was not a harsh **occupation**. The British military rulers did not wish to cause any further disruption in the colony of New France and did not make any great changes to life in the colony during this three-year period.

Canadiens—French-speaking people born in New France (Quebec). The name shows that the *Canadiens* were distinct from the French in Europe.

Occupation—the control of an area by a foreign military force

Life of the *Canadiens*

This period of British Military Rule—from 1760 to 1763—was a time of uncertainty for the *Canadiens*. Until a peace treaty was signed, there was uncertainty in New France about how daily life and government might become different under British rule.

The *Canadien* soldiers in the militia were allowed to return to their homes, and they were promised that their property would not be taken away. However, many found that their property had been destroyed. Many farms along the St. Lawrence River east of Quebec had been burned by British soldiers during the summer of 1759. Much of the Lower Town of Quebec, which the British had been able to reach with cannon shots all through the summer of 1759, had been destroyed. This meant that many homes and businesses had been destroyed.

The *Canadiens* were uneasy, remembering the deportation of the French Acadians during British occupation in 1755. They had questions about whether or not they would be asked to swear an oath of loyalty (allegiance) to Britain or face deportation. They also had questions about maintaining their French language and culture, and Roman Catholic religion.

The Jesuits were forced to return to France. Since they had run the schools, the educational system of the *Canadiens* was seriously weakened. However, because the orders of nuns were allowed to stay, the hospitals that they ran continued to operate. In fact, there are stories about the French nuns knitting stockings to help keep the British soldiers warm during the winter of 1759–60.

Many of the business people of New France were actually from France. When they returned to France, their place in business was often taken over by British merchants, many of these coming from the Thirteen Colonies.

Some aspects of life in New France changed very little under British Military Rule. The French language and Roman Catholic religion were maintained. The role of the Catholic priests in meeting the needs of the people also continued. French **civil law** and the French language were used in the courts. The seigneurial system continued.

The British wanted to co-operate with the French during this time of uncertainty, so daily life in New France changed little between 1760 and 1763. However, during the time of British Military Rule, New France lost its main political, business, and religious leaders who returned to France.

The Treaty of Paris (Peace Treaty 1763)

In 1763, the war in Europe between Britain and France ended and The Treaty of Paris was signed. By the terms of this treaty, France surrendered all of its possessions in New France and Acadia to Britain. The French kept two tiny islands, St. Pierre and Miquelon, off the coast of Newfoundland.

Effects of the Treaty of Paris

- Economic stability was restored as the British troops paid for goods with coin money.*
- The military courts used French civil law.
- The French were assured they would not be deported.
- The Roman Catholic religion was retained.
- The seigneurial system was retained.

Treaty of Paris, 1763

Legend:
- Britain
- Spain
- France
- French fishing rights
- Russia
- Territory unclaimed by Europeans

Pacific Ocean

Atlantic Ocean

St. Pierre and Miquelon (France)

0   1000 km

An Exercise in Problem Solving

1. Return to the five groups of the role play activity you just did on pages 75 to 77 (Native people, seigneurs, French clergy, habitants, and British merchants).

2. Analyse the facts presented in the Treaty of Paris. How do they affect your role play group?

3. List these facts on large notepaper (wall chart).

4. Reorder or regroup the facts you listed, placing those items that are similar together. Record them on a graphic organizer or chart.

5. Analyse the facts again.

6. Hypothesize what you think may happen to your particular group as a result of the Treaty of Paris.

7. Share your hypothesis with the rest of the class.

Civil law—having to do with private rights of citizens, especially property disputes; as opposed to criminal law, which has to do with public wrongs

*There was considerable economic chaos in New France after the Seven Years' War. The British introduced a variety of economic changes, which added to the economic uncertainty in New France.

Alternatives Open to the British

The British colonial policy was ethnocentric.* Many British believed that their culture was superior to the French and the Native peoples' cultures. This belief in ethnocentrism was central to the British policies in interacting with both the French and the Native peoples. Another key part in British policy was their belief in claiming and ruling conquered lands.** When the French signed the Treaty of Paris in 1763 they surrendered to Britain all claims over French lands in North America except the islands of St. Pierre and Miquelon.

Britain felt that the French *Canadiens* were still too much of a threat to North America. Approximately one-third of the continent of North America still had French people living there, with French militia and their Native allies. Britain still considered the French a threat to their colonies to the south—the Thirteen Colonies. The British also had to consider the large number of Native peoples living in North America. The British had to make a decision as to what they would do with these people.

After the Seven Years' War was over and the Treaty of Paris was signed, the British had to make some major decisions as to what they should do with the large numbers of French and Native peoples living on the lands that were now part of the British Empire. The British basically had five alternatives:

1. **Deportation:** force the *Canadiens* to leave Quebec, just as the British did with the Acadians from 1755 to 1762.

2. **Maintain the status-quo:** allow the French to keep their system of doing things—French laws, customs, language, and religion; maintain existing reserves for the Native people.

3. **Isolation:** create separate territories, which are sometimes called reserves: one for the British, one for the French, and one for the Native peoples. Each territory would have its own system of government, language, and religion. People living in these reserves were to be protected by the government.

4. **Assimilation (when a culture is absorbed into another):** make the French and/or the Native peoples into British subjects by enforcing British laws, customs, language, and religion. British immigration was encouraged to create a majority. This alternative is also called Anglicization.

5. **Biculturalism (having two cultures):** allow British and French ways of doing things. The term biculturalism is a modern one. The British did not seriously consider biculturalism in 1763.

For Your Notebook

1. Use a mind map, web, paragraph, or outline notes to summarize each of the alternatives. Design an icon for each alternative.

2. Apply one or more of the textbook icons (power, co-operation, decision-making, or conflict) to each of the alternatives. There is no single correct icon to apply to each alternative. Be prepared to defend your choice.

Exploring Further

1. Divide your class into five groups. Your teacher will give you one of the five alternatives to work on.

   (a) Consider what Canada would have been like today if that alternative had been followed exclusively.

   (b) Design a mobile to illustrate the alternative you have been assigned. Your teacher will be asking you to add illustrated examples to your mobile as you progress through this textbook.

C-357, National Archives of Canada, Ottawa.

A view of the Church of Notre Dame de la Victoire. During the seige of Quebec in 1759, many buildings were destroyed by cannonballs and fire.

---

*See page 24 for a further explanation of ethnocentrism.
**Note: British claim over conquered lands was not unique to Britain. It was standard European policy to claim and rule conquered lands.

An Exercise in Decision-Making

Divide your class into two groups with one half of the class working on each exercise.

Exercise 1: There were over 60 000 French-speaking, Roman Catholic people who were used to French laws and customs living in Quebec. What was to be done with the French people and with the colony of Quebec? What kind of government should there be? The government in Britain had to make a decision.*

(a) Earlier in this chapter you looked at the British occupation of Quebec mainly from the point of view of the people who lived there. In this exercise you were asked to take an alternative point of view—that of the British government. As advisors to the British government, discuss in pairs the alternatives and consequences, then decide what you would do if you were the British government. Refer to the information on page 80, "Alternatives Open to the British," to help you in your decision-making. You may wish to use the chart below in making your decision. Be ready to defend your choice.

(b) With your partner prepare an official report to the British government outlining your points of view.

Exercise 2: In the past most Europeans disregarded the fact that the lands they were moving onto had been occupied by Native peoples for thousands of years. They believed that the lands were theirs because they had planted their country's flag, established control and set up homes. Britain did not have a formal policy towards the Native peoples. By the mid-eighteenth century the British Parliament began to think about and write down their policies on how they should formally deal with the Native peoples of the New World.

(a) In this exercise you are to pretend you are advisors to the British government. Discuss in pairs the alternatives and consequences, then decide what you would do about the Native Peoples. Refer to page 80, "Alternatives Open to the British," to help you in making a decision.

(b) With your partner prepare an official report for the British government outlining your point of view regarding what you think should become part of British policy on what to do with the Native peoples.

A few tips:

- Use brainstorming for alternative ideas, to decide on the best possibilities, or to look at positive and negative outcomes before you predict.

- Either create your own decision-making model, or use the one from Chapter 1 of this textbook, the example on page 67, or the one on this page.

An Exercise in Critical Thinking

Each group is to read its reports written for the above exercise. After listening to the reports, discuss the following questions in class:

1. Find words in the reports that tell how the writers feel about the issue.
2. Define "point of view."
3. What point of view are the writers taking?
4. Do you feel the writers have enough information about the issue to arrive at a good decision? Why or why not?

Decision-Making Chart

Issue to be Solved	Alternative	Consequences	Decision
	1.		
	2.		
	3.		
	4.		
	5.		

*Note: The British had strict anti-Catholic laws (e.g., Roman Catholics could not hold public office or vote).

The Proclamation of 1763*

Introduction

In 1763, the British government issued a royal proclamation outlining what was to be done in Quebec. This is known as the Proclamation of 1763.

Aims: to make Quebec British (Assimilation)

- to ensure that British institutions and laws, customs, language, and religion were enforced in Quebec
- to attract British settlers to Quebec
- to limit the size of Quebec, cutting the Montreal fur traders out of the western fur trade
- to reassure the Native peoples that their interests in the fur trade and their hunting grounds in the Ohio Valley would be protected

Part of the population in Quebec consisted of long-time British subjects, who were still loyal to Britain. Britain believed they should give these people what they wanted over the next decade or so to create a strong, loyal base. They believed that in time the French could be assimilated or absorbed into the British way of doing things.

The British government realized that the Native peoples were unhappy because of the many people from the Thirteen Colonies who were moving west across the Appalachian Mountains into their territory.** If the boundaries of Quebec were limited, the Native peoples would be happy since traders, trappers, and settlers were forbidden to enter their territory unless they had a special government licence.

Key Terms

Settlement Patterns: Settlement in the Ohio and Mississippi river valleys was forbidden. Trappers, traders, and settlers had to have special government licences to enter lands set aside for the Native peoples.

Language: The French language was allowed to continue.

Religion: The Roman Catholic religion was allowed to continue but the Church had no official status; the Protestant religion was to be introduced and promoted.

Government: Quebec was to be ruled by an appointed British governor and an appointed Executive Council (to be drawn from the English-speaking military and merchant elites) and an elected Legislative Assembly (as soon as the population was large enough to warrant it).

- British laws and court system were created to replace French laws (except for French civil laws, which were allowed to continue for settling property disputes).
- Roman Catholics were to be barred from legal positions and were not allowed to be elected to the Legislative Assembly.

Exploring Further

1. In your role play groups established on page 75, predict how your "characters" (seigneurs, French clergy, Native people, habitants, and British merchants) would have felt about the Proclamation of 1763. Record your predictions on large chart paper and display on the wall.

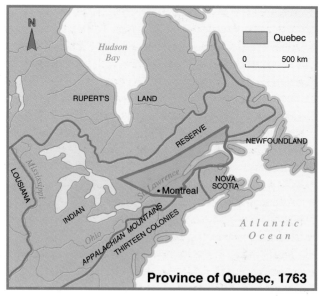

Province of Quebec, 1763

The Proclamation of 1763 reduced the size of Quebec.

---

*The Proclamation of 1763 is sometimes referred to as the Royal Proclamation of 1763.
**Also the Native peoples had lost their traditional trading partners, the French.

After the Proclamation of 1763

As a result of the Proclamation of 1763, civil rule replaced military rule in Quebec. The British found that the Proclamation did not result in assimilation (absorbing one culture into another) of the French the way they had hoped.

The Anglo-Americans from the Thirteen Colonies did not come north to live in Quebec (instead they moved westward). The French greatly outnumbered the British in Quebec. For every 100 Europeans in Quebec, 97 were French and three were British. Thus there was no British culture into which the French could be assimilated. The priests and the seigneurs tried hard to maintain the French culture. The Native peoples had been promised a western reserve where colonists from the Thirteen Colonies could not go. The colonists were moving west into Native lands even though the Proclamation of 1763 forbade settlement in the Ohio and Mississippi valleys.

British Governors in Quebec

Governor James Murray

C-26065, National Archives of Canada, Ottawa (detail).

The first appointed British governor general to Quebec was James Murray. He had been one of General Wolfe's officers and was the military governor of Quebec during the period of British Military Rule (from 1760 to 1763). It was Governor Murray's job to enforce the conditions of the Proclamation of 1763. However, Britain and the creators of the Proclamation were a long distance away from the colony. Thus the officials in Quebec had a certain amount of freedom in interpreting and enforcing the Proclamation of 1763.

Murray grew to like and respect the *Canadiens*—especially the clergy and the seigneurs. The many **concessions** that Murray made towards the French provoked the hostility of the British merchants. They wanted to control the colony through an elected assembly so they could vote on and pass whatever laws benefited them the most.*

The conditions of the Proclamation of 1763 were difficult for Governor Murray to enforce. The British merchants revived the fur trade but their attitudes and opinions contrasted sharply with those of the habitants of New France. The British wanted the Proclamation of 1763 enforced so that they could have political power and make profits from the fur trade. Governor Murray interpreted the Proclamation in favour of the *Canadiens* and allowed French to be spoken in the smaller courts. Some of Murray's concessions were quite important:

- In an effort to maintain harmony with some 60 000 *Canadiens,* Murray did not call the assembly although the Proclamation of 1763 made provision for this.**

- He believed that co-operation with the Catholic Church could strengthen the loyalty of the population. When the Roman Catholic Church chose Briand as bishop, the British Government confirmed him as Superintendent of the Roman Catholic Church in New France.

The British merchants wanted the Proclamation of 1763 enforced. Through their many influential contacts in the British Parliament and their many letters of complaint, they pressured the British government to recall Murray. Sir Guy Carleton was sent out to be the colony's new governor.

Governor Guy Carleton

Sir Guy Carleton became the governor of Quebec in 1768. He saw that British control of Quebec was dependent on the support of the large population of *Canadiens*. Loyalty and support were important because at this time, the people in the Thirteen Colonies to the south were starting to have disagreements with the officials in Britain. He wanted to make sure that the *Canadiens* would be loyal to Britain. To ensure this support, Carleton made friends with the leaders of the *Canadiens*, the seigneurs and the clergy. He thought that if the leaders accepted British rule, the rest would also agree. Carleton encouraged the British government to allow the French people to keep their system of laws and their Catholic religion. Therefore Carleton rejected the policy of assimilation in favour of an acceptance of allowing the two cultures to exist side by side.

Although they did not use the term biculturalism, this policy of allowing two cultures—French and British—to exist side-by-side is a forerunner of the biculturalism we have in Canada today. These ideas were officially recognized and supported by the British government when they passed the Quebec Act of 1774.

Concession — giving in
*Note the Proclamation of 1763 did not allow for an elected assembly, which made the British merchants quite angry.
**Had Murray done so, he would have given the British minority political control over a huge French majority.

The Quebec Act, 1774

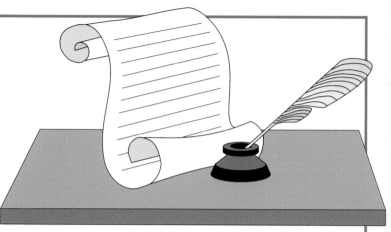

Introduction

The Quebec Act was passed by the British government in an attempt to keep the loyalty of the *Canadiens*.

Aim: to allow the French and British ways of doing things (Biculturalism)

The British hoped the Quebec Act would combine the French and British ways of doing things while maintaining the French character of the colony.

This was an example of biculturalism—where two cultures (British and French) exist side by side in the same country. The British government decided that the best way to gain the loyalty of the *Canadiens* was to allow them to maintain the French character of Quebec and preserve the French culture. Quebec was to become both British and French.

Province of Quebec, 1774

The boundaries of Quebec were enlarged to include the rich fur trading areas between the Ohio and Mississippi rivers.

Key Terms

Language: The French language was allowed to continue.

Religion: The Roman Catholic Church was allowed to continue and to collect tithes (church taxes).

Government:

- Quebec was to be ruled by an appointed British governor and an appointed council.
- An elected assembly (although promised earlier) was not introduced at this time.
- Roman Catholics could hold government positions.
- French civil law was to continue along with English criminal law.

British Government
- made the important decisions
- appointed the governor

Council (appointed)
- advised the governor on policy and law-making

Governor
- tried to carry out wishes of the British government
- was very powerful
- had the power to veto suggestions

Land Holding System: The seigneurial system was allowed to remain. The governor could also grant land according to the British freehold system.

An Exercise in Critical Thinking

Reactions to the Quebec Act

Who	Reaction	Why
Who?	anger	• westward expansion cut off (French had control of Ohio Valley) • fear of tighter British control • called the Quebec Act intolerable
Who?	delight anger	• extended boundary into very large area would increase fur trade business • less political power as a result of no assembly
Who?	pleasure	• kept religious influence and ability to tithe (tax)
Who?	pleasure	• kept land and privileges • kept French civil law • implied that French language will remain
Who?	indifferent	• kept *Canadien* way of life but under control of Church and seigneurs
Who?	upset	• north of the Ohio River not much change • south of the Ohio River great numbers of settlers moved west from the Thirteen Colonies

1. Use this list to decide who held each point of view described in the following chart. Select from: British merchants in Quebec, British, Thirteen Colonies, Native people, French seigneurs, French habitants, French Catholic Church officials.

2. Form into your role play groups established on page 75 (seigneurs, French clergy, and others). Compare the predictions you recorded on the wall chart (*see* page 82) with the way the various groups reacted to the Quebec Act (above). Share your results with your classmates.

3. In your role play groups decide what new problems your group thinks the Quebec Act would create. Present these hypotheses to the class as a bulletin board display, mural, collage, poster, story, play, or mobile.

4. Why is it important to look at an issue from different points of view?

Review ●

Summarizing the Chapter

- The European rulers' desire for power and wealth caused conflict in Europe and in North America.

- European wars between France and Britain resulted in British–French hostilities in North America.

- Treaties ending British–French wars often resulted in North American land possessions being given up or returned to the other country.

- British–French conflict in North America centred on control of fur trade lands and control of strategically located lands (Atlantic Coast and St. Lawrence River Valley).

- The British and French built many forts to control the fur trade and control important locations. Louisbourg was a famous French fort. Halifax was a famous British fort.

- Acadia became British as a result of the Treaty of Utrecht in 1713. In 1755, the French Acadians were still refusing to take an oath of allegiance to Britain, so they were deported.

- The British–French conflict in North America reached its climax in 1758 when the British captured Louisbourg and other French forts in the Ohio Valley. This made it possible to attack Quebec.

- The British captured Quebec at the Plains of Abraham in 1759 and Montreal in the spring of 1760, thus defeating the French in North America.

- The British army ran the government of New France between 1760 and 1763. This was known as the period of British Military Rule.

- The Treaty of Paris, 1763 officially ended the British–French war in Europe.

- The Proclamation of 1763 aimed to make Quebec British. This is an example of the theory of assimilation.

- The Quebec Act of 1774 aimed to make Quebec both British and French. This is an example of the theory of biculturalism.

Checking Predictions

1. At the beginning of this chapter you made some predictions based on the Overview and what you already knew. Now use what you learned from reading the chapter to fill in the third column of the chart that you began earlier.

2. Refer to the "Questions to Talk About" on page 41. Discuss the questions based on the type of government in Quebec as a result of the Quebec Act. How did the system of government change from royal government (as you studied in Chapter 3) to the government established by the British in the Quebec Act?

Working with Information

1. Here are some main ideas from this chapter. Use one of the following approaches to make a permanent set of notes: mind map, web, paragraph, or outline. Show the relationships among these main ideas.

   - areas of British–French conflict in North America
   - War in America: a Three-Pronged Attack
   - the Proclamation of 1763
   - alternatives open to the British in dealing with the French and Native peoples
   - Native land claims and the Proclamation of 1763
   - Quebec Act, 1774

2. Review all the different examples of decision-making and conflict found in this chapter. Work with a partner to draw a mind map that organizes all of these examples on one sheet of paper. Show how the conflict between the French and the British and the methods of decision-making affected the colony of Quebec. A sample mind map is shown on page 16. Share your mind map with others in the class.

3. Prepare visual definitions for biculturalism, assimilation, and isolation.

4. Do research to find out why the Proclamation of 1763 is considered the basis for Native land claims (aboriginal rights).

Building Thinking Strategies

Point of View

1. In small groups reread the "Alternatives Open to the British" on page 80, the Proclamation of 1763 (page 82), and the Quebec Act (page 84). Identify some attributes (traits or characteristics) that appear in both acts. List these on the left side of the chart. Then describe the importance of each attribute from the British and from the *Canadien* point of view.

Points of View		
Attributes	British Side	*Canadien* Side

SAMPLE

2. Select an issue from your school, work, or personal life, or find a newsclipping about some important issue. Describe the issue you choose from several points of view. Why is it important to look at an issue from several points of view?

Decision-Making Review

1. Make up a list of five different issues that have forced you to make decisions within the last year. Simply outline what the questions/problems were. Do not give any hint of your decisions. Now exchange your list with someone else in the class. Read the new list carefully, and choose one of the decision-making situations it presents. Use the decision-making model discussed in this chapter to help you to analyse the issue thoroughly. After you have written up the model and weighed all the alternatives and consequences, come to a decision. Now get back together with your classmate and discuss the conclusion you have drawn. Examine each of the problems separately. Does your decision match the decision that was made by your classmate? Why? Why not? Which decision do you think is better?

Remember that decision-making becomes better with time and practice. Good decisions take careful thought. Simply having made a decision does not always ensure that it was the best one possible. Keep an open mind while discussing your choices. Strive to improve your decision-making skills.

Communicating Ideas

Reading

1. Read the story "Antoine Boulanger" by Marie Moser in *Ordinary People in Canada's Past*.

Writing

1. Work in groups to develop an imaginary newspaper that could have existed during the time of the capture of Quebec in 1759, the Proclamation of 1763, or the Quebec Act of 1774. Include political, social, and economic events. Select a name for your newspaper.
2. Do research to find out about the western expansion of the Thirteen Colonies into Native lands. Do research on the Cherokee and "The Long March" into Oklahoma. Present your findings in a written report.
3. Which person from this chapter would you like to have met? Explain why you find that person interesting.

Creating

1. Using the eyewitness account on pages 71–72, and the map and pictures on pages 71–73, make a visual presentation of the Battle of the Plains of Abraham.

Canada Revisited

Quebec City was protected by a fortified wall. Shown is one of the two gates in the wall.

Section III

Toward Representative Government 1774–1815

The Students' Council at Fairmont School is discussing an issue that must be resolved before the next school dance.

Act I

John: Some of the kids want to bring friends from other schools to our dances.

Farrah: I don't think it should be allowed. Our dances are crowded enough as it is!

Tammy: Yes, but I know how they feel. My boyfriend goes to Marpole School and I'd like to bring him to our dances.

Saul: Yes, and we can go to the dances at some of the other schools, so they should be able to come to ours.

John: Maybe we should ask the Fairmont students to vote on this issue.

Sam: What's the point of that? They elected us as Students' Council so we could make decisions on their behalf. I think we should vote.

John: Okay, how many in favour?

How many against? Okay, we've voted in favour of letting students from other schools come to our dances.

Act II

The school principal, Mrs. Cherniak, reads the minutes of the meeting, and asks that a special meeting be called so that she can speak with the Council.

Mrs. Cherniak: I'm afraid that I can't allow you to have students from other schools at your dances. I made a school rule, with the agreement of the other staff members, that prohibits it.

Farrah: But, as the Students' Council, we voted on this issue, on behalf of all of the other students at Fairmont!

Mrs. Cherniak: I'm sorry. It doesn't matter. This is a school rule. As the Students' Council you have been elected to represent other students in our school by making decisions that affect them. This is a type of representative government. But you are still students who are under my authority as principal. I have to agree to the decisions you make.

Exit Mrs. Cherniak.

Act III

The Students' Council continues to discuss the situation.

Tammy: I think the school rule not allowing other students to attend our dances is unfair.

Saul: I think we should refuse to attend classes in protest!

John: You know we can't do that! Maybe we should write a letter to Mrs. Cherniak giving our point of view.

Farrah: We could ask her to read it at the next staff meeting.

Tammy: Yes, I know that the final decisions

are made by the principal and other staff members, but I think that they should at least know that we don't agree with them.

Farrah: Yes, maybe they'll change their minds! ▪

Questions to Talk About

Discuss the following questions by referring to the section story you just read. Keep these questions in mind while you read the rest of the chapter. At the end of the chapter you will be asked to review them in light of the information you have gained about representative government.

1. In a representative government, who makes the decisions—the people, or elected representatives?
2. Who makes the final decisions? Who has the power? How does this make the situation unlike a representative government?

3. What are your alternatives when you do not agree with the decisions made by the person or people who have the power?
4. Which alternative was chosen by the students you read about?

Chapter 5 Focus

The two chapters in this section will answer the question: what factors contributed to Canada's expansion? Both chapters also trace the development of representative government. The concepts of power, co-operation, decision-making, and conflict underlie the events in Chapter 5. The concept of conflict will be the focus of the chapter.

Power

Co-operation

Decision-Making

Conflict

Overview/Prediction Chart

Examine the Overview found on the following page. In pairs or small groups, use the Overview and what you already know to predict answers to the questions in the Prediction Chart. Put your predictions in the "My Predictions" column. Once you have finished the chapter, complete the "What I Found Out" column to help you review and summarize. Your teacher will provide you with a full-sized working copy of the Prediction Chart.

Prediction Chart—What Do You Think?		
Questions	**My Predictions** (fill out now)	**What I Found Out** (fill out at end of chapter)
1. What might be the major events?		
2. Who might be some of the important people or groups?		
3. Who might hold power?		
4.		

SAMPLE

Chapter 5
The American Revolution
(1775–1783)

O v e r v i e w

Use this Overview to predict the events of this chapter.

1774

The Thirteen Colonies, along the east coast of North America, had a population of about 2.5 million people. The colonists elected representatives and decided how the colonies were to be governed. The First Continental Congress of the Thirteen Colonies met. Grievances were discussed.

1775

The Thirteen Colonies protested British taxes. The first battle of the American Revolution was fought at Lexington and Concord.

1775

Soldiers of the Thirteen Colonies invaded Quebec.

1776

The Declaration of Independence stated that the Thirteen Colonies were free and independent of British control. The United States of America came into existence in 1783 after many long years of fighting.

The Thirteen Colonies

By 1763, Britain had defeated France in the Seven Years' War. You have read about how New France became a British colony at that time. The Thirteen Colonies to the south of New France, along the coast of the Atlantic Ocean, had been British colonies. Settlers had been sent to the Thirteen Colonies to produce raw materials that would add to the wealth of Great Britain. Others went to gain religious or political freedom.

As in New France, settlers had begun to come to the Thirteen Colonies in the early 1600s. But by 1775, the population of New France was only about 70 000. The Thirteen Colonies had a European population of about 2.5 million people at this time.

Each of the Thirteen Colonies was different, but they can be divided into three groups based on their location.

Location

New England

Most of the New England settlers came from England and Scotland. These colonies were first settled by religious groups whose beliefs were not accepted in England. The economy was based on wheat farming and trade with the islands in the Caribbean Sea to the south. The seaport towns, such as Boston, with a population of 15 000, were prospering. Many people in the seaport towns made their living from the sea, or as craftspeople and merchants.

The Middle Colonies

The middle colonies had many different religions and nationalities compared to the other colonies. They were settled by Dutch, Swedes, English, Germans, Scots, and Irish, as well as others. These colonies were known as the "breadbasket" of the New World because most people were farmers. Ships loaded with crops from the Middle Colonies left from the harbours of New York and Philadelphia. These crops were sold in Britain and the West Indies.

The Southern Colonies

Many of the southern colonists were from England. Others were Scots, French, and Germans. Many British workers were needed for the huge tobacco, sugar, and rice farms, which were called plantations. These plantations were owned by a small, powerful group of people. Since few settlers were willing to work for wages on the plantations when they could have small farms of their own, the plantation owners used slaves from Africa as workers. These slaves were bought from slave traders. They were not paid wages. They were given food, clothing, and shelter.

The only large cities in the southern colonies were Charleston, with a population of 10 000, and Baltimore, with 5000.

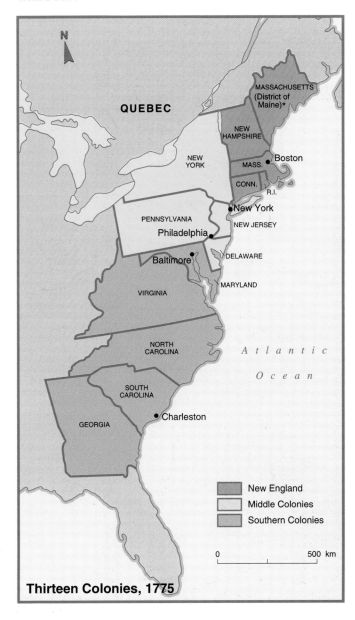

Thirteen Colonies, 1775

*Note; Maine became a state in 1820. Prior to that, it was under the jurisdiction of Massachusetts and referred to as "District of Maine."

Government

The colonists had two levels of government: one to handle local affairs, the other to deal with provincial issues.

Community Government

Communities in the New England colonies had a form of local government to look after day-to-day problems. This form of local government came to be called the town meeting. All free adult males were encouraged to take part in the decision-making process. This is an example of participatory democracy. Citizens would gather together to decide on how much they should be taxed, to discuss town problems, and to elect town officers. The elected town officers did not make the laws, they just administered and enforced them.

Representative Government

Citizens elect people who represent them in their Legislative Assembly (decision-making body). Every individual has a voice in government, but only a small group actually makes the decisions.

Veto — the right or power to forbid or reject
*The colony of Nova Scotia also had representative government. It was granted an assembly by Britain in 1758.

Colonial Government

Each of the Thirteen Colonies had a form of representative government. The first representative assembly in North America was called the House of Burgesses. It was in Williamsburg, Virginia, one of the Thirteen Colonies. The governor invited each community in the colony to send two representatives to the Legislative Assembly. This assembly could pass laws for the colony, as long as the laws did not go against the laws of Britain. But the laws could be **vetoed** by the governor.

This photograph was taken at the reconstructed Williamsburg. It shows the interior of the House of Burgesses, the first representative assembly in North America.

Each of the other colonies established a system of government similar to that of Virginia.* In most cases, the government consisted of a governor (as a representative of the British government), a council of men who helped the governor, and a representative assembly, which made the laws. The governor and his council were appointed by the king and the members of the representative assembly were elected. The colonies of Rhode Island and Connecticut were exceptions to this. In these colonies the voters elected the governor and the council, as well as the representative assembly.

The number of people who could vote was much more limited than it is today. Only the free adult males of the colonies and the small number of women who owned property could vote for their representatives. Slaves and most women could not vote; neither could men who did not own property of a certain size or could not prove that they had an income and paid taxes of a certain amount. Also, many people who could vote did not because they did not have the time to make the journey from their isolated pioneer farms. Thus the representatives were elected by a very small proportion of the population.

Even though the laws passed by the assemblies could be vetoed by the governor, the assemblies had a surprising amount of power. That is because they controlled how the money was spent. This means that they could decide whether or not the governor could have the money to carry out the things he wanted to do.

The colonists were used to having a form of representative government, even though many decisions were still made in Britain by the British government and they were still subject to the laws of Britain.

Colonial Government

Like a Representative Government	Unlike a Representative Government
• People voted for representatives who acted for them in a Legislative Assembly.	• Only a small group of people were eligible to vote.
• The representatives made laws.	• Laws passed by the representative assemblies could be vetoed by the governor.

For Your Notebook

1. In some ways the representative assemblies in the Thirteen Colonies were like a representative government and in other ways they were not. Your Students' Council is also a form of representative government. Design a chart like the one above comparing your Students' Council to a representative government.

The Thirteen Colonies Protest

Due to Britain's victory over France in the Seven Years' War, New France now belonged to Britain. However, Britain's troubles were far from over after the Seven Years' War. The war had been expensive and had resulted in a high national debt. It was also expensive to maintain an army in the Thirteen Colonies. Britain decided to impose certain taxes on the people of the Thirteen Colonies to help pay these costs.

Many of the colonists did not see the need for a British army in the colonies since they no longer needed protection from French forces at Quebec or Louisbourg. To them, the army was a waste of tax money.

The people of the Thirteen Colonies protested vigorously against taxation without representation. Because they had no elected representation in the British Parliament, the colonists objected to British taxes. Some of their protests are shown on page 95. They felt it was unfair that their taxes were being used to help run the British government when they were not allowed to elect representatives to speak for them in the British Parliament.

Taxation without Representation
Being taxed without benefit of elected representatives to speak on your behalf.

The people of the Thirteen Colonies and the British government had different points of view for many years. Between 1660 and 1774 the British government passed a series of laws or acts that many of the colonists did not like. They felt that the British government had no business interfering in their lives in this way. The British government felt that its laws were fair and just. Here are the opposing points of view of the people of the Thirteen Colonies and the British government on the Navigation Acts of 1660 and 1668, on the Proclamation of 1763 (*see* page 82), and on taxation without representation. Below are two imaginary points of view based on actual historical accounts. Read the colonists' point of view first and then read across the page to the point of view of Great Britain.

The Navigation Acts: 1660 and 1668

Colonists

These Acts will not allow us to use our own ships to carry goods to and from Britain. This prevents us from making money on the transport of these goods. Furthermore, goods from other countries in Europe are very expensive in the colonies because they have to go to Britain, where you tax them, before they come here. We also think it is unfair that we have to sell most of our goods to you. We should be able to sell them to whom we please.

Great Britain

Do not forget that our trade laws also do not allow British merchants to buy tobacco that isn't grown in one of our colonies. These laws help you. Besides, the American colonies belong to us. Therefore you should be helping us, not some other country. Further, the mother country needs to be strong in order to protect you from enemies.

The Proclamation of 1763

Colonists

You have ordered the settlers who live west of the Appalachian Mountains to move back into the Thirteen Colonies. These people have made their homes there. You are forcing them to start all over again. This is very unfair. This land is already ours anyway, since some of our colonies were given it in their charters. Also, you aren't allowing any fur traders to cross the mountains without your permission. You are destroying the livelihood of these men.

Great Britain

We are trying to prevent another war between the Native people and the settlers. There is still lots of room for settlement in the Thirteen Colonies. More land is not needed yet. Also, if we allow the land west of the Appalachians to become settled, the fur-bearing animals will be driven away. The fur trade is almost the only way we can make any money from our North American colonies.

Taxation without Representation

Colonists

Why should we pay so many taxes to Great Britain? This makes us very angry. We should have elected representatives in the British Parliament who will stand up for our rights.

Great Britain

We have stationed an army of 10 000 men in the colonies to enforce law and order and to protect you from further Native attacks. This army is very expensive to support. Why should the people of Britain have to pay for this army? The members of the British Parliament keep your interests in mind and represent you just as well as they represent the people of Britain.

Events Leading Up to the American Revolution

This chart shows some of the events leading up to the American Revolution. They involve taxes imposed by the British and describe the colonists' protests against the taxes. You will see that some of these protests were peaceful and some were violent. The British actions are in red. The colonists' reactions are in purple.

1764 Sugar Act
- Taxes were put on imported goods such as sugar and molasses.
- Some colonists **boycotted** sugar.

1765 Stamp Act
- All legal documents and newspapers had to be stamped at a cost ranging from one cent to several dollars.
- Angry speeches were made in colonial assemblies.
- Merchants boycotted British goods.
- Tax collectors were terrorized.
- The house of Governor Hutchinson of Massachusetts was wrecked by a mob.
- In 1766 the Stamp Act was withdrawn.

1767 Townshend Acts
- Taxes were placed on glass, tea, silk, paper, paint, and lead.
- The sale of British goods fell by almost two-thirds.
- In 1770 taxes were dropped on everything but tea.

1773 Tea Act
- The East India Company was given the sole right to sell tea in North America.
- East India Company ships were refused admittance to the harbours of New York and Philadelphia.
- At the Boston Tea Party, about 40 or 50 people from Boston, disguised as Native people, dumped three boatloads of tea from British ships into the harbour.

1774 Intolerable Acts
- Boston was closed to all shipping until all the destroyed tea was paid for. Public meetings were forbidden, and 4000 British troops were stationed in the area (one soldier for every four Bostonians).
- The Quebec Act was considered to be an Intolerable Act. It gave Quebec, with its relatively tiny French-speaking population, control of the largest piece of land in British North America—the Ohio Territory. This seemed to be an attempt to prevent the colonists from expanding westward.
- The people of the Thirteen Colonies boycotted British goods.
- Many colonists secretly began to collect arms and ammunition.
- The colonists began to raise an army of their own with 122 000 men, of whom two-thirds were **Minutemen.**
- In September 1774, the first Continental Congress was held.

Boycott—refusal to trade with a country or company or to buy its products
Minutemen—armed men ready to fight at a moment's notice

The American Revolution

In 1775 the protests broke into the armed conflict known as the American Revolution, or the War of Independence. This resulted in the formation of the new United States of America, independent of Great Britain.

United States, 1783

You may be wondering why we are talking about the American Revolution in a book about Canada's history. One reason is to learn about protest. The Thirteen Colonies chose violent protest to get the changes they wanted. The people in the two other major British colonies of Quebec and Nova Scotia did not choose violent protest at this time, although they had many of the same complaints as the Thirteen Colonies. The people of Quebec and Nova Scotia were different from the American colonies; in fact the Americans were their long-term enemies. The people of Quebec and Nova Scotia chose to remain part of the British Empire rather than join with the Thirteen Colonies in their fight for independence against Britain.

The People of British North America Remain Loyal to Britain

It occurred to the American revolutionaries that the people of the colonies of Nova Scotia and Quebec must also have many complaints against the British. The Stamp Act of 1765, for instance, caused them some hardship. *The Quebec Gazette* printed the following notice:

This is to inform the public that the printers of this gazette find themselves obliged to stop publication as of this day, given the small number of subscribers they now have, caused by the Act for the imposition of a stamp tax!

In Halifax, the owner of *The Halifax Gazette* lost his contract as official printer for the Nova Scotia government because he refused to put the required stamp on his newspaper. In fact, on the day that the Stamp Act came into effect, he used a skull and crossbones in place of the official stamp.

The Thirteen Colonies thought that the *Canadiens* in Quebec, having been so recently defeated by the British, would be ready to rebel against them. Also, Quebec and the Thirteen Colonies were neighbours since they shared a long border. Nova Scotia was farther away, but three-quarters of its population was from the Thirteen Colonies.

Quebec
Conflicting Messages

George Washington

In 1775, two messages were delivered to the people of Quebec. General Washington, who was later to be the first president of the United States, tried to convince them that they should join the revolution.

Come, then, my brethren, unite with us ... let us run together to the same goal. We have taken up arms in defence of our liberty, our property, our wives, and our children; we are determined to preserve them or die. We look forward with pleasure to that day ... when the inhabitants of America shall have one sentiment, and the full enjoyment of the blessings of a free Government ... the grand American Congress have sent an Army into your Province... not to plunder, but to protect you. ...

Bishop Briand of Quebec reminded the people of Quebec of their duty to the British king:

The remarkable goodness and gentleness with which we have been governed by his very gracious Majesty, King George the Third . . . the recent favours with which he had loaded us, in restoring to us the use of our laws and the free exercise of our religion . . . would no doubt (cause you to support) the interests of the British Crown.

The Soldiers of the Thirteen Colonies Invade Quebec

The American revolutionaries decided to send a two-pronged attack into the colony of Quebec. One army, under General Richard Montgomery, took the well-travelled route up the Richelieu River to Montreal. He was able to capture Montreal easily. Guy Carleton, the governor of the colony, escaped disguised as a French trapper, or he probably would have been captured. Montgomery then continued on to Quebec City.

General Benedict Arnold and his troops had a much more difficult time. They took the overland route from Maine to Quebec, finding their way through dense forests and foul swamps. They ran out of food and were forced to eat candles and roasted moccasins. Due to starvation, disease, and desertion, Arnold had only half of the 1200 men he had started with when he finally joined Montgomery at Quebec City. By the time the two armies camped outside the walled fortress at Quebec, they were facing both the hardship of a cold winter and the ravages of smallpox. In spite of Montgomery's boast that he would eat Christmas dinner in Quebec City, the armies were not able to attack until New Year's Eve, in the middle of a driving snowstorm. Two hundred Americans, including General Montgomery, were killed, while the British defenders lost only six men. The American revolutionaries were left with little choice but to call off the attack. They remained camped outside the city for the rest of the winter. In May of 1776, the British navy arrived with reinforcements and the Americans were forced to return home. The American invasion of the colony of Quebec had failed.

If Montgomery and Arnold had been successful in their invasion attempt on the colony of Quebec, there was a slight possibility that British North America may have taken part in the American Revolution. The French subjects, however, were deeply distrustful of their English-speaking American neighbours. The British newcomers to Quebec still felt a strong loyalty to Britain.

Soldiers from the Thirteen Colonies attacked Quebec City on New Year's Eve, 1775. They expected that the *Canadiens* would welcome them as liberators, but instead they were seen as invaders.

Nova Scotia

The Americans did not attempt to invade the colony of Nova Scotia, as they had done with Quebec. Nova Scotia was quite isolated from New England and did not participate in pre-revolutionary activity. Nova Scotians' attention at that time was taken up with a Christian religious revival called the Great Awakening. It might seem surprising that the people of Nova Scotia did not decide on their own to join the American rebellion against British rule. Many Nova Scotians actually were Americans. Either they or their parents had been born in the Thirteen Colonies. In fact, in 1767, the total population of Halifax was 2822 people. Of these, 1351 people called themselves Americans. The people of Nova Scotia were sometimes called "Neutral Yankees." Yankees is a term for Americans. Calling them Neutral Yankees referred to the fact that Nova Scotians would not join the Americans in rebelling against British rule.

Focus On: British North American Feelings about the American Revolution

In British North America, there was a wide variety of points of view on the American Revolution. Fourteen points of view follow.*

The People of Quebec's Response

The British have treated us fairly. The Quebec Act protects our Roman Catholic religion. The Americans might force us to give it up.

I sold supplies to the American army. The money they gave me was worthless! I won't help them again!

I wish the Americans would just go away and leave us alone! What would we gain by joining them?

What have I to gain by helping the Americans? They have never helped me. They compete with me for trade with Britain.

We must defend our homeland against the Americans. The British have protected our seigneurial system of land ownership. The Americans would take it away.

But there are so many Americans! Some of them are our cousins! And Quebec is so much closer to the Thirteen Colonies than to Britain!

I'm for loyalty to the British. They've been good to me. I say take up arms against the Americans!

The People of Nova Scotia's Response

We should join the Americans! We too are taxed unfairly by the British!

I agree that the British are taxing us unfairly. But if we decide to fight against the British, we will get no help from the Americans. They have no extra ammunition to send us.

We have fathers, brothers, and sons fighting in New England. We should not side with the British against our loved ones.

Yes, but we are becoming rich from providing for the needs of the British troops. Why should we side with the Americans? Besides, General Washington was asked to invade Nova Scotia and he refused.

I also think we should join the Americans in fighting against the British. But with our small communities, which are scattered everywhere, it is impossible to get people to unite for a common cause.

I am a Halifax merchant. Don't forget that we depend on Britain for trade. We would be poor without Britain. Besides, the British navy controls the ocean. The navy would destroy any American ships bringing troops here.

I used to be on the American side. But I don't know how they can expect us to be on their side when their **privateers** attack our coastal settlements.

For Your Notebook

1. Make a chart showing the positions of the colonists in Quebec and Nova Scotia.
2. Summarize the reasons why the people in Quebec and Nova Scotia either supported or opposed the American cause.
3. Imagine that you are a 15-year-old Nova Scotian living in or near Halifax. Your father came to Nova Scotia from Boston, and your mother came from Britain. Write a passage of dialogue that includes a family discussion of whether Nova Scotians should join the Americans. You might want to include other people, such as a neighbour who used to live in Quebec.

*Note: these are imaginary points of view based on actual historical information.

Privateer—privately owned and staffed armed ship

Review

Summarizing the Chapter

- In 1775, when open rebellion against Britain broke out in the Thirteen Colonies, they were a prosperous group of colonies with a population of 2.5 million people. They had representative assemblies which, because they controlled the spending of money, were surprisingly powerful for the times.

- The war against Britain, which became known as the American Revolution, ended in 1783 with the Treaty of Paris. The Thirteen Colonies became the United States of America, a nation independent of British rule.

- The people of the British colonies of Quebec and Nova Scotia did not join in the revolution. The French-speaking people of Quebec saw the Americans as a threat to their Roman Catholic religion and their seigneurial system of land ownership. The English-speaking people had nothing to gain by joining the Americans.

- Even though three-quarters of Nova Scotia's settlers were former New Englanders, they too remained loyal to Britain, in spite of the fact that they were sympathetic with the Americans. The power of the British navy was one factor that influenced the people of Nova Scotia against joining the Americans. Also, settlements were scattered and it would have been difficult to unite for a war effort. By the end of the war, many of those who had sympathized with the Americans had turned against them because of the frequent attacks on coastal settlements by American privateers.

Checking Predictions

1. At the beginning of this chapter you made predictions based on the Overview and what you already knew. Now, use what you learned from reading the chapter to fill in the third column of the Prediction Chart.

2. Refer to the "Questions to Talk About" on page 89. Discuss the questions based on what you have learned about government in the Thirteen Colonies.

Working with Information

1. Here are some main ideas from this chapter:
   - participatory democracy
   - representative government
   - taxation without representation
   - violent protest
   - peaceful protest
   - loyalty to Britain

   Write a paragraph that shows the relationship among these points. You may want to brainstorm as a pre-writing activity.

2. Review different examples of conflict in this chapter. Choose one point of view and write a position paragraph describing whether you think peaceful protest would have been just as effective in this situation.

3. Prepare a visual definition for representative government.

Building Thinking Strategies

Evaluating Arguments

1. Reread the arguments made by Bishop Briand and George Washington on page 96. Evaluate the arguments by asking yourself the following questions:
   - (a) What reasons are given to support the arguments?
   - (b) Were there any contradictions in the points made to support the arguments?
   - (c) Were irrelevant facts cited?
   - (d) What would someone who disagrees with this argument say?
   - (e) Which argument do you think is strongest and why?

2. Work with a friend to describe the strategies one uses when evaluating arguments.

Communicating Ideas

Listening

1. Choose two students who will stage an interview between a newspaper reporter for *The Boston Gazette* and an American **Patriot**. In response to the reporter's questions, the Patriot will give his reasons for engaging in violent protest. Listen to the interview and then decide whether or not you agree with his reasons. Write a position paper describing why you agree or disagree with the Patriot's point of view.

Sympathetic—in agreement with
Patriot—a colonist who rebelled against British rule

Chapter 6
The Loyalists
(1776–1815)

1783
Loyalist migration to British North America after the American Revolution.

After the American Revolution, Thayendanegea, a Loyalist and leader of the Iroquois Six Nations Confederacy, led his people to settle on a reserve in British North America.

The Loyalists started new lives in British North America.

1791
Passage of the Constitutional Act. Quebec divided into Upper and Lower Canada, each with its own laws and system of government. Representative government established.

Upper Canada

Lower Canada

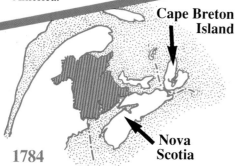

1784
New Brunswick created. Cape Breton Island established as a colony separate from Nova Scotia (reunited in 1820).

Cape Breton Island

Nova Scotia

War of 1812–1815
War between British North America and the United States of America.

George Pearkes Junior Secondary School
1390 Laurier Street
Port Coquitlam, B.C.

932761

Chapter 6 Focus

Chapter 5 dealt with the American Revolution and its effects on British North America. Chapter 6 covers approximately the same time period as Chapter 5, but provides details about how the areas that were to become Canada and the United States began to distinguish themselves as separate countries. Chapter 6 also examines how representative government was established in British North America. The concepts of power, co-operation, decision-making, and conflict underlie the events of this chapter. The concept of decision-making is the focus of Chapter 6.

| Power | Co-operation | **Decision-making** | Conflict |

Overview/Prediction Chart

The Overview for Chapter 6 highlights some of the events that occurred from 1776 to 1815. Work in pairs or small groups to fill in the "My Predictions" column on the chart provided by your teacher. Use what you already know and the Overview to predict. After you have read the chapter, you will fill out the "What I Found Out" column.

Prediction Chart—What Do You Think?		
Questions	My Predictions (fill out now)	What I Found Out (fill out at end of chapter)
1. What might be the major events?		
2. Who might be some of the important people or groups?	*SAMPLE*	
3. Who might hold power?		
4.		

Patriots
(Rebels)

Patriots (Rebels) were loyal to the Thirteen Colonies. They wanted to separate from Britain to form the United States of America.*

Tories
(Loyalists)

Tories (Loyalists) were loyal to Britain. They did not want to separate from Britain. Most Loyalists came to the remaining British North American colonies of Quebec and Nova Scotia.*

C-96362, National Archives of Canada, Ottawa.

Loyalists Drawing Lots for Their Lands, 1784

*Both the Patriots and the Tories had uniforms of several different colours and styles.

The King's Friends

Tory Refugees on Their Way to Canada. During and after the American Revolution, thousands of Loyalists travelled north by land and sea to settle in British North America.

Tories with their brats and wives
Should fly to save their wretched lives.

Beginning in 1776 and continuing for a decade, a steady stream of political **refugees**, called Tories, came to the British colonies of Quebec and Nova Scotia from the 13 American colonies. After the Treaty of Paris in 1783, these people came to be known as Loyalists.

Refugee — person who leaves home or country to seek safety elsewhere

The Tories fled from the Patriots because they did not agree with the Patriots' belief that British rule should be overthrown. They left the Thirteen Colonies in order to get to safer British territory. Since the colonies to the north had remained British and were close by, they settled there.

An Unusual Kind of Punishment

Some Tories were killed by the Patriots. Others endured a punishment called being "tarred and feathered." Prospective victims sometimes received a warning in the form of a ball of cold tar with a couple of feathers attached. After this warning, the potential victims could usually be seen on their way to British North America.

A victim who remained was often pulled out of his home by a crowd of men and taken to a bonfire. He was usually forced to watch the tar being melted over the fire, so that he could think about the pain he was going to experience. He was then stripped of his clothing, and the boiling tar was poured over him. The victim was then made to roll in a pile of feathers. Often he was made to sit with his legs on either side of a sharp rail, and his tormentors would carry him around the town so that everyone could see what happened to people who were loyal to their king. Removal of the tar was very painful. Often the person's blistered skin would peel off along with the cold tar.

Loyalists

Many of these Tories had been physically mistreated by the Patriots, their businesses destroyed, and their homes taken away from them. In the Treaty of Paris of 1783, which ended the American Revolution, the Americans promised to repay the people whose homes or other property had been destroyed. This promise was never kept.

The coming of the Loyalists changed British North America greatly. Their arrival resulted in the creation of two new colonies. The new colony of New Brunswick was formed from a part of the colony of Nova Scotia. Also, the colony of Quebec was split into Lower Canada (now the province of Quebec) and Upper Canada (now the province of Ontario). You will read about this later in the chapter.

There Were Many Kinds of Loyalists

The Patriots described a Loyalist as "someone whose head is in England, whose body is in America, and whose neck should be stretched." This saying meant that the Loyalists should be hanged for their loyalty to Britain and the British government. But did all of the Loyalists leave the Thirteen Colonies because they were loyal to Britain? Read the examples below to find out about some of the other reasons why people left the Thirteen Colonies.

One of the Loyalists fled to Halifax when the rebels captured his home town of Boston. Nine days before he left, he had married a poor woman because he believed that she was rich. When he discovered that she was not, he abandoned her. In Halifax, he pretended to be a bachelor, and married a widow there. We can only wonder whether it was for her money.

A commonly held opinion has been that the Loyalists were mainly of British descent. It is now known that their nationalities varied. As well as the English, the Irish, and the Scots, there were Loyalists of German, Dutch, French, Iroquois, and African ancestry. These people hoped that Britain would protect their special customs and traditions.

Some groups feared the democratic ideas of the Americans. They knew that if they stayed in the United States their children would be forced to become like everyone else (**homogeneous**). Many of the people came to America to keep their own culture and religion. They felt all this would be lost if they stayed in the United States, so they packed up and moved north to British territory, where they felt their way of life would be protected.

Some blacks came to British North America because they had no choice in the matter. They were slaves and went where their masters went. Many blacks came as free people, like the other Loyalists.*

Most of the Iroquois, such as Thayendanegea (Joseph Brant),** were Loyalists. They had fought alongside the British regiments. Many of the Iroquois believed that they had more to fear from American farmers, who wanted to move onto lands where the Iroquois lived, than from the British.

The Loyalists were people of many different religions. There were Presbyterians, Anglicans, Methodists, Lutherans, Roman Catholics, Quakers, and Mennonites. Some of these religious groups were afraid that their religion would be lost. They wanted Britain's protection.

Most Loyalists came from colonies controlled by the British army. Loyalists who held British government jobs had no choice but to leave.

Some people became Loyalists on the basis of which recruiter, British or American, offered the best deal to settlers. Loyalists were offered free land in British North America. This greatly influenced their decision to go there.

Some Loyalists may have thought that it would not be long before their new home would be part of the United States anyway. Therefore, they were not leaving their own country forever.

Some people became Loyalists because they expected Britain to win the war. They wanted to be on the winning side. When Britain did not win, if their support of the Loyalist cause was known, they had to flee. Those who had not voiced their opinions as openly quickly became Patriots.

Homogeneous — similar; like everyone else
*The British offered the black slaves their freedom if they helped the British cause.
**See page 113.

Where the Loyalists Went

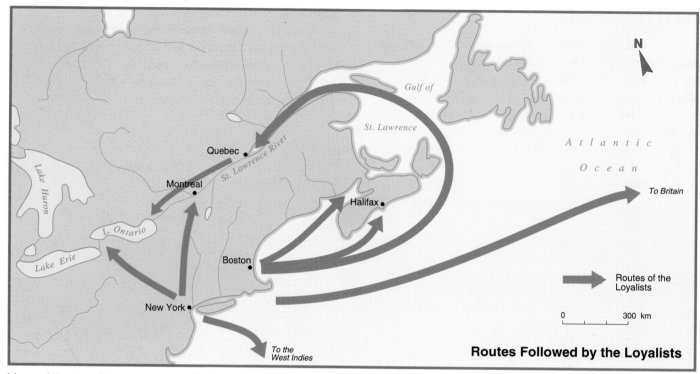

Many of the Loyalists who went to Quebec travelled by land. This map shows the major routes they used. Most of them arrived between 1776 and 1785. The Loyalists who went to Nova Scotia travelled by sea.

The Loyalists had been leaving the Thirteen Colonies since 1776. In the Treaty of Paris of 1783,* which ended the American Revolution, the American Congress agreed to ask the American states to pay the Loyalists back for any of their property that had been taken away or destroyed during the revolution. The American states refused to do this. In fact, after the revolution was over, there was still a great deal of anger against the Loyalists who remained in the United States. Some of them had their farms and businesses burned; others were beaten. The practice of tarring and feathering continued after the peace treaty as well.

By 1785, two years after the end of the revolution, as many as 100 000 Loyalists may have left the Thirteen Colonies. The Loyalists did not have many choices for places to go. Some went to Britain. Others went to the West Indies. Between 40 000 and 45 000 went to British North America.**

*Note that there are two treaties called the Treaty of Paris. The treaty of 1763 ended the Seven Years' War; the treaty of 1783 ended the American Revolution.

**Figures for the number of Loyalists who settled in present-day Canada are not exact. Some did not apply for aid and therefore did not make it into the official records. Also, some who came did not stay. Some returned to the United States. Others came to Nova Scotia and then moved on to other places.

British North America

The Treaty of Paris of 1763,* which ended the Seven Years' War between France and Britain, gave the colonies of Newfoundland, Nova Scotia, Quebec, and Prince Edward Island to Britain.

Newfoundland and Prince Edward Island had very small populations. Nova Scotia had a population of about 20 000, most of whom were of British or German descent.

The province of Quebec was given to Britain, but it was definitely not British. Most of the people—about 98 000 of a population of 113 000—spoke French and had French traditions, but their government was British.

The Loyalists in British North America

Because of their loyalty to Britain, the Loyalists would be protected by the British government in British North America. Also, the British government would give each Loyalist family or individual a piece of land and some supplies to help them start a new life. About 34 000 Loyalists went to the British colony of Nova Scotia. About 7000 went to the British colony of Quebec.**

The British Colony of Nova Scotia

At the end of the American Revolution, in 1783, the only major port in the American colonies still held by the defeated British was New York. Many Loyalists went there so that the British could protect them from the victorious American Patriots. At New York the Loyalists awaited British ships that would take them to Nova Scotia.

The Loyalists who went to New York included those who had fought in Loyalist regiments for the British army during the revolution. At the end of the revolution the British government gave them a choice between being sent back to their homes with three months' pay or being transported to Nova Scotia.

Actually, there was no real choice because the Loyalists were in danger of being persecuted if they returned home. Many of the former soldiers decided that they would be much better off to take their families to Nova Scotia, where they could start a new life.

Here is part of a letter written by the wife of a Loyalist soldier, on June 6, 1783:

Kind husband,

I am sorry to acquant you that our farme is sold . . . they said if I did not quitt posesion that they had aright to take anythink on the farme or in the house to pay the cost of a law sute and imprisen me—I have suffered most every thing but death it self in your long absens pray grant me spedy releaf or God only knows what will become of me and me frendles children. . . . They say my posesion was nothing youre husband has forfeted his estate by joining the British Enemy with a free and vollentary will and thereby was forfeted to the Stat and sold. All at present from you cind and loveing wife.

Phoebe Ward

For families like the Wards, Nova Scotia seemed like a good place to go. Even though it was a British colony, very few people lived there. The low population ensured that there would be plenty of land available for the Loyalists.

Some of the Loyalists were so thankful to arrive on British soil that they knelt and kissed the ground. One Loyalist, the Reverend Jonathan Beecher, wrote:

As soon as we had set up a kind of tent, we knelt down, my wife and I and my two boys, and kissed the dear ground and thanked God that the flag of England floated there. We resolved that we would work with the rest to become again prosperous and happy.

C-168, National Archives of Canada, Ottawa.

The Coming of the Loyalists, 1783. Many Loyalists faced great hardships when they had to start new farms or businesses in British North America.

Unfortunately, some Loyalists were soon disappointed in their new home. They called it "Nova Scarcity." The winters were harsh, and food was scarce. In many areas the land was unproductive. They complained bitterly at how poorly the British government had rewarded them for their loyalty to Britain during the revolution.

By 1785, about 34 000 Loyalists had made the journey to Nova Scotia. This was over one and one-half times as many people as the 20 000 already there. The Loyalists settled in three main areas—Halifax, Shelburne, and the St. John River Valley.

Areas Where the Loyalists Settled

Halifax

Halifax was founded in 1749. By the time the Loyalists began to arrive in 1783, Halifax was a well-established community, with schools, churches, and stores. It was the British military centre and capital of Nova Scotia. The British-appointed governor and many soldiers, as well as families, lived there. Only a small number of Loyalists settled in Halifax. In Halifax, the Loyalists had to fit into the community, rather than make their own new life, as they did in Shelburne and the St. John River Valley.

The Church of St. Paul, and the Parade at Halifax in Nova Scotia.

Shelburne

About 10 000 Loyalists went to settle at Port Roseway. They renamed it Shelburne and made it, for a short time, one of the largest cities in all of North America. The Loyalists had high hopes for the new lives they would have in Shelburne. There was an excellent harbour and few people, which meant that they would be able to live their own lives and not have to fit into an established community, as the Loyalists who settled in Halifax had to do.

A thriving town developed, with stores, taverns, churches, three newspapers, and a shipbuilding industry. Benjamin Marston, a resident of Shelburne, describes how early in 1784 some 50 citizens of the city "danced, drank tea, and played cards in a house where six months ago there was an almost impenetrable swamp."

Unfortunately, though, the land around Shelburne was unsuitable for farming, and when the British government's food rations began to run out, people began to leave. In a short time, it went from a boom town of 10 000 people to a few hundred people. Many of the new houses were either taken apart and shipped to Halifax, where they were set up again, or they were destroyed for firewood. Soon much of the city looked like a grassy ghost town with stone fireplaces scattered about.

The St. John River Valley

About 15 000 Loyalists settled in the St. John River Valley. This was the area that would later become the colony of New Brunswick. Before this could happen, problems between the Loyalist settlers and the British government needed to be solved.

This group of Loyalists began to ask for a separate colony almost immediately. They did not want to be part of the colony of Nova Scotia. They felt that Halifax, the capital, where most of the government officials were located, was too far away.

The government was not well prepared for the arrival of the Loyalists. The first night after landing, the Loyalists had to hack away bushes and trees in order to find room to set up their tents. Some were so dismayed by this situation that they simply sat down and cried.

The government did not provide enough tools and building materials to help the Loyalists build their new homes. As a result, some of the women and children died from cold weather or starvation during the first winter.

The distribution of land to the Loyalists was another major problem. The land had not been divided into lots when the first Loyalists arrived. Therefore, they could not be sure that they actually owned the land upon which they were building their homes. In fact, some of the first Loyalists had already built 1500 frame houses and 400 log huts near the harbour, when the government informed them that the area was needed as a refugee settlement area for new arrivals.

Later arrivals were unhappy because the lots that they were given were much smaller than the lots given to Loyalists who had arrived earlier. In fact, in Parrtown (later renamed St. John) the last town lots were one-sixteenth the size of the first lots.

Favouritism was also a problem. Loyalists who had held important positions in the Thirteen Colonies received more land than Loyalists who were not so important.

Thomas Peters (1738–1792)

Thomas Peters was a former slave. He served with the Black Pioneers, an all-black regiment, during the American Revolution. In 1783, Peters and other veterans of the Black Pioneers were transported to Nova Scotia, where they had been promised town lots of approximately eight hectares each, outside of the city of Shelburne.

Instead, the British government gave them only poor land outside of Shelburne. When they built on this land, their homes were burned down by people from Shelburne. They finally settled in an all-black community called Birchtown.

After six years of waiting for the land he had been promised, Peters went to Britain for help. There he met William Wilberforce, a famous anti-slavery crusader. Wilberforce organized the start of a new colony in Africa, called Sierra Leone. About 1200 black people, including Thomas Peters, sailed from Nova Scotia to Sierra Leone. There was to be equality between blacks and whites in this new colony.

Unfortunately, the colony only lasted a year. There were many difficulties from the beginning. Many colonists died on the voyage to Africa. Droughts, tornadoes, fever, and feuds among the colonists made the first year a disaster. However, even though the colony collapsed, there are still descendants of the Nova Scotia colonists in Sierra Leone today.*

The British Colony of New Brunswick

A New Colony Is Formed

In 1784, Nova Scotia was divided along the Missiquash River and the British colony of New Brunswick was created.

The Loyalists Want a New Colony

The Loyalists in the St. John River Valley had many reasons for wanting a new colony. They felt that they were too far from the government capital in Halifax. They felt that the distant government treated them unfairly. The Loyalists also believed that they were unlike the people who were already settled in the colony of Nova Scotia. Many of these people were formerly from the New England colonies and had remained neutral, favouring neither side during the revolution. They had not been forced to leave their homes.

The Loyalists thought that all they had suffered during and after the revolution made it difficult to live with people who had not suffered or taken part in the revolution. They thought a separate Loyalist colony where they could live with people like themselves would be better.

This idea was expressed by Edward Winslow, one of the Loyalist leaders:

A large proportion of the old inhabitants of this country are natives of New England, or descendants from New Englanders. They never experienced the violence of political bad feelings. They remained quiet during all the persecutions. They kept an affection for their former country. On our side are people who served in the military. They are angry from a series of misfortunes and are jealous to an extreme. Either of these kinds of people may form useful societies among themselves, but they can't be mixed.

A final reason had to do with the possibilities of the area. The St. John River was easy to navigate. The soil was fertile. Fish and timber were plentiful and the coastline had many good harbours. It looked like a place where new settlers could become prosperous.

The British Government Agrees

The British government recognized certain advantages in the formation of a Loyalist colony separate from the colony of Nova Scotia.

- If the colony of Nova Scotia were split, it would be less difficult to control because there would be a governor in each of the two colonies. The governor in Halifax would no longer have to worry about governing a place so far away.

- A new colony would provide government positions for wealthy and well-educated Loyalists who were demanding them.

- A strong Loyalist colony on the American border would provide protection against the American idea that colonists should rebel and govern themselves. The British government did not want the people in its remaining North American colonies to be influenced by this idea.

New Brunswick developed representative government soon after its formation as a colony. The first Legislature met in 1786, just two years after it became the separate colony of New Brunswick. Representative government means that the people of New Brunswick could "rule" by choosing others to act for, or represent, them in government.

---

*Note: there are thousands of descendents of the Black Loyalists living in Nova Scotia today.

The British Colony of Prince Edward Island

In 1763, by the Treaty of Paris, Île St. Jean (as Prince Edward Island was called then) became British property. The British renamed it St. John Island. It was called St. John Island until 1799, when it took the name of Prince Edward Island.

In 1767, the British divided the island into 67 townships of approximately 8000 hectares. The townships were given to British noblemen or officers. These people were absentee landlords, which meant they owned the land but did not choose to live on it. The owners chose to live in Britain instead of the colonies.

The landowning system on St. John Island was like an English version of New France's seigneurial system. All the land was owned by a favoured group of people. The difference between the landholding system in St. John Island and that in New France was that the St. John Island landholders did not bring in settlers as they had promised and many of them did not even pay their taxes.

In 1774, when the Thirteen Colonies had their First Continental Congress (a meeting to discuss their complaints about Britain), the people of St. John Island, as well as the people of Quebec and Nova Scotia, were invited to attend. They were not worried about gaining independence from Britain, but did want to gain some rights as colonies. But these colonies decided not to send any representatives to the meeting.

By 1784, there were still only about 1000 people living on St. John Island. Approximately 600 Loyalists decided to try to settle there. They found that they had to pay high rents and could not buy their land, since it was already owned by the absentee landlords.

Eventually some of the Loyalist farmers decided that if the British landlords did not have to pay taxes, then they should not have to pay the high rents. The story is told that the first person in a neighbourhood to see a rent collector coming would blow on a large seashell to sound an alarm. Then the farmers would drive away the collector with clubs and pitchforks.

Some of the farmers were so discouraged by the fact that they could not own their own land that they left St. John Island. Others stayed on in the hope that one day the land would be theirs.

The British Colony of Cape Breton Island

Like New Brunswick, Cape Breton was made a separate colony from Nova Scotia in 1784. Up to this time the British government had not allowed people to settle there. There was coal on the island but the British government did not allow factories to be built because they would compete with the factories in Britain. However, in 1784 Cape Breton Island was opened to the Loyalists. About 3000 settled there. Most did not stay long. They did not like the fact that they could only rent, not buy, their land. As on St. John Island, most of the land on Cape Breton Island was owned by absentee landlords who lived in Britain. In 1820, Cape Breton was **re-annexed** to Nova Scotia.

C-13954, National Archives of Canada, Ottawa.

Cape Breton Council, by Charles Walter Simpson. The Cape Breton council had to deal with the large numbers of Loyalist refugees moving into the area.

The British Colony of Newfoundland

The British still showed no interest in having Newfoundland grow in population. All of the attention of the British government was still directed toward the fishing industry there. As a result, settlement was not encouraged. The government did not transport any Loyalists to Newfoundland.

Re-annex— to unite with a province or country again

By the 1760s, semi-permanent fishing stations were settled in many of Newfoundland's harbours.

C-105230, National Archives of Canada, Ottawa.

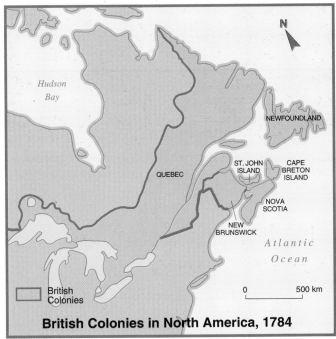

British Colonies in North America, 1784

Britain gained Quebec in 1763, then lost the Thirteen Colonies during the American Revolution. The result was a very different British North America by 1784.

For Your Notebook

1. In which three areas did the Loyalists settle in Nova Scotia? Briefly summarize the Loyalist experience in each of these places.
2. Why did the Loyalists in the St. John River Valley want the British government to create a new colony for them?
3. Why did the British government agree that a new colony should be created in the St. John River Valley?
4. Explain the landholding system on St. John Island (later called Prince Edward Island) at the time of the arrival of the Loyalists.

Exploring Further

1. Benedict Arnold is an interesting person from these times. He began as a Patriot, married a Loyalist, and then offered to spy for the British. He escaped from the Patriots on a British ship, but left his British contact behind to be hanged as a spy. After the war he was hated by both Patriots and Loyalists (for abandoning his contact). Read more details about Benedict Arnold. Decide whether you think he was a Patriot, a Loyalist, or an **opportunist.** Justify your answer.

Opportunist—a person who takes advantage of a situation for his or her own benefit

The British Colony of Quebec

The Loyalists had been coming to Quebec since 1776. By 1783, of the 7000 who had come, 6000 were crowded into temporary refugee camps on the seigneury of Sorel, waiting for the government to decide what to do with them.

The British government was urging Governor Haldimand to encourage the Loyalists to go back home. They complained too much and cost the government too much money.

However, Governor Haldimand realized that it was highly unlikely that they would return to the United States. There was too much hatred against them there. Also, their farms, homes, businesses, and any other possessions left behind had all been taken over by the Patriots. They really did not have any good reasons to return. The Loyalists had given up everything and expected the British government to make up for their losses.

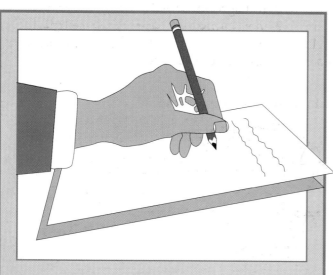

A Petition

A petition is a document containing a request directed to the government. It contains statements describing what the petitioners want changed and has space for the petitioners to sign their names. People might sign a petition requesting anything from the construction of a road to the lowering of taxes. People who want others to sign their petitions often go door-to-door or stand in markets or other places where many people will see them.

An Exercise in Problem Solving

1. Divide into groups of four. Imagine you are a member of a Loyalist family of two parents and four children leaving from one of the Thirteen Colonies for Quebec. Your father's life is in danger and you have only a few hours to prepare for your journey. You have two horses and a small cart. List the possessions you would take with you.

2. Imagine that your family is travelling toward the colony of Quebec. You decide to write a petition to Governor Haldimand, to be delivered when you arrive.
   In the petition you describe the following:

   - what you will need (land, food, clothing, seed, farm and household tools)
   - the hardships you expect in your new home
   - the help you expect Governor Haldimand to give you.

A Loyalist Petition

Governor Haldimand did not want the Loyalists mixing with the French-speaking population. Even though the Loyalists had left their own country so that they could live in a colony under the king's rule, they still had been exposed to the American ideas of liberty, equality, and representative government. He did not want them passing these ideas to the French-speaking inhabitants of Quebec.

Governor Haldimand decided to give the Loyalists land on the frontier to the west, as far away from the French as possible. Another reason for putting them there was so that they could serve as a first defence in the case of an American attack.

The Loyalists decided that they would need many things if they were going to be pioneers in a new land. A copy of the petition that they sent to Governor Haldimand is shown on the next page.

An Example of a Loyalist Petition

To His Excellency General Haldimand, Governor-General and Commander in Chief:

The Loyalists, going to form a settlement at Cataraqui, ask:

- That boards, nails, and shingles be given to each Loyalist family so that they may build houses and other buildings; that eight squares of window glass also be given each family.
- That arms, ammunition, and one axe be given to each male, aged fourteen or more.
- That the following things be given to each family:
  - one plow shear and coulter
  - leather for horse collars
  - two spades
  - three iron wedges
  - fifteen iron harrow teeth
  - three hoes
  - 2.5 cm and 1.25 cm auger
  - three chisels
  - one gouge
  - three **gimlets**
  - one hand saw and files
  - one nail hammer
  - one drawing knife
  - one frow for splitting shingles
  - two scythes and one sickle
  - one broad axe
- That one grindstone be given for every three families.
- That one year's clothing be given to each family.
- That two years' provisions be given to each family, enough according to their number and age.
- That two horses, two cows, and six sheep be delivered at Cataraqui for each family.
- That seeds of different kinds such as wheat, Indian corn, peas, oats, potatoes, and flax be given to each family.
- That one blacksmith be established in each township.

(Adapted from the Loyalist Petition to Governor Haldimand, written at Sorel.)

Gimlet—a small hand tool used for boring holes in wood

Government Help

Provisions and Tools

The Loyalists were not given all of the things they had requested. However, they were given enough supplies to last for three years. Each family was given one tent. One musket was given to every five men (with one kilogram of powder and two kilograms of lead balls). There were lots of army muskets available, but Governor Haldimand thought that if the men could not spend their time hunting, then they would spend it clearing the land and planting crops. Each man was given an axe, a spade, and a hoe for this purpose. Small groups of families were given an ox, a plough, and building tools to share. Clothes were provided for three years' wear. Flour, beef, pork, salt, and butter were given to each family.

The following seed supply was given to the members of the community: 2 kg of onion seed, 5 kg of Norfolk turnip, 4 kg early Dutch turnip, 5 kg large Dutch cabbage, 6 kg celery seed, 8 kg orange carrot, 2 kg short top radish, 1 kg parsley seed, 36 dm^3 of marrowfat peas.

It is interesting to note that the wheat seed had to be purchased from Americans in Vermont and the Mohawk Valley. Some of the wheat must have come from farms once owned by the Loyalists who had left those areas.

Land Grants (imaginary quote)

I brought my family all the way up north to find this alien land system—the seigneural system. The people here don't own the land. They rent it! That's not for me! I demand the British Freehold System, where we own our own land.

To accommodate the Loyalists, the British system of owning land was introduced. It was decided that land would be given out according to the Loyalists' army rank and the number of people in their families. Army officers could draw more land than others, but they were not allowed to choose the land they liked best.

The land was divided into lots of about 80 hectares. Each lot was given a number. The numbers were written on pieces of paper and placed in a hat. Each man picked one of the lot numbers out of the hat and then hurried off to inspect his land.

Because there were no roads, the most valuable land was located along the waterways. Land that proved to be too poor for farming could be left and another lot, farther inland, could be drawn.

Building a New Life

The Loyalists had many hardships to endure. Although some merchants and **artisans** were able to continue their occupations, many people with no farming experience were forced to become farmers.

They lived in tents at first until a small shanty or hut could be built in preparation for winter. Then they began to clear the land to plant crops. Trees were cut down using handaxes. Those trees that were too big for the pioneers' small handaxes were circled with a cut 1.5 metres above the ground. This would kill the tree by the next year. The stumps were often left to rot in the ground. Later, when oxen became available, they were used to pull the stumps out.

The Loyalists were so busy building houses, clearing land, and planting crops, that they had little time to worry about other things.

An Eyewitness Account

James Dittrick, a boy whose family was Loyalist, described one hardship that he experienced:

We none of us had any shoes or stockings, winter or summer, as those we brought with us were soon worn out. At length my father tanned some leather, and I recollect the first pair of shoes he made which fell to my lot, greased and putting them too near the fire, on returning to my grief found that my shoes were all shrivelled up, so that I could never wear them. I[t] was twelve months before I obtained another pair, so many daily occurrences of life having to be attended to.

The Hungry Year

The year 1788 has become known as the "Hungry Year." The winter of 1787–88 was extremely cold. It was followed by a summer drought. The lack of rain caused the crops to wither and die. To make matters worse, this was the year when the British government ended its assistance to the Loyalists. The government thought that they could now manage on their own.

James Dittrick describes the Hungry Year:

The most trying period of our lives, was the year 1788 called the year of scarcity . . . .

All the crops failed . . . for several days we were without food, except that the various roots we procured and boiled down to nourish us. We noticed what roots the pigs eat; and by that means avoided anything that had any poisonous qualities . . .

. . . Our poor dog was killed to allay the pangs of hunger, the very idea brought on sickness to some, but others devoured the flesh quite ravenous.

A few of the settlers starved to death. Most survived until 1789, when emergency supplies arrived. It has been estimated that half of the Loyalist population would have died if these supplies had not arrived when they did.

Fortunately, the harvest of 1789 was an excellent one. The Loyalists continued to live in their new homes. Many eventually became very prosperous farmers, but they never forgot the Hungry Year.

C-10717, National Archives of Canada, Ottawa (detail).

Sir Guy Carleton (1724–1808)

Sir Guy Carleton, later named Lord Dorchester, was commander-in-chief of the British forces at the end of the American Revolution. He worked long and hard on behalf of the Loyalists. He was responsible for the evacuation of the Loyalists from New York. All of the Loyalists were supposed to have gone by September 3, 1783, but Carleton stalled until November. By stalling for time, he allowed all the Loyalists who wished to escape New York time to reach safety.

Carleton had been governor of Quebec before Haldimand. He had been responsible for convincing the British government to proclaim the Quebec Act of 1774. (You read about it on page 84.) He became governor of Quebec again in 1786. In 1791, when the Constitutional Act divided Quebec into Upper and Lower Canada, Carleton became the first governor general of Canada. You will read about the Constitutional Act later in this chapter.

For Your Notebook

1. Ask your parents or other adults if they have ever signed a petition. What did it request? Did the petition get results?

2. Compare the actual petition sent by the Loyalists to the petition that you wrote to Governor Haldimand in the exercise on page 110. Did you forget anything important? Did the Loyalists ask for anything that you do not consider important?

Artisan — worker very skilled in his or her craft

An Exercise in Problem Solving

(a) Refer to pages 80 and 84. Describe and/or make a chart illustrating the type of government in existence in Quebec when the Loyalists arrived.

(b) Read the two stories on pages 114 to 117. Under the headings language, religion, and land ownership, describe the Quebec that the Loyalists would have preferred. In groups, draw on chart paper a government diagram showing the way in which the Loyalists would have liked to have seen the government organized. Present your government diagram to the rest of the class.

(d) Write a letter from a Loyalist to Lord Dorchester describing how Quebec should be changed. A brief biography of Lord Dorchester (formerly called Sir Guy Carleton) is found on page 112. Read the biography of Thayendanegea (Joseph Brant) so as to consider a Native person's point of view as well.

Native People

The Six Nations lived in what is now New York State. During the American Revolution most of the Iroquoian people were loyal to Britain and fought on their side.

When the revolution was over, Britain invited the Iroquoian people to move to British North America. Many of them did. Thayendanegea (Joseph Brant), a war leader of the Iroquois Six Nations Confederacy during the American Revolution, led his people to the Grand River area (now called the Six Nations Reserve). In the years that followed, several other Native groups moved to British North America as well.

After the American Revolution, American settlers moved westward by the thousands into the lands set aside for Native peoples by the Proclamation of 1763.

Exploring Further

1. Find instances today of Native land claims. What are the issues involved? How are they the same as or different from those faced by Thayendanegea (Joseph Brant)?

2. Find information about Molly Brant, Joseph Brant's sister (*see* biography above right). Prepare a report about this important Native leader.

Thayendanegea (1742–1807)

Thayendangea, which meant "Two Sticks of Wood Bound Together for Strength" became a man of two worlds—the world of the Mohawks and the world of the Europeans. He attended school and could read and write English, Latin, and Greek—at a time when schooling was available for only a favoured few. While at school he became a devout Christian and received his Christian name—Joseph Brant.

Thayendangea became war leader of the Iroquois Six Nations Confederacy during the American Revolution. Under his leadership most of the Six Nations remained loyal to the British government. He and his men fought many battles against the Patriots.

After the war Thayendanegea led his people to British North America. There, most settled on a reserve that extended to a width of 10 kilometres on either side of the Grand River in what is now southwestern Ontario.

He spent many years fighting for the right of his people to treat the land around the Grand River as their own. In 1784 Governor Haldimand of Quebec signed a formal deed on behalf of King George III of Britain that gave the land to the Mohawks with the words "which they and their posterity are to enjoy forever." In 1793 Lieutenant Governor Simcoe of Upper Canada issued a new deed that stated that the land belonged to the Native people only so long as they remained on it. If they left it, the ownership would go back to the British government. They could not sell or transfer it. When the British government was appealed to, they agreed with Simcoe. This issue was not resolved in Thayendanegea's lifetime.

Thayendanegea was an exceptional leader during difficult times. He was a strong Loyalist during the American Revolution. However, after the revolution he was not afraid to stand up for his people against what he saw as injustices of the British government. He served as a bridge for his people between the old ways and the new, while at the same time working to maintain their distinct culture.

#5777, National Gallery of Canada, Ottawa (detail).

On a Loyalist Farm

The coming of the Loyalists greatly changed the lives of the people living in the colony of Quebec. The Loyalists wanted the representative governments they had been used to in the Thirteen Colonies. The French also had concerns and wanted to ensure that their way of life continued. You will read about their differing points of view in the following stories.

Andy burst through the door in his usual energetic way, shouting "Is dinner ready yet?"

A peaceful scene greeted him. The baby was sleeping in her cradle. His little sister, Jane, sat near the fire, singing a lullaby as she rocked her cornhusk doll to sleep.

His mother smiled fondly as she turned from the fire, where she had been stirring stew in the large black pot the family had brought with them from their old home in New York. Father had complained that it would take up too much room in their small wagon, but Mother had insisted, pointing out that it would be needed for baths and for washing clothes, as well as for cooking. She pushed her blond hair off her brow and looked at him. "Just go call your father and your brother. They're in the barn. Come back and wash up. Then we'll eat."

A few minutes later the Smith family members sat down to their dinner of stew made from a deer shot by Father and vegetables grown by Mother and Jane. The roaring fire made the small cabin warm and snug in spite of the chill of the October evening. It would not be long before the winter winds began to blow.

"It's hard to believe," commented Father, "that it has only been six years since we spent the winter at Sorel, sleeping in a tent and living off government rations of salt pork and peas."

"It is also hard to believe that it has been only two years since the Hungry Year," Mother quietly added.

"Do you think we will ever have another Hungry Year, Mother?" Jane looked at her mother, her eyes anxious in the flickering candlelight.

"No, silly," interrupted John, who, as the eldest, often felt it his duty to explain the ways of the world to his younger brother and sister. "It will never be as bad as that. Even if we do have poor crops again, we will always have something saved from the year before. In the Hungry Year there was nothing to fall back on because there was nothing left over. Father and I had been too busy building the house and clearing the fields to plant a large crop that year. We ate everything we grew as well as our government rations. Then, in the Hungry Year, the government rations stopped and we had poor crops. People almost starved. We never want to see times like that again!"

"Yes, we are very fortunate," Mother commented as she looked proudly around the table at her family. "The harvest this year has been bountiful. There will be plenty of food to last the winter, even with six hungry mouths to feed. Our home is warm and snug thanks to the way in which Andy and Jane worked to chink the logs so that the wind wouldn't get in."

"We are also fortunate that Father wasn't tarred and feathered by the Patriots in the Thirteen Colonies," added Jane, who adored her father. "My friend Jenny's father took off his shirt when he was plowing the fields last summer. You can still see the scars on his back from the hot tar. It is a good thing that we left our former home in New York in the middle of the night like we did."

As the family continued to sit contentedly around the table, there was a loud rap on the door. Jane rose to open it. What a surprise! There stood their nearest neighbours, Mr. and Mrs. Thornton.

"I hope we're not interrupting your dinner," began Mr. Thornton as he and his wife came through the door, "but we were on our way home from the grist mill and decided to stop for a few minutes. The harvest has been so good this year that there has been little time for visiting."

"You are right about that, my friend," replied Father, as he and his family rose and joined the Thorntons around the crackling fire. Mother went to dip into her carefully hoarded supply of coffee to make a pot to offer the visitors.

"It's good to sit in front of a warm fire and enjoy a cup of hot coffee," began Mr. Thornton. "There was a time not so long ago when luxuries like coffee were unheard of. Quebec is beginning to seem like home. Our lives are getting much better. During the long evenings this winter I intend to spend my time making some decent furniture for our home. I would like to replace those blocks of wood we call chairs."

"It's about time that we had some of the things we had to leave behind," agreed Mrs. Thornton. "I am sure that all of our old things have either been destroyed by now or are sitting in the homes of whichever Patriots could get to them first. How I wish I had my beautiful china set," she sighed.

"Never mind your china set, my dear," responded Mr. Thornton. "What about payment for the prosperous farm we had to leave behind?"

Mother, who was always practical, interrupted firmly, "I have given up worrying about ever getting paid for the property we left behind in the new United States. It will never happen. We must put all that behind us and get on with making a new life here in Quebec."

Here she paused while she tackled a difficult part of the sweater she was knitting for the baby. "Speaking of a new life," she continued after a moment, "I am certainly displeased with the present type of government under the Quebec Act. I can understand why the civil laws have been based on the system in France since most of the people here were French-speaking. But, since the arrival of so many Loyalists, that is no longer the case. We Loyalists have proven our loyalty to Britain by taking Britain's side in the American Revolution. We have paid for our loyalty by having to leave our homes and possessions behind and moving here to start a new life. But we certainly didn't come here to live under French civil law. We expect our own British law."

"Not only that, my dear," added her husband. "We need to have an elected **Legislative Assembly**. We don't want a governor, even a British one, and an appointed council, to tell us what to do. We had elected assemblies in the Thirteen

Colonies, the people who live in Britain have an elected assembly, and we must have the same here!" he finished emphatically.

"If Governor Dorchester is wise, he will make sure that we have a Legislative Assembly so that we can have a say in how we are governed," agreed Mr. Thornton. "The British government was very wrong to impose taxation without representation on the people of the Thirteen Colonies. But the means of protest should have been peaceful, not the violent ones chosen by the Patriots."

"And what about protection for the Protestant churches?" asked Mrs. Thornton. "The Roman Catholic church is protected by the Quebec Act, but many of the newcomers like us are not Catholics. We need protection too."

"It is not just the churches," added Mr. Thornton. "We want to own our land. Right now, since there are no seigneuries in this part of Quebec, we are tenants of the king instead of tenants of a seigneur. But what is the difference? We are still renters instead of owners!"

"Oh, well," laughed Mr. Thornton, as he rose from his chair. "We will not solve all of Quebec's problems during one evening's discussion. I am sure that the British government will be fair to those of us who have sacrificed so much for our loyalty."

"I hope so," replied Father. "But sometimes people do have to stand up for their rights," he added, "although certainly not with the violent means used by the Patriots in the Thirteen Colonies."

"Well, good evening, friends," said Mrs. Thornton. "Tomorrow is another day, with more grain to be taken to the grist mill, and glad we are that we have it to take."

"Yes," agreed Mother. "We may have problems in our new home, but life is getting easier. We are no longer in danger of starving and the British government will soon give us the Legislative Assembly we are asking for," she concluded confidently. ■

Legislative Assembly—the group of representatives elected to the Legislature who represent the people of each province; a law-making body

On a Seigneury

Spring was in the air that day in 1790 as 14-year-old Henri de Coursière walked with his family to the May Day celebration at the home of the seigneur. They made a pleasant-looking group as they walked down the village street. Monsieur Jean de Coursière carried little Jean-Pierre on his shoulders. Madame de Coursière walked along beside them. Strung out across the road were Henri and his five younger brothers and sisters, all dressed in their Sunday best, their faces still shiny from the scrubbing they had received with their mother's lye soap. Madame de Coursière and the girls wore little white bonnets on their heads and their good dresses, the ones they saved for church. Madame de Coursière, who was often chilly, had thrown a soft gray homespun shawl over her shoulders. Monsieur de Coursière and his sons wore leather breeches, wool shirts, leather jackets, and leather moccasins on their feet.

As the family walked along they greeted their friends and neighbours, most of whom were also on their way to the celebration. This was the day when all the *censitaires,* or seigneurial tenants, paid their *cens,* which was a token payment to their seigneur for living on his land. There was an actual rent payment to be made, but Henri knew that his parents would not have to pay that until November 11, which was the day rents were due to the seigneur and **tithes** paid to the priest.

Both May Day and November 11 were days that the *censitaires* eagerly awaited. May Day was a welcome break from spring planting and November 11 a pause before the long winter set in. Most of all they were holidays and a chance to meet with friends and neighbours for some merry-making. Henri secretly hoped that he would be able to talk

This is a detail from the painting called *Circular Dance of the Canadians,* by George Heriot.

C-251, National Archives of Canada, Ottawa (detail).

Tithe— a tax of one-tenth of the produce of one's land or the amount in money, paid to support the church

to Suzanne Grenier during the day. If he was really fortunate, perhaps he would even be able to sit beside her at the feast provided by the seigneur. It was too much to hope that he might hold her hand during the round dances that would follow the feast. She was beautiful and there would be others hoping for the same chance.

Henri sighed as he remembered that she was 15 and would probably be married before the next May Day celebrations, and likely to someone much richer than himself. He might inherit at least part of his father's river front farm one day. In the meantime he would have to try to rent a small piece of land farther inland, since all the river front property on the seigneury already had tenants.

As Henri was daydreaming, his father's friend Jacques Rivard and his family came into view. Monsieur Rivard called out to them, "Hello, friends. Your seigneur has invited me and my family to the May Day celebrations on his seigneury."

"That is good news, Jacques," replied Henri's father. Henri knew that his father had not expected his friend to be at the celebrations since he was not a tenant on the seigneury, but earned his living as a notary. His father would enjoy the day even more now. Henri was glad for him. His life was not easy with seven children to support.

Monsieur Rivard joined Henri's father as Madame Rivard began to chat with Henri's mother and the Rivard children paired up with Henri's brothers and sisters. Since Monsieur and Madame Rivard had no children his age, Henri continued to amble along on one side of his father.

Monsieur Rivard walked on the other side. At first Henri continued with his daydream, but Monsieur Rivard's raised voice drew his attention to the conversation between the two men.

"I am growing impatient with Lord Dorchester," Monsieur Rivard was saying. "He doesn't do anything. When he was here as governor before and was known as Guy Carleton, he ran the government well. Since he changed his name to Lord Dorchester he has become like a new person. He can't make a decision anymore. The Quebec Act must be reformed. If we had a system of representative government we French-speaking people, who are in the majority, would have a greater say than the English-speaking people in the way the government is run. Why should the Loyalists, who have been here only a short time, have more influence than we *Canadiens* whose fathers and grandfathers were born and died here?"

"You are right, my friend," Henri's father calmly replied. "The Quebec Act must be reformed, but it is not necessary to take things as far as you suggest. We do not need to have an elected assembly, but we do need to demand that *Canadiens* take a greater part in governing the colony. We have to make sure that *Canadiens* are on the appointed councils. We have to protect our ways of doing things, such as our laws and our system of land ownership, from the influence of all these English-speaking people who keep arriving."

"Speaking of our system of land ownership," exclaimed Monsieur Rivard, "I wouldn't mind if we did change to the English system! I

think people should be able to own their own land. I know you and the seigneurs disagree with me, Jean," he said. "You habitants seem content to live as you always have, as tenants of a seigneur; but I would like to see people have the opportunity to own their own land."

"The thing I am most concerned about is our religion," said Henri's father. "We *Canadiens* are Roman Catholics. Most of the newcomers to Quebec are Protestants. They are demanding rights for their religion. We must make sure our Roman Catholic Church continues to be protected. For instance, we must not let a Protestant governor take away the right of Roman Catholics to hold government positions."

"Our language must also be protected," added Monsieur Rivard. "The newcomers speak English. We must be able to speak French in our new Legislative Assembly, our laws must be written in French, and court cases must be tried in French."

Henri was just starting to get interested in the conversation. He wanted to ask whether or not either man thought that Lord Dorchester would soon reform the Quebec Act, but they had arrived at the Maypole. The conversation stopped as everyone gathered round to watch the seigneur wet the pole with brandy and fire a blank from his musket to blacken the pole. Then the other men raised their flintlocks and also fired blanks at the pole, blackening it from top to bottom. This was the first event of the May Day celebrations and Henri forgot the Quebec Act as his thoughts returned to Suzanne Grenier and his eyes began to search for her in the crowd. ■

An Exercise in Decision-Making

What Should the British Government Do?

After the arrival of the Loyalists the British government was faced with the problem of governing two groups of people with very different views and backgrounds, both living in Quebec.

British: (imaginary quotes)

- We fought for Britain during the American Revolution. We risked our lives and lost our homes for Britain. We deserve to have British laws and government now. We want an elected Legislative Assembly to make laws for us.

- We do not like the French seigneurial system of landholding. We want to own our own land.

- We want land set aside for our Protestant churches and schools.

- Since we are English-speaking, we want English as an official language. It will certainly be the language spoken in our Legislative Assembly since we will be electing English-speaking people like ourselves.

- We expect to be rewarded for our loyalty to Great Britain. If these changes are not made, we will feel like strangers in our new home.

French: (imaginary quotes)

- We were in Quebec first. Why should we have to change our laws and system of government because of these new people?

- There are more French-speaking people. We want to keep our seigneurial system. It has worked well for many years and will continue to work well.

- We want protection for our Roman Catholic religion. We do not want our children to attend Protestant schools.

- There are four times as many of us French-speaking people as there are English speakers. French must stay as the official language here in Quebec.

- Why should we have to change our ways for these new people?

- The Quebec Act of 1774 guaranteed us certain cultural rights, especially to our language and religion.

A decision had to be made. How could the British government best meet the needs of both the 30 000 English-speaking and 140 000 French-speaking people in Quebec?

1. Refer to the section on page 80 entitled "Alternatives Open to the British." As advisors to the British government, discuss each alternative and decide what you would do if you were the British government. Use the two stories on pages 114–117 and the information on this page as reference material. Record your information on a decision-making chart. Write a letter to the British government outlining your point of view.

The Constitutional Act, 1791

Introduction

The Constitutional Act of 1791 gave the people of Upper and Lower Canada their own Legislative Assemblies, thereby giving them representative government. Because the British government did not repeal the Quebec Act, its terms continued in existence.

Aims: to recognize the bicultural nature of Quebec by dividing it into two colonies: Upper Canada and Lower Canada

- to provide a government satisfying both British and French
- to give the people an elected Legislative Assembly, but limiting the assembly's power.

By giving the people elected assemblies with limited power, the British government attempted to ensure that the situation in the Thirteen Colonies, where the legislative assemblies had too much power and a revolution occurred, did not happen in British North America.

Upper and Lower Canada, 1791

Quebec was divided into two colonies: Upper Canada ("up" the St. Lawrence River), which is part of the present-day province of Ontario, and Lower Canada ("down" the St. Lawrence River), which is part of the present-day province of Quebec.

Bicultural—having two cultures (British and French) existing side by side in the same country or province

Key Terms

Language: Upper Canada to be English-speaking and Lower Canada mainly French-speaking

Religion: one-seventh of all public lands in Upper Canada to be set aside for Protestant schools and churches. In Lower Canada the system established under the Quebec Act was to be continued (protection for the Roman Catholic Church).

Government—Who Makes the Laws (Legislative)

- governor general for Lower Canada would control affairs in both colonies; Upper Canada to have its own lieutenant-governor
- each colony to have an Executive Council (appointed) to advise governor, and a Legislative Council (appointed) to propose laws and approve those laws passed by the Assembly
- each colony to have representative government, with (elected) Legislative Assembly, and power to impose taxes, make laws, and serve local needs. Only male landowners allowed to vote. Women with property in Lower Canada could vote until the 1830s. Women in Upper Canada could not vote.
- power of Legislative Assembly very limited, councils and governor can block laws.

Government—Who Enforces the Laws (Executive)

- Upper Canada to have English civil law and criminal law; Lower Canada same system as Quebec Act (English criminal and Canadian [based on French] civil law)

Refer to the government diagram on page 120.

Government Structure of Upper Canada
Under the Constitutional Act, 1791*

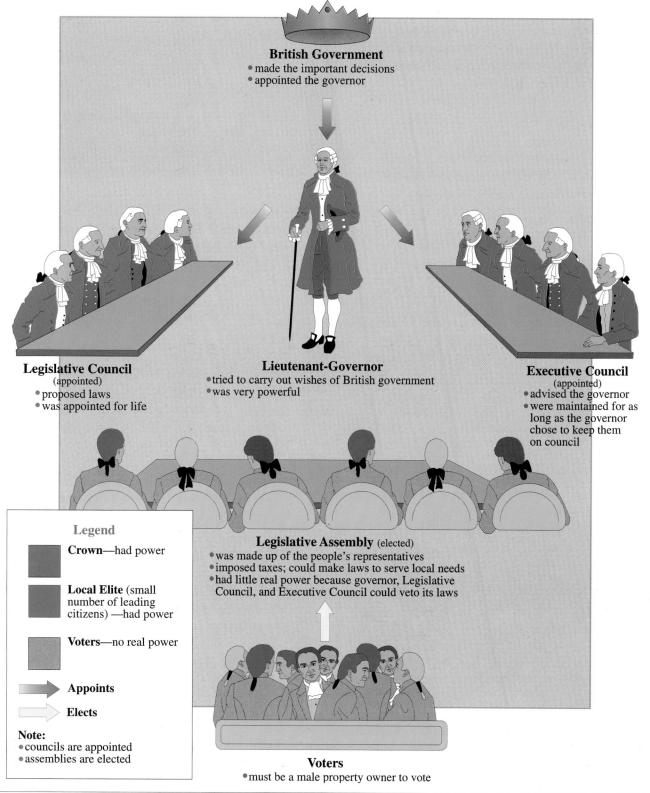

British Government
- made the important decisions
- appointed the governor

Lieutenant-Governor
- tried to carry out wishes of British government
- was very powerful

Legislative Council
(appointed)
- proposed laws
- was appointed for life

Executive Council
(appointed)
- advised the governor
- were maintained for as long as the governor chose to keep them on council

Legislative Assembly (elected)
- was made up of the people's representatives
- imposed taxes; could make laws to serve local needs
- had little real power because governor, Legislative Council, and Executive Council could veto its laws

Voters
- must be a male property owner to vote

Legend

Crown—had power

Local Elite (small number of leading citizens) —had power

Voters—no real power

➡ **Appoints**

➡ **Elects**

Note:
- councils are appointed
- assemblies are elected

---

*Lower Canada had the same government structure but they had an entirely separate government. Refer to the complete government diagram on page 128. Note: The colony of Lower Canada had a representative government after the passage of the Constitutional Act in 1791.

An Exercise in Decision-Making

1. Turn back to page 84 and read the description of the Quebec Act of 1774. List the ways that Quebec stayed the same and ways that it changed with the Constitutional Act of 1791.

2. Return to the chart on page 80, entitled "Alternatives Open to the British." Five alternatives are listed. The British government chose one of these with the Proclamation of 1763 and another with the Quebec Act of 1774. Which alternative is represented by the Constitutional Act of 1791?

3. The power of the assemblies was intentionally limited in the Constitutional Act. Why was this done?

4. Throughout this book we have looked at three major ideas: Who participates in the government? Who has the power to make the decisions? Does majority rule exist? Answer these three questions for Upper Canada and Lower Canada now that representative government has been established.

5. Compare the government diagrams that you drew in the exercise on page 113, "An Exercise in Problem Solving," to the diagram on page 120. Discuss reasons for similarities and differences.

6. In the lefthand column of the chart below, decide who would fit in each of the six "Who" spaces. Select your answers from: Loyalists, French Seigneurs, French Habitants, British Government, British Merchants in Lower Canada, and the Roman Catholic Church.

7. Divide into six groups—one for each of the perspectives represented in the chart. As a group, write a letter to the lieutenant-governor of your new colony explaining how you feel about the Constitutional Act and why. Read your letter to the rest of the class.

Reactions to the Constitutional Act

Who	Reaction	Why
1. Who?	pleased	Could not be accused of taxation without representation. Satisfied wishes of people for Legislative Assembly while keeping the real power in the hands of the British government.
2. Who?	angry	Cut off from rest of English-speaking Protestant population. Worried about power of *Canadien* Legislative Assembly.
3. Who?	pleased	Kept religious influence and ability to tithe.
4. Who?	pleased	Kept seigneurial system.
5. Who?	indifferent	Kept *Canadien* way of life but still under control of Church and seigneurs. No influence in the government.
6. Who?	pleased/displeased	Established English-speaking colony with own Legislative Assembly, but only male property owners could vote.

The War of 1812

On July 12, 1812, an army of more than 1000 Americans marched into British North America. They thought it would be a quick and easy job to push the British out of North America.

Causes of the War

By 1812, Britain and France had been at war for almost 20 years. As a result European ports were **blockaded**. This angered the Americans who held a neutral position. Because of the blockade they could not deliver their cargo to the European ports. A second war practice of the British angered Americans. A number of deserters from the British navy were working aboard American ships, where the pay was higher and working conditions were better. The British began to stop American merchant ships at sea and search them for deserters. When they discovered sailors whom they suspected of being deserters, they were removed and pressed back into the British navy. A number of innocent Americans who were not British deserters were taken in this way.

There was a group of influential men in the United States who were called War Hawks because they were pushing for war. British North America had rich farmland that would be useful to the United States. Most of the good farmland in the United States was very expensive. In British North America, particularly in Upper Canada, there was plenty of inexpensive, good farmland available. Some Americans saw the British North American colonists as possible allies for the Native peoples who were resisting westward movement by American colonists. The Native leader, Tecumseh, had already gone to British North America to see if he could enlist help for the Native cause there. If the Americans could take over British North America, there would be no more danger from the Native peoples.

Modern-day historians tend to place national honour as the major cause for the War of 1812. By 1812, the British still had not accepted the Americans as their equals. They continued to look upon the Americans as colonials (as children), not as a full **sovereign nation**. The Americans reasoned that if they were equals the British would not take sailors off American ships. One nation should not treat another nation in such an insensitive manner.

Blockade—closed off; usually done to a harbour or port in wartime to prevent supplies from reaching their destination
Sovereign nation—a country that is independent of the control of other governments

A Heroine of the War of 1812

C-10717, National Archives of Canada, Ottawa (detail).

Laura Secord (1775–1868)

Laura Secord and her husband lived in Queenston in the Niagara region. She became a heroine of the War of 1812 when she fearlessly risked her life to help the British.

James Secord was injured in the Battle of Queenston Heights in October 1812. While he was at home recovering from his wounds, Laura overheard some American soldiers discussing a surprise attack on the British. Laura decided to warn the British commander, Fitzgibbon. Because the American troops guarded the roads, she walked 23 kilometres across fields and through forests. The attack occurred as planned, but the Americans ended up surrendering to Fitzgibbon.

Native Role in the War

Tecumseh (1767–1813)

Chief Tecumseh of the Shawnee was a well respected Native leader. He wanted to protect Native lands from the Americans who were pressing westward and hoped that the British would help him.

He turned out to be a powerful ally of the British forces during the War of 1812. He and his men helped General Brock capture Detroit in August of 1812. By October of 1813 the Americans were advancing well into Upper Canada while the British retreated. Tecumseh finally persuaded the British commander to take a stand at the Thames River, not far from present-day Stratford, Ontario. Forty-eight of the British were killed and the rest surrendered. The courageous Tecumseh was also killed in this battle. With him died the Native hope for their own separate territory.

Events of the War

As you will see from the map timeline, both sides had victories. There was no winner. By the end of the war, Britain had possession of some American territory but they returned it in the Treaty of Ghent. The War of 1812 has been called "the war that nobody won."

C-276, National Archives of Canada, Ottawa (detai

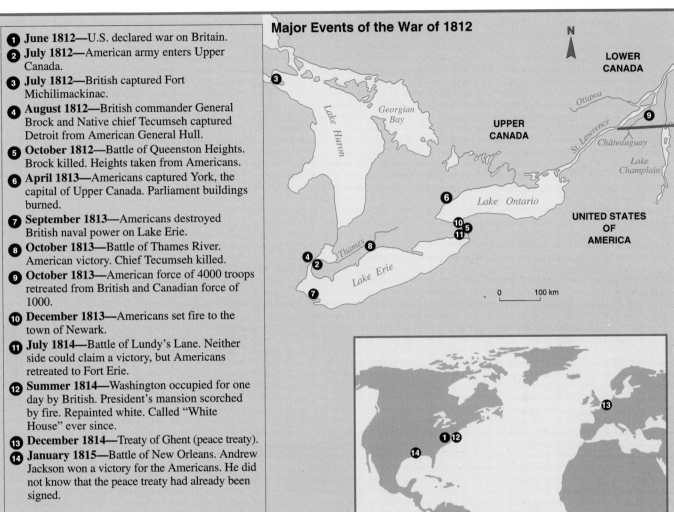

❶ **June 1812**—U.S. declared war on Britain.
❷ **July 1812**—American army enters Upper Canada.
❸ **July 1812**—British captured Fort Michilimackinac.
❹ **August 1812**—British commander General Brock and Native chief Tecumseh captured Detroit from American General Hull.
❺ **October 1812**—Battle of Queenston Heights. Brock killed. Heights taken from Americans.
❻ **April 1813**—Americans captured York, the capital of Upper Canada. Parliament buildings burned.
❼ **September 1813**—Americans destroyed British naval power on Lake Erie.
❽ **October 1813**—Battle of Thames River. American victory. Chief Tecumseh killed.
❾ **October 1813**—American force of 4000 troops retreated from British and Canadian force of 1000.
❿ **December 1813**—Americans set fire to the town of Newark.
⓫ **July 1814**—Battle of Lundy's Lane. Neither side could claim a victory, but Americans retreated to Fort Erie.
⓬ **Summer 1814**—Washington occupied for one day by British. President's mansion scorched by fire. Repainted white. Called "White House" ever since.
⓭ **December 1814**—Treaty of Ghent (peace treaty).
⓮ **January 1815**—Battle of New Orleans. Andrew Jackson won a victory for the Americans. He did not know that the peace treaty had already been signed.

Major Events of the War of 1812

Results of the War

Even though the War of 1812 had no winner, there were some long-term effects:

- American immigrants were discouraged from coming to British North America.
- The war stabilized the border between the United States and British North America at the 49th parallel, from the Lake of the Woods west to the Rocky Mountains. The fur country of Oregon Territory was to be jointly occupied.*

*This arrangement lasted until 1846 when the 49th parallel was chosen for that boundary as well.

- The Rush–Bagot Agreement of 1817 demilitarized the Great Lakes.
- Britain began to respect the United States as a separate nation. There was still distrust, though, as the British built Fort Henry at Kingston for protection from possible American invasion. The Americans turned their attention away from British North America and looked southward and westward for expansion.
- A very small feeling of unity began to develop in the Canadas, especially in the colony of Lower Canada. Here the French and English had fought side by side against their common enemy, the Americans.
- The Maritime colonies became more prosperous as a result of the war.

Fur Traders

Competition between Hudson's Bay Company and North West Company

As you read earlier, the Hudson's Bay Company (HBC) was formed in 1670. The British government granted the company a monopoly on the fur trade in Rupert's Land, the land drained by rivers flowing into Hudson Bay. From 1720 to 1763, many Cree carried their furs from the tribes in the West to the fur forts that the company built around Hudson Bay.

From 1731 to 1743 the La Vérendryes built trading posts on the rivers farther to the west to encourage the Native peoples to trade with independent traders from Quebec instead of travelling all the way to the fur forts built by the Hudson's Bay Company on Hudson Bay.

In 1763, as a result of the Seven Years' War, the British gained control over New France. They hoped that by gaining control of the land, they had also gained control of the fur trade. However, this was not to be the case. French traders from Quebec continued to travel to the interior and to get the best furs.

In 1774 Samuel Hearne built Cumberland House, the first HBC fort in the interior. Even this step did not increase trade to the HBC posts. In 1778 an independent trader named Peter Pond built Fort Chipewyan, northwest of Cumberland House, to encourage the Native traders to take their furs there rather than continuing on to Cumberland House.

In 1783 the independent traders from Quebec decided that they would be more effective if they joined together. Some formed the North West Company and others the XY Company. The North West Company took over the XY Company in 1804.

The North West Company had wintering partners, who spent the winter in the Northwest trading with the Native peoples. They then brought their furs to Fort William, where they were met by the Montreal partners, who took the furs to Montreal, to be shipped to Europe.

By 1804 the rivalry between the two companies was intense. There were rival fur-trading posts along the entire length of the Saskatchewan River. The North West Company built Pine Island, Fort George, Fort Augustus, and Rocky Mountain House. The Hudson's Bay Company built posts at Manchester, Buckingham, Edmonton, and Acton House.

After 1812, the rivalry led to violence. The Hudson's Bay Company allowed a group of settlers, led by Lord Selkirk, to begin a settlement at Red River. The North West Company and the Metis were concerned that the settlers would be used to interfere with their fur trade and supply routes. You will read about these events and some of the accomplishments of the Metis Nation in more detail in Chapter 10.

In 1774 the Hudson's Bay Company sent Samuel Hearne to build their first inland post, Cumberland House, on the Saskatchewan River.

Captain James Cook traded European goods for furs with the Nootka peoples on the West Coast.

Explorers of Western Canada

The exploration and settlement of what is now western Canada was a direct result of Europeans looking for furs and for a Northwest Passage leading from eastern North America to the Pacific Ocean. Between 1741 and 1867, Russian fur traders built posts on the west coast of North America. The Spanish explored and traded as far north as the Queen Charlotte Islands during the 1700s. However, British explorers were the most dominant in this exploration.

Sea Explorers

Captain James Cook

Captain Cook made three voyages for Britain. During his first two voyages he explored the coasts of New Zealand and Australia, and visited Tahiti and Hawaii. He sailed closer to the South Pole than any European before him. His third voyage, which began in 1776, took him to the west coast of North America. His tasks were to make scientific studies, claim undiscovered land for Britain, and search for an outlet to the still undiscovered Northwest Passage. He travelled north from what is now the American state of Oregon to the Bering Sea. On his way he met and traded for furs with the Nootka people of Vancouver Island. Cook intended to trade the beautiful sea otter furs that he got from the Nootka for unusual and interesting items from China, which could be sold for high prices in the eastern United States and Britain. After travelling to China, Cook returned to the Hawaiian Islands, where he died in a quarrel with some Native people.

Captain George Vancouver

On a voyage that began in 1791, Captain Vancouver explored and mapped the Pacific coast of North America from the Strait of Juan de Fuca north to Alaska. He also met the Spanish commander, Bodega y Quadra, in 1792 at Nootka Sound on the west coast of Vancouver Island, to arrange for the transfer of Spanish territory there to Britain. The Spanish had decided to abandon this piece of their extensive empire. This gave control of the fur trade on the west coast to the British.

The Nor'Westers—the Men of the North West Company

Alexander Mackenzie

Over the course of two long journeys, Alexander Mackenzie, with the help of Native guides, mapped one of the largest rivers in North America and became the first **Caucasian** to cross the continent. On his first trip in search of a Pacific route in 1789, Mackenzie arrived at the Arctic Ocean instead. He called the river that carried him to the Arctic "Disappointment," but it is now known as the Mackenzie. Samuel Hearne had reached the Arctic Ocean by land 18 years earlier. However, Mackenzie was the first Caucasian to descend the Mackenzie River.

In July of 1793, Mackenzie finally reached the Pacific. Under the direction of Native guides, his men travelled overland to the river that was later to be called the Fraser. When they were warned by some Native people not to travel any farther because of rapids, they went overland again and explored the Bella Coola River. At what they called the "Friendly Village," some Native people gave them canoes to carry them to the sea.

Mackenzie's explorations provided the North West Company with some of the richest fur territory in British North America. He was able to claim for Britain the north and northwest of North America. He was knighted by the king for his explorations.

Simon Fraser

Simon Fraser worked for the North West Company as a trader until he became a full partner in 1801. He built the first trading posts in what is today the northern interior of British Columbia—Fort McLeod, Fort St. James, Fort Fraser, and Fort George.

In 1808 he set out with 21 fellow Nor'Westers and two Native guides to follow what he thought was the Columbia River, looking for a safe fur trade route to the ocean. The river proved to be treacherous. The men were often forced to leave their canoes and creep along the steep cliffs beside the river, as they followed it to its mouth.

Fraser eventually realized that it was not the Columbia. Even though it was not navigable, the land near the river was claimed for the North West Company.

Fraser passed a river that flowed into the river that he was following. He named this river the Thompson after Nor'Wester David Thompson. Later Thompson was to give the name Fraser to the river that Simon Fraser followed.

"We had to pass where no human beings should venture," wrote Simon Fraser about the Fraser Canyon.

David Thompson

David Thompson, another Nor'Wester, was a mapmaker, explorer, and fur trader. Thompson was the first Caucasian to explore the Columbia River to its source. He travelled about 50 000 kilometres in all and made maps of the main travel routes through almost two million square kilometres of western North America.

Thompson was often accompanied by his Metis wife, Charlotte, and their children. He and Charlotte were married for almost 60 years. They had 13 children.

David Thompson explored and surveyed the headwaters of the Mississippi before travelling to the Columbia. He built a number of fur-trading posts on the Columbia and its **tributaries**. He also explored the mountain passes of the Rockies and mapped a route through the Athabasca Pass, which became the most travelled pass between the Prairies and the mountains on the other side of the Rockies.

In 1810, David Thompson was asked by the company to explore the Columbia River to its mouth and to claim the land through which he passed as North West Company fur-trading territory. However, when he arrived at the mouth of the Columbia in 1811, he found the Americans and their Fort Astoria already there. This meant that the Americans held claim to the fur territory in this area.

David Thompson retired from his explorations in 1812 to develop his great map of the West. Parts of this map were still in use in the twentieth century.

Caucasian— member of the white race

Tributary— stream feeding larger streams, rivers, or lakes

Focus On: Canada Revisited—The Reconstructed Fort William

Below: The reconstructed Fort William. Here, at the western end of Lake Superior, the wintering partners brought their furs, picked up more trade goods, and had exuberant celebrations before returning to the woods.

Right: The house of Mr. Boucher, one of the important officials of Fort William. The smaller building in front is the oven where bread was baked for people at Fort William.

Left: A discussion of fur-trade business. At Fort William, the business partners from Montreal met the wintering partners, who spent their winters trading with the Native peoples in the North-West.

Review

Summarizing the Chapter

This chapter discussed a number of changes in British North America caused by the arrival of between 40 000 and 45 000 Loyalists.

- The Loyalists transformed huge areas of relatively unpopulated lands in the colony of Nova Scotia. In what is now Ontario, Loyalists developed prosperous farming communities.

- The colony of New Brunswick was formed in 1784 to meet demands from Loyalists who settled in the St. John River Valley for the creation of a new colony.

- The population balance of British North America changed from being mostly French-speaking, with French traditions, to mostly English-speaking, with British traditions.

- While the Loyalists brought **conservative traditions** to British North America, they also brought their experience with the democracy of the American colonies. As a result, the people of British North America began to demand more say in the colonial government. You will learn about these developments in Chapter 8.

- The Constitutional Act of 1791 divided the colony of Quebec into the colonies of Upper Canada (English-speaking majority) and Lower Canada (French-speaking majority). Each colony was given a form of representative government.

- The War of 1812 has been called "the war that nobody won." As a result of this war the Americans were discouraged from settling in British North America.

- For many years there was an intense rivalry between the Hudson's Bay Company and the North West Company for dominance over the fur trade. Rival fur-trading posts were built along the entire length of the Saskatchewan River. The North West Company had wintering partners, who spent the winter in the North-West trading with the Native peoples. They then brought their furs to Fort William, where they were met by the Montreal partners, who took the furs to Montreal, to be shipped to Europe.

- Nor'Westers explored much of what is now western Canada. Mackenzie was the first Caucasian to cross the continent. Fraser followed the Fraser River to its mouth. Thompson was the first Caucasian to explore the Columbia River to its source. He also developed a great map of the West. All of these explorers and fur traders relied on the assistance of the Native peoples.

Checking Predictions

1. At the beginning of this chapter, you made some predictions based on the Overview and what you already knew. Now, use what you learned from reading the chapter to fill in the third column of the chart that you began earlier.

Working with Information

1. Here are some main ideas from this chapter:
   - influx of the Loyalists to British North America
   - formation of new colonies
   - political change (representative government)
   - use of petitions
   - war between Britain and the United States
   - European fur traders explore the West

   Use one of the following approaches to make a permanent set of notes: mind map, web, paragraph, outline to show the relationship among these main ideas.

2. Use this diagram and the one on page 120 to write a paragraph explaining how representative government works.

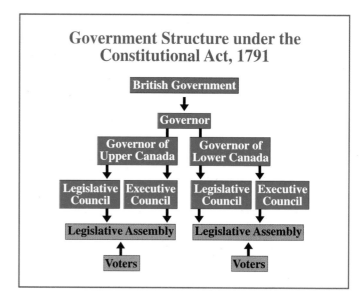

Government Structure under the Constitutional Act, 1791

British Government → Governor → Governor of Upper Canada / Governor of Lower Canada → Legislative Council / Executive Council → Legislative Assembly → Voters

---

Conservative tradition— customs, opinions, and habits that are cautious and opposed to change

3. Review all of the different examples of decision-making found in this chapter. Work with a partner to draw a mind map that organizes all of these examples on one sheet of paper. Show how these examples helped bring about representative government. Use simple line drawings and at least three different colours. A sample mind map is shown on page 16.

4. Reread the story at the beginning of Section III (pages 88 and 89) and review the definition of representative government on page 92. In what ways do the students of Fairmont School have a representative government?

Building Thinking Strategies

Transferring Ideas to New Contexts

1. The text points out that the Loyalists were refugees—people who leave their homes or countries to seek safety elsewhere. Because of the political situation in their home colonies, they sought refuge in the colonies of Quebec and Nova Scotia. Think of a group of people today who have become refugees for political reasons. Compare and contrast the Loyalists and this group of people.

Communicating Ideas

Reading

1. Read "Jim Jones" by Brenda Bellingham in *Ordinary People in Canada's Past* by Nancy Sellars Marcotte. Evaluate the story according to how realistic you consider it to be, based on what you have learned in this chapter.

2. Read about one of the following people in the book *Great Canadian Lives: Portraits in Heroism to 1867* by Ford, MacLean, and Wansbrough: Muquinna (Moachat trader and peacemaker), Vancouver, Pond, Hearne, Matonabbee, Mackenzie, English Chief, Caleb Seely, Brock, Tecumseh, Secord, De Salaberry, Fraser, Thompson, Gaboury. Would you have liked to have been this person? Why or why not? Share your findings with a friend.

3. During the War of 1812–1814, Washington, DC (the American capital) was occupied for one day by the British. The President's mansion was scorched by fire, only to be painted white later. It has been called the "White House" ever since. Do research to find out more about this story.

Writing

1. Lady Tennyson, wife of the famous British poet, Alfred Lord Tennyson, once said: "You Canadians should be proud of the founders of your country. The United Empire Loyalists were a grand type of loyal, law-abiding, god-fearing men. No country ever had such founders, no country in the world." Do you agree with Lady Tennyson? Explain your answer.

2. Which person in this chapter would you have liked to have met? Tell why.

3. Carry out research to find out what part the Native peoples played in the fur trade.

Speaking

1. In pairs, write a conversation that might have taken place between an American Patriot and his best friend, whom he has just discovered is a Loyalist. The conversation might begin like this:

   Patriot: John, they say you have refused to join arms with those of us who will be in the Continental Army.
   Loyalist: I cannot take up arms against my king, Caleb.

   Present the conversation to your class.

2. Debate either a) or b):
   a) The Constitutional Act of 1791 was the best compromise between the differing views held by the English- and French-speaking people of Quebec,
   b) The current English-French conflict began as a result of the Constitutional Act of 1791.

Listening

1. Choose students to engage in a debate on the effectiveness of the Constitutional Act as a way of dealing with the demands of the people of Quebec. Listen to the debate and then write a paper, making and defending your personal position for or against the Constitutional Act.

Creating

1. Imagine that you are a Loyalist travelling to Quebec after the American Revolution. Make three journal entries—one during the journey, the second upon arrival in Quebec, and the third after a year there.

2. Design a poster depicting the changes in British North America caused by the arrival of the Loyalists.

Section IV

The People's Voice Is Heard 1815–1855

Do you remember the difficulties the Students' Council at Fairmont School were experiencing in dealing with the issue of whether friends from other schools should come to their dances? The Students' Council voted in favour of letting the friends come, but its decision was overruled by the principal. Some Council members wanted to refuse to attend classes in protest against the principal's action. Others wanted to engage in peaceful protest by informing the principal and other staff members of their disagreement with the action.

The Students' Council has a form of representative government. The council members are elected representatives of the other students in the school and make decisions for them, but the Students' Council has an authority figure (the principal) who can overrule any decisions made by the students' elected representatives.

Act I

All is not well at Fairmont High. Let's eavesdrop on a conversation that is taking place among several of the students at this very moment.

Tollel: I don't know what's the matter with that bunch on Students' Council! The way I hear it from a friend, Tammy, who's on Students' Council, a few of them seem to be making all the decisions for the rest!

Janis: But everybody on Students' Council has a vote.

Tollel: Yes, but Bruce and his crowd on Mrs. Cherniak's Special Council always try to talk the rest into voting their way.

Kyle: It's not just that. They're the ones Mrs. Cherniak has picked to come and talk to her about decisions Students' Council has made.

Jennifer: Whatever the principal says goes! It's "Yes, ma'am; no ma'am; whatever you say, ma'am." They never even try to convince her that Students' Council might have made a good decision.

Act II

We join a Students' Council meeting in progress. Mrs. Cherniak is making an important announcement.

Mrs. Cherniak: I have some news for you. I have had a memo from the Superintendent of Schools. As you know, the Superintendent is almost the top authority in our district. He, in consultation with others, has decided that the Students' Council is mature enough to be responsible for their actions. From now on there will be certain areas where Students' Council can make decisions and the principal cannot overrule those decisions. I will leave this list with you so you can discuss it.

Exit Mrs. Cherniak.

Sam: I have a suggestion. It sounds like we're

going to have a lot more responsibility from now on and there's going to be a lot more talking with Mrs. Cherniak. I think we should vote for a couple of kids who could be the ones to go and talk with her rather than have her select them for her Special Council. They can then come back and tell us what she said.

Tammy: I think that would be okay. It's better than always having certain people, like Bruce and his friends, taking over things! This way we'll have the kids we want talking with her!

Farrah: Don't get so worked up, Tammy. I think it's a good idea too. I also think that if we vote these students onto Mrs. Cherniak's Special Council, we should be able to vote them out of power if we don't like the job they're doing and if they are not responsible to us.

Todd: That's a great idea, Farrah! Throw them out on their ears if they don't vote for what the students want. Let's vote.

The meeting continues.

Act III, Scene I
We join a Special Council meeting in progess.

Tammy: Some kids have asked me to bring up the question of whether Honour Roll students should be able to miss classes to listen to a guest speaker on Friday afternoons.

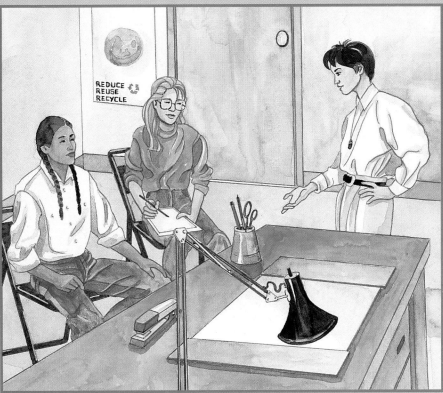

Todd: Great idea! I wish I'd thought of it!

John: I don't think Mrs. Cherniak would go for it.

Farrah: Maybe she won't be very happy about it, but that's just too bad! That's in one of the areas where we can make decisions and she has to go along with our decisions now.

Sam: Aren't you guys getting just a bit carried away here? Let's decide if we think it's a good idea first.

Then we can worry about Mrs. Cherniak's opinion.

Tammy: You're right as usual, Sam. Let's use one of our decision-making models to reach a decision here.

Act III, Scene II
Again we join a Special Students' Council meeting.

Farrah: I guess after talking to the students on council to find out their wishes and those of the school, we've

decided that Honour Roll students should get out of Friday afternoon classes to listen to a guest speaker.

Todd: Yeah!

Farrah: *(ignoring the interruption):* Now, Sam and I will have to go and tell Mrs. Cherniak our decison, since we are the ones who were elected for the job.

Act IV
Mrs. Cherniak's office.

Mrs. Cherniak: Hello, Sam and Farrah. I have thought very carefully about this and I am ready to let you know what I have decided. First, I want you to know that I still do not agree with your decision to allow Honour Roll students to miss Friday afternoon classes. However, as you know, the Superintendent has said that I am not supposed to interfere with your decisions in certain areas. He wants you to have a type of responsible government. Therefore, I feel that I have to go along with the decision of the majority, even though I know that many parents, and possibly some students who are not on the Honour Roll, will be very unhappy. I may have to face a lot of criticism over this, but, under the circumstances, I will go along with your decision. ■

Answer "Questions to Talk About" on page 134.

Chapter 7
Upper and Lower Canada (1815–1838)

Overview
Use this Overview to predict the events of this chapter.

1821
Rivalry between the North West Company and the Hudson's Bay Company ended in 1821. The new company was called the Hudson's Bay Company.

1815–1850
The Great Migration brought thousands of new settlers to Upper Canada and Lower Canada.

A thriving timber industry developed in Upper Canada and Lower Canada.

Towns were slowly built.

Most of the new pioneers moved into the forested areas of Upper Canada. Many faced great hardship as they felled the trees and built new homes.

With the arrival of the newcomers, the First People were pushed farther inland.

In both Upper Canada and Lower Canada, small groups of powerful and conservative men appointed by the governor controlled the government. They shaped policy and provided favours for their friends.

Executive Council

The ordinary people felt they had little influence in the government. Only property owners had the vote. Laws put forward by the elected assembly (the Legislative Assembly) could be stopped by the Executive Council.

Legislative Assembly

Upper Canada

Lower Canada

1837–1838
Rebellions broke out in Lower Canada and Upper Canada.

Section IV Questions to Talk About

Discuss the following questions by referring to the section story on pages 130 and 131. Keep the questions in mind while you read the rest of the chapter. See if there are similarities between how the government of Upper and Lower Canada between 1815 and 1838 is similar to Mrs. Cherniak's Special Council at Fairmont School and the changes brought about by Students' Council.

1. (a) In small groups discuss some criteria for acting in a responsible way. Share your ideas with the rest of the class and compile a master list. (b) What two things did the students on the Special Council do to indicate they were acting in a responsible way?
2. Discuss the following questions by referring to the story on pages 130 and 131. **For Act I:** Who participated in the student government at Fairmont School? How were decisions made? Who had the final authority? **For Act II:** How did the situation change? **For Act III:** In what ways did the Special Council operate as if they had a government that was responsible to the student body? **For Act IV:** Who lost some power when the Special Council operated as though they were responsible to the Students' Council? Who gained more power?
3. Draw a diagram to illustrate the type of government the students at Fairmont School had at the end of Act IV.

Chapter 7 Focus

Chapter 6 described the events of Canada's history from 1776 to 1815. This chapter is about political reform—changes to make the government reflect what some people wanted.

The concepts of power, co-operation, decision-making, and conflict underlie the events of this chapter. The concept of conflict is the focus of Chapter 7.

Power   Co-operation   Decision-making   **Conflict**

Overview/Prediction Chart

Examine the Overview found on the previous pages. In pairs or small groups, use the Overview and what you already know to predict answers to the questions in the Prediction Chart. Put your predictions in the "My Predictions" column. Once you have finished the chapter, complete the "What I Found Out" column to help you review and summarize. Your teacher will provide you with a full-sized working copy of the Prediction Chart.

Prediction Chart—What Do You Think?		
Questions	My Predictions (fill out now)	What I Found Out (fill out at end of chapter)
1. What might be the major events?		
2. Who might be some of the important people or groups?	SAMPLE	
3. Who might hold power?		
4.		

Bush Farm Near Chatham. When European and American settlers started farms in Upper and Lower Canada, their first task was to clear away the dense forests. Many of the trees were burned; others provided lumber for homes and furniture.

C-11811, National Archives of Canada, Ottawa.

Changes to Upper and Lower Canada: 1815–1838

There were three major changes in Upper and Lower Canada between the end of the War of 1812, which you read about in the last chapter, and the rebellions of 1837, which you will read about in this chapter. Two of these changes, a population explosion and the development of a thriving timber trade, affected both Upper and Lower Canada. The other change, the end of competition in the fur trade, affected only Lower Canada.

Population Explosion

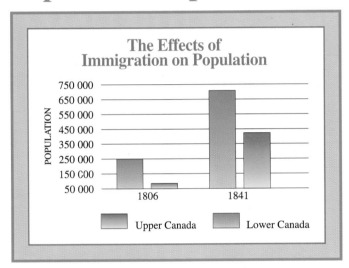

The Effects of Immigration on Population

Lower Canada

The population in Lower Canada increased from 250 000 in 1806 to 717 000 in 1841. This population explosion was caused mainly by a very high birth rate among the French-speaking people of Lower Canada. In addition, some British and many American immigrants settled in the Eastern Townships of Lower Canada. This was an area of Lower Canada that had been set aside for settlement by English-speaking farmers.

Upper Canada

Upper Canada was originally settled by Loyalists leaving the United States during and after the American Revolution; then, until the War of 1812, by other American settlers.

After the War of 1812, American settlers were no longer welcome in Upper Canada. A wave of settlers from Great Britain (Ireland, Scotland, England, and Wales) took their

place. Historians call the period between 1815 and 1850 "The Great Migration."

Many tenant farmers in Great Britain were being forced by their landlords to leave their small farms because it was more profitable for the landowners to use the farms for grazing sheep than to rent them to the farmers. Many artisans were finding themselves unemployed because machines used in the Industrial Revolution were taking over their jobs. In Ireland in the 1840s, many people were starving because of poor potato crops.

These immigrants came to seek new lives for themselves in British North America. Many of the immigrants bought land and became farmers. Others came to the cities. They often worked as servants, labourers on canals and railways, in the forest industry, or at whatever job was available. By 1860, the majority of English-speaking people in Canada* were of Irish descent.

As a result of British immigration, the population of Upper Canada increased from 71 000 in 1806 to 432 000 in 1841. In 1815, the population was 80 percent American-born. In 1841, almost 50 percent were recent British immigrants.

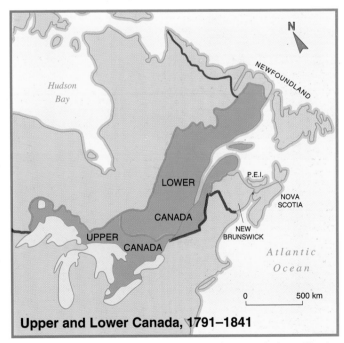

Upper and Lower Canada, 1791–1841

During the late 1700s and early 1800s, the population of both Upper and Lower Canada increased greatly.

---

*Sometimes Upper and Lower Canada were called the Canadas or Canada, and the people were called Canadians.

Most British immigrants that came to British North America left behind a life of unemployment and poverty. In spite of leaving family and friends and most of their possessions behind, they were prepared to venture into the colonies of the New World, where their lives could begin again.

Exploring Further

1. Pretend you are one of the people in the illustration below. Write a journal account of your thoughts and feelings (both positive and negative) about leaving your homeland and going to a new country.

Aboard the Immigrant Ship

The sea journey to British North America lasted from 20 days to more than two months. Most of the immigrants travelled in the holds of cargo ships. These ships were not meant to transport people but for carrying timber. Living conditions were primitive, unsanitary, cramped, and rat-infested. The variety of food was limited due to a lack of refrigeration. Food and water had to be taken along. Because of the many ocean storms sea sickness was common. Diseases such as typhus, cholera, and dysentery spread quickly in such close quarters. Many became ill on the long voyage and large numbers died.

In fact, so many people died that the vessels became known as "coffin ships." The first stop for the ships, upon reaching British North America, was Grosse Isle, an island in the St. Lawrence River just below Quebec City. A doctor would come on board to inspect the passengers. Anyone who was sick was removed to wooden sheds on the island, where they were cared for. Once the ship was given a clean bill of health, it was allowed to sail on to Quebec or Montreal.

Some immigrants chose to stay in Quebec or Montreal. Most travelled on to Upper Canada or to the United States. To reach Upper Canada, the newcomers travelled in smaller boats down the St. Lawrence to Kingston and farther. Once in Upper Canada, they tried to find jobs or to search for land. A person who bought land received a "location ticket," which described where to find the land. Once they had this, they would travel on foot or in carts through the backwoods to find their new homes.

An Eyewitness Account:

In many cases in bad weather, they would not go on deck; their health suffered so much that their strength was gone, and they had not the power to help themselves. Hence the between-decks were like a loathsome dungeon. When the hatchways were opened under which the people were stowed, the steam rose and the stench was like that from a pen of pigs.

Exploring Further

1. Continue the journal you started on the previous page. In it describe the conditions on board the ship and some of the events that happened to you and your family.
2. Do research to find out about typhus, cholera, and dysentery. What are the causes, symptoms, and cures? Do we still have these diseases today?

The Timber Trade

A second major change in Upper and Lower Canada in the early 1800s occurred because the pioneers began to use trees as a way of making a living. Before that time they had used some to build their homes, but most were cut down and burnt in order to clear land for planting crops.

In 1839, wood made up 80 percent of all goods exported from Upper and Lower Canada. It provided jobs for thousands of people in Lower Canada. Much of it was sold to Britain. The United States also bought some. The rest was used in Nova Scotia and New Brunswick in the shipbuilding industry.

Among the dangers faced by lumbermen were the log jams. The man in this picture is attempting to break up a log jam.

Uses for Trees

Potash was used for making soap and glass in Europe. It was made from ashes of trees. The pioneers could sell potash and have a little extra money to buy a few luxuries.

Masts made of white pine were needed for the ships of the British royal navy. A supply of new masts was particularly needed until 1815 because Britain was involved in European wars until then.

Square timber was needed in Europe for building. The men would fell the trees, cut off the limbs, and square the trunks. Next, they would lash the timber together in huge rafts that could hold as many as 50 or 60 men and then float the rafts downstream to the ports of Quebec and St. John. There, the timber was loaded onto large ships and transported to Europe. Sawn lumber was needed for the larger homes that pioneer families wanted as their lives became more settled. By 1854 there were 1618 sawmills in Upper Canada. They produced boards for Europe and for local use.

The shipbuilding industry in the colonies of Nova Scotia and New Brunswick required lumber. The ships built in Nova Scotia were for local use, but the New Brunswick ships were exported. By 1800, British North America supplied more ships to Britain than any other country. Nearly 500 ships were built in the peak year of 1875. Most of these ships came from New Brunswick and Quebec.

Philomen Wright (1760–1839)

Philomen Wright was the first lumberman in the Ottawa Valley. He came from the United States. With a small group of pioneers, Wright founded the village of Hull in 1800. By 1805, the community was running short of money and Wright came up with a brilliant idea for saving the community.

He knew Great Britain had developed a great need for timber. France had conquered much of Europe at this time and was cutting off Britain's timber supply. If Britain was to keep building ships for its navy, then it would need timber from its colonies.

All one winter, Wright and his men chopped down trees. Next, they lashed the logs together to form a huge raft they called "The Columbo." In June, Wright and three others rode the raft down the swift Ottawa River and the St. Lawrence all the way to Quebec. This proved that timber from the Ottawa Valley could be successfully delivered to market.

The End of Competition in the Fur Trade

The third major change in the Canadas in the early 1800s involved the fur trade. The fur trade was still an important part of the economy of Lower Canada. The rivalry between the French and the British over the fur trade could have ended in 1763 when the British took control of New France—but it did not. Instead, traders from Montreal returned to the woods and extended the vast fur-trading system even farther than it had gone before.

In 1783, a group of Montreal merchants formed the North West Company to compete for furs with the Hudson's Bay Company. The North West Company proceeded to build trading posts far to the west so that it would be easier for the Native peoples to bring in their furs. The Hudson's Bay Company was forced to build posts inland as well. Sometimes the trading posts of the two companies were in sight of one another.

The Hudson's Bay Company had an advantage in that it had posts on Hudson Bay itself and could ship furs and trading goods in and out of the Bay. The North West Company had to use the slower overland route to Montreal. However, the voyageurs who worked for the North West Company were so skilled that they provided stiff competition.

The fur frontier was moving farther north all the time. This meant that it was becoming more and more expensive for the North West Company to take their furs to market and to transport trading goods and supplies to the trading posts.

In 1821, the rival companies decided to unite under the name of the Hudson's Bay Company. The new company took over all the trading posts in the West. There would be no more need for voyageurs to carry furs and trading goods to and from Montreal.

The Spring Brigade, by Franklin Arbuckle. Fur traders set off from Montreal to go to the fur trading posts in the West.

C-2774, National Archives of Canada, Ottawa.

Shooting the Rapids, by Frances Anne Hopkins. The artist has included herself in the painting.

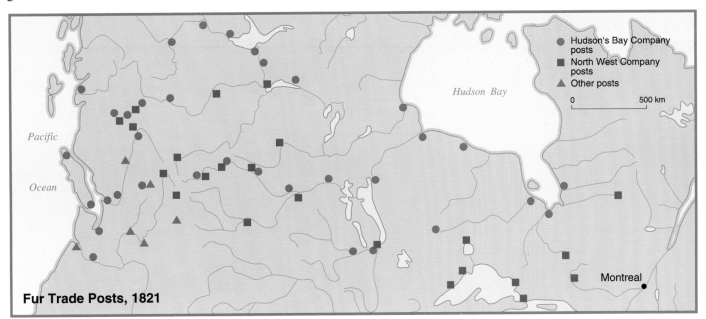

Fur Trade Posts, 1821

Hudson's Bay Company posts
North West Company posts
Other posts

Hudson Bay

0   500 km

Pacific

Ocean

Montreal

Life in Lower Canada: 1815–1838

Groups in Lower Canada

In the male-dominated society of Lower Canada there were three major groups at this time. They were the French-speaking habitants, the English-speaking merchants, and the French-speaking professional men.* Each group had special concerns they wanted the government to implement.

Habitants

The French-speaking tenant farmers, or habitants, continued to live much as they had done for the past 150 years. They worked their long, narrow farms and paid their rent to the seigneur. But change was threatening their lifestyle. Population growth was filling up the available farmland. The narrow farms were becoming even narrower as farmers divided them among their sons. New rows of farms appeared behind the original row fronting on the St. Lawrence, Richelieu, and Ottawa rivers. As available farmland dwindled, young people left to work in the towns or the lumber camps of Lower Canada or they went to the United States.

Extreme poverty was common after 1810. Some faced starvation. The economic situation was made worse by the low prices fetched by wheat at the time, and by the fact that much of the wheat was ruined by bad weather, disease, and insects.

The habitants were anxious over the scarcity of land and the poor economic conditions. The huge number of English-speaking newcomers made them fearful of losing their French language, Roman Catholic religion, and agricultural way of life.

Merchants

Compared to the habitants, the English-speaking merchants were newcomers to Lower Canada. They had arrived following the events in 1763, when New France became a British colony. The merchants were rich and powerful. They made their money from the export of furs and timber, as well as wheat from the habitants' farms. They wanted improvements, such as harbours, canals, and roads, all of which were to be paid for by government taxes.

Professional Men

The French-speaking professionals were the newest group in Lower Canada. This group did not become prominent until after 1800. They were educated people, mostly lawyers and doctors. They wanted to be the leaders of the colony and they believed that they spoke for all the French-speaking people of Lower Canada.

These professional men began to dream of and speak of a separate French Canadian nation. This nation would preserve the French Canadian way of life: the French language, Roman Catholic religion, and traditional agricultural lifestyle. They saw the British as a cultural threat. They formed a new political party called the "Parti Canadien."

Louis-Joseph Papineau (1786-1871)

Louis-Joseph Papineau was a wealthy seigneur and a strong supporter of the old French order in Lower Canada. This meant he favoured doing things in the old ways, as they had been done before the British came.

Papineau served as an officer in the militia, defending British North America from the Americans during the War of 1812.

He had been elected to the Legislative Assembly of Lower Canada in 1809. He served as the Speaker of the Assembly almost continuously from 1815 to 1837.

As Speaker, Papineau became the leader of the Parti Canadien, which, after 1826, was called the Parti Patriote. These were the people who wanted **political reform** in Lower Canada.

---

*Note: Women did not enter the professions (become doctors, lawyers, judges) at this time or become involved in the government. While Native people also lived in the area they were not involved in the government at this time and are thus not included on this page.

Political reform—changes to make the government better

Government in Lower Canada

The system of government in Lower Canada during this time was that which had been established by the Constitutional Act of 1791.* (*See* pages 119 and 120 in Chapter 6.)

The power of the elected Legislative Assembly was limited by the governor and the Councils. However, after 1817 the Legislative Assembly controlled revenues in Lower Canada. Its laws could be vetoed by the Legislative Council and the Executive Council, and by the British-appointed governor. Members of the Legislative Council and the Executive Council were appointed for life, so they could not be voted out at election time. Since the governor was English-speaking, the council members appointed by him also usually spoke English. Their interests and concerns were usually different from those of the French-speaking habitants and professional men.**

Château Clique

One group in Lower Canada held most of the power in the government. This group came to be known as the Château Clique. This group was well named, since château means "castle" and clique means "a small group unfriendly to outsiders." The Château Clique:

- was a small group of powerful people (mostly in businesses) in the colony of Lower Canada
- were either of British background or were wealthy French Canadians who allied with the British
- believed power should be in the hands of a few capable people (themselves)
- wanted the Roman Catholic Church to stay powerful; in turn the Church supported their political aims
- favoured the British point of view and the British system of government
- wanted more English-speaking settlers in the colony.

Parti Canadien

Some people in Lower Canada wanted the old French ways to remain. These people formed the Parti Canadien, later the Parti Patriote (after 1826). They favoured traditional French ways, which were tied to the past. They viewed most new ideas as negative and change as a threat. They appealed to the *Canadien* professional **elite**.

The Parti Canadien was almost exclusively French, but there were a few English-speaking people who took up the cause. The leader of the Parti Canadien was Louis-Joseph Papineau, a lawyer and a long-time member of the Legislative Assembly.

Shortly after 1800 the French-speaking professional group won control of the Legislative Assembly. Even though the Legislative Assembly had little power they were able to vote against improvements such as canals, thereby blocking the plans of the merchants. Their name for the French-speaking people of Lower Canada was *Canadiens*.

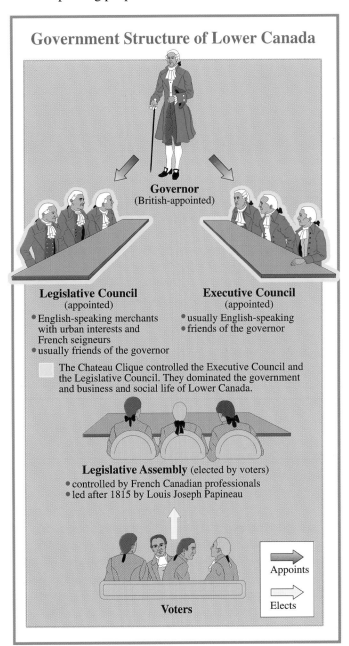

Government Structure of Lower Canada

Governor
(British-appointed)

Legislative Council
(appointed)
- English-speaking merchants with urban interests and French seigneurs
- usually friends of the governor

Executive Council
(appointed)
- usually English-speaking
- friends of the governor

The Chateau Clique controlled the Executive Council and the Legislative Council. They dominated the government and business and social life of Lower Canada.

Legislative Assembly (elected by voters)
- controlled by French Canadian professionals
- led after 1815 by Louis Joseph Papineau

Voters

Appoints

Elects

---

*Upper Canada had the same government structure but had an entirely separate government.
Elite—special group, usually more educated or richer than others

**Note: Women with property in Lower Canada could vote until the 1830s, at which time they lost their vote. Women in Upper Canada could not vote.

Unrest in Lower Canada
Points of View

The French-speaking people and the English-speaking merchants wanted different things for Lower Canada. For instance, the merchants wanted to improve canals, harbours, and roads to make it easier to transport wheat and timber to Britain. They suggested that all landowners be taxed to pay for these improvements. The habitants were not interested in these improvements, which they felt would help only the merchants.

Immigration was also causing problems. The Château Clique was encouraging emigration from Great Britain, but the *Canadiens* looked on the immigrants with dismay. If enough immigrants arrived, the French-speaking inhabitants of Lower Canada could lose their language rights and protection of their Roman Catholic religion. They saw the immigrants settling on land in the Eastern Townships and wondered where their own young people would be able to farm. In June of 1832, an immigrant ship brought a deadly disease, cholera, which resulted in an epidemic in the colony. By September, it had claimed almost 5500 victims. Not only did the British "cast their beggars on the Canadian shore," according to the Parti Patriote, "they must do still more; they must send us, as the final outrage, pestilence and death."

Another area of concern for the French-speaking people of Lower Canada was the fact that the Executive Council and the Legislative Council were dominated by people who were either English-speaking or who supported Great Britain. It was difficult for the Legislative Assembly to get its laws passed when the goals and values of the council members and the governor were so different from the members of the Legislative Assembly, the majority of whom were French-speaking.

Appeal to Great Britain

In 1822, the English-speaking merchants asked Britain to unite Upper and Lower Canada. They thought that the English majority that would result from the union of the two colonies would agree to build the canals, harbours, and roads they wanted.

In response, Papineau took a protest petition to Britain. He managed to persuade the British Parliament to forget the idea of uniting the two colonies, at least for the time being.

In 1834, the Legislative Assembly put together a list of its grievances, which they called the Ninety-Two **Resolutions.** They decided that they would vote for no taxes until their concerns were resolved. This meant that government workers would not be paid and that the building of roads and bridges would stop.

The British response to the unrest in Lower Canada was to send out Lord Gosford as the new governor in 1835. He had special orders to investigate the grievances in the Ninety-Two Resolutions. He was not well received. Papineau and the Patriotes despised him as a **puppet** of the British. The Montreal merchants were angry with him for trying to please the Patriotes (formerly the Parti Canadien).

Then, as if things were not bad enough, crops failed in much of North America in 1836. Many people in Lower Canada faced starvation.

In January of 1837 Governor Gosford sent a report of his study of the Ninety-Two Resolutions to Britain. In response, the British Colonial Secretary issued 10 resolutions. These were a blow to Papineau and the Patriotes. Britain refused to give the Legislative Assembly any more power. British immigration would continue to be encouraged. It was also decided that if the Legislative Assembly refused to vote for taxes, the governor could simply take from the treasury the money needed to pay his officials.

Then, later in 1837, economic depression hit the United States, Britain, and British North America. Prices dropped and many businesses failed. The situation had a disastrous effect on the rich Canadian timber trade. The *Canadiens* took out their anger on the English-speaking merchants.

For Your Notebook

1. In the 1820s and 1830s who had the power in Lower Canada? What role did ordinary people play in making decisions?

Resolution—formal statement of the way one feels; usually written down and sent to one in a position of power and authority; may be followed as a guideline for ruling a group of people

Puppet—leader who is not independent, who waits for orders or does what someone else tells him or her to do

Armed Rebellion in Lower Canada

By the end of November, the *Canadiens* were ready to fight. Papineau supported the rebellion, but fled when he was threatened with arrest. The people listened to another leader, Wolfred Nelson, who cried, "The time has come to melt our spoons into bullets!"

The actual rebellion in Lower Canada lasted only a few weeks. It began on November 23, 1837, at St. Denis, where the rebels won a victory.* Following this successful battle, about 200 of the rebels built a log fort at the village of St. Charles. But this battle was not nearly as successful. The British troops fired their cannon, charged, and the rebels fled. Of the Patriotes, 40 were killed, 30 wounded, and over 500 captured. Papineau and other rebel leaders fled to the United States.

The biggest battle took place on December 14 at St. Eustache. Over 1000 Patriotes gathered there and fortified the church and several other buildings. The British attacked the church with cannons and then set fire to it. The rebel leader, Dr. J.O. Chenier, and 70 other rebels died as they tried to escape the flames. The British troops then robbed and burned the village. This ended any hopes of a successful rebellion. A second, small rebellion in November of 1838 was quickly put down.

In the end, 12 of the rebels were hanged and 58 were sent in chains to a prison colony in Australia. The remaining 1200 prisoners were set free. Papineau and others who had fled to the United States were to be executed if they returned to the Canadas.

C-393, National Archives of Canada, Ottawa.

After the British attacked the Patriotes at St. Charles, Papineau and other rebel leaders escaped to the United States.

The Battle of St. Eustache, December 14, was the end of the Rebellion of 1837 in Lower Canada.

---

*The term rebels refers to the popular movement known as the Patriotes. Most were French-speaking professionals, merchants, farmers, labourers, and crasftsmen. The key leaders were Papineau and Wolfred Nelson. Refer to page 141 under "Parti Canadien" for additional information.

Life in Upper Canada: 1815–1838

A New Home

#6673. National Gallery of Canada, Ottawa.

Behind Bonsecours Market, Montreal (1866), by William Raphael. Many immigrants to Upper Canada stopped in Montreal.

Role Card*

Name: .... Alex MacIntosh, age 19
Country of Origin: .... Scotland
Family Information: ...... 2 females, wife 17 and
one-year-old daughter
Education/Skills: .... unskilled, illiterate
Wealth: .... poor
Religion: .... Presbyterian

Other: All of your family died of cholera on the passage from Scotland. You met your wife on the ship. Her family also died aboard the ship.

**Month you purchased
your lot:** .... April

Equipment/Supplies you have:
1 broad axe, some nails, garden seeds

Location Ticket: .... Concession 3, Lot 13

To help you better understand what life was like in Upper Canada from 1815 to 1838, you are to take part in the following four-part activity. Carefully examine the above painting. Imagine what it might have been like to have arrived in Montreal and to wait on the dock before you proceed to your new home in Upper Canada. Your teacher will give you a role card. You are to pretend you are the person described on this card throughout this activity. The concluding part of this activity is on page 156. A sample role card is on the left.

All Settlers Must Perform the Following Duties:

1. Clear and fence 2.03 hectares for every 40.5 hectares you have been granted.
2. Build a dwelling house, 4.88 metres x 6.1 metres.
3. Clear one half of the road in front of each lot.

These duties must be performed within two years of the date of the ticket.

---

*Additional Role Cards are in the Teacher's Resource Package.

continued on page 146

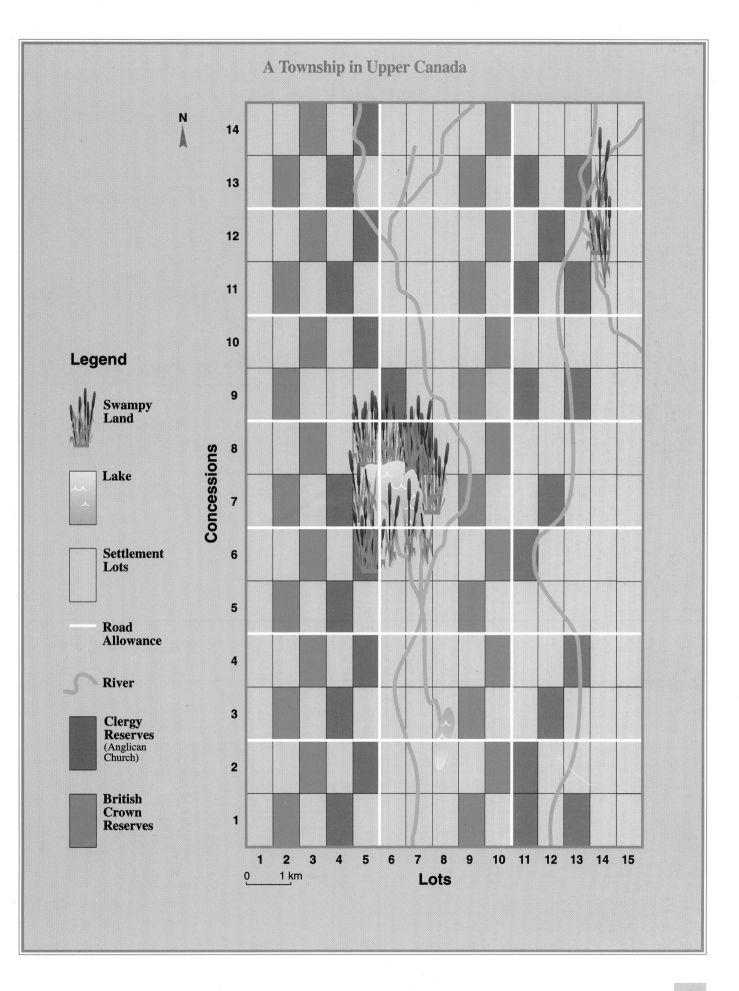

Legend

Swampy Land

Lake

Settlement Lots

Road Allowance

River

Clergy Reserves (Anglican Church)

British Crown Reserves

N

Concessions

Lots

Part 1

(a) Work with a partner for Part 1 to share and discuss how to deal with your role card. Examine the map provided on page 145. Locate your lot and study the map's legend.

(b) Visualize in your mind what the land you have purchased would look like. Imagine yourself walking across the land that you are seeing for the first time. Notice the smells, sights, and sounds around you. Look at the reactions of your family members. Experience walking throughout your land and then answer the following questions.

- Is your land flat? hilly? Is it covered with trees? rocks? water? swamps? What is the soil like? Is it good for growing crops? What is the drainage like? What wild animals are in the area? Do you have fresh water available for drinking? Is there a river nearby? Will it be beneficial or harmful?

(c) Think about and make plans of what you would do for your first three months. Make brief notes of your decisions.

Consider:

- What skills do you have?
- What equipment do you have?
- What assistance is available from family members, the religious community, hired help, the Native people?
- What food supplies have you brought with you?

(d) Think about and make plans for the next two years. (Remember duties you are required to do by law before you get the deed to your land.)

---

*Potash was one way for settlers to earn cash after the land was cleared. The large hardwood trees were collected and burned in huge bonfires. Water was poured through the ashes. The liquid was boiled in iron pots until it evaporated. The remaining grey powder, known as potash, was sold to European factories where it was used in the manufacture of soap and cosmetics.

**Grist mills for grinding grain and saw mills for planing logs into lumber were needed in pioneer communities. These mills were located near rivers as running water was necessary in the milling process.

Crown reserve—one-seventh of all public land was set aside for the British government by the Constitutional Act of 1791. By 1825 these lands were finally sold because they prevented compact settlement, making it difficult to complete roads

Clergy reserve—one-seventh of all public land was set aside for Protestant schools and churches by the Constitutional Act of 1791 (*see* Chapter 6, page 119).

Speculation—the act of buying or selling land, at some risk, with the hope of making large profits from future price changes

---

- How do you plan to survive through the first winter?
- What will you do if someone in your family is injured or becomes sick?
- If you are going to grow a crop how will you harvest it?
- How do you plan to meet others in your area? Or does the isolation not bother you?
- Do you feel it is important to co-operate with others in your area? If so, how?
- Do you feel a school should be built nearby? A church? If so, who will build it and how?
- Is transportation a problem? What about roads? Waterways? Do you feel you should be involved in building them?
- How do you "pay for" the goods and services you need and use?
- What ways are there for making money?*
- Check back to page 144. Have you completed all the duties you are required to do?

(e) Think about and make plans for the next five years.

Consider:

- How will the area in which you live change over the next five years?
- How do you plan on looking after the soil so it does not become depleted?
- What will you do if you need more land?
- What industries do you think should be developed in the area?** How should this be done?
- Is there a need for a village or town to be built in your area? Where would it best be built?
- Would you provide assistance to newcomers? If yes, what kind of assistance? If no, why not?
- What problems have you had in keeping the roads in good condition?
- How have the **Crown reserves** and the **clergy reserves** interfered with your building and maintaining the roads?
- How has the land-granting system encouraged **speculation?**

146

Part 2

You have lived in Upper Canada for years. Write a letter to relatives in Great Britain telling them about your new life. Describe your accomplishments and the hardships you have encountered. You may wish to encourage them to come to Upper Canada by giving them reasons why this is a good place to settle.

Part 3

As a class, brainstorm about the following. Record your contributions on huge chart paper or the chalkboard.

(a) What circumstances forced the majority of the immigrants to come to Upper Canada?

(b) What problems were involved in travel to Upper Canada?

(c) What hardships were encountered during

    i.   the first three months
    ii. the first year
    iii. the first five years?

(d) What was the importance of family, friends, and Native neighbours?

(e) What geographic features hindered settlement? What other factors hindered settlement? What factors helped settlement? How could settlement of Upper Canada have been carried out more efficiently?

(f) How did your area change during the first five years?

(g) What cultural groups settled in your township? Is there evidence of a pattern of kinship (or cultural) settlement? Why did people (in history) settle in cultural groups? What advantages does this type of settlement have? What disadvantages are there?

(h) Suppose that someone from the government (the Legislative Assembly) comes to your community. He asks you to fill out a questionnaire on how you have cleared the land, how many animals you own, and other questions. He also asks you to name things you feel prevent the improvement of your township. What complaints or grievances would you give him? List these on large chart paper. Keep this list for later reference.

Note: Part 4 of this activity is on page 156 and is to be done later.

Below: The first task of many settlers was clearing the land.

C-17, National Archives of Canada, Ottawa.

Focus On: Daily Life on a Pioneer Homestead

C-12632, National Archives of Canada, Ottawa.

Above: Once new roads were built, it became easier to travel.

Right: A pioneer homestead in the early years of settlement was usually a one-room log cabin with a dirt floor.

Below: Fifteen years later, this family had built a larger house with several rooms.

For their homesteads the pioneers selected lands where the First People had lived for thousands of years. The land was still in its natural state—an uncleared dense forest—home to the First People and the various species of wildlife. As the trees were cut and the swamps drained, the First People and the wildlife were forced farther inland, away from the newcomers who were making Upper Canada their home.

Clearing a forested area of thousands of trees and building a new home was a time-consuming and difficult task.

But gradually life on a homestead became more comfortable as time went on. The pictures show a pioneer homestead in the early years of settlement, 15 years after settlement, and 30 years after settlement.

The first house of a pioneer family was usually a one-room log cabin with a dirt floor and a wooden chimney. A blanket might be used to divide the room into two for sleeping purposes. These homes were cold and draughty. As the logs dried, they shrank, making the gaps between

them even larger. These gaps were filled with mud or lime plaster, which had to be replaced every year.

After a year or two, when there was a little more time, a larger and more comfortable house would be built. It would have several rooms on the main floor, with a loft or attic as well. The fireplace would be stone or brick. Once this house was finished, the old log cabin would be turned over to the pigs or other farm animals for shelter.

Focus On: Daily Life on a Pioneer Homestead
continued

Thirty years after settlement, a pioneer homestead might look like this.

A few years later, the family might add on to the log house, or build a new home of fieldstone or sawn lumber, if there was a sawmill in the district. This house would have glass windows instead of the oiled paper or rags that covered the windows on the other houses. Glass was expensive because, until 1825, it had to be imported. After that it was manufactured in Upper Canada.

A Summary of Rural Life in Upper Canada in the Early Years of the Nineteenth Century

Most inhabitants:
- lived on the forest frontier
- used physical labour to fell the trees and remove the stumps
- persisted through years of hard work and effort to create a home
- were **subsistence farmers**
- had to work daily to provide their necessities
- were isolated from their neighbours
- received the little education they had from their parents or a **literate** neighbour
- visited nearby towns to use the mills to grind their grain or the sawmill to get lumber

- attended "bees" to get big projects accomplished and to have some social activity
- depended on their own ingenuity for their survival.

Left: These men are threshing to separate wheat from chaff.
Above: This man is winnowing—allowing the chaff to blow away so only wheat remains.

C-73395, National Archives of Canada, Ottawa.

C-73396, National Archives of Canada, Ottawa.

Subsistence farmer—only grew enough food for the family; none was left to sell for much-needed cash to buy other products and supplies
Literate — educated; having the ability to read and write

Focus On: Daily Life in the Towns of Upper Canada

As more fields were cleared in Upper Canada, more wheat was grown. Farmers could sell wheat for cash. Villages began to grow at places that were convenient for the farmers, like crossroads or mill sites. In the villages the farmers could sell their wheat and purchase goods with the money. A fairly large village could be expected to provide the following services for its local farmers: stores, taverns, shoemaker, blacksmith, miller, carpenter, lawyer, doctor, wagonmaker, tinsmith, tailor, school, church, and newspaper.

Eyewitness Account

Catherine Parr Traill, an early settler, describes the changes that took place in her community over a few years:

When we first came up to live in the bush . . . there were but two or three settlers near us and no roads out . . . . Very great is the change that a few years have effected in our situation . . . .

A village has started up where formerly a thick pine-wood covered the ground; we have now within a short distance of us an excellent sawmill, a grist mill and store, with a large tavern and many good dwellings.

(from *The Backwoods of Canada* by Catherine Parr Traill)

Kingston

Kingston developed as a British military and naval base for Lake Ontario and was the largest and most important town in Upper Canada for many years.

Eyewitness Account

Here is a description of Kingston, written about 1820:

Kingston, although the largest town in the Upper Province, contains only 2,336 inhabitants, most of whom are the descendants of those loyalists who sought asylum in Canada after the revolutionary war. The rest are English, Irish, and Scotch, with a few Germans and Frenchmen. The streets are laid out with considerable regularity; but the houses, like almost all others in the Canadas, are very irregularly built. In consequence of the neglected condition of the roads in this as well as in every other part of the Province, it is scarcely possible in wet weather to walk out without sticking fast in the mire. The public buildings of Kingston are of such an inferior description as scarcely to be worthy of notice.

(from *Five Years' Residence in the Canadas* by Edward Allen Talbot)

York

The Queen's Rangers began clearing land to build a fort at York in 1793. Governor Simcoe decided to build a temporary capital here. In 1834, it was renamed Toronto and has been the capital ever since.

York became more important as the newcomers moved westward. It became their business centre and their government centre.

Eyewitness Account

Here is a description of York, written about 1820:

The streets of York are regularly laid out, intersecting each other at right angles. Only one of them, however, is yet completely built; and, in wet weather, the unfinished streets are, if possible, muddier and dirtier than those of Kingston.

(from *Five Years' Residence in the Canadas* by Edward Allen Talbot)

C-1669, National Archives of Canada, Ottawa (detail).

This painting shows King Street, which is still one of Toronto's main streets.

Mire — wet, soggy ground

Focus On: Canada Revisited— Upper Canada Village

These pictures are from a reconstructed Upper Canada Village.

Right: As communities developed, lumber mills made possible the construction of frame houses.

Below: One of the early industries was weaving woolen and linen fabrics.

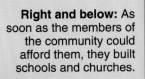

Below: On winter and summer evenings, travellers were relieved to find food and shelter at an inn. This picture shows the livery stable behind the inn.

Right and below: As soon as the members of the community could afford them, they built schools and churches.

Right: Later there would be a more elaborate centre of government, such as this city hall.

Services Provided in the Towns

Services, running water, natural gas for home heating, sewers to take away water and waste, garbage collection, sidewalks, paved roads, police and fire protection—none of these were available in the early 1800s in Upper Canada.

You have read the description of how the unpaved roads turned to mud in the rain. People threw their garbage onto roads or into streams and lakes. Many got their drinking water from the same streams where they disposed of their garbage. By the 1840s, cities were installing sewer systems to take away used water.

Toronto had a water system by 1841, but its main purpose was not to provide clean water for drinking. It was for firefighting. Fire was a serious threat to the wooden buildings of early towns, with their poorly constructed or open fireplaces. There were no paid firefighters. The firefighting was done by the people of the town. By law, every house had to have a water bucket and a ladder on its roof near the chimney. When a fire broke out, people from all around came with their buckets to help fight it. Some towns were lucky enough to have a fire engine that could be pulled by men or horses to the fire. In the 1820s and 1830s towns began to establish volunteer fire departments. This was more effective, since the volunteers received some training.

By the 1840s cities were beginning to have gas lights. Pipes were installed to bring flammable gas to light posts on streets and to light fixtures in houses. The gas was lit with a flame to produce light.

C-69849, National Archives of Canada, Ottawa.

Mail was delivered by coach in the 1800s.

Transportation in Upper Canada

Walking was often the safest and fastest means of getting about in Upper Canada, since the first roads were often nothing better than wide, muddy footpaths. Even in the towns the unpaved streets turned to mud when it rained. By the 1830s, a few main streets had been macadamized, which meant they were paved using crushed stone or gravel. But most streets remained unpaved. In the countryside, corduroy roads were used. Logs were laid side by side across them in order to create a hard surface. The result looked like the bumps on a piece of corduroy. These roads were very uncomfortable to walk on or drive over.

Eyewitness Account

Here is one traveller's description of such a road:

. . . Indeed, "corduroy" is dreadful. When we came to it I tried every thing to save my poor bones—sitting on my hands, or raising my body on them—but it was of little use; on we went, thump, thump, thumping against one log after another, and this, in the last part of our journey, with the bare boards of an open wagon for seats . . . But we got through without an actual upset or breakdown, which is more than a friend of mine could say, for the coach in which he was went into so deep a mud-hole at one part of the road, that it fairly overturned, throwing the passengers on the top of one another inside, and leaving them no way of exit, when they came to themselves, but to crawl out through the window.

(from *Adventures in Canada; or Life in the Woods* by John C. Geikie)

Waterways, as well, were often used for transportation. In the winter, horse-drawn sleighs could travel swiftly over the ice. The rest of the year, many types of boats were used. By the 1820s, steamboats were going back and forth across Lake Ontario, carrying passengers and cargo between the falls of Niagara and the beginning of the St. Lawrence at Kingston.

Government in Upper Canada

In the 1830s the system of government in Upper Canada, as in Lower Canada, remained as it had been set out in the Constitutional Act of 1791 (*see* pages 119 and 120). There was an elected Legislative Assembly, appointed Legislative Council and Executive Council, and a British appointed lieutenant-governor. As in Lower Canada, the elected Legislative Assembly had limited power. Laws passed by the Legislative Assembly had to be approved by the Executive Council and the Legislative Council and the lieutenant-governor. There were two political groups in Upper Canada: the Tories, led by the Family Compact, and the Reformers.

Family Compact

Just as Lower Canada had its elite powerful people called the Château Clique, Upper Canada also had an elite. This group came to be known as the Family Compact. Members of this group were in the Executive Council and Legislative Council, so they had the power to veto or stop any laws passed by the Legislative Assembly that they did not like. They took for themselves and gave to their friends favours such as jobs, land, and contracts for canal and road work. Most of the Family Compact members were of Loyalist descent, or were British immigrants who arrived before 1800. They claimed that those who had not proven their loyalty to Britain by fighting against the Thirteen Colonists in the American Revolution and the Americans in the War of 1812 were not true Upper Canadians. They did not want Americans to be part of the government of Upper Canada and some even said that Americans should have their land taken away from them.

The Family Compact:

- was a small group of powerful people in the colony of Upper Canada
- along with their friends and supporters were known as Tories
- did not want people from the United States to be part of the government of Upper Canada
- defended tradition (the things that had always been done) and opposed change
- believed power should be in the hands of a few capable people (themselves)
- believed the Church of England should be powerful in the colony
- were loyal to Great Britain and to the British system of government.

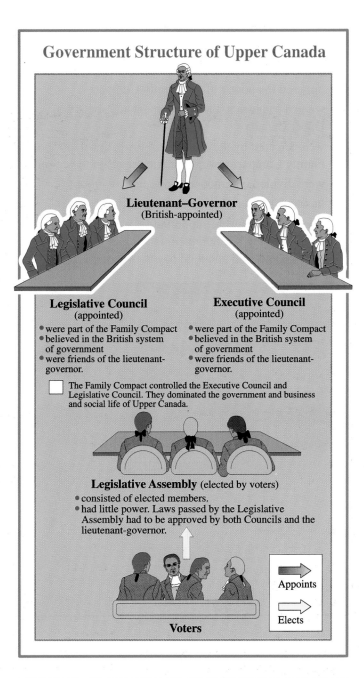

Government Structure of Upper Canada

Lieutenant–Governor
(British-appointed)

Legislative Council
(appointed)
- were part of the Family Compact
- believed in the British system of government
- were friends of the lieutenant-governor.

Executive Council
(appointed)
- were part of the Family Compact
- believed in the British system of government
- were friends of the lieutenant-governor.

☐ The Family Compact controlled the Executive Council and Legislative Council. They dominated the government and business and social life of Upper Canada.

Legislative Assembly (elected by voters)
- consisted of elected members.
- had little power. Laws passed by the Legislative Assembly had to be approved by both Councils and the lieutenant-governor.

Voters

➡ Appoints

⇨ Elects

Bishop Strachan (1778–1867)

John Strachan was born in Scotland. After he arrived in Upper Canada in 1799, he taught school. His leadership of Upper Canadians and his bravery were noted when the Americans attacked York during the War of 1812, and during his tireless work to help victims of the cholera epidemic of the 1830s.

Strachan was a powerful spokesman for and advisor to the Family Compact. By the 1820s he and his friends in the Family Compact largely controlled the government of Upper Canada.

In 1839 Strachan became the first Anglican bishop of Toronto.

The Reformers

The Reformers in Upper Canada:

- opposed the power of the Family Compact
- wanted changes in the government and society of Upper Canada
- were angered by the attitudes of the members of the Family Compact toward the Americans in the colony
- were divided into moderate and radical groups
- included some radicals who later became rebels.

The Reformers were supported by some of the people represented in the simulation you took part in on pages 144 to 147, and read about on pages 148 to 152.

Robert Gourlay (1778–1863)

Robert Gourlay arrived in Upper Canada in 1817 from Scotland. He had a plan to bring poor people from Britain over to farm. He said that without land, "no good can be expected of us."

Gourlay sent a questionnaire to farmers in Upper Canada, asking them about their progress in clearing land, the number of animals they owned, and so on. He also asked them to name things they felt prevented the improvement of their township or province.

Gourlay was criticized by members of the Family Compact for attempting to stir up discontent because the farmers began to have meetings to voice their concerns over the land. They felt that the land should be owned by those who lived and worked on it, not by those who did not improve it, or by the church (clergy reserves) or government (Crown reserves). Between the clergy reserves, the Crown reserves, and the land owned by rich people who did not work it, there was a great deal of land in Upper Canada that was not available for farming. These land reserves made it difficult to build roads and it took farmers much longer than necessary to get their crops to market.

The Family Compact saw Gourlay as someone who caused trouble. He was thrown in jail and then banished from Upper Canada in 1819.

C-1993, National Archives of Canada, Ottawa (detail).

William Lyon Mackenzie (1795–1861)

Mackenzie was another Reformer. He was born in Scotland and came to Canada in 1820. He began as a shopkeeper, but in 1824 he established *The Colonial Advocate,* a newspaper for which he was publisher, editor, writer, and paper carrier. He used his newspaper to speak out on the land problems, the power of the Family Compact, and the question of who was an Upper Canadian.

On June 8, 1825, 15 young men from wealthy, well-known families of York (now Toronto) smashed their way into the offices of *The Colonial Advocate* and threw the printing equipment into the street. They then tossed the type (letters used for printing) into the harbour.

Fortunately for Mackenzie, he was able to turn this disaster into a triumph. He became a public hero. The young men were tried, and convicted, and ordered to pay Mackenzie $2450. Before the raid *The Colonial Advocate* had been in financial trouble. Afterwards, he was able to pay off his debts and buy new equipment.

Mackenzie was first elected to the Legislative Assembly in 1828. He used his new position to suggest government changes. He thought that the elected people in the Legislative Assembly did not have enough power and suggested that Upper Canada adopt the American system of government.

Other members of the Legislative Assembly did not always like Mackenzie's ideas and voted to expel him. Mackenzie was expelled from the Legislative Assembly a total of six times and each time the people re-elected him.

Mackenzie often became very agitated during his speeches. He had lost his hair as a result of a fever and it was a common sight to see him tear his bright red wig off his head and fling it on the ground to make a point.

As the 1830s wore on, Mackenzie became more radical. He decided to resort to armed rebellion in an attempt to destroy Upper Canada's system of government.

Sir Francis Bond Head

C-18789, National Archives of Canada, Ottawa (detail).

Sir Francis Bond Head was appointed lieutenant-governor of Upper Canada in 1835. He was welcomed as a friend and ally by the Reformers, but they soon changed their minds. He included two leading Reformers among his official advisors, but when he ignored their advice, they quit in anger.

The Legislative Assembly decided not to co-operate with him. The Reformers would not vote to pass money bills. As a result, without money, all work on bridges, roads, and docks came to an immediate halt.

Sir Francis called an election in which he personally fought for the Tories.* The people of the colony, worried about their roads and bridges and the pro-Americanism of the Reformers, voted for the Tories. William Lyon Mackenzie and many other Reformers went down in defeat in this 1836 election. **Moderates** like Robert Baldwin simply did not run because they rejected the increasing **radical** Mackenzie.

Focus On: Elections in Upper and Lower Canada

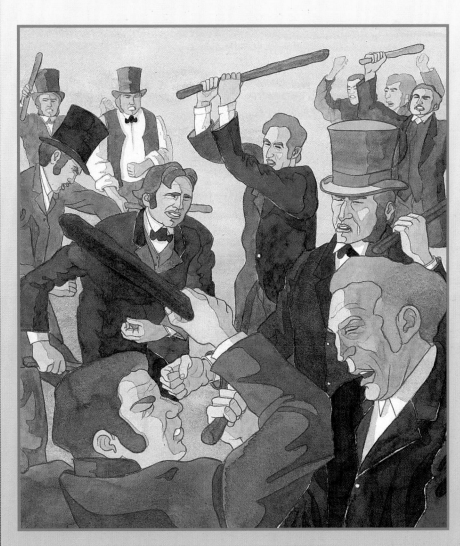

Strong disagreements, fueled by alcohol, often turned elections of the 1830s into violent confrontations.

Election violence in the 1830s was very common. There was no secret ballot as there is today. Instead of voting in private booths and then depositing their ballots in a box, the voters shouted their choices for everyone to hear. The choice was often greeted by insults from people who were voting for an opponent. Voters threw stones and even swung clubs at one another. In Montreal in 1832, one candidate hired bullies who threatened and beat anyone who declared his support for the opponent. The resulting riot caused the deaths of three people.

Exploring Further

1. What difference would a secret ballot have made in elections in the 1830s?
2. Compare a Canadian election with one in the 1830s.

---

*The Family Compact, along with their friends and supporters, were known as Tories. *See* page 153.

Moderate—a person who does not hold extreme opionions
Radical—holding extreme opinions; wants fundamental social, economic, and political changes

Simulation Conclusion
(Continued from page 147.)

Part 4

Mentally place yourself back into the role you played in the simulation on pages 144 to 147. It is now 1837 and you have lived in Upper Canada for a number of years. You and your neighbours have gathered at a bee to build a community hall.

People are talking about the recent election and the resulting political unrest. The Reformer William Lyon Mackenzie arrives to try to convince you to join his armed rebellion against the government.

In your role, decide whether you will join Mackenzie or not. Your teacher will tell you what group to work with.

Either select one of the decision-making models used in this textbook or design your own model. Use that model to decide as a group whether you will join with Mackenzie. Be prepared to share your decision-making process and your decision with the rest of the class.

Armed Rebellion in Upper Canada

Mackenzie decided to take advantage of the political unrest. He began to ride about the countryside north of Toronto, stirring up people against the government. Those who became most rebellious were called Radicals. They wanted Upper Canada to have a government like the Americans had in the United States.

On October 9, 1837, news came that Papineau's Patriotes in Lower Canada were ready to spring into armed action. British troops had left Toronto to defend the government of Lower Canada and thousands of weapons were left unguarded in Toronto. Mackenzie decided the time was ripe for armed rebellion. He suggested to his rebel followers that they seize the weapons; capture Sir Francis Bond Head, the lieutenant-governor of Upper Canada; and proclaim a new government. His followers were not yet ready for armed rebellion. They sent Mackenzie north of the city to collect names of people in favour of the proposed new government, but he was not to speak of armed rebellion. Mackenzie collected 4000 names on his petition.

On December 5, Mackenzie, wrapped in several overcoats to keep out bullets, led a group of about 800 men down Yonge Street into Toronto. A few of the men had guns. Others carried pitchforks, clubs, and even carving knives strapped to poles. They were fired on by a small band of defenders, who turned and ran as soon as they fired. In response to the attack, the leading rebel riflemen threw themselves down and returned fire. In the confusion, those behind thought the riflemen had been killed. They turned and fled back the way they had come.

On December 6, with cannon and rifles, 600 of the colony's militia marched up Yonge Street. Before long the rebels were running for their lives. Mackenzie stayed until the bitter end and then, in spite of the fact that Sir Francis Bond Head had offered a $5000 reward for his capture, was able to escape to the United States. There, he tried to raise an army to liberate Upper Canada by offering 120 hectares of free land to anyone who would join him. He was arrested for breaking the legal neutrality between the Province of Canada and the United States and was imprisoned for 11 months.

Two other rebels, Samuel Lount and Peter Matthews, were hanged on April 12, 1838, for the crime of **treason.**

Mackenzie returned to Canada in 1849. He began another newspaper and was elected to the Legislative Assembly, but he never regained his earlier influence.

T-1316 #1, Art Gallery of Ontario, Toronto

During the Rebellion of 1837, radicals were eager to take up arms with Mackenzie.

Treason—the crime of betraying one's country

DEATH OF COL. MOODIE.

The Rebellion of 1837 was violent.

Aftermath of the Rebellions

Lower Canada ended up, at least temporarily, worse off than before the rebellion. The colony's Legislative Assembly was suspended until 1841, and the governor and a Special Council ruled. In Upper Canada, people were afraid to speak out because even moderate reformers were branded as rebels.

C-13493, National Archives of Canada, Ottawa.

Twelve Patriotes were executed after the rebellions of 1837 and 1838.

The British response to the rebellions was one of shock. The prime minister decided to send John George Lambton (Lord Durham) as governor general. He was told to investigate the causes of the rebellions and to suggest solutions to the problems. You will read about Lord Durham's suggestions and the British response in the next chapter.

Exploring Further

1. Lord Durham was sent by the British to investigate the rebellions in Upper and Lower Canada. Imagine you are Durham. What would you report to the British government about the causes and possible solutions for the rebellions?

C-3653, National Archives of Canada, Ottawa.

Soldiers captured rebels who spoke out against the government.

Review

Summarizing the Chapter

- Upper and Lower Canada underwent three major changes between the end of the War of 1812 and the Rebellions of 1837. These were a population explosion due mainly to a high birth rate in Lower Canada and immigration to Upper Canada, the development of a successful timber industry, and the end of competition in the fur trade through the union of the Hudson's Bay Company and the North West Company. The latter change affected only Lower Canada.

- The system of government during this period remained as it had been established by the Constitutional Act of 1791. Laws passed by the elected Legislative Assembly could be vetoed by the appointed Legislative Council, the Executive Council, or by the governor.

- A small group of powerful people held much of the power in each colony. In Lower Canada this group was known as the Château Clique; in Upper Canada, the Family Compact. A reform movement developed in the Legislative Assembly of each colony led by Louis-Joseph Papineau in Lower Canada and William Lyon Mackenzie in Upper Canada. The Patriotes in Lower Canada and the radical Reformers in Upper Canada demanded that Executive Council and Legislative Council members as well as members of the Legislative Assembly be elected rather than appointed. They thought the people should have more say in how the colonies were run.

- By 1837, there were brief armed rebellions. The rebellions were quickly put down. The rebel leaders fled to the United States.

- The British response was to send Lord Durham to the Canadas as governor, with orders to study the situation and make recommendations.

Checking Predictions

1. At the beginning of this chapter you made some predictions based on the Overview and what you already knew. Now, use what you learned from reading the chapter to fill in the third column of the chart that you began earlier.
2. Refer to the "Questions to Talk About" on page 134. Discuss the questions based on what you have learned about the government in Upper and Lower Canada.

Working with Information

1. Here are some main ideas from this chapter. Use one of the following approaches to make a permanent set of notes: mind map, web, paragraph, or outline to show the relationship among these main ideas.

   - increased population and settlement in Upper Canada
   - timber trade
   - the end of competition in the fur trade
   - French-English conflict
   - rebellion in Lower and Upper Canada
   - rural and urban life

2. Review all of the different examples of conflict found in this chapter. Work with a partner to draw a mind map that organizes all of these examples on one sheet of paper. Show how this conflict affected the ordinary people's attempts to have more say in governmental decisions. Use simple line drawings and at least three colours. A sample mind map is shown on page 16.
3. Using either the government of Upper Canada or Lower Canada as your reference point, answer these three questions: Who participates in the government? Who has the power to make decisions? Does majority rule exist?

Building Thinking Strategies

Evaluating Information

This excerpt is from William Lyon Mackenzie's newspaper, *The Constitution*. It was written on July 12, 1837, and criticizes the Executive Council (the Family Compact).

Ye false Canadians! Tories! Pensioners! Placemen! Profligates! Orangemen! Churchmen! Spies! Informers! Brokers! Gamblers! Parasites and knaves of every cast and description, allow me to congratulate you! Never was a vagabond race more prosperous. Never did successful villainy rejoice in brighter visions of the future than ye may indulge. Ye may plunder and rob with impunity—your feet [are] on the people's necks, they are transformed into tame, crouching slaves, ready to be trampled on. . .

1. What is Mackenzie's message?
2. What colourful words and phrases does Mackenzie use to make his point? What other devices does he use?
3. Do you think that Mackenzie is successful in getting his point across?
4. Rewrite Mackenzie's message using today's language.

Looking at a Situation from Another Point of View

1. How do you think the Native peoples felt when the settlers moved into and settled on their traditional lands? What problems do you think developed?

Conceptualizing

1. Settlement is a major concept in this textbook. Review the steps on concept formation as found on page 39. Make a bulletin board display of your triad's idea of settlement. Use the Great Migration as your example.

Communicating Ideas

Writing

1. Read about the experiences of the men and the women who worked in the timber industry. Put yourself in the role of a worker in Lower Canada. Write three journal entries: the day you made the decision to take your job after considering its merits over working on a farm; a day during your winter in the woods; and a day during the raft journey downstream.
2. Write a character description of a wife or mother of a Château Clique or Family Compact member. Include how she dressed and lived, and what she believed.
3. Which person in this chapter would you have liked to have met? Tell why.
4. What role did the ordinary people have in the government of Lower and Upper Canada before the rebellions?
5. Do research in your school library to find out what part Baldwin and Ryerson played in the rebellion. Write a biography for each.

Speaking

1. You are a newspaper reporter interviewing immigrants as they step off their ship in Montreal. Ask them about their reasons for leaving their homeland, their experiences during their journey, and their expectations for life in Canada.

Listening

1. Conduct a campaign for election to the Upper or Lower Canada Legislative Assembly. Create campaign posters and write a major campaign speech. Deliver your speech to a group of other students. Remember that politicians often use very forceful language while seeking election.

Creating

1. Create a newspaper issue in Upper Canada or Lower Canada devoted to the 1837 Rebellion. Include:
   a) articles describing events of the rebellion
   b) columns analyzing causes and effects
   c) columns speculating on what Lord Durham's recommendations might be
   d) "Letters to the Editor" and
   e) an editorial.

2. Create a collage that visually describes the Family Compact and the Château Clique.

Canada Revisited

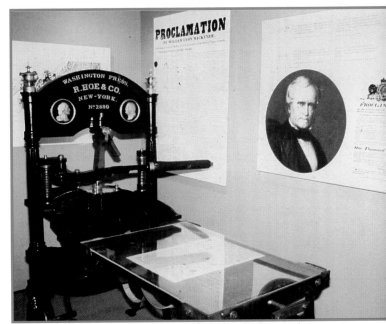

William Lyon Mackenzie's printing press in a reconstructed print shop in Mackenzie House, Toronto.

Chapter 8
Planting the Seed of Nationhood
(1838–1855)

O v e r v i e w

Use this Overview to predict the events of this chapter.

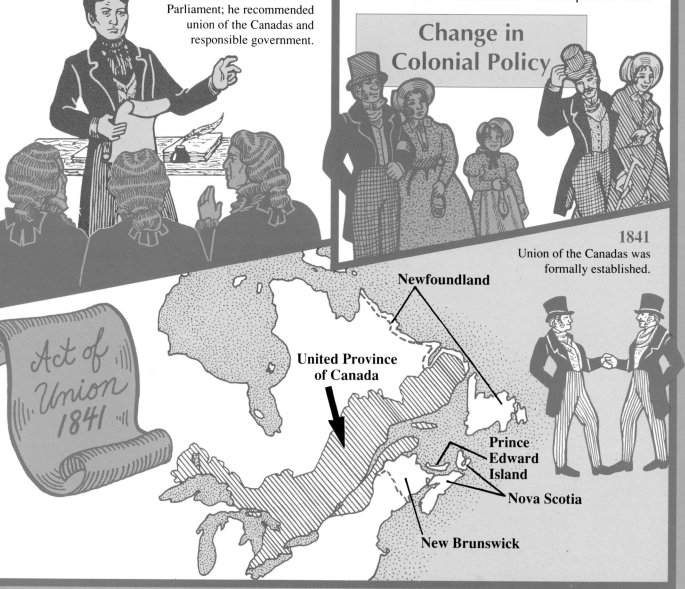

1838

The British government sent Lord Durham to investigate the rebellions in Upper and Lower Canada. Lord Durham presented his report on the affairs of British North America to the British Parliament; he recommended union of the Canadas and responsible government.

1840s

The British government wanted the colonies to take more control of local matters. Ordinary men should be given more influence in the government. The British government wished to become less involved in the government of British North America. It also adopted free trade.

Change in Colonial Policy

1841

Union of the Canadas was formally established.

Act of Union 1841

Newfoundland

United Province of Canada

Prince Edward Island

Nova Scotia

New Brunswick

The first steam railway in British North America had been in operation since 1836.

1849
Rebellion Losses Bill

Rebellion Losses Bill

The Rebellion Losses Bill was to pay the people of Canada East for property damaged or destroyed during the Rebellion of 1837. Riots broke out immediately after Lord Elgin, the governor general, signed the bill, and the Parliament Building was set on fire.

1850s
Some cities were beginning to get modern conveniences—gaslight in some houses and along a few streets, simple sewers to carry away used water. Photography came to Canada.

Chapter 8 Focus

Chapter 7 introduced you to the many changes that occurred in Upper and Lower Canada from 1815 to 1838. Chapter 8 shows how the people's voice became increasingly important in government decision-making after 1839. Power, co-operation, decision-making, and conflict are all important concepts for this chapter. The concept of conflict is the special focus of Chapter 8.

Power

Co-operation

Decision-making

Conflict

Overview/Prediction Chart

Examine the Overview found on the previous pages. In pairs or small groups use the Overview and what you already know about the events that occurred in Canada to predict answers to the questions in the Prediction Chart. Put your predictions in the "My Predictions" column. Once you have finished the chapter, complete the "What I Found Out" column to help you review and summarize. Your teacher will provide you with a full-sized working copy of the Prediction Chart.

Prediction Chart—What Do You Think?		
Questions	**My Predictions** (fill out now)	**What I Found Out** (fill out at end of chapter)
1. What might be the major events?		
2. Who might be some of the important people or groups?	SAMPLE	
3. Who might hold power?		
4.		

Definition Review*

The British Government:
- made the important decisions; had the real power
- appointed the governor to run the colony on its behalf

The Governor:
- was appointed by the British government
- tried to carry out the wishes of the British government
- was very powerful

The Executive Council:
- consisted of members appointed by the governor for as long as he chose to keep them on the council
- advised the governor
- ran the government

The Legislative Council:
- consisted of members of the local elite who could be appointed by the governor for life
- advised the governor
- proposed laws

The Legislative Assembly:
- was elected by the people
- consisted of the representatives of the people
- imposed taxes and made laws to serve local needs
- had limited power since the governor, Legislative Council, and Executive Council could veto its laws

Legend and Notes

▇ Monarchy (Crown)

▇ Elite (a small number of powerful citizens)

▇ People (whose participation makes this government a democracy)

Note:
- Councils were appointed.
- Assemblies were elected.
- During this time period, voters had to be male property owners in order to vote.

 Power was held by the monarchy and the local elite.

*The positions represented on this page are those as set out in the Constitutional Act of 1791 (see pages 119 and 120).

Upper and Lower Canada

Lord Durham was sent by the British government to study the situation in Upper and Lower Canada, investigate the grievances that had sparked rebellions, and search for a solution. Durham stayed only five months in the Canadas. During this time he and his team of experts talked to many people. Upon his return to Britain, he wrote his "Report on the Affairs of British North America," which became known as the Durham Report.

C-5456. National Archives of Canada, Ottawa.

Lord Durham (1792–1840)

John George Lambton, better known as Lord Durham, arrived in Quebec City as governor general of British North America in May of 1838.* He was sent to investigate the causes of the Rebellions of 1837.

Lord Durham was especially interested in educating the poor and giving people more control over the government. He had been nicknamed "Radical Jack" in the British House of Commons because of his **radical policies**.

His most immediate task, upon arrival, was to decide what to do with the Patriotes—those who supported the Rebellions in 1837 in Lower Canada—who were still in jail in Lower Canada. He decided to set most of them free and to **exile** the leaders to Bermuda. Louis-Joseph Papineau and others who had fled to the United States were to be executed if they tried to return to the Canadas.

Durham resigned as governor general toward the end of 1838 because he felt that he was not getting enough support from the British government. He returned to England and took two months to write his report. He died soon after, on July 28, 1840.

The Durham Report

Durham made two major recommendations in his report:

1. **The two colonies of Upper and Lower Canada should become one colony called the United Province of Canada.**

Uniting Lower and Upper Canada would place the English in the majority. This was intended as a way of uniting the English-speaking people and giving them a majority in the Legislative Assembly.

2. **The new united colony should have responsible government.**

- British imperial powers would be set out in writing. All other local powers would be handled by the colonies.

- On matters involving only colonists, the governor would be advised only by his Executive Council, with no input from the British government.

- The governor would not take sides, but would sign into law any bills recommended by the Executive Council.

- The Executive Council members would be chosen by the leader of the largest group in the Legislative Assembly rather than by the governor. This would mean that members of the Executive Council would really be chosen by the people's representatives. This is called responsible government. **

- Members of the Executive Council would keep their jobs only as long as they had the support of more than half the members of the Legislative Assembly, rather than for as long as the governor chose to keep them on the council.

---

*Lord Durham was appointed governor general of British North America—not lieutenant-governor of Upper Canada and Lower Canada—but governor general of all of British North America.
Radical policy—plan for extreme changes
Exile—to officially order someone to leave the country
**This is what happens in the federal or provincial government's Cabinet today.

The Act of Union, 1841

Introduction

The British government decided to act on one of Lord Durham's recommendations. The Act of Union of 1841 joined Upper and Lower Canada together as the United Province of Canada. The Act of Union was the first step toward Confederation (the union of the British North American colonies). It was hoped that the English-speaking members from both areas would unite and control the Legislative Assembly by having the majority of votes.

Aim: to unite the two colonies of Canada into a single unit, and to give the English-speaking people control of the newly named colony.

Key Terms

- Eliminate separate governments in Upper Canada and Lower Canada and create a single government with equal representation from Canada West and Canada East.* The system of government was to be the same as in the past.

- Establish English as the official language of government.**

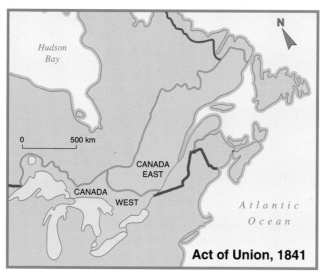

The Act of Union of 1841 joined Upper Canada and Lower Canada to become the United Province of Canada.

*Refer to pages 120 and 128 to review the type of government in existence before the Act of Union.
** By 1848 the Government of the Province of Canada recognized both English and French as the languages of government. In 1969 English and French became the official languages of Canada.

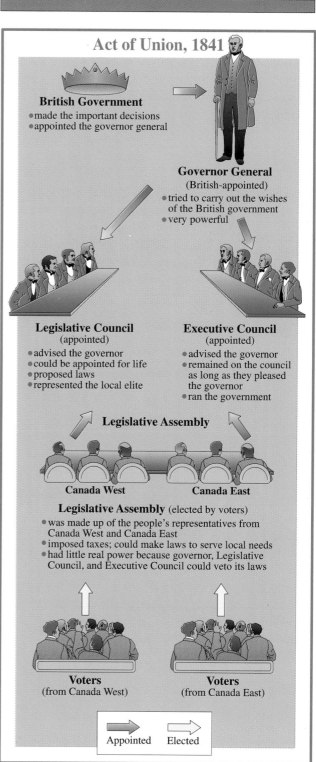

Act of Union, 1841

British Government
- made the important decisions
- appointed the governor general

Governor General
(British-appointed)
- tried to carry out the wishes of the British government
- very powerful

Legislative Council
(appointed)
- advised the governor
- could be appointed for life
- proposed laws
- represented the local elite

Executive Council
(appointed)
- advised the governor
- remained on the council as long as they pleased the governor
- ran the government

Legislative Assembly

Canada West   Canada East

Legislative Assembly (elected by voters)
- was made up of the people's representatives from Canada West and Canada East
- imposed taxes; could make laws to serve local needs
- had little real power because governor, Legislative Council, and Executive Council could veto its laws

Voters
(from Canada West)

Voters
(from Canada East)

Appointed   Elected

Colonial Policy in Great Britain

Britain was beginning to rethink its imperial (colonial) policies in the 1840s. After all, the point of having colonies was so that they could provide natural resources for the imperial power. Instead, they seemed to be very expensive. Finally, in 1846, the British government decided to stop giving its colonies special trading protection and to freely trade with all nations. This affected Britain's attitude toward her colonies. There is no point in being involved in the internal politics of the British North American colonies if they were no longer important to Britain's economic well-being.

Lord Elgin

In 1847, James Bruce, the Earl of Elgin, was appointed to be the new governor general of Canada. His instructions were to permit responsible government in British North America.

Rebellion Losses Bill

The first test of responsible government came in 1849, when the Rebellion Losses Bill was presented to the Legislative Assembly. The purpose of the **bill** was to pay the people of Canada East for property damaged or destroyed during the Rebellion of 1837. The people of Canada West who had suffered losses had already been repaid.

The Tories were strongly opposed to this bill. They did not want any of the rebels to receive payment. The Tories were strongly opposed to the Rebellion Losses Bill because they felt the rebels were traitors. They did not want any of the rebels to receive payment. Governor Elgin did not like the bill either, but he was committed to the principle of responsible government, which meant that he must follow the wishes of the majority in the Legislative Assembly. They wanted the bill passed.

Reaction to the Rebellion Losses Bill

On April 25, 1849, Lord Elgin signed the Rebellion Losses Bill. The Tory reaction was immediate. There were riots in Toronto and Kingston. But the most violent protest was in Montreal. On the night the bill was signed, an angry mob stormed the Parliament Building and set it on fire. The building was destroyed. The governor was pelted with rotten eggs and stones. Vegetables, dead rats, and garbage were thrown at members of the Legislative Assembly.

After a few months the protests faded away, but the Rebellion Losses Bill remained in effect. In frustration, some of the English-speaking Tories began to look elsewhere. Three hundred of them signed the **Annexation Manifesto,** which proposed that the Province of Canada drop its ties with Britain and join the United States.

Lord Elgin rode home in this coach on April 25, 1849, the day he signed the Rebellion Losses Bill. The angry crowd threw rotten eggs and stones at Lord Elgin's coach.

Bill—a proposed law that is presented to the Legislative Assembly to be debated and voted on. When it becomes law it is called an Act.
Annexation—joining of one territory to a larger political entity
Manifesto—a public declaration of intentions by an important group of people

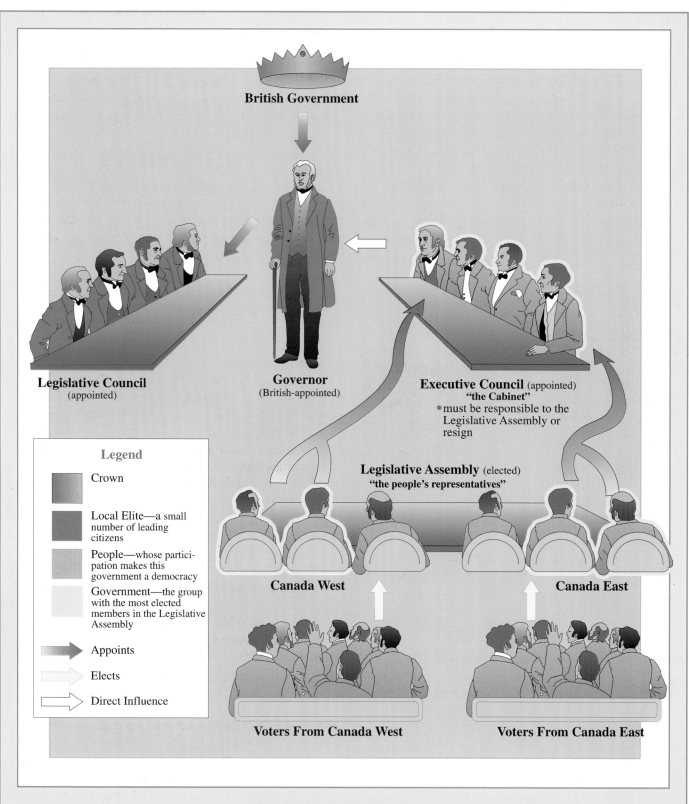

British Government

Legislative Council
(appointed)

Governor
(British-appointed)

Executive Council (appointed)
"the Cabinet"
- must be responsible to the Legislative Assembly or resign

Legislative Assembly (elected)
"the people's representatives"

Canada West

Canada East

Voters From Canada West

Voters From Canada East

Legend

Crown

Local Elite—a small number of leading citizens

People—whose participation makes this government a democracy

Government—the group with the most elected members in the Legislative Assembly

Appoints

Elects

Direct Influence

Responsible Government

Members of the Executive Council (today known as the Cabinet) are chosen from the group with the most elected members in the Legislative Assembly (rather than by the governor). The most powerful voice in the government is the Cabinet. The Cabinet is thus responsible to the representatives of the voters for its conduct of public business. If the Cabinet loses the confidence of the majority of the Legislative Assembly, it must resign. In other words, the government can function only if it has the support of the Legislature; it is *responsible* to the Legislature.

Formation of Political Parties

Before the signing of the Rebellion Losses Bill, the governor and councils held most of the power. Once responsible government was in place, the group with the most elected members controlled the Legislative Assembly. Thus they formed the government. It now made sense for members to unite in political parties in order to achieve power. Several new parties emerged at this time.

Political Party

A group of people with similar beliefs about government, who work together to get their candidates elected as representatives.

Life in the Province of Canada

In 1840, over 80 percent of the male workers of British North America worked in either agriculture or lumbering. The lumbering industry provided timber for Europe, as well as timber and sawn lumber for local use. Many farmers burned the trees from their property and made potash to sell. (*See* page 146.)

Most of the people of Canada East (formerly Lower Canada) were habitants. Their land was still held under the seigneurial system. They worked their long, narrow farms in much the same way as their ancestors had done.

In 1841, the two largest cities in Canada East were Quebec City, with a population of 31 700, and Montreal, with a population of 40 000. Life for city dwellers was showing more signs of change as the cities were the centres of business activity. Montreal was the capital for the Province of Canada from 1844 to 1849.

In Canada West (formerly Upper Canada), the main agricultural crop was wheat. From 1843 to 1846, Britain had lower import duties on wheat from British North America than from other countries. This made farmers from Canada West, millers, and other people involved in the wheat trade very prosperous.

By 1841, Toronto had a population of 15 000; Kingston, which was the capital of the Province of Canada from 1841 to 1844, had a population of 3000.

During the 1840s the cities of the Province of Canada began developing some gas lights as well as some sewer systems to take away waste water along the main streets.

Transportation and Communication

Since the 1820s transportation in Upper and Lower Canada had been made easier by the construction of canals. In 1825 the Lachine Canal was completed. About 10 kilometres in length, it took ships around the Lachine Rapids south of Montreal.

By the 1830s, the Welland Canal had by-passed Niagara Falls. This made it possible for ships to travel all the way to Fort William, at the western end of Lake Superior.

The Rideau Canal, completed in 1832, provided a safe route from Bytown (later called Ottawa) to Kingston. The authorities feared that the St. Lawrence River, bordered on the south by the United States, was vulnerable to attack by the Americans. The Ottawa River and the Rideau Canal provided a route between Upper and Lower Canada that was completely in British North American territory.

The first railway in British North America was a 24-kilometre line south of Montreal built in 1836. Most of the early railways connected waterways. They were built because railways were cheaper than canals. Throughout the 1840s, less than 100 kilometres of track were built in British North America. Throughout the 1850s, about 3200 kilometres of track were built in British North America. Several of the lines connected British North American cities with American port cities such as New York and Portland, Maine.

During the 1840s, mail service in British North America improved. By 1847, messages could also be sent by telegraph to most of the cities of British North America.

The 1840s and 1850s were times of great population increase, as well as development of cities and transportation networks, in the Province of Canada and the Maritimes.

Exploring Further

1. Do research to find out what roles women and children had in the Province of Canada during the 1840s.

After the Rebellions

by Nancy Sellars Marcotte

Just now it is late, late at night on April 25, 1849. In the past few hours I have witnessed some of the most perplexing events of my 16 years. When I came to Montreal from Toronto I knew I would hear in the streets a language I do not understand—French. But I did not expect to see Tories acting with violence against the government.

My name is Robert McKinney. I am the son of Douglas McKinney the Reformer, who in 1837 was one of William Lyon Mackenzie's Rebels who marched down Yonge Street on a December night. A few years ago it might have cost my father his life if he had admitted that.

My parents think I was too young to remember the Rebellions of 1837, but I recall as though it were yesterday when I was four years old and my father came home late one night with a bullet hole in the shoulder of his coat. My mother leaned close to the light of a single candle and mended the hole so it would look like part of the shoulder seam.

It is now 12 years later, and that coat is the one I wore to keep me warm on the long trip through the woods of Canada West between Toronto and Montreal.

My father never did publicly admit to being one of the men who marched with Mr. Mackenzie in 1837, although he longed to shout with pride that he had been there. Instead of joining the men in prison, he was the lawyer who defended many of them. I remember my parents being upset when some of the men were exiled, and their tears when Mr. Lount and Mr. Matthews were hanged.

I was too young to realize that another rebellion happened in 1837. It was in Lower Canada, and had many more deaths.

My father was born on a farm north of York—the city we now call Toronto—in 1800. He is now a lawyer in Toronto, and I am his apprentice.

One late afternoon earlier this month—April 1849—I was busy closing up the office for the evening. The fire in the fireplace had died down. I had already put the day's incoming letters away in the desk, and had made a trip to the post office to mail the outgoing letters, the ones I had hand-written so carefully according to my father's instructions. Lawyer's letters could be funny or sad or boring. Somebody in Toronto had better return somebody else's cow, which had wandered into the wrong yard; an employer regretted to inform a family in Queensville that their 12-year-old son had been killed when his arm got caught in some mill machinery; somebody's debts relating to some business had not been paid.

I pulled Father's old grey coat over my shoulders and, as I always did, lightly touched the stitches hiding the old bullet hole. It reminded me of how hard Mr. Mackenzie and his friends had fought for our rights. Then I stepped out onto the wooden sidewalk of Yonge Street. The lamplighter passed me, his long pole swinging over his shoulder. I was glad of the yellow light that he set going in the streetlamp. The streets of Toronto could be very frightening at night. Even though begging could land a person in jail, many a poor person, desperate for a penny to buy some food for himself or his family, would be sleeping in the alleyways of Toronto that night. Some of these people were off the ships from Ireland. People who got too near them sometimes came down with cholera.

No one came near me as I hopped the mud puddles and ditches of the six blocks to our home. However, as I entered the gate of my father's property, a figure slipped out of the bushes. I was startled until I realized that it was my sister Charlotte, who is 13.

"Robbie, did father tell you?" she asked. Knowing that he hadn't, she went on, "Next week he's going to Montreal! Imagine! None of our family has ever travelled so far— except Grandmother and Grandfather when they came here on the ship from Scotland. Father has to go to see about some property that someone here in Toronto has inherited in Montreal. Anyway, Father is taking you to Montreal!"

"Don't be silly, Charlotte," I scolded. "Father wouldn't take me so far. And he certainly won't go to Montreal next week. Why, the ice is barely out of Lake Ontario, and the steamships to Montreal haven't started running yet this spring."

But at dinner that night, over the roast beef and potatoes and carrots,

Father told me sternly that I must pack my travelling box and prepare for a trip to Montreal. Mother started planning out loud the things that she must get ready for our trip.

"I must arrange for the laundress

although there is always the danger of the ship catching fire, or going aground."

"They say that some day we'll be able to travel by railway from Toronto to Montreal," said Charlotte.

week as Father and I rode in the stage-coach until the movement made us feel sick. Then we walked. Twice on the first day Father and I had to get out and help push the coach through mud puddles. I remembered the words Charlotte had hissed at me as we were leaving home: "Be sure to remember every inch of the trip so you can tell me all about it." I would show her a good many of those inches in the mud on my breeches.

At night we stayed in inns along the road. They had only a few rooms for travellers to sleep. We spread our blankets on dirty old mattresses. The food at the inns was little more than bread, potatoes, and salt beef, with the occasional addition of cheese and pickles. Even so, Father usually paid a dollar each night for our food and lodging.

There was one good thing about the trip. For once Father was not working at his papers, and he talked to me.

"I remember when I was a boy going to a little house in a clearing just like that," he

to wash your shirts before the trip. And the cook will pack you some food. Although I have heard that many people lose their appetites on that coach. Goodness knows, I would like to see Montreal some time, but I would rather travel by steamer—

"Charlotte, don't be silly," I told her. "They'll never be able to lay railway tracks though the woods of Canada West. Why, in some places, the road disappears into the mud every spring."

I remembered my words the next

would say. "The woman there grew up in Scotland, and she could read and write very well. Whenever we could, the children in the neighbourhood would go to her house. It was usually two days a week—Mondays and Thursdays—but not when there was too much snow or at planting time or at harvest. She would teach us how to read and write and do arithmetic."

"And that was probably enough learning for anyone," said a deep voice from the opposite corner of the coach. I jumped. I had forgotten that there was anyone else with us.

A man with huge side whiskers and a very rumpled suit struggled upright. "Have you heard what this man Egerton Ryerson is saying?" he asked. "He's in charge of schooling in Canada West, and he says every child should have schooling, no matter whether the parents can pay or not! He says that the rest of us should pay taxes to support schools, even if we have no children. Furthermore, Ryerson is visiting other countries to see what they are teaching in their schools. Reading, writing, and arithmetic aren't good enough for this man Ryerson, oh no! He says every child should also be learning history, and about government, and drawing and music as well. And not only learning, but also exercises to help them be strong!"

The very idea of all this learning seemed to be too much for the rumpled man in the corner of the coach. He slumped back into his corner. Father winked at me. We each knew what the other was thinking. Mother had read a little about what Mr. Egerton Ryerson was hoping to do with the schools of Canada West.

"I would like to be able to hire a nurse for the younger children who could read to them from the Bible," she said. "And it would be nice to have a cook who could read one of the new cookery books. As it is, I have to read any new recipe to the cook and we make it together until she has learned how to do it. And imagine if the laundress could read. We could deliver the laundry to her house, with written instructions, and not have to see her to tell her anything special we want done."

When we finally arrived at Montreal, after five days of jolting and shaking, we went to the home of a lawyer with whom Father often had correspondence. I found that the lawyer had a son who, like me, was being apprenticed to become a lawyer.

This young man—his name was Peter Sherwin—offered to take me for a walk about Montreal. I was delighted to go, and to talk to him. However, I soon found that Peter Sherwin had some very different ideas than I had. He and his friends were angry about a law that was to be passed in the Legislative Assembly that very day.

"They say that the governor general, Lord Elgin, will sign this new bill, and it will become law," said Peter. "It is called the Rebellion Losses Bill. It will repay people for property that was destroyed in the Rebellion of 1837. Can you imagine? The very people who rebelled 12 years ago will now be paid back for the things they lost!"

"But the old Reformers are now the people in the Legislative Assembly of Canada," I protested. As though I were scratching my shoulder, I reached up and touched the mended bullet hole in the shoulder of my grey coat. "They are our legal government. The governor general is supposed to sign any laws they pass, whether he agrees with them or not. That is what responsible government means. And besides, people in Upper Canada—Canada West—have already been repaid for their losses."

"Well, it isn't right. You don't sound like a good Tory to me," said Peter. "My grandfather left the Thirteen Colonies and came to British North America because he was determined to remain loyal to Britain. He would not support the so-called Patriots in the Thirteen Colonies in 1776. But now in 1849 our taxes have to go to repay those Patriotes in Lower Canada—Canada East—who were traitors to Britain in 1837."

I did not want to be rude to Peter, but I could see that we had very different ideas of how Canada should be governed. I could tell that Peter's family was part of the Château Clique, the wealthy people in Canada East who did not think the colony should be governed according to the wishes of the majority. This was like our Family Compact in Canada West. The Family Compact were the people who controlled the government that my father and Mr. Mackenzie had marched against in 1837. If they had been in Canada East, my father and Mr. Mackenzie would have been with the Patriotes fighting against Peter Sherwin's people, the Château Clique. How embarrassing!

It got worse than embarrassing when we ran into some of Peter's friends. They were so angry that the governor general was about to sign the Rebellion Losses Bill that they went to the Parliament Buildings to wait for the governor general, Lord Elgin, to leave. I think they meant to just shout their anger at him, but one of the Tories threw a rock. Vegetables, eggs, rocks, dead rats—the coach was bombarded with garbage both disgusting and dangerous.

I hung back, thinking that this would be the end and that soon we would go home. But Peter and his friends continued to walk the streets, shouting their anger that the Patriotes would be paid back for their losses in the rebellion of 12 years ago. Darkness was coming down, and I would have liked to go back to the Sherwin's home to find my father, but I was completely confused by the unfamiliar streets. It was dark when we arrived once again at the Parliament Buildings.

Rocks flew through the air. I found

The Burning of the Parliament Buildings, Montreal, by Joseph Légaré. Tories, angry that the Rebellion Losses Bill was passed by Parliament, burned the building.

it hard to believe that Tories actually decided to throw rocks at the Parliament Buildings. Then somehow the crowd was surging into the Parliament Buildings. The windows became just shards of glass. Chairs were smashed. I do not believe that anyone decided to set the building on fire. Surely that was an accident, caused by the broken glass lamps.

Just when it seemed that we must escape or be burned, an old man shouted for help. Through the flames he was dragging a portrait of Queen Victoria. Peter and I—Tory and Rebel, who were on opposite sides of this conflict—

helped to carry a picture of Queen Victoria out of the flames.

Can you see what has happened in Canada in 12 short years? And not just once, but twice—in both Upper Canada and Lower Canada. The Rebels in Upper Canada, who 12 years ago were traitors being exiled and hanged, are now the legal government of Canada West. The Patriotes in Lower Canada, who 12 years ago were traitors being exiled and hanged, are now the legal government of Canada East.

They are now one government of the United Province of Canada. They are

supposed to meet in the Parliament Buildings in Montreal, but these buildings are now burning in a fire caused by the Tories, the people who used to control the government.

The governor general has signed a law that he didn't agree with because it was passed by the majority of the representatives in the Legislative Assembly. This is responsible government.

Of course, Charlotte will say that we won't really have responsible government until women can vote too. But Charlotte thinks that one day there will be railway tracks from Montreal to Toronto! ■

Education

Until the mid-1800s, education was considered to be a privilege for children whose parents could afford to pay for it. In some areas, families got together to build schools. These schools were often little more than log cabins. Sometimes students met in the home of the teacher. Students were expected to bring wood for the school stove, and candles if it was too dark.

Books and papers were rare, so students often wrote on pieces of **slate.** Students stayed away from school to help when they were needed at home, particularly at times of planting and harvesting. Even though both boys and girls attended schools, they were sometimes expected to have little contact with each other. In some schools, boys and girls had separate entrances and schoolyards.

By the 1840s, under the influence of Egerton Ryerson, people in Canada West were beginning to think that schools should be supported by the government. When school attendance was made **universal** and **compulsory** in Ontario (formerly Canada West) in 1871, many more teachers were needed. This opened up a profession that was considered suitable for women.

Egerton Ryerson (1803–1882)

Even to this day, the person who has had the most influence on education in Canada was probably Egerton Ryerson. Ryerson was descended from Loyalists. He believed in many of the goals of the Reformers of the 1820s, but he did not support the radical policies of William Lyon Mackenzie.

Ryerson spent several years as a Methodist circuit rider, riding throughout Upper Canada to preach to people in different places. Later, when he became a newspaper editor, he was able to spread his ideas about education.

From 1846 until 1876, Ryerson was superintendent of education for Canada West (called Ontario after 1867). He visited Europe and the United States to gather ideas about education. He wanted schools to teach more than the basics of reading, writing, and arithmetic. Amongst other subjects, Ryerson wanted to include history, geography, government, art, music, and physical education.

Ryerson saw many of his ideas come into practice when Ontario passed the Schools Act in 1871, making education in Ontario universal and compulsory. Many other provinces have adopted Ryerson's ideas for education.

Left: Education was considered to be a privilege for children whose parents could afford to pay for it.

Slate—thin slice of bluish-grey rock on which people wrote
Universal—for everybody
Compulsory—required

The Atlantic Provinces

Nova Scotia

Nova Scotia was the first British colony to achieve responsible government. This occurred in 1847, when the governor of Nova Scotia was told by Britain to bring in responsible government. His instructions were to choose all of the Executive Council members from the largest political party in the Legislative Assembly.

An election was held and the Reform Party, led by J.B. Uniacke and Joseph Howe, won a majority in the Legislative Assembly. The governor asked Uniacke to choose the Executive Council members. He chose them all from the Reform Party. The Executive Council was now called the Cabinet.

C-22002, National Archives of Canada, Ottawa.

Joseph Howe (1804–1873)

Joseph Howe was a colourful politician with a reputation for good **oratory.**

He started work as an apprentice printer in his father's shop at the age of 13. At 24, he bought his own newspaper, *The Nova Scotian.* He used his newspaper to support changes in the government.

In 1835 Howe was charged with **libel** after an attack on the Halifax magistrates, who were appointed by the Executive Council. Howe chose to defend himself in court. He gave a six-hour speech to the jury, in which he described many injustices such as the unfair tax system and the way in which magistrates foreclosed on the poor. He pleaded for freedom of the press. It took the jury only 10 minutes to decide that Howe was not guilty. Afterwards, people carried him home on their shoulders. The victory celebration lasted for two days.

Howe was elected to the Legislative Assembly of Nova Scotia as a Reform candidate in 1836.

Joseph Howe had an important role to play following Confederation in 1867. You will read more about him later in this textbook.

C-73708, National Archives of Canada, Ottawa.

This painting by C.W. Jeffreys shows Joseph Howe being carried out of the courtroom by a cheering throng after his 1835 libel case.

New Brunswick, Newfoundland, and Prince Edward Island

Responsible government was also granted in the colony of New Brunswick in 1854. The colony of Newfoundland asked for it in 1846, but it was not granted until 1855.

The members of the Legislative Assembly of the colony of Prince Edward Island petitioned Britain for responsible government until they decided that petitions were not helping. Then the Legislative Assembly decided not to pass any laws or vote for the money needed to run the government. Britain granted Prince Edward Island responsible government in 1851.

Oratory—the art of public speaking
Libel—a printed statement or picture that unjustly injures a person's reputation

Review ●

Summarizing the Chapter

- Lord Durham arrived to take up his duties as governor general of British North America in May of 1838. His job was to investigate the situation in Upper and Lower Canada and to suggest solutions. The Durham Report made a number of recommendations. Two major recommendations came from the report. First, Durham recommended that the colonies of Upper and Lower Canada be united. Second, he urged that the new united colony have responsible government.

- The Act of Union of 1841, which joined the colonies of Upper and Lower Canada into the United Province of Canada, was the British government's response to the Durham Report. The British government decided in 1846 to stop giving its colonies special trading protection. Since Canada was no longer important to Britain's economic well being, there seemed no point in being so involved in its internal politics.

- The Rebellion Losses Bill paid the people in Canada East for property that had been damaged or destroyed during the Rebellion of 1837.

- The Rebellion Losses Bill became the first test of responsible government. The Tories were strongly opposed to the bill, even though the people of Canada West who had suffered losses had already been repaid. There were riots in Toronto, Kingston, and Montreal. Governor General Lord Elgin was opposed to the bill, but because he was committed to the principle of responsible government, he signed it.

- During the 1840s and 1850s, many people immigrated to Upper and Lower Canada.

Checking Predictions

1. At the beginning of this chapter you made some predictions based on the Overview and what you already knew. Now, use what you learned from reading the chapter to fill in the third column of the chart that you began earlier.

2. Discuss the following questions by referring to the Section IV story on pages 130 and 131. Answer these questions in light of the information you have gained from Chapters 7 and 8.

   (a) In what two ways did the Students' Council become more like a responsible government?

   (b) Did the Students' Council have more power before or after it became like a responsible government?

   (c) Who lost some power when the Students' Council became like a responsible government?

Working with Information

1. The title of Section IV is "The People's Voice Is Heard." Provide examples from Chapters 7 and 8 to show why this title was chosen. Suggest alternative titles.

2. Here are some main ideas from this chapter:
   - Durham Report
   - political change
   - Act of Union, 1841
   - Rebellion Losses Bill
   - violent protest
   - development of cities
   - railways
   - education

   Construct a pictorial overview showing the above ideas. Use a long strip of paper and put each idea in correct sequence with the appropriate date or dates. Provide a simple graph or illustration for each idea, depicting its importance during this period of Canada's development.

3. Use the information in Chapters 7 and 8 to prepare a game to illustrate the social or political events in the Province of Canada in the 1840s and 1850s.

Building Thinking Strategies

Evaluating Actions

As you read in this chapter, after Lord Elgin signed the Rebellion Losses Bill, mobs of people reacted angrily, pelting him and members of the Legislative Assembly with various objects and setting the Parliament Buildings on fire.

1. Why do you think people reacted in these ways?

2. What other ways of responding to Lord Elgin's decision were available to them?

3. How do you think the governor and members of the Legislative Assembly felt?

4. Do you think their actions were fair and reasonable? Why or why not?

5. How do you think you would have responded to Lord Elgin's decision had you lived in Upper or Lower Canada? Why?

Communicating Ideas

Reading

1. Read about one of the following people in the book *Great Canadian Lives: Portraits in Heroism to 1867* by Ford, MacLean, and Wansbrough: Archibald Chief of McNab clan, Strachan, Papineau, Chenier, William Lyon Mackenzie, Ryerson, Elgin, Lafontaine, Howe. Would you have liked to have been this person? Why or why not? Share your findings with a friend.

Writing

1. In his report, Lord Durham wrote: "I expected to find a contest between a government and people: I found two nations warring in the bosom of a single state: I found a struggle, not of principles, but of races; . . . " How did Lord Durham attempt to end the problems in Upper and Lower Canada? Explain your answer.

Debating

1. On page 167 you read about the new political parties that emerged in the late 1840s. Divide the class into two. Now, divide each group into four subgroups. Each subgroup will represent one of the four political parties. Because there are two sets of political parties, there will be two debates. Your teacher has additional information about your political party, or use the information on the chart on page 181.

   a) **Prepare**

   - Discuss what you know about your party's beliefs. Choose a recorder to list these ideas in point form.

   - Brainstorm other points you need to know in order to have your leader participate effectively in this debate. Record these questions. Here are examples of the kind of questions you might need to ask: How much is our party willing to co-operate with English (or French) Canadians? What is our opinion of westward expansion?

   - Come back together as a group and pool your new information. Again, have a recorder list the major points. Record your political platform (your party's beliefs) onto a wall chart. Use drawings to make it more interesting. You may wish to make up a slogan or buttons for your political party.

   - Choose a party leader from the members of your group. Help your leader to practice answering the questions you prepared previously by making suggestions for improvements.

   b) **Debate**

   - Choose a moderator from the class. Carry out the two debates. During the debate, each party leader will have a chance to respond to each of the questions. Then each leader should give a brief rebuttal to the other leaders' responses. Decide on time limits for the responses and rebuttals. Carry out the debate.

   c) **Debrief**

   - As a class, discuss and evaluate the two debates.

   - In Chapter 9 you will read that, in June 1864, three parties joined together in what was known as the Great Coalition. Based on what you have learned about the party platforms, which three do you think joined forces? Why? Write a paragraph or two in which you give your opinion.

Canada Revisited

The Rideau Canal, completed in 1832, is still in use today.

Section V
Building the Canadian Nation
1800–1911

Do you remember the last time we listened in at Fairmont School? The system of student government was in the process of undergoing a major change. Instead of the principal dealing with representatives from the council, who were of her choice, the Students' Council chose its own representatives. Also, within certain areas the Students' Council could make its own decisions, which could not be overruled by the principal.

As you discovered by reading Chapters 7 and 8, this situation was remarkably similar to the situation in the British North American colonies in the 1840s and 1850s. It was during this period that they were granted responsible government. This meant that members of the Executive Council were chosen from the group with the most elected members in the Legislative Assembly, rather than by the governor. If the Exective Council lost the confidence of the Legislative Assembly, then its members had to resign. The Governor

was to go along with the decisions made by the people's elected representatives although some subjects were still closed to them.

Act I

We join a Fairmont School council meeting in progress.

Farrah: I have an incredible idea! I was at the mall the other day looking for a CD and I ran into my friend, Pam, from Thompson School. She said that Students' Council representatives from four or five different schools are getting together to talk about a way to join forces.

John: What do you mean ?

Farrah: Well, we would have a mega-council that would be made up of representatives from all the

schools that joined.

Tammy: Come to think of it, maybe there is strength in numbers.

Sam: The only thing is, if we join the others are we going to lose the power to make decisions in our own school?

Todd: I don't see why we would. We could have a separate election in our school for a representative who would be part of this mega-council. Our own Students' Council would be the same as it has always been.

Farrah: Well, what do you think? The first meeting is next week. Should one of us go?

Sam: Why don't you go, Farrah? At least you know someone there. You can report back to us at our next meeting.

Farrah: Okay, if it's all right with everyone, I'll do that.

Act II

Next meeting.

Tammy: Well, Farrah, how did the big meeting go? Did anything interesting happen?

Farrah: The meeting went really well. We

listened to the pros and cons of forming a mega-council and all the kids there decided it was a good idea. Everyone has now gone back to try to convince the other kids in their schools to go ahead with it.

Todd: Okay, Farrah, what were the pros and cons? Don't bore us. Just summarize.

Farrah: Well, one advantage of joining would be to keep in touch with what's going on at other schools. We could learn from their experience and not repeat the same mistakes.

Another advantage would be that we could trade.

John: Like what?

Farrah: Well, ideas for one thing. We could trade good ideas for dances, fund-raising, new cheers, and lots of other things.

Sam: Maybe we could even trade actual things like unused sports or lab equipment, art supplies, and things like that. We could trade things we aren't using in return for other things that we need. That way we could save money for things that we wouldn't normally be able to buy.

Todd: Don't forget the advantages of power in numbers! Maybe we could even pool money once in awhile to buy something really expensive that could be shared among the schools.

John: Yes, like a set of great telescopes so we could really get into astronomy!

Todd: Well, whatever.

Sam: Come to think of it, there's more to this idea of power in numbers than meets the eye. What if all the kids in this mega-council decide that it would be a good idea to make some change in their schools? Say, for instance, they all decided that there should be no fines for overdue library books. Wouldn't they have a lot of power if their principals knew that the same topic was being discussed in all the schools that had reps on the mega-council?

John: I'm starting to like this mega-council idea.

Tammy: Maybe after it's been going for awhile, the mega-council could take responsibility for some decisions that would apply to all the schools. Then we could do a better job on our own school councils of the things that we are responsible for.

John: What a great idea! Maybe the mega-council could take over the planning of dances. If we did that, we could probably get special rates on the music, decorations, and whatever else we needed to buy.

Tammy: What about disadvantages?

Farrah: Well, the only one we thought of was that one Sam brought up last time about losing our own power. We would be turning over some of our power to a central Student's Council government. But none of us could see how that could actually happen. We decided there weren't any disadvantages.

Todd: Let's go for it!

Sam: Let's have a vote! ∎

Questions to Talk About

Discuss the following questions by referring to the story you have just read. Keep them in mind while you read the following three chapters. At the end of the three chapters you will be asked to answer similar questions based on the information you have gained from your reading.

1. How would student representatives joining together in a mega-council be helpful to all the individual schools?
2. Would the distance between the various schools be a problem? Explain.
3. How would decisions be made in this new situation?
4. How important is leadership in the mega-council?
5. What are the advantages of joining the mega-council?
6. Would there be advantages to not joining?
7. Who would hold the power in this new situation?
8. Would there be fears of any one group dominating the larger group? Explain.

Chapter 9

The Drive to Nationhood
(1854–1868)

Overview
Use this Overview to predict the events of this chapter.

1854–1866
Reciprocity Treaty with the United States—the British colonies in North America were prosperous. Reciprocity ended in 1866. If the colonies would join together and trade amongst themselves, economic prosperity would perhaps continue.

1857–1864
A political deadlock occurred in the Legislative Assembly of Canada, making it impossible to pass important laws.

Legislative Assembly

1850s
Railways were built to improve transportation and communication. If the colonies joined together they could all share in the costs of railway building.

1860s
Britain was changing her attitude about her British North American Colonies. Britain told the governors of each colony to encourage the colonies to join together.

1864
In spite of their differences, some of the politicians in the Canadas decided to join together and form a federal union for the good of the country.

1864
Pressure was exerted for a Maritime Union.

MARITIME UNION!

1864
Charlottetown Conference (September)

1864
Quebec Conference (October).
The 72 Resolutions
were drafted.

1866
The Fenians, a group of Irish Catholics in the United States, wanted to end British rule over Ireland. They led several armed raids across the border into British North American colonies.

1866
London Conference drafted the British North America Act.

1867
On July 1, Nova Scotia, New Brunswick, Quebec, and Ontario joined together to form the Dominion of Canada.

Quebec

New Brunswick

Ontario

Nova Scotia

Chapter 9 Focus

Chapter 8 detailed specific events and people who worked to give more people a voice in government. Chapter 9 is about some of the many problems Canada faced on the way to nationhood and what attempts were made to solve them. This chapter will emphasize co-operation and decision-making during the period from 1854 to 1868.

| **Power** | **Co-operation** | **Decision-making** | Conflict |

Overview/Prediction Chart

Examine the Overview on the previous pages. In pairs or small groups, use the Overview and what you already know about Canada's formation as a nation to predict answers to the questions in the Prediction Chart. Put your predictions in the "My Predictions" column. Once you have finished the chapter, complete the "What I Found Out" column to help you review and summarize. Your teacher will provide you with a full-sized working copy of the Prediction Chart.

Prediction Chart—What Do You Think?		
Questions	My Predictions (fill out now)	What I Found Out (fill out at end of chapter)
1. What might be the major events?		
2. Who might be some of the important people or groups?		
3. Who might hold power?		
4.		

Discussion

1. Lord Durham in his statement on page 175 says: "I found two nations warring in the bosom of a single state." As a group develop definitions for the terms nation, nationhood, and state. You may want to refer to the definition of nation on page 7.

   a) Based on the definitions you developed discuss whether you agree with Lord Durham or not.

   b) Canada is made up of "two founding peoples—the British and the French." Speculate what problems may occur when two such groups attempt to bring about nationhood.

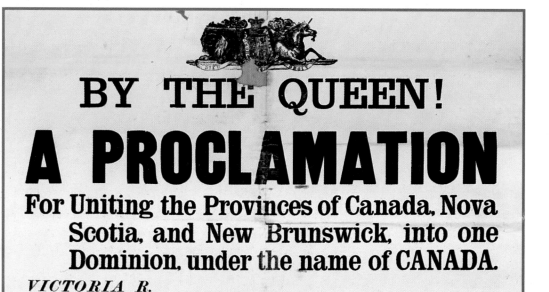

On Monday, July 1, 1867, market squares and open places in front of public buildings were packed with people eager to hear Queen Victoria's proclamation that the Province of Canada, Nova Scotia, and New Brunswick had been united into one Dominion under the name of Canada.

The Province of Canada: 1854–1867

The union of the two Canadas, which had taken place in 1841 (the Act of Union, *see* page 164), was not successful. Not one political party could seem to get the support of a majority of the Legislative Assembly and implement any changes.

The *Canadiens* (French) believed that the English Canadians were trying to make them lose their cultural identity (their language, religion, and culture). The English Canadians accused the *Canadiens* of trying to run everything their way. Refer to the chart below when reading this page.

"Rep by Pop"

One of the disagreements between French- and English-speaking members of the Legislative Assembly was representation by population or "**rep by pop**." In rep by pop the number of elected members of the Legislative Assembly is based on the number of voters.

The reformers in Canada West, led by George Brown and his Clear Grit party, were pushing for rep by pop. This would mean that, since its population was larger, Canada West would have more representatives in the Legislative Assembly than Canada East would have. The representatives from Canada East, led by George-Étienne Cartier, were against rep by pop, since it would result in less power for them in the Legislative Assembly. It seemed unfair since, in the past when Canada East had a larger population than Canada West, the two had equal representation in the Legislative Assembly.

Political Deadlock

 There was disagreement in the Legislative Assembly at this time. Since there was an equal number of representatives from Canada West and Canada East, the two groups often voted against one another and major legislation could not be passed. A deadlock resulted.

Fortunately, George Brown, the leader of the Clear Grits, and John A. Macdonald, the leader of the Tories, were able to save the situation.* Even though the two men had been bitter enemies for years, they put aside their personal feelings and acted for the good of the country. George Brown stood up in the Legislative Assembly and said that he would work with Macdonald and George-Étienne Cartier, the leader of the Bleus. Together they could form a **federal union** of the Province of Canada (Canada West and Canada East), the Atlantic colonies, and the North-West Territories. The offer was accepted and the groups united to work for a federal union. A government where the political parties work together is called a coalition.

Political Party Chart			
Canada West		**Canada East**	
POLITICAL PARTY AND LEADER	**BELIEFS**	**POLITICAL PARTY AND LEADER**	**BELIEFS**
Clear Grit Party George Brown	**Reformers** (wanted to change and improve things)	**Le Parti Rouge** A.A. Dorion	**Reformers** (favoured rights of *Canadiens*)
Liberal-Conservative Party (Tories) John A. Macdonald	believed in British system of government (against change in government)	**Le Parti Bleus** (Bleu) George-Étienne Cartier	favoured co-operation between *Canadiens* and English-speaking Canadians

---

Rep by pop —The number of elected members of a Legislative Assembly (the representatives) is based on the number of voters (based on the population). "Rep by pop" is an abbreviation for representation by population.

*The Tories are today called the Conservatives.
Federal union — a political union in which the members have certain powers over their own affairs, and certain powers are turned over to a central government

Reasons for Federal Union (Confederation)

Why do you think the political parties in the Canadas decided to work towards a federal union (Confederation) at this time? Many changes had taken place during the 1850s and early 1860s that had led to this decision. There were basically five reasons why the politicians of the 1860s were in favour of Confederation:

1. When there is a political deadlock, no laws can get passed. That was when the Great Coalition was formed. (You have already read about the problems in the government of the United Province of Canada [Canada East and Canada West].)
2. A railway was needed to link the colonies.
3. Trade with the United States was ending.
4. There was a threat of an American expansion into British North America.
5. Britain was changing her attitude about the British North American Colonies.

1. Political Deadlock and the Great Coalition

The Great Coalition was formed in June of 1864. The parties joined together in a new political party that they called the Confederation Party. The purpose of the Confederation Party was to create a federal union in the Province of Canada (Canada East and Canada West) and seek a larger union with the other British North American colonies: the colony of Newfoundland, the colony of Nova Scotia, the colony of Prince Edward Island, and the colony of New Brunswick. Eventually, they hoped that the colonies of Vancouver Island, British Columbia, and the North-West Territories would become part of the union.

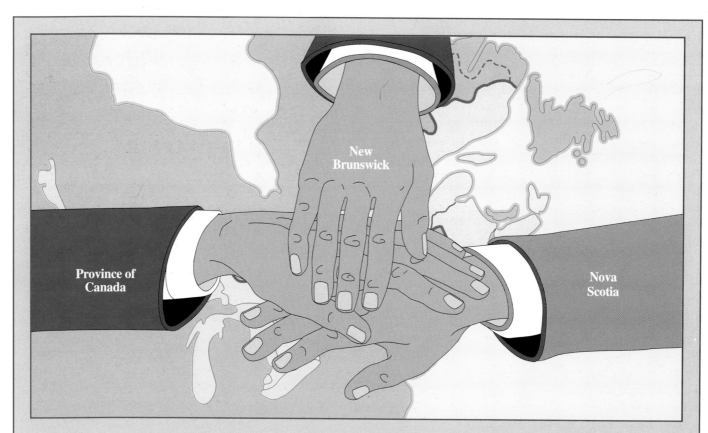

Confederation

In 1867, the British North American colonies of New Brunswick, Nova Scotia, and the Province of Canada (Canada East and Canada West) agreed to join together to form a nation that would be a federal union. This was Confederation. The members in this union would retain some power over their own affairs and would turn some powers over to a more powerful central government. This central government, located in Ottawa, is Canada's federal government.

2. A Railway Was Needed

The Province of Canada was separated from the Atlantic colonies by the mountains in Gaspé and northern Maine, and by the ice that closed the St. Lawrence River each winter. The railways made the distance between the colonies seem much shorter. Before the railway, mail delivery took a week. After the railway was built it took a day. The first important railway line ran from Montreal to Portland in the United States. This gave merchants in Montreal a means of getting their goods out of Canada East even in the winter. They no longer had to worry about the St. Lawrence River freezing over.

The railway enabled mail and goods to go to the colonies in a shorter amount of time.

Focus On: The Railway-Building Era

This is the Great Western station at London, Ontario, in 1858. The large building in the background is Tecumseh House. It was the largest hotel in British North America at this time.

In British North America there was an obsession with building railways in the 1850s. By 1860 Nova Scotia, New Brunswick, Canada West, and Canada East all had their own railways. Travel by water was very slow and the rivers froze in the winter, making it impossible to get goods to market. The railways made it possible to get farm crops and manufactured goods to market quickly and cheaply. This provided a tremendous interest in Canadian manufacturing.

Unfortunately, it did not take long before the railways were in financial difficulty. By 1860 the Grand Trunk Railway, which ran from Sarnia in the west to Rivière-du-Loup in the east, was virtually bankrupt. In 1861, it declared a deficit of 13 million dollars. The Great Western Railway, which ran from the Niagara River to Windsor, also ended up in financial trouble.

The government could not let the railways go bankrupt because of their importance to the economy. As a result, the railway companies did not have to repay most of their loans.

This was very expensive for the taxpayers of Canada.

After 1860, railway building in the British North American colonies came to a virtual halt. By this time a new dream was beginning. This was the dream of a new nation united by a railway, built from sea to sea. If the colonies joined together and they all shared in the costs, an **intercolonial railway** and a railway to the Pacific Coast would be possible.

Intercolonial railway—a railway that joins the various colonies

C-18737, National Archives of Canada, Ottawa (detail).

This painting depicts a battle between Fenians and British soldiers that took place in 1866 at Ridgeway near Niagara. The Fenians wore green and carried a green flag with a gold harp. The British wore red.

3. Trade with the United States

Because the British North American colonies were part of the British Empire, they received favoured status when they traded with Britain. This meant that owners of products such as timber and wheat either paid low taxes (**tariffs**) or no taxes when they entered Britain. People importing products from places that were not part of Britain's empire were forced to pay high tariffs and did not receive tariff protection.

In 1846 Britain entered a period of **free trade.** This meant that Britain bought goods from whichever country sold them at the lowest price. The colonies of British North America lost their special status with Britain and as a result lost most of their markets. Economic hard times resulted.

The economic situation improved in 1854 when a trade agreement, called the Reciprocity Treaty, was signed between British North America and the United States. Reciprocity meant that there would be free trade in natural products between the British North American colonies and the United States. It meant that the British North American colonies could sell their products to the United States without paying tariffs whenever products entered or left an area. Soon new American markets joined old British markets.

In 1865 the United States decided to end the Reciprocity Treaty. Soon an idea began to spread among the colonies of British North America: if the colonies joined together and traded among themselves, removing the tariffs between their various colonies, economic prosperity would continue.*

4. Threat of American Expansion Northward

During the 1860s the Northern and Southern American states had been at war with one another. Southern raiders had used Canadian territory as a base from which to attack the Northern states. At the end of the Civil War, in 1865, the Northern states accused the British colonies of helping Southerners who were fleeing from Northern troops. The British government, to some extent, had sided with the South. There was talk of invading the British North American colonies.

In 1866 the Fenians made several armed raids across the border into the British North American colonies. The Fenians were a group of Irish Catholics in the United States who wanted to end British rule over Ireland. Since they could not get at Britain directly, they decided to attack her North American colonies. Fenian border raids were another example of a threat from the American states.

Tariff—a tax paid on goods brought into a country or colony
Free trade—trade between countries where taxes or tariffs are not involved
*Each of the colonies of British North America had tariffs on goods entering them.

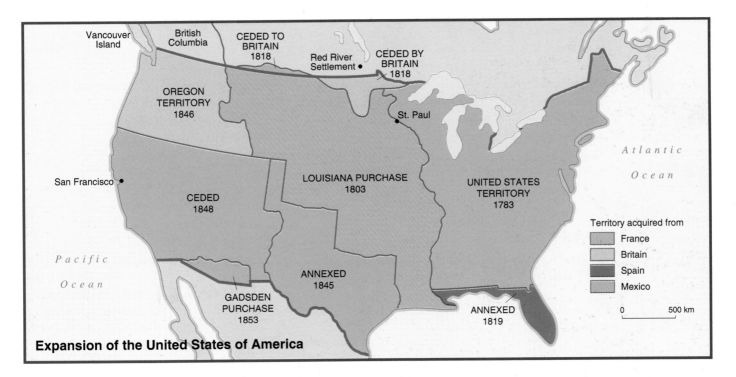

Expansion of the United States of America

Territory acquired from
- France
- Britain
- Spain
- Mexico

0   500 km

After the American Civil War the Americans entered into a period of western expansion. They had obtained land from Spain, Mexico, France, and Great Britain (Oregon) as their people moved westward. Many people in the colonies were concerned about the American threat to western lands in British North America. Would the Americans try to buy land in British North America from Britain? Would they invade as they had done in the past (during the American Revolution, during the War of 1812, and recently during the Fenian border raids)?

The Americans in the colony of Red River wanted it to join the United States. There was already a great deal of trade going on between Red River and the American community of St. Paul.

There was also a danger that the most western colonies of Vancouver Island and British Columbia could be taken over by the United States. Many American miners, who had flooded in during the gold rush in the late 1850s and early 1860s, had settled in the area. Also, there was much trade going on between the two British colonies and the American port of San Francisco.

Good farmland in Canada West was getting more difficult to obtain. Many people in Canada West looked to the lands to the west (present-day Manitoba, Saskatchewan, and Alberta) as a possible area for settlement; but the Americans too were thinking about moving into these western lands. If the colonies of British North America were to join together and annex these western lands, they would get the land before the Americans did.

Many people in the British North American colonies were concerned about the American threat. They thought that if they united they would be better able to defend themselves.

5. Changing British Attitudes

The British were also concerned about the American threat. It was very expensive to defend the British North American colonies. They thought that if the colonies united they would be able to defend themselves, and the British army would not have to help them. The British governors in each of the colonies were told to encourage the colonies to unite (Confederation).

Britain's decision to encourage union was very important because the British North American colonists were still intensely loyal to Britain. If Britain wanted Confederation, then many people would be inclined to favour it for that reason alone. Britain's change in attitude towards her British North American colonies meant Britain was in favour of these colonies taking on more responsibility for governing themselves. This factor played an important part in Canada's struggle for self-government.

> *As fragments, we shall be lost; but let us be united and we shall be as a rock.*
>
> **Thomas D'Arcy McGee**
> Canada East
>
> *If we desire to obtain England's support for our defence, we must help ourselves. When we are united, the enemy will know that if he attacks any province he will have to deal with the combined forces of the Empire.*
>
> **George-Étienne Cartier**
> Canada East

185

The Atlantic Colonies: 1854–1864

By the early 1860s the Atlantic colonies of Newfoundland, Nova Scotia, Prince Edward Island, and New Brunswick were facing some serious problems. For one thing, there was little industrial development in the region. As a result, there was little population growth. Many people were forced to leave to look for work elsewhere.

Trade was another problem. The United States was planning by 1866 to end the special trade treaty (the Reciprocity Treaty of 1854), whereby many goods passed across the border without duty. Also, the British policy of free trade with all nations, which Britain had put in place in 1846, had meant less demand in Britain for goods from the Atlantic colonies. The dwindling American and British markets meant that it was very important to develop new markets within the British North American colonies.

The Atlantic colonies were also concerned about the threat of American expansion and knew they would be stronger if they banded together.

For these reasons, the Atlantic colonies began to look at the idea of a maritime union. A conference was scheduled for September of 1864 in Charlottetown, Prince Edward Island, to discuss the possible union of the Atlantic colonies.

Left: Saint John, New Brunswick, prior to Confederation.

Below: 948 140 17, courtesy of the Royal Ontario Museum

Above: Halifax was the oldest city in the Atlantic colonies.

Left: Charlottetown, Prince Edward Island, was where the Charlottetown Conference was held in 1864.

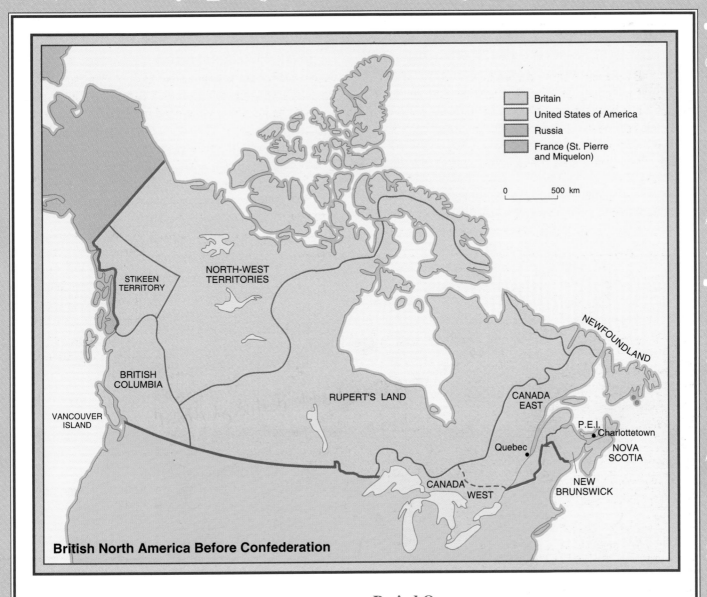

British North America Before Confederation

Map legend:
- Britain
- United States of America
- Russia
- France (St. Pierre and Miquelon)

0   500 km

Labels on map: STIKEEN TERRITORY, NORTH-WEST TERRITORIES, BRITISH COLUMBIA, VANCOUVER ISLAND, RUPERT'S LAND, CANADA WEST, CANADA EAST, Quebec, NEWFOUNDLAND, P.E.I., Charlottetown, NOVA SCOTIA, NEW BRUNSWICK

An Exercise in Decision-Making

The colonies of Nova Scotia, New Brunswick, and Prince Edward Island are meeting to discuss maritime union. The Province of Canada asked to join the discussion. It is August 1864. You are one of the delegates at this conference. Since there are representatives from four colonies (Nova Scotia, New Brunswick, Prince Edward Island, and the Province of Canada—made up of Canada East and Canada West) at this meeting, you are to divide your class into four groups.* Each group should represent one of the colonies of British North America and should move to one part of the classroom. As a group, you are to perform a number of tasks. You will be asked later on in this activity to meet as a large group and carry out a role play activity.

Period One

Task 1 (one period with homework)—Do research in the library to find out what your colony was like in 1864. Prepare a large chart containing the following information to display in your colony's work area: the name of your colony, your capital city, your location on a map of British North America, the names (and perhaps pictures) of your colony's political leaders, your population, your main economic activities, and your colony's special needs. Pick a recorder and a leader for your group. The leader should assume the name of the actual leader of the colony. Your teacher has role play cards for the members of your group to use.

---

*Newfoundland did not attend this conference.

Period Two

Task 2 (10 minutes of Period 2)—The members of your group have mixed feelings about this new idea of political union. Some of you are in favour of union and some are against it. In character and as a group, brainstorm your feelings about having your colony join with the other colonies of British North America. The note-taker should write the ideas from brainstorming on chart paper. What problems is your colony facing? Is it to your advantage to have your colony join with the other colonies? What will your colony gain? What will your colony lose? What type of government do you want in order to protect your colony's special needs?

Task 3 (20 minutes of Period 2)—In chart form make a list of all the factors your colony should consider when deciding whether you should join Confederation. Remember, you must consider the wishes of everyone in your colony when you make up your list of factors. (Just make up a list—do not discuss or evaluate any of the factors. Before you start, make sure everyone in your group understands the issues you are working on.)

Task 4 (10 minutes of Period 2)—Referring to the chart your group did in Task 3, prioritize up to six factors that your group feels are the most important for your colony. List them on the Charlottetown Conference 1864 Chart, and on the large chart your teacher will provide for you.*

Period Three

Task 5 (25 minutes of Period 3)—As a group review the factors your colony should consider if it is to become part of Confederation. Examine the consequences of each factor (both short- and long-term) by deciding how these factors will affect you personally (as per your role card) and how they will affect the other people in your colony. Fill in the consequences section of the Charlottetown Conference 1864 Chart. It is not necessary that you fill in four consequences for each factor, but try to think of as many outcomes as you can for each factor.

Task 6 (5 minutes of Period 3)—Thinking About Thinking: take approximately five minutes of quiet time to reflect upon the procedure your colony/group went through while doing tasks three to five.

Task 7 (5 minutes of Period 3)—Considering other people's points of view is an important critical thinking exercise. Think about why other people see the issue of political union (Confederation) differently than you do. If someone sees an issue differently than you do, does this mean that their way is the wrong way?

Task 8 (5 minutes of Period 3)—Discuss: Why did some of the people in your colony think their way was the best way?

Period Four

Task 9 (20 minutes of Period 4)—In character, make a decision about the issue: Should your colony join Confederation? Consider all the factors and the consequence of each factor that your group listed on the Charlottetown Conference 1864 Chart. As a group, reach a consensus as to what your colony should do. Record it in the space, "Your Colony's Decision."

Task 10 (10 minutes of Period 4)—Critical thinkers sometimes change their decisions in light of new evidence. There is nothing wrong with this. As a group, critically think about and then discuss: Does your decision really solve the issue? Do this by referring to the factors and consequences that were noted on the Charlottetown Conference 1864 Chart, and by brainstorming the following questions: How does the decision you reached solve the issue? What other solutions can you think of? What are their advantages and disadvantages? Do you wish to change your solution?

Task 11 (10 minutes of Period 4)—In your next social studies class, your colony's leader will meet with the leaders of the other colonies to debate the issue of Confederation. If your colony decided to join the other colonies, help your leader prepare for this debate by making sure the special concerns of your colony are not lost in the proceedings. If your colony decided not to join the other colonies, help your leader prepare arguments against joining Confederation.

Period Five

Task 12 (40 minutes of Period 5)—It is September 1, 1864. Your colonial leader is sitting in one of the chairs around the "Confederation table" at Charlottetown, Prince Edward Island. Have a debate to decide whether your colony should join the other colonies of British North America, forming the new country of Canada.

In the next social studies class you will find out what actually happened at the Charlottetown Conference of 1864.

---

*Masters for Charlettown Conference 1864 Chart are located in the Teacher's Resource Package.

Charlottetown Conference: 1864

The colonies of Nova Scotia, Prince Edward Island, and New Brunswick decided to meet in Charlottetown, Prince Edward Island on September 1, 1864 to discuss the idea of a union of the Atlantic colonies. Newfoundland decided not to attend the meeting.

The Province of Canada (Canada East and Canada West) decided to take advantage of this opportunity to convince the Atlantic colonies (Nova Scotia, New Brunswick, and Prince Edward Island) to join with them in a larger union. They were told that they could attend the conference.

John A. Macdonald, George Brown, George-Étienne Cartier, Alexander Galt, and Thomas D'Arcy McGee went in order to state why they thought there should be a British North American union. The Province of Canada promised to build a railway connecting Canada and the Atlantic colonies. George Brown (Canada West) promised "that our farmers and manufacturers and mechanics shall carry their wares into every village of the Maritime Provinces and that they shall with equal freedom bring their fish, and their coal, and their . . . produce to our three millions of inhabitants."

By the end of the Charlottetown Conference the decision had been made to work toward a Confederation of all the British North American colonies. It was decided that a second meeting should be held in a month's time at Quebec.

Above: People celebrated at a grand dance held on the final night of the Charlottetown Conference.

Fathers of Confederation, by Rex Woods. Delegates met in Charlottetown in 1864 to discuss the formation of a united Canada.

Quebec Conference: 1864

  Delegates from the British North American colonies met again in October, but this time they met in Quebec City. There were representatives from the Province of Canada, as well as all of the Atlantic colonies, including Newfoundland, which had not attended the Charlottetown Conference. The Quebec Conference lasted for over two weeks.

The result of the Quebec Conference was a list called the Seventy-Two **Resolutions**, which were to form the basis upon which the new nation of Canada would be built. The highlights of the Seventy-Two Resolutions appear to the right.

Seventy-Two Resolutions

At the Quebec Conference, Seventy-Two Resolutions were drawn up. Some of the major ideas follow:

- A strong central government (federal government) would handle common affairs, notably economic development and defence.

- Provinces would have limited powers (thus they would be weaker than the federal government) to handle local affairs, and social and cultural issues.

- A federal Parliament would be composed of a lower house called the House of Commons and an upper house, known as the Senate.

- Members of the House of Commons would be elected according to the notion of representation by population.

- Members of the Senate would be appointed. Canada East, Canada West, and Atlantic Canada would each be considered a region and would be given about the same number of members. Each region had 24 members. This would provide some protection for the small Atlantic colonies, which would each have very few elected members in the House of Commons.

- The federal government was to legislate for "peace, order and good government."

The Quebec Conference was held in the temporary Parliament Building at Montmorency–Laval in Quebec.

This photograph, taken on October 27, 1864, the last day of the Quebec Conference, shows delegates from the five colonies of British North America: the Province of Canada, New Brunswick, Nova Scotia, Prince Edward Island, and Newfoundland.

Resolutions — a list of guidelines or rules that are to be followed as a basis for ruling a group of people

The Confederation Debates

In the Province of Canada

The Confederation Debates included intense discussions of serious disagreements.

The job of the delegates who were at the Quebec Conference was to go home and convince the anti-Confederates (those against Confederation or Union) to change their minds. In order for the Seventy-Two Resolutions to be passed, they had to be approved by the colonial assemblies in the Province of Canada.

In the Province of Canada the debate continued for six weeks, but in the end the Great Coalition (*see* page 182) had an overwhelming majority on its side. The vote in the assembly was 91 to 33 in favour of Confederation.

Here is an imaginary conversation that might have taken place among some of the members of the Legislative Assembly after the vote:

I voted for Confederation because if we are united we will be able to defend ourselves better against the Americans. Britain does not seem very interested in helping us, so we must help ourselves.

That is perfectly true, my friend. However, what is more important, trade will improve within the British North American colonies. We will send our manufactured and our farm goods to the Atlantic colonies and will receive their goods in return.

As a *Canadien* and a representative of my people, I am more interested in protecting the *Canadien* way of life. I think that a separate provincial government for Canada East will do that. I'm in favour of guaranteeing **La Survivance**, not Confederation.

I am also a *Canadien*, but I do not share your feelings about Confederation. I think our way of life will be threatened, because the central government will be too strong and will be run by English-speaking people. We *Canadiens* will have to stand up for ourselves at every turn in the future.

I feel as you do about Confederation, even though I am not a *Canadien*. What good are the Atlantic colonies to the Province of Canada? We don't need to unite with them in order to trade with them.

You nay-sayers are forgetting about the possibility that Confederation will allow us to build a trans-continental railway. Then we will be able to unite with the colonies and territories to the west, and become a nation from sea to sea. Look at all the good farmland we'll be able to take over for the younger generation.

La Survivance—cultural survival, especially of the French language and culture, and of the Roman Catholic religion

In the Atlantic Colonies

There was strong opposition in the Atlantic colonies to the Seventy-Two Resolutions and thus to Confederation. Many people thought that they were doing fine on their own and could see no reason to join Canada and take on its problems. The people of the Atlantic colonies were in the fishing, lumbering, and shipbuilding industries. They felt that they had little in common with the farmers of the Province of Canada.

Briefly, here is what happened before 1867, in the Atlantic colonies:

- The people of New Brunswick and Nova Scotia reversed their initial opposition to Confederation and voted for it.
- The people of Prince Edward Island and Newfoundland rejected the idea of Confederation.

The following includes more details about the story of the debates in each of the Atlantic colonies.

New Brunswick

In 1865 Premier Tilley's pro-Confederation government (those in favour of Confederation or Union) fought an election on the issue of Confederation and lost. His opponents stressed that New Brunswick would lose control over its own affairs in Confederation and the people believed them.

In 1866 the lieutenant-governor, appointed by Great Britain, was instructed to encourage Confederation in the colony. He pressured the anti-Confederation government into resigning and appointed a pro-Confederation government. He then called another election. Tilley was re-elected and the new assembly voted for Confederation. This seems like a surprising turnaround, but circumstances changed between the two elections. First, the fear of an American invasion had been reawakened by Fenian raids across the border. People felt it would be much easier to have a strong army if New Brunswick united with Canada. Second, Great Britain announced that it supported the idea of union. People who were worried about breaking ties with Britain were reassured that some links would remain. Third, people had time to think about the possible economic benefits of union. They became convinced that union would mean an enlarged, protected market for New Brunswick goods. Also, people thought union would mean more money for railway construction, which in turn would mean more jobs for the labour force in the colony. Railways were also needed to open up forested land for settlement. Another reason for the pro-Confederation victory was that Tilley was able to wage a strong campaign with money from sources such as shipping, timber, and railway interests, as well as from the government in the Province of Canada.

Sir Samuel Leonard Tilley (1818–1896)

Samuel Leonard Tilley was born to Loyalist parents who had come north following the American Revolution. He had a profitable medical supply business before entering politics. Tilley was one of the Fathers of Confederation. He represented New Brunswick at both the Charlottetown and Quebec Conferences. As premier he led the fight to convince the people of New Brunswick to join Confederation. Following Confederation Tilley joined John A. Macdonald's Conservative government first as minister of customs, then as minister of finance. He was lieutenant-governor of New Brunswick from 1873 to 1878. He returned to the Macdonald government as finance minister in 1878. In 1885 he became lieutenant-governor of New Brunswick.

All in the Family. This 1865 cartoon from *Le Perroquet* shows Upper and Lower Canada arranging to marry Nova Scotia and New Brunswick. They plan to adopt little Prince Edward Island, but the U.S. is not invited.

Nova Scotia

People in Nova Scotia had been quite interested in a union of the Maritime colonies. Nova Scotia was largely responsible for the Charlottetown Conference of 1864. There was a strong emotional pull for a maritime union in Nova Scotia. This was because New Brunswick and Prince Edward Island had been part of one colony (Nova Scotia) during the 1700s.

By 1867 Halifax was already an important port and military centre.

Confederation was tied to railway building in the minds of the pro-Confederation people in Nova Scotia. They wanted to see Halifax linked by railway to the Province of Canada (Canada East and Canada West). The access to Canadian markets would greatly help industrial development in Nova Scotia. The reaction of communities in Nova Scotia to the idea of Confederation often depended on their nearness to the proposed railway. If they were not close, then they were not particularly interested.

Many anti-Confederates led by Joseph Howe were concerned about how much influence a small province like Nova Scotia would have in Confederation. They were also worried about higher taxes to support railway development.

Premier Charles Tupper, who was pro-Confederation, watched the 1865 election loss of the pro-Confederation candidates in New Brunswick and decided not to call an election until Joseph Howe lost some of his support. Nova Scotia could not very well join without New Brunswick anyway, since New Brunswick was between Nova Scotia and the Province of Canada. Finally, in 1866 pro-Confederation Premier Tilley of New Brunswick was swept back into office.

A new pro-Confederation lieutenant-governor was appointed in Nova Scotia. Sir Fenwick Williams was well liked because he was a native of the colony and had been a hero in the British navy. With his help, Premier Tupper was able to win the support of the Legislative Assembly for Confederation.

Charles Tupper (1821–1915)

Tupper was a third-generation Nova Scotian, descended from a family of early North American settlers. He became a doctor and was the first president of the Canadian Medical Association. In 1864 Tupper became the premier of Nova Scotia and attended the Charlottetown and Quebec conferences during that same year. He is one of the Fathers of Confederation and is credited with his province's entry into Confederation. After Confederation, Tupper held many Cabinet posts in the federal government, including that of minister of railways and canals from 1870 to 1884, while the Canadian Pacific Railway was being built. He replaced Sir Mackenzie Bowell as prime minister in May of 1896, but resigned July 8 after he and his Conservatives were defeated by Wilfrid Laurier's Liberals. He led the Opposition for another four years before retiring from politics.

Joseph Howe

The popular Joseph Howe led the fight against Confederation in Nova Scotia. His 12 "Botheration Letters" were printed in the *Halifax Morning Chronicle* from January to March, 1865. This is an example of what he said:

Comparing Confederation to a piece of cloth, it is a weak and poorly planned piece of material. Is it a good idea to put new wine [Nova Scotia] in an old bottle [Province of Canada] or to attach new cloth to an old item of clothing? Is union strong when a wise man, doing a steady business, is tricked into joining a gambler? Was Samson stronger when combined with Delilah, who tied him with ropes and cut off his hair?

Prince Edward Island

In Prince Edward Island there was widespread opposition to the idea of Confederation. People were concerned that the island's five representatives in the House of Commons would have little power or influence. Also, the Quebec Conference had refused to guarantee a £200 000 loan to buy out the absentee landlords who owned most of the island. Islanders saw no advantage in the proposed customs union, because the island's government operating revenues came almost entirely from duties on trade with other colonies.

Newfoundland

The people of Newfoundland were really not very interested in Confederation. They felt that they had little in common with the people of the united Province of Canada. When they heard about the anti-Confederation events in the other Atlantic colonies, they lost the little interest they had.

The London Conference

  Sixteen delegates from the Province of Canada, Nova Scotia, and New Brunswick sailed to London in 1866 to present the Seventy-Two Resolutions to British officials. During the meetings in London, the delegates from Nova Scotia and New Brunswick were able to make some changes that were to their benefit. New Brunswick got assurances that the intercolonial railway would be built. Provincial government **subsidies** were increased.

On February 12, 1867, the bill containing the Seventy-Two Resolutions (the British North America Act) was introduced in the British House of Lords. It passed through both houses quickly, and on May 22, 1867, Queen Victoria proclaimed that the Dominion of Canada would become a nation on July 1, 1867. John A. Macdonald was to be the first prime minister.

London Conference on Confederation, by J.D. Kelly. The London Conference lasted from December 1866 to February 1867.

Subsidy — loan of money that the government contributes or sets aside for a given year's budget. It is usually for a specific project.

C-8449, National Archives of Canada, Ottawa (detail).

Personal Summary

John Alexander Macdonald was born in Glasgow, Scotland. He came to Canada as a young boy. He later said that he did not have a boyhood because he left school at the age of 14 and went to work in a law office at 15. By the time he was 19 he had started his own law practice. He served in the militia during the Rebellion of 1837 in Upper Canada.

In 1843 Macdonald married Isabella Clark. Their first son died in 1848. Their second son, Hugh John, served briefly as premier of Manitoba in 1900. Isabella was ill most of her married life and died in 1857.

In 1867 Macdonald married Susan Agnes Bernard, who was 20 years younger than John A. She was very interested in Macdonald's political career and would often sit in the gallery of the House of Commons in order to watch him in action. When she accompanied him on a trip to British Columbia by train in 1886, she rode part of the way on the cowcatcher—a metal framework at the front of the train—in order to better enjoy the scenery. Macdonald's second marriage, like his first, was tinged with sadness. The only child of the marriage was born severely handicapped. However, John A. believed in making the best of things. Lady Macdonald once wrote:

Oftentimes he comes in with a very moody brow, tired and oppressed, his voice weak, his step slow; and ten minutes after he is making very clever jokes and laughing like any schoolboy with his hands in his pockets and his head thrown back. . . . I tell him his good heart and amiable temper are the great secrets of his success.

Macdonald was knighted by Queen Victoria for his work and thereafter was called Sir John A. Macdonald.

Political Summary

John A. Macdonald helped to create the Liberal-Conservative Party in Canada West in 1854. In 1856 he became joint premier of the Province of Canada. In 1867 he became the first prime minister of the Dominion of Canada.

Sir John A. Macdonald 1815–1891

Dates as Prime Minister—1867–1873, 1878–1891
Party—Conservative

● ● ● ● ● ● ● ●

He presided over the union and expansion of Canada. The first provinces joined together in 1867 (Confederation). In 1870 the North-West Territories were brought into Confederation and the province of Manitoba came into being. In 1871, the province of British Columbia entered Confederation, and in 1873, the province of Prince Edward Island joined. In 1880 the British government transferred the Arctic Islands to Canada.

Sir John A. was responsible for the building of the Canadian Pacific Railway, which resulted in the West becoming populated and then joined to the rest of Canada. He once said that he would be quite willing to not have Canadians settle the far West for the next half century, but he was afraid to do so because of the threat of an American takeover. Large numbers of Canadians were needed to fill the West before the Americans did. The Pacific Scandal, which caused Macdonald and his Conservative Party to resign from office in 1873, was related to the building of the railway. In 1872 the Conservatives had received a large campaign contribution from Sir Hugh Allan, the man who had been awarded the contract to build the railway. Macdonald and his Conservatives won the election with a reduced minority, but the opposition accused them of accepting bribes from Allan and his company. The Conservatives resigned in 1873 and lost the election of 1874. However, they were returned to office with a majority in the election of 1878.

Wilfrid Laurier, a Liberal opponent of Macdonald and a later prime minister, summed up Macdonald's accomplishments after his death in 1891:

It may be said, without any exaggeration whatever, that the life of Sir John Macdonald, from the day he entered Parliament, is the history of Canada, for he was connected and associated with all the events, all the facts which brought Canada from the position it then occupied—the position of two small provinces, having nothing in common but their common allegiance, united by a bond of paper and united by nothing else—to the . . . state of development which Canada has reached.

The British North America Act, 1867

Introduction

The British North America Act* (BNA Act) created the Dominion of Canada in 1867, stated the powers of the provincial and federal governments, outlined the way in which the government would be structured, and guaranteed protection for minority groups.

Constitution Act, 1867

Aim: to create a federal union (Confederation) of the colonies of British North America, associated with Great Britain.

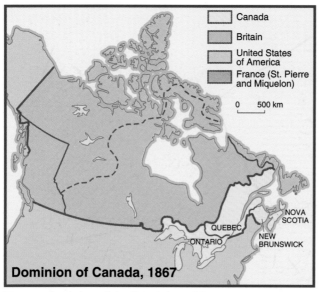

Dominion of Canada, 1867

Legend:
- Canada
- Britain
- United States of America
- France (St. Pierre and Miquelon)

0   500 km

Map labels: NOVA SCOTIA, QUEBEC, NEW BRUNSWICK, ONTARIO

The proclamation of the Dominion of Canada was announced at Windsor Castle in Great Britain in May 1867. The Dominion of Canada was to consist of the provinces of New Brunswick, Nova Scotia, Ontario, and Quebec.

Federalism

The most important question that the writers of the Constitution Act, 1867 had to decide was whether there should be both national and provincial levels of government, or just a national level. John A. Macdonald and others had not wanted provincial governments. However, Quebec felt that if it lost its provincial government, it would also lose its identity: its French language, its culture and traditions, as well as its civil laws. Many people in the provinces of New Brunswick and Nova Scotia were anxious to have their own provincial governments.

The result was a system of federalism. This meant that the Dominion of Canada would have two levels of government: national or federal (or central) and provincial. The federal government would handle matters affecting everyone. Each provincial government would handle matters affecting only the people it governs within its boundaries.

Canada's System of Federalism

- It would be a system with a central government and provincial governments.

- The central government would have more power than the provincial governments. The provincial governments would have little power and few rights.**

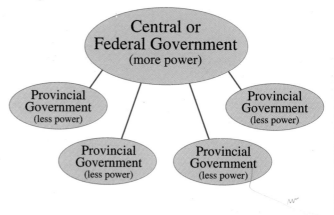

Central or Federal Government (more power)

Provincial Government (less power)
Provincial Government (less power)
Provincial Government (less power)
Provincial Government (less power)

---

*The BNA Act was renamed the Constitution Act, 1867 because of the changes made to the Constitution in 1982.

**In 1982 some changes were made to the Canadian Constitution. For example, the provinces gained more power.

Form of Central Government

It was decided that the central government of the Dominion of Canada would have three parts. (1) The head of the government of Canada is the monarch and is represented by a governor general. Parliament—the law-making body of the government—is composed of (2) the House of Commons and (3) the Senate.

Representatives from each province are elected to the House of Commons. They are called Members of Parliament.

The number of Members of Parliament from each province depends on the size of the population in that province (representation by population). This means that the smaller provinces of Nova Scotia and New Brunswick have far fewer Members of Parliament to represent their interests.

The Senate is meant to represent regional interests. Ontario was given 24 representatives, Quebec 24, and Nova Scotia and New Brunswick 24 together. Senators are appointed.

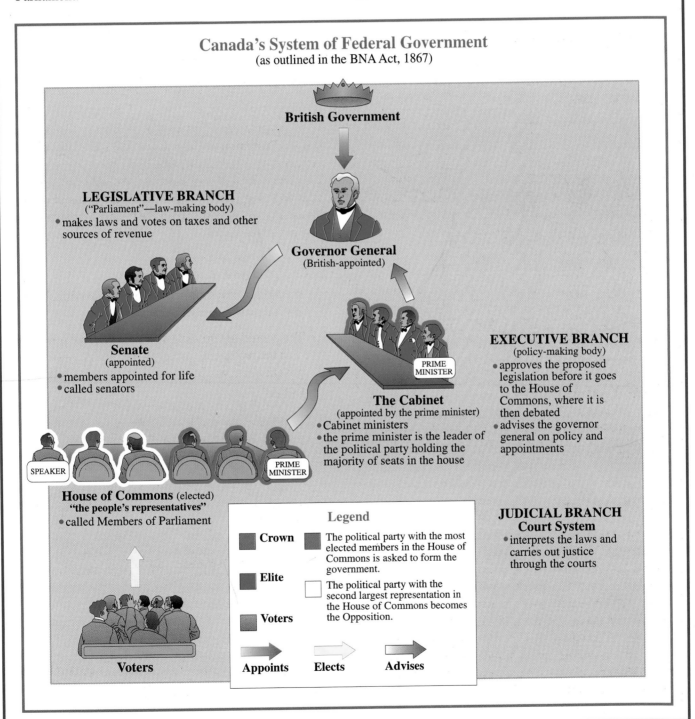

Canada's System of Federal Government
(as outlined in the BNA Act, 1867)

British Government

Governor General
(British-appointed)

LEGISLATIVE BRANCH
("Parliament"—law-making body)
- makes laws and votes on taxes and other sources of revenue

Senate
(appointed)
- members appointed for life
- called senators

The Cabinet
(appointed by the prime minister)
- Cabinet ministers
- the prime minister is the leader of the political party holding the majority of seats in the house

PRIME MINISTER

EXECUTIVE BRANCH
(policy-making body)
- approves the proposed legislation before it goes to the House of Commons, where it is then debated
- advises the governor general on policy and appointments

SPEAKER
PRIME MINISTER

House of Commons (elected)
"the people's representatives"
- called Members of Parliament

JUDICIAL BRANCH
Court System
- interprets the laws and carries out justice through the courts

Voters

Legend

- Crown
- Elite
- Voters

The political party with the most elected members in the House of Commons is asked to form the government.

The political party with the second largest representation in the House of Commons becomes the Opposition.

Appoints   Elects   Advises

197

A Strong Central Government

The central or national government was to be very strong. This was partly because the American Civil War, in which the states fought against each other, was still fresh in the minds of the Fathers of Confederation. They were afraid that if the provinces were too powerful, they might fight in the same way that the American states had.

 Here is how the central government became strong:

1. The central government was given authority over matters of general concern. These powers were vague. They included everything that was not specifically covered by the provinces. Here is an example: "The federal government shall make laws for the peace, order, and good government of Canada in regard to all subjects not specifically given to the provinces . . . ."*
2. It was given the power to veto or reject any provincial laws within one year of their passage.

Division of Powers in the Constitution Act, 1867

Just as you cannot play hockey without rules, so you cannot govern a country without rules. The rules that govern a country are called a constitution. There are basically two types of constitutions: written and unwritten. The United States has a written constitution. If questions arise, one refers to the constitution for the answers. Britain has an unwritten constitution, where the courts make decisions based on customs and traditions and previous court rulings. Canada's constitutions (the 1867 Constitution and the 1982 Constitution) are written in some areas and unwritten in other areas. Actually, the 1982 Constitution moved Canada closer to a written constitution and farther from custom and tradition.

---

*This is known as the POGG clause—a government for Peace, Order, and Good Government. The United States created a government to provide for life, liberty, and the pursuit of happiness.

**As the years went by these powers often overlapped and blurred, so that the division of powers is no longer easy to explain. It is also a current issue.

Powers Specified in the 1867 Constitution

Among the 29 items that were specifically stated as powers and thus the responsibility of the federal (central) government were:

- trade and commerce
- raising money by taxation
- postal service
- armed forces and defence
- fisheries
- money
- Native peoples and lands reserved for them
- divorce
- criminal law
- penitentiaries

While matters of national interest were to be legislated by the federal government, matters of a particular or local interest were the responsibility of the four provincial governments. These matters were:

- direct taxation within the province
- management and sale of public lands belonging to the province
- provincial prisons
- hospitals and asylums
- local works and projects
- education
- administration of justice and provincial courts
- issuing licences to shops, saloons, taverns, and other businesses

As you can see from the provincial list of responsibilities, the provinces were given authority over social and cultural areas such as education, and local matters such as provincial courts.**

Shared Powers in the Constitution Act, 1867

In addition to the powers specified in the Constitution Act, 1867, Canada also has some powers that are shared by the national (federal) government and the provincial governments. All other powers in the Constitution Act, 1867 are covered by the POGG clause. This clause gave the federal government all the powers necessary to carry out peace, order, and good government. It made the federal government very powerful.

Issues Raised by Confederation

The Fathers of Confederation believed that the division of powers between the federal and provincial governments would not be a cause of tension. However, **provincial rights** almost immediately became an issue in the Maritimes. You will read about this later in the chapter.

The issue of biculturalism was not settled as a result of Confederation. Biculturalism refers to having two cultures. In Canada it was the French and English cultures that lived together in one nation.

French Canadian and Roman Catholic institutions that had been established in Quebec were protected by the Constitution Act, 1867. Both English and French were declared the official languages of the federal Parliament, the federal courts, and the government and courts of Quebec. This was an example of what we now call bilingualism. French civil laws were protected in Quebec. Whatever rights and privileges that separate schools in each province had at the time of Confederation were supposed to remain.

However, the question of whether bilingualism was just to be protected in Quebec or was to be extended throughout Canada was not clear. This issue was to be raised in the North-West. You will read about this later on in the textbook.

First People and Other Minorities

The Constitution Act, 1867 only has one direct reference to the Aboriginal peoples: section 91 (24) gives the Parliament of Canada exclusive authority over "Indians and lands reserved for the Indians." The First People, as Canada's original people, did not have any input in the Confederation negotiations or in policies affecting them. The Province of Canada had already worked out its Aboriginal policy; thus when the new Canadian government had to make decisions regarding the First People, they adopted the policy already in effect in the Province of Canada: Aboriginal lands were to be acquired by treaty; the people were to be settled on reserves; and a government department was to be created in Ottawa to manage how they were to live. Because they surrendered their traditional lands, the First People received reserves and services such as education and health care. Some First People believe that this was too high a price to pay.

While the rights of the French Canadians were guaranteed in the Constitution Act, 1867, the rights of the other minorities in Canada were not guaranteed at this time.

The aim of the new government of Canada in regard to minority peoples was to force the minorities to live by the will of the majority. This meant that there would be an attempt to assimilate the Aboriginal peoples into the dominant Canadian culture. They would have to give up their customs and traditions, their language, and their religion. They were to become like Canadians of English or French backgrounds. You will learn more about this in Chapters 10 and 11.

For Your Notebook

1. Canada has a federal system of government. Explain how this works.
2. Which of these government responsibilities are provincial? Which are federal? (Hint: Check in the government pages of your telephone directory.)
   * vehicle licensing
   * making new coins
   * hospitals
   * Native land claims
   * pensions
   * highway maintenance
   * international boundary disputes
   * unemployment insurance
3. When was bilingualism introduced? Briefly explain why Canada is a bilingual country.
4. Who has the most power—the federal government or the provincial government? In what ways could you see this causing problems in Canada today?

Exploring Further

1. The U.S. Civil War between the Northern and Southern states took place between 1861 and 1865. How do you think that the Canadian system of federalism, brought in by the Constitution Act, 1867, might prevent a war between the Canadian provinces?
2. Optional: The Constitution Act, 1867 gave the central or national government (the federal government) a great deal of power. If the Meech Lake Accord had passed in 1990, what effect would it have had on the powers of the federal government?
3. Optional: Monitor the media for a week. Record any constitutional issues.

Provincial rights—the powers maintained by the provincial governments, usually involving cultural, social, and local issues

Confederation Celebrations

On March 29, 1867, the British Parliament passed the British North America Act, now known as the Constitution Act, 1867. The Constitution Act, 1867 created the Dominion of Canada. The new dominion was to consist of the four provinces of Ontario (formerly Canada West), Quebec (formerly Canada East), New Brunswick, and Nova Scotia. Provision was made for other provinces to join later.

On Monday, July 1, 1867, a Toronto newspaper announced: "A united British North America takes its place among the nations of the world." There were fireworks, cheering crowds, fine speeches, parades, and gun salutes to celebrate the occasion.

Below: The Confederation Medal was ordered by John A. Macdonald in 1867 to commemorate Confederation.

C-14989, National Archives of Canada, Ottawa.

Above: This crowd of people has gathered in Kingston's Market Square on July 1, 1867, to hear the proclamation announcing Confederation.

Right: One of Canada's early postage stamps shows a profile of Queen Victoria. In 1868 it cost 3 cents to send a letter within Canada, 6 cents in the United States, and 12.5 cents to Britain.

Below: Viscount Monck was Governor of British North America from 1861 and Canada's first governor general.

C-10813, National Archives of Canada, Ottawa (detail).

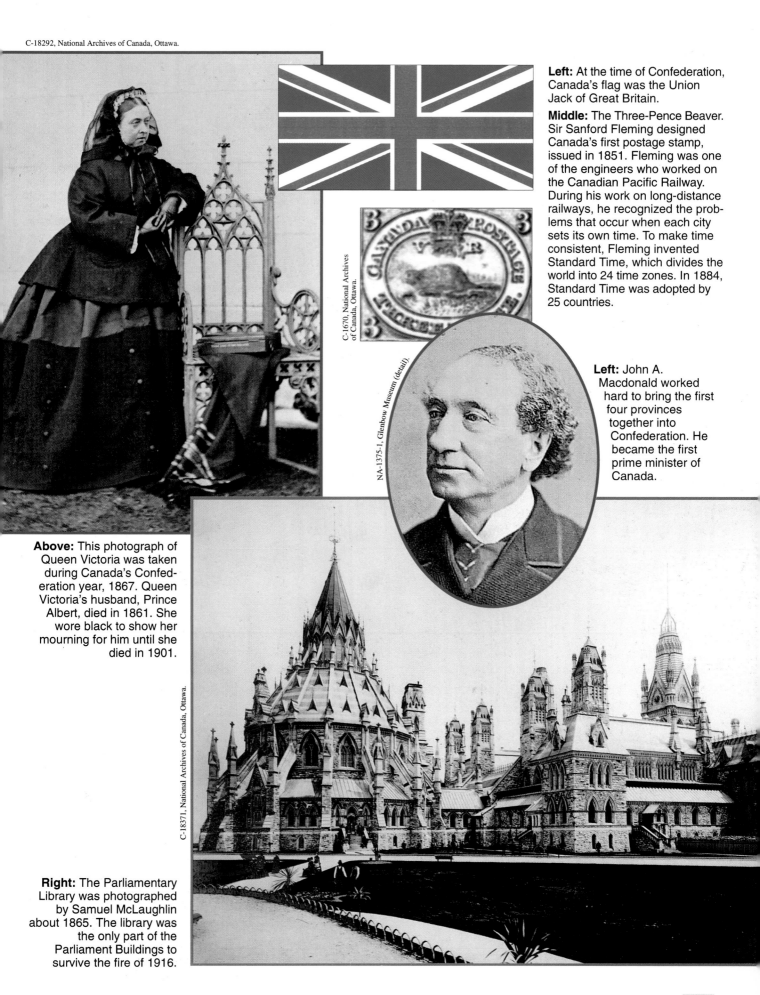

C-18292, National Archives of Canada, Ottawa.

Left: At the time of Confederation, Canada's flag was the Union Jack of Great Britain.

Middle: The Three-Pence Beaver. Sir Sanford Fleming designed Canada's first postage stamp, issued in 1851. Fleming was one of the engineers who worked on the Canadian Pacific Railway. During his work on long-distance railways, he recognized the problems that occur when each city sets its own time. To make time consistent, Fleming invented Standard Time, which divides the world into 24 time zones. In 1884, Standard Time was adopted by 25 countries.

C-1670, National Archives of Canada, Ottawa.

NA-1375-1, Glenbow Museum (detail).

Left: John A. Macdonald worked hard to bring the first four provinces together into Confederation. He became the first prime minister of Canada.

Above: This photograph of Queen Victoria was taken during Canada's Confederation year, 1867. Queen Victoria's husband, Prince Albert, died in 1861. She wore black to show her mourning for him until she died in 1901.

C-18371, National Archives of Canada, Ottawa.

Right: The Parliamentary Library was photographed by Samuel McLaughlin about 1865. The library was the only part of the Parliament Buildings to survive the fire of 1916.

The Years After Confederation

Federal/Provincial Conflict in Nova Scotia

 Not everyone in the new Dominion of Canada felt like cheering on July 1, 1867. In Nova Scotia many people were having second thoughts about Confederation. The July first Halifax *Morning Chronicle* newspaper appeared edged in black like an obituary notice. It declared that "the free and intelligent Province of Nova Scotia" had "died last night at twelve o'clock." In Yarmouth, Nova Scotia, pro-Confederation politicians were burned in **effigy**, along with a dead rat.

The anti-Confederation feeling in Nova Scotia became evident to the rest of Canada after the September elections of 1867. In the first federal election to be held in Nova Scotia, 18 anti-Confederation candidates won and only one pro-Confederation candidate won. In the Nova Scotia provincial election held on the same day, the anti-Confederates won 36 of the 38 seats.

The anti-Confederates in Nova Scotia were led by Joseph Howe. Howe and his followers had gone to Britain in 1866* to **lobby** against the union of Nova Scotia with the other provinces to form the Dominion of Canada. The British legislators listened but did not agree. They were firmly convinced that Confederation was in the best interests of both the colonies of British North America and the British Empire as a whole.

Separatist Movement

Following Canada's first federal election, the Nova Scotian members of Parliament, led by Howe, presented a motion in the House of Commons in Ottawa. It stated that Nova Scotia should be released from Confederation. The motion was overwhelmingly rejected by the powerful Conservative majority. They wanted Nova Scotia to remain as a part of Canada.

Back in Nova Scotia, public discontent toward Confederation was being expressed by massive petitions and discussions in the provincial Legislature.

Howe and members of the Nova Scotian anti-Confederation group again went to London to ask the British government to allow Nova Scotia to withdraw from Confederation. They were told in no uncertain terms that they would not be released and that any complaints about the way in which Confederation was working should be taken up with the government of Canada.

Compromise

 Some members of the Nova Scotian anti-Confederation group began to talk of joining the United States. However, Howe and most of the members of the Nova Scotian anti-Confederation group remained loyal to Britain. Howe returned to Nova Scotia from London having decided to **compromise**. He wanted to "accept the situation, repair the mischief, and make the best of a bad business." The only path left was to stay in Confederation and to try to arrange a better agreement with the Canadian government.

Prime Minister Macdonald was not particularly pleased about the separatist movement in Nova Scotia. To encourage them to stay in Confederation, he decided to offer better terms to the province. The yearly grants were increased by $20 000. Macdonald also asked Howe to become a member of the federal Cabinet.

When Howe accepted the position as a federal Cabinet minister, he left the anti-Confederation movement in Nova Scotia without a leader. Leaderless, the movement lost steam. It faded and was no longer a threat to a united Canada.

Ontario, Quebec, and New Brunswick

People in these provinces seemed satisfied with Confederation, although the Confederation agreements had passed with a small majority among French members. English-speaking members from Canada East were overwhelmingly in favour of Confederation. No strong anti-Confederation movements like the one in Nova Scotia arose in the other provinces.

Exploring Further

1. Find out more about Joseph Howe. Hold a debate between Howe and Sir John A. Macdonald on the subject of Nova Scotia's withdrawal from Confederation.
2. Do research to find out more about separatist movements in Canada between 1867 and the present.

Effigy — an imitation, made of cloth, of a person who is disliked
*Note this was the year before the passing of the Constitution Act, 1867 (Confederation).
Lobby — represent a special interest to the government. A lobbyist tries to get lawmakers to introduce or vote for measures favourable to the lobbyist's special interest.
Compromise — an agreement in which each side gives up some of its demands

Cultural Groups in Canada

When studying the history of Canada, it is very important to remember that Canada is a varied mixture of many cultures. These cultures have added so much to our history.

Germans

The first record of the arrival of Germans to this country was to the colony of Quebec as soldiers in the French army. After their military service ended they chose to stay in New France. Hans Bernard is thought to have been the first German settler in New France, having purchased land near Quebec in 1664. Edward Cornwallis, the governor of the colony of Nova Scotia and founder of Halifax, later preferred German immigrants because of their skills at farming, and because they were Protestant, like the other settlers in the area. In an organized effort to bring German newcomers to Nova Scotia, King George II of England offered free land and enough supplies for one year to farmers from Germany who were willing to become British subjects and immigrate to British North America. One reason he offered free land was because he was also German. By 1753 approximately 1500 Germans set up a colony at Lunenburg, Nova Scotia.

During the American Revolution many of the soldiers in the British army were German mercenaries. At the end of the war some of these soldiers who were stationed in British North America chose to remain as permanent colonists.

After the American Revolution a large number of the Loyalists who came to British North America were Germans. They were primarily Amish from Pennsylvania and New York, and they settled mainly in the area between Lake Ontario and Lake Huron. Others settled along the St. Lawrence River in eastern Upper Canada. It has been estimated that one-third of the Loyalists who came to Upper Canada spoke German.

By 1867 there were approximately 200 000 German-speaking people in Canada. Between 1874 and 1876 roughly 6000 Germans came to the Red River area from Russia, the United States, and Europe. Most were Mennonites. They were joined by groups of Germans from Ontario. Soon a large settlement was established around Berlin, Ontario (later renamed Kitchener).

Ukrainians

The first Ukrainian immigration to the western world began in 1812. Information as to who actually came first is not clear, but they were probably mercenary soldiers who came to fight in the War of 1812 and then stayed on as settlers. Andrew Yankovsky and Peter Komdrovsky were among the Selkirk Settlers who settled in the Red River area in 1812. In 1874 Mennonites from the central Ukraine settled in Manitoba. In the 1880s groups of Ukrainians left the United States and came to Winnipeg.

Blacks

By 1850 there were close to 40 000 blacks in Upper Canada. Roughly 1000 had been taken to Quebec as slaves under French rule. They mostly worked as household servants. While slavery was still legal in Britain's colonies, any slave joining the British army was granted his freedom. After the American Revolution approximately 3500 black Loyalists, all having achieved their freedom, moved to the British colony of Nova Scotia (and later to the newly formed colony of New Brunswick). Most black Loyalists expected that they also would receive free land, but many did not receive that land from the British government, nor were they allowed to vote or have access to the law courts. Some blacks (approximately 2000) came as slaves to British North America. Some non-black Loyalists brought their slaves with them. During the War of 1812 blacks from the United States moved to British North America, mainly to Nova Scotia, where they received land from the British as a reward for joining the British side.

In 1793 Upper Canada abolished slavery, but it remained legal in parts of British North America until 1834, when a new law stopped slavery in the British Empire. Thus, Canada became a place of safety for slaves escaping from the United States. Close to 30 000 came to Canada. The route to freedom in Upper Canada was called the Underground Railway. Years later when black people were given their freedom in the United States, many returned to their former homeland.

Chinese

The first Chinese person to come to British North America came because of the Pacific fur trade. The Chinese did not establish any permanent place of residence until the gold rush in British Columbia in the 1850s. While some became involved in the search for gold, most provided services such as restaurants, laundries, and hotels to the miners. Many returned home to China after the gold rush. Close to 1500 stayed on to become involved in other mining operations, or to work as servants or in the new fishing industry developing on the West Coast.

Review

Summarizing the Chapter

- The political deadlock in the Province of Canada was finally broken when the Grits, the Tories, and the Bleus united under their leaders, George Brown, John A. Macdonald, and George-Étienne Cartier. This union was called the Great Coalition. Its goal was to create a union between Canada and the other British North American colonies.

- There were several reasons for this decision. One was the need to build railways to increase trade among the colonies as the Reciprocity Treaty with the United States was ending. The fear of American expansion was another. Armed border raids by the Irish-American Fenians were also a concern. It was thought that if the colonies joined together, then they would be able to defend themselves better. The British colonial governors were instructed by the British government to encourage the union. The British government did not want to spend a great deal of money to defend the colonies.

- In September of 1864 the Atlantic colonies scheduled a conference at Charlottetown, Prince Edward Island to discuss a union among themselves. Representatives from the Province of Canada attended and persuaded the Maritime delegates to discuss a larger union among all of the British North American colonies at Quebec in October.

- The result of the Quebec Conference was a list called the Seventy-Two Resolutions. They called for a federal system with a strong central government and provinces with limited powers. The federal Parliament would consist of a House of Commons with members elected according to the principle of representation by population, and a Senate whose members would be appointed by region.

- The task of the delegates at the Quebec Conference was to go home and convince people that Confederation was a good idea. In the Province of Canada, the Legislative Assembly voted 91 to 33 in favour. The task was more difficult in the Atlantic colonies.

- In New Brunswick, Premier Tilley's pro-Confederation government lost an election on the issue in 1865. However, he was re-elected the next year and the people of New Brunswick decided to join Confederation. That year, 1866, was also the year when Premier Tupper of Nova Scotia was able to win the support of the assembly for Confederation. In Prince Edward Island there was widespread opposition. In Newfoundland most people were simply indifferent to the issue. They saw no particular advantage to joining with the united Province of Canada.

- Delegates met again at the London Conference in late 1866 and early 1867, to work out the final details. On May 22, 1867, Queen Victoria proclaimed that the Dominion of Canada would become a nation on July 1, 1867. John A. Macdonald was to be the first prime minister.

Checking Predictions

1. At the beginning of this chapter you made some predictions based on the Overview and what you already knew. Now use what you found out by reading the chapter to fill in the third column of the chart that you began earlier.
2. Refer to the "Questions to Talk About" section on page 177. Discuss the questions based on what you have learned about Confederation in Canada.

Working with Information

1. Here are some main ideas from this chapter:
   - representation by population
   - political deadlock
   - the Great Coalition
   - Confederation (federal union)
   - intercolonial railways
   - decision-making
   - co-operation
   - lobby
   - compromise
   - nationhood

   Choose one main idea and use one of the following approaches to making a permanent individual record: mind map, web, paragraph, or an outline.

2. Put yourself in the place of one of the people mentioned in this chapter. Write a journal entry or entries describing what the above ideas are and your opinion of them.
3. Refer to page 7 for the definition of nation. Based on this definition and what you learned in Chapter 9, is Canada a nation? Give reasons for your answer. You may wish to debate this question.
4. Canada's government consists of three branches. What are they? Describe each branch.
5. Refer to the last footnote on page 196. Provide examples of the new powers the provinces gained.

Building Thinking Skills

Conceptualizing

Refer to the visual definitions of nation on page 7, Confederation on page 182, and the definitions you developed at the beginning of this chapter. Make a poster of your triad's concept of nationhood based on what you have learned. You may wish to review the steps in concept formation as found on page 39.

Evaluating Arguments

On page 193 reread the quote from Joseph Howe's "Botheration Letters," which he wrote in 1865. You will see that Howe is arguing against Nova Scotia joining Confederation.

Here is a quote by Premier Charles Tupper from a speech made the same year. Premier Tupper tells why Nova Scotia should join Confederation.

The fact is, if we are known, at all across the Atlantic, notwithstanding, the immense resources of these Maritime Provinces, it is because we happen to be contiguous to Canada. Everything connected with our interests tells us of the insignificance of our position.

- Briefly summarize Joseph Howe's argument against Confederation.
- Briefly summarize Premier Tupper's argument for Confederation.
- Which argument do you consider to be stronger? Tell why. With which side do you agree? Tell why.

Communicating Ideas

Reading

1. The strong anti-Confederation movement in Nova Scotia was an example of federal/provincial conflict. Check newspapers and other media for a period of two weeks. List examples of federal/provincial conflict that you find. You could put the information in a chart.

Writing

1. Check the newspapers and other media daily for a period of two weeks.

   (a) Make a list of individuals and groups who are lobbying provincial and federal governments today, and tell what their special interests are.

   (b) Make a list of requests made in petitions to provincial or federal governments.

Speaking

1. Discuss or debate the following: To become a nation an area must have the legal right to control its own affairs. Find proof to show that Canada, at the time of Confederation, did not have this right. Was Canada really a super colony and not a nation?

2. What rights do minorities have guaranteed in the Constitution Act, 1867? Check the newspaper and other media to find examples of how provincial and federal governments are protecting the rights of minorities. Tell a classmate about what you found.

Creating

1. Use the information in Chapter 9 to prepare a game to illustrate the reasons for Confederation, the events leading up to Confederation, and the government of Canada as determined by the British North America Act, 1867.

Canada Revisited

Prime Minister Pierre Trudeau watches as Queen Elizabeth II signs the Constitution Proclamation on April 17, 1982.

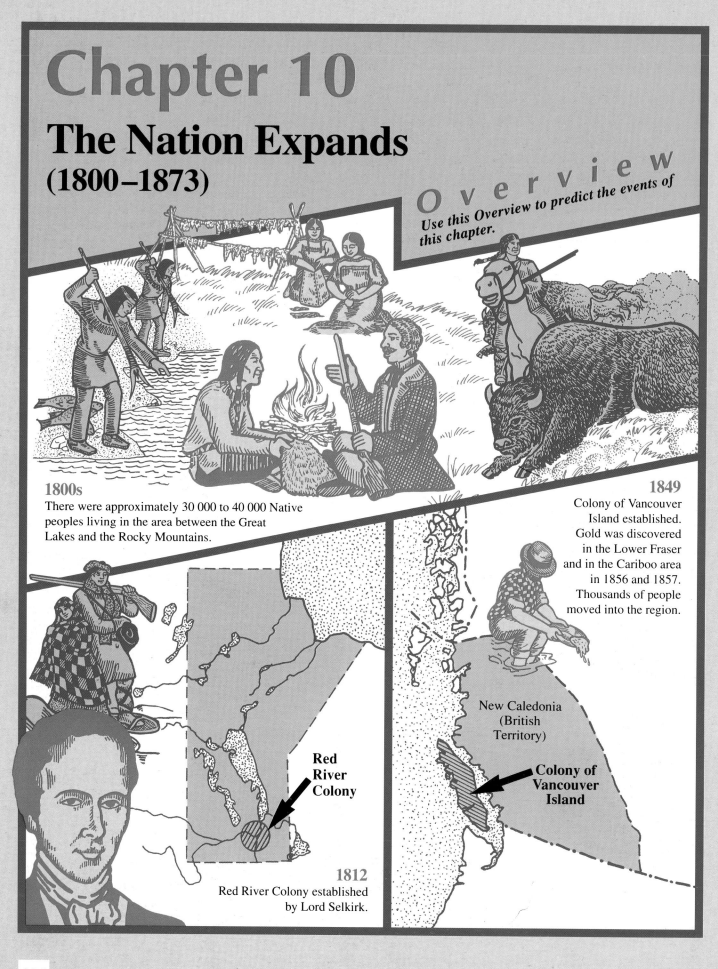

Chapter 10
The Nation Expands
(1800–1873)

Overview

Use this Overview to predict the events of this chapter.

1800s
There were approximately 30 000 to 40 000 Native peoples living in the area between the Great Lakes and the Rocky Mountains.

Red River Colony

1812
Red River Colony established by Lord Selkirk.

1849
Colony of Vancouver Island established. Gold was discovered in the Lower Fraser and in the Cariboo area in 1856 and 1857. Thousands of people moved into the region.

New Caledonia (British Territory)

Colony of Vancouver Island

1860s
About 9800 Metis lived in the Red River area.

1868
Rupert's Land Act was passed and HBC lands were transferred to the Canadian government in 1869. The government sent surveyors to the Red River area in 1868 and 1869.

1869–1870
Riel became leader of the Metis people. The Red River Resistance occurred.

1870
The Province of Manitoba was created and entered Confederation after the Red River Resistance.

1871
British Columbia entered Confederation.

1873
Prince Edward Island entered Confederation.

Chapter 10 Focus

In 1867 the new Dominion of Canada contained only four provinces: Ontario, Quebec, New Brunswick, and Nova Scotia. Between 1867 and 1905, five new provinces joined the Dominion of Canada. Chapter 10 tells how Manitoba, British Columbia, and Prince Edward Island joined the Dominion of Canada. The concepts of power, co-operation, decision-making, and conflict underlie the events of this chapter. The concepts of co-operation and conflict are the special focus for the chapter.

Power   Co-operation   Decision-making   Conflict

Overview/Prediction Chart

Examine the Overview on the previous pages. In pairs or small groups, use the Overview and what you already know about Canada's formation as a nation to predict the answers to the questions in the Prediction Chart. Put your predictions in the "My Predictions" column. Once you have finished the chapter, complete the "What I Found Out" column to help you review and summarize. Your teacher will provide you with a full-sized working copy of the Prediction Chart.

Prediction Chart—What Do You Think?		
Questions	My Predictions (fill out now)	What I Found Out (fill out at end of chapter)
1. What might be the major events?		
2. Who might be some of the important people or groups?	SAMPLE	
3. Who might hold power?		
4.		

The Growth of Canada, 1867–1873

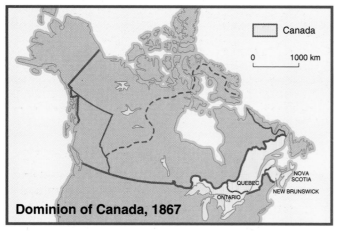

Dominion of Canada, 1867

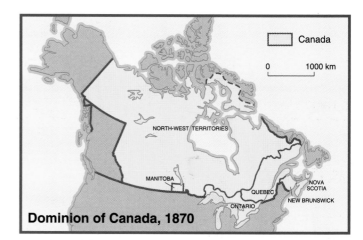

Dominion of Canada, 1870

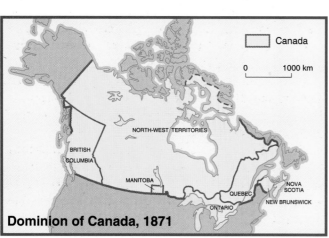

Dominion of Canada, 1871

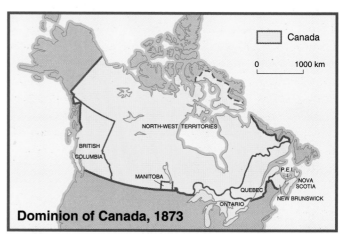

Dominion of Canada, 1873

When Canada became a nation in 1867, there were four provinces: Ontario, Quebec, New Brunswick, and Nova Scotia. Manitoba became the fifth province in 1870, British Columbia became the sixth province in 1871, and Prince Edward Island became the seventh province in 1873.

Manitoba Joins Confederation

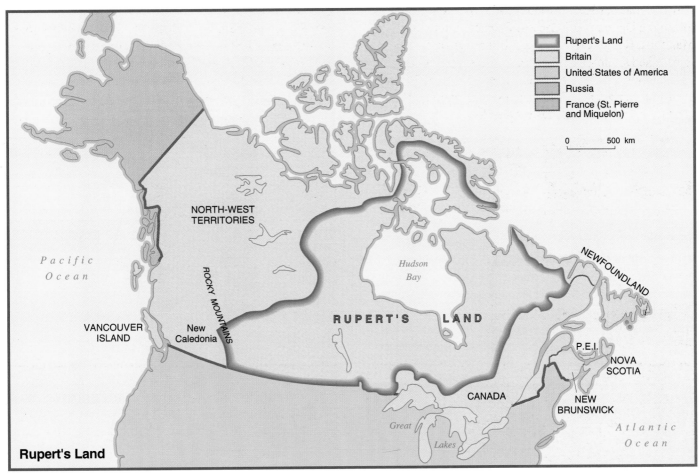

	Rupert's Land
	Britain
	United States of America
	Russia
	France (St. Pierre and Miquelon)

0   500 km

NORTH-WEST TERRITORIES

Pacific Ocean

ROCKY MOUNTAINS

Hudson Bay

RUPERT'S LAND

NEWFOUNDLAND

VANCOUVER ISLAND

New Caledonia

P.E.I.

NOVA SCOTIA

CANADA

NEW BRUNSWICK

Great Lakes

Atlantic Ocean

Rupert's Land

This map shows British North America before Canada became a country in 1867.

Rupert's Land

To the west of the Dominion of Canada was the vast (7 770 000 square kilometres) area known as Rupert's Land. Rupert's Land referred to all of the territories that were granted to the Hudson's Bay Company by Charles II in 1670. This area had been controlled by the Hudson's Bay Company for 200 years. Eventually, the area to the north and west of the Great Lakes came to be called the "North-West" even though it was still technically "Rupert's Land." In this chapter you will read about how, in 1870, part of Rupert's Land became Canada's fifth province—the province of Manitoba. Manitoba was but a fraction of the entire area of the North-West. The next chapter will continue with the history of the North-West.

In 1870, there were approximately 30 000 to 40 000 Native peoples living in the area between the Great Lakes and the Rocky Mountains. They were spread out over a huge area and had different cultural characteristics. The main tribes were the Ojibwa, the Cree, the Sarcee, the Assiniboine, and the Blackfoot. The Ojibwa were part of the Algonkian Nations. The Assiniboine and Blackfoot were Plains people. The Cree and Sarcee tribes included both Algonkian and Plains peoples.*

The Algonkian peoples lived mainly by hunting, fishing, and trapping. The Plains people were buffalo hunters. However, there were some changes as a result of the fur trade. Native men trapped, traded furs, and acted as guides. Native women made **pemmican** and exchanged it for goods at the trading posts. They made canoes, moccasins, snowshoes, and other items. They helped with the trapping and acted as interpreters. From the trading posts the Native people obtained European goods such as metal pots and tools, cloth, and guns. The guns made hunting easier and allowed more time for trapping furs.

---

*Refer to First People chart on page 8 for further explanations.
Pemmican— a food made of dried buffalo meat, buffalo fat, and berries. One kilogram of pemmican was considered equal to four kilograms of ordinary meat and it would last for years. It was an ideal food for long journeys.

Assiniboia
The Red River Settlement

A Scottish nobleman, Thomas Douglas, Earl of Selkirk, wanted to help the **crofters** of Scotland who had been forced off their small rented farms by the large landowners so they could use the land to raise sheep. Wool was fetching a high price and the landowners thought they would make more money by raising sheep than they would by renting their land to the farmers.*

Lord Selkirk asked the British government for a land grant in the Red River Valley in Rupert's Land, the land the British government had given to the Hudson's Bay Company for fur trading. He was refused, but Lord Selkirk was very determined. When the price of shares of the Hudson's Bay Company went down, he and Sir Alexander Mackenzie, the famous explorer, bought enough shares to gain control of the company. Because of his position of power in the Hudson's Bay Company, Selkirk was able to get a land grant of 300 000 square kilometres in the valley of the Red and Assiniboine rivers, in what is now Manitoba. The area also stretched south into what is now the United States. Selkirk's land grant was called Assiniboia. It is shown on the map below.

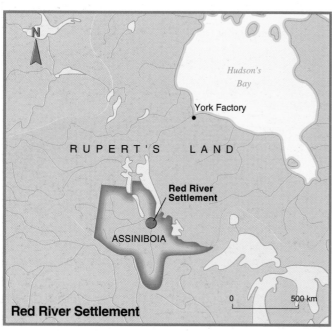

Red River Settlement

Rupert's Land was controlled by the Hudson's Bay Company for the purpose of fur trading. The land granted to Lord Selkirk was called Assiniboia and was part of Rupert's Land. The Red River Settlement was located in Assiniboia along the Assiniboine and Red rivers.

Another reason for choosing the Red River area for a colony was to try to stop the North West Company from competing with the Hudson's Bay Company for furs. The Nor'Westers (people who worked for the North West Company) relied on the Metis of the Red River area to provide them with pemmican and other provisions. The Red River area was also an important part of the route the Nor'Westers used when taking furs to Montreal.

C-1346, National Archives of Canada, Ottawa (detail).

Lord Selkirk (1771–1820)

Thomas Douglas, the fifth Earl of Selkirk, was the seventh son of a Scottish Earl. In those days, the younger sons of men with titles and money usually prepared themselves for careers in law, the ministry, or the military because it was always the eldest son who inherited the estate and titles. Lord Selkirk decided to go to university to be educated as a lawyer. While he was there he became interested in **social problems**.

One by one Lord Selkirk's older brothers died unexpectedly and eventually he was left as heir to the family fortune and titles. He decided to do some good for others with his money. He was concerned about the Scottish farmers who were being displaced from their lands. Some of them ended up living in wretched conditions in the poor districts of Britain's industrial cities. Many others were no longer living in the British Empire, because they chose to settle in the United States, which was no longer a colony of Great Britain. Lord Selkirk decided to use his own money to help many Scots settle in Prince Edward Island and in Upper Canada. Later, he established a settlement at Red River.

---

*In Chapter 7 you read about the "great migration" of settlers to Upper Canada from Great Britain that took place between 1815 and 1850. Many of those settlers were also tenant farmers who had been forced off their small farms by their landlords.

Social problems—problems concerning life in a community, problems between people that arise in day to day living

---

Crofter—a person who cultivates a small farm

Selkirk's First Settlers

The first group of 80* Scottish settlers arrived at York Factory, a Hudson's Bay Company fur fort, in the winter of 1811. They spent a difficult winter there enduring homesickness, cold, poor food, and **scurvy**.

In the spring they set out on the 420-kilometre journey to the Red River Valley, arriving in August of 1812. They arrived too late to plant crops and no special preparations had been made for their arrival. Another difficult winter was to follow. The settlers survived mainly because of the help they received from the First People and because they were able to buy food from the local **Metis**.

In the spring of 1813 Lord Selkirk sent another group of settlers from Scotland. They too endured many hardships.

Conflict

All of Lord Selkirk's land grant was in Rupert's Land, the lands granted to the Hudson's Bay Company. However, Selkirk's land grant was in the midst of the transportation route and trading territory that was used by the North West Company. The Nor'Westers were angered and thought that the Hudson's Bay Company was trying to purposely disrupt their trading practices and block the supplies of pemmican that were being brought in to the fur trading posts.

The settlers met with considerable opposition. The Metis and Cree felt that the Selkirk settlers, who were farmers, would bring to an end their traditional hunting patterns. In spite of this the Metis and First People were helpful to the newcomers by providing them with food and other assistance. Gradually the Metis came to realize that the Red River Settlement would interfere with their hunting of buffalo. Many of the Metis people were farmers near the Red and Assiniboine rivers. They had no legal rights or title to the land even though they had farmed it for generations. The Nor'Westers warned the Metis that they would lose their land to the settlers. They also told the Metis that food, especially pemmican, would become scarce and perhaps it would become unavailable for the North West traders.

By January of 1814 things were desperate in the settlement. The governor of Assiniboia, Miles Macdonnell, was worried that the Selkirk settlers would starve. He issued a law called the "Pemmican Proclamation." It stated that, for the next year, no food could be taken from Assiniboia without a licence that only he, acting as governor, could issue. This affected the Metis because they made pemmican to sell to the fur traders, who ate it on their long trips to the North-West. The Metis were greatly angered because pemmican was an important source of income for them, as was buffalo meat, which was also restricted. They felt that Governor Macdonnell had no right to pass laws in their land. A very tense situation developed.

The North West Company told the Metis that if they destroyed the crops and homes of the settlers, then maybe they would leave, and the land would be returned to the Metis. By 1815, only 60 settlers remained. The situation grew worse, under the leadership of Cuthbert Grant, when a group of Metis decided to barricade Fort Douglas until the colonists inside the fort came out desperate for food. Robert Semple, the Governor-in-Chief of Rupert's Land, and a group of armed men went to find out what Grant and the Metis were doing. Semple met Grant near a group of trees called Seven Oaks. There is no agreement among historians as to which side fired the first shot, but at the end of the brief battle one Metis and 20 settlers, including Governor Semple, were dead.

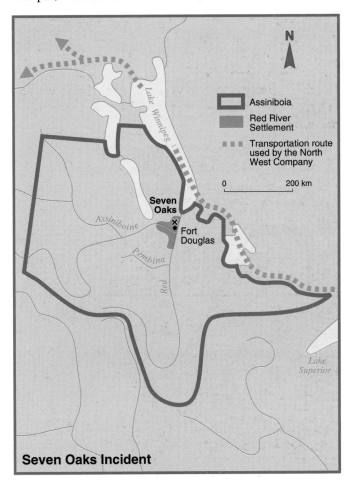

Seven Oaks Incident

Settlers in the Red River Settlement would interfere with the North West Company's fur trade route.

---

*Sources vary from 70 to 105 people.

Scurvy—a disease caused by a lack of Vitamin C
Metis—people of mixed North American Indian and European ancestry

Women of the Red River Settlement

There were few non-Native women in the West in the early days. Marie-Anne Lagemodière is often referred to as the first non-Native woman in the West.* She was the grandmother of Louis Riel, the Metis leader whom you will read about later in this chapter. She was born in Quebec, where she married a fur trader, Jean Baptiste Lagemodière. Marie-Anne and her husband travelled by the fur traders' route from the St. Lawrence, a journey of 3218 kilometres, to come west in 1807. Their first child was born in a wigwam near the bank of the Pembina River on January 6, 1807. Julie, the second youngest of Marie-Anne's children, was to become the mother of Louis Riel. After Marie's death, Abbé Dugas wrote down the story of her life as she told it to her children. Here is a story about the time when she was riding a horse that was a trained buffalo runner.

As soon as her horse caught sight of the buffalo, without a thought of his burden he took the bit in his teeth and galloped after the herd. Embarrassed by the two bags which hung, one on each side of the horse, in one of which was her child, the poor woman expected every moment that she would be thrown to the ground. She commended herself to God, and clung with all her strength to the horse's mane. She did not know how long her mad career continued—she knew only that it was horribly long. When her husband, by wheeling and cutting across her horse's path, succeeded in stopping his flight, she was on the point of succumbing. This was about three o'clock in the afternoon. They pitched their tent on a rising piece of ground near some trees, and there, some hours after that furious race, Madame Lagemodière gave birth to her second child, whom they nicknamed Laprairie, because he was born in the middle of the prairie.

The second party of Selkirk settlers included the first group of European women to come to the West. There were, according to Owen Keveny, who was in charge as Lord Selkirk's representative, 18 women older than the age of 15, one girl, and 11 children under the age of eight. One woman gave birth to a child while on ship, during a furious storm in Hudson Bay. There was also a great deal of an illness known as ship fever on board the ship.

Among the women in this group was Catherine McPherson. Catherine was admired by the others because of the way she risked her own health to care for those who were ill. She was always positive and encouraged the others during the long journey from Hudson Bay to the Red River Settlement. A young man named Alexander Sutherland was in the same group of settlers as Catherine McPherson. He too admired her courage and strength. The two were married shortly after their arrival in the Red River Settlement.

Many other Red River women showed great courage during the time of the beginning stages of the Red River Resistance in the winter of 1869–70. At one point Riel's followers were looking for a Mr. Eccles and came to the home of his mother-in-law in search of him. His mother-in-law made him crouch under a chair. She quickly sat down on the chair, and spread her large skirt over it to hide him. He had to stay in the same position for two hours while Riel's men searched the house and then waited, hoping that he would arrive home.

After Confederation, in 1867, many people from the East began to come to settle in Red River. They brought their custom of having large dances and fancy dinners with them. Lack of proper clothing was a common problem:

Dinners of ceremony were attended by ladies in imported gowns, wearing moccasins in lieu of dancing slippers, which could not easily be obtained. At the first ball after the rebellion there were not enough evening shoes to supply the men so some of them went in dress suits and moccasins. For certain of the more formal affairs dress clothes were obligatory. More than one story is told of two friends who tossed a coin to see which should wear the one dress suit owned by them jointly.

Caroline Sinclair (née Pruden) and Maggie Stewart (née Mowat)

*There was actually a woman from the Orkney Islands who lived in the West from 1806 until 1808. We do not know her name, but she travelled on a Hudson's Bay Company ship disguised as a young man. She gave birth to a "a fine boy" on December 29, 1807, at the trading post at the mouth of the Pembina River, according to the journal of the fur trader, Alexander Henry. The following summer she and her son returned to Scotland.

The Metis
Before 1867 (Confederation)

The largest group of people in the Red River Settlement were the Metis. In 1843 there were 5000 people in the Red River Settlement. Of this group 1000 were Caucasian; the Metis made up the remaining 4000.

The Metis nation began when English, Scot, or French fur traders married Indian women. As a result of these intermarriages, the Metis had a varied background. They were able to draw upon the cultures of all of their ancestors. Most of them spoke English or French and at least one Indian language. Some of the boys had been educated in schools in the cities of British North America or in Great Britain. Girls learned Indian ways from their mothers. The Metis who were of a French background were generally Roman Catholic, and those from an English or Scottish background were usually Protestant.

Before 1867, the Metis had supported themselves in many different ways. Many worked in the fur trade. Some of these worked at the fur posts as labourers, interpreters, and company clerks. Others worked for the fur trading companies as hunters, trappers, or as York boat "tripmen" who transported trade goods and furs to and from the fur forts, or as freighters in brigades of **Red River carts**. Many Metis women worked to supply the fur trading companies with pemmican. Other Metis who worked in the fur trade chose to trap and hunt independently, rather than work for the large fur-trading companies. Still others preferred to stay in the Red River Settlement and farm for most of the year.

The Buffalo Hunt

 The buffalo hunt was an important part of Metis life. The buffalo was a major source of food and the pemmican that the women made from the meat could be traded at the fur posts for other items. The hunt itself was an opportunity for the hunters to display their hunting skills and to earn the admiration of the others.

Buffalo hunts took place at least once a year. The hunters would travel in their Red River carts until a buffalo herd was sighted. These hunts grew larger over time. In 1820 there were 540 Red River carts on the hunt; in 1830 there were 820 carts; and in 1840 there were 1210.

There were strict rules of conduct for these hunts. The four basic rules were:

- No hunting on Sunday.
- No one was to lag behind, go ahead, or go off in a different direction from the main hunting group.
- No one was to start the buffalo running before the order was given.
- Anyone caught stealing was to be publicly humiliated.

The first time one of the rules was broken, the offender's saddle and bridle were cut up. The second time his coat was cut up. The third time a rule was broken, the person was whipped. It was very important that the rules be obeyed. For instance, if someone started the buffalo running before the order was given, others could be caught off guard and injuries might result.

Following the hunt, the women skinned the buffalo and cut them up. That night everyone feasted on fresh buffalo meat that had been roasted over the campfire. The meat that was not eaten immediately was dried in order to make pemmican.

Metis Farms

The Metis farms (and those of the Scottish settlers) were usually in strips about three kilometres long. They often had a 100-metre frontage on the rivers. These long, narrow farms allowed each farmer to take his animals to the river to drink and to the meadow to eat hay. The Metis did not like the block method of dividing land that was used in Upper Canada. If the block method, which resulted in square farms, was introduced into the Red River Settlement, it would cause the Metis to lose either land used for hay or access to water.

C-73392, National Archives of Canada, Ottawa (detail).

A Metis buffalo hunter of the mid–1800s

Red River cart—a strong two-wheeled cart pulled by horses or oxen

Focus On: The Red River Settlement in 1869

The following contains a summary of some of the facts about the Red River Settlement in 1869:

- The Red River Settlement was located in the Assiniboia region, the 300 000-square-kilometre area in Rupert's Land that was granted to Lord Selkirk by the British government.

- The population of the Red River Settlement was about 11 300. About 5700 were French-speaking Metis and 4100 were English-speaking Metis. These Metis were farmers, Hudson's Bay Company employees, and self-employed fur traders and trappers. About 1500 of the population of Red River were settlers—Roman Catholic missionaries, Scottish farmers, Hudson's Bay Company employees, and English-speaking Protestants from Ontario, some of whom were merchants and land speculators.

- The Hudson's Bay Company had bought back the land after Lord Selkirk died. Thus, the Red River Settlement did not have the status of a separate colony. It was governed by a governor and a council that was appointed by the Hudson's Bay Company.

- Fort Garry, built in 1835 to serve as the main Hudson's Bay Company post in the region, was the centre of government. Fort Garry was located at the present-day site of Winnipeg.

- The farms in the Red River Settlement were long, narrow strips that fronted onto the river. Most of the farms had not been bought. The farmers had simply settled down and begun working them. This kind of ownership was recognized by the community as being valid.

- The people of the Red River Settlement had developed a distinct culture and identity over the years. They had little contact with the people of Ontario or Quebec.

Above: A group of Metis hunters and traders photographed on the Plains by the Boundary Commission in the early 1870s

Above: A Metis hunter

Left: The paddlewheeler *Dakota* on the Red River at Fort Garry

C-79643, National Archives of Canada, Ottawa.

Canada's Interest in Rupert's Land

The government of Canada was interested in Rupert's Land for several reasons. For one thing, Rupert's Land had good farmland. There was very little farmland left to buy in Ontario. People who wanted to be farmers were starting to look farther west.

There was also the Canadian government's goal of expanding Canada from the Atlantic Ocean to the Pacific Ocean. This was part of John A. Macdonald's Conservative government's policy of *"A Mari usque ad Mare"*—meaning "From Sea to Sea." For the government to achieve that goal, Rupert's Land would have to become part of Canada.

The Canadian government felt that if they did not move quickly and make Rupert's Land part of Canada, the Americans would take over Rupert's Land. Some American settlers had already moved into the area. Minnesota, a state south of the Red River Settlement, already had a population of 300 000 by 1865. Trade had begun between the Red River Settlement and St. Paul, which was the capital of Minnesota.

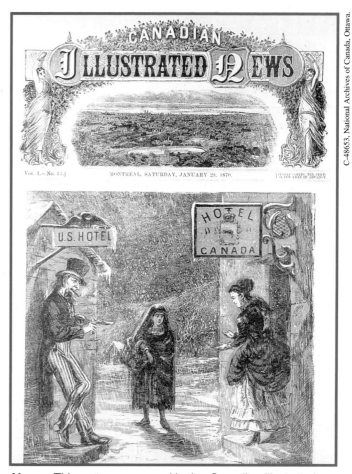

C-48653, National Archives of Canada, Ottawa.

Above: This cartoon appeared in the *Canadian Illustrated News* on January 29, 1870. What are the choices facing the Red River Settlement? What impression of the Red River Settlement does the cartoonist present to the viewer?

Below: This painting of Fort Garry was done by Ernest J. Hutchins in 1872. The Hudson's Bay Company built Fort Garry in 1835 at the junction of the Red and Assiniboine rivers to provide a base for governing Assiniboia.

The Rupert's Land Act, 1868

The government of Canada decided to buy Rupert's Land. They paid the Hudson's Bay Company $1 500 000 for this land. In 1868 the British government passed the Rupert's Land Act. This act allowed the British government to transfer the Hudson's Bay Company lands to the Canadian government. The transfer was to take place on December 1, 1869. The Hudson's Bay Company also kept its fur forts and was given some large land grants in the West. After gaining control of the area, the Canadian government called the entire area the North-West Territories. They did not plan to make any part of the area into a province.

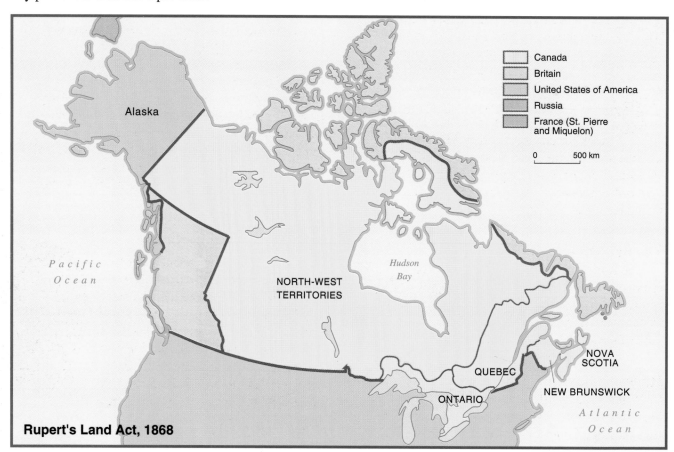

Rupert's Land Act, 1868

Legend:
- Canada
- Britain
- United States of America
- Russia
- France (St. Pierre and Miquelon)

0   500 km

Alaska

Pacific Ocean

NORTH-WEST TERRITORIES

Hudson Bay

QUEBEC

ONTARIO

NOVA SCOTIA

NEW BRUNSWICK

Atlantic Ocean

In the Rupert's Land Act of 1868, the lands of the Hudson's Bay Company were sold to the government of Canada.

Government Surveyors

The Canadian government decided to begin surveying the land for the location of townships before the official transfer of Rupert's Land on December 1, 1869. A survey crew was sent to the Red River area in the autumn of 1868. A second crew arrived in the summer of 1869. The surveyors began dividing the land into large squares similar to the block system used by the people in Ontario.

The people of the Red River Settlement, both the settlers and the Metis, were surprised to see the surveyors. No one from Ottawa had ever been sent out to ask the people for their opinions about becoming part of Canada, or even to inform them of the government's plans.

An Exercise in Critical Thinking

Points of View

In the fall of 1869, there were several different groups involved in the Canadian government's proposed takeover of Rupert's Land. The following are some points of view on the issue.

Prime Minister Macdonald

The settlement of the North-West was necessary to fulfill Macdonald's dream of a Canada that stretched from sea to sea. Since farmland was mostly settled in Ontario, he saw the North-West as a place for new settlers to go. The possible American takeover of the area was a concern. The people of the North-West were not consulted in the decision to make the area part of Canada. Macdonald took for granted that they would go along with the union of the North-West and Canada. Macdonald did not think there was any need to grant the North-West provincial status and felt that the area should remain as a territory.

The British Government

The British government had approved the sale of the Hudson's Bay Company lands to the Dominion of Canada in 1869. They felt it was now Canada's responsibility to govern the area.

Hudson's Bay Company

William Mactavish, governor of the Hudson's Bay Company territory, felt that the authority of the Hudson's Bay Company over Rupert's Land had ended, since the transfer to Canada was to take place on December 1, 1869.

(The fact that the governor was unwell may have been part of the reason why he did not want to become involved in the events in the Red River Settlement at this time.)

Settlers

Many of the English-speaking Protestants from Ontario belonged to the Canada Party. This was a group of Red River settlers who were urging the Canadian government to make the Red River Settlement a province of Canada. Their leader was Dr. John Christian Schultz. Schultz was an important man who owned a store in the Red River Settlement and published a newspaper. Members of the Canada Party wanted the English-speaking Protestants from Ontario to settle on the Metis farms and govern the area. Schultz carried on a campaign for the Canada Party in his newspaper, *The Nor'Wester*, to promote union with Canada and to attack the Metis and the Hudson's Bay Company. Schultz later became lieutenant-governor of Manitoba. The members of the Canada Party felt political union with Canada would put an end to the traditional Metis strip farms. They looked forward to the Metis land being passed on to the settlers who would arrive from Ontario. The settlers were bitterly disappointed that Rupert's Land would not have an elected government when it was taken over by Canada, but they felt that this would only be temporary.

Metis

The Metis were uncertain about the Canadian government's plans for their homeland. They were concerned that the English-speaking newcomers might take over their lands. They also wanted the culture, especially religious and language rights, of the Roman Catholic French-speaking Metis to be respected. They were angry that their opinions were not sought in regard to union with Canada.

Discussion

1. Identify the issue debated on this page. Relate it to the Canadian government's purchase of Rupert's Land.
2. With which point of view would you have agreed? Give reasons for your answer.
3. Why is it important to look at an issue from various points of view?
4. Can you predict some problems that may have resulted because of the points of view expressed here?

Red River Resistance

In the summer of 1869, Canadian government surveyors arrived in the Red River area. The Metis were upset because the boundaries of their long, narrow river-lot farms were being ignored as the land was surveyed into square blocks. The Metis decided to put a stop to the surveying of their lands by taking away the chains that were being used by the surveyors for measuring. The surveyors gave up and left.

The Metis were also angry upon hearing the news that the government was planning to appoint William McDougall as lieutenant-governor of the North-West Territories. McDougall was known to the Metis as the federal minister who favoured westward expansion. He was the person responsible for sending the road and land surveyors.

At this time Louis Riel emerged as a leader of the Metis. Riel was well educated. He had been born in the Red River Settlement, but was sent by Bishop Taché to Montreal to study for the priesthood. He was a persuasive speaker who was fluent in both French and English.

Riel helped to set up *Le Comité National des Métis* (the National Committee of Metis). He was the secretary and John Bruce was the president. The purpose of the committee was to bargain with the Canadian government for the lands, language, and religious rights of the Metis people.

One of the first acts of the National Committee of Metis was to stop the newly appointed lieutenant-governor, William McDougall, from entering the Red River area on November 2, 1869. McDougall's way was blocked by 14 armed Metis. They gave him a message from the National Committee telling him not to enter the Red River Settlement until he had permission from the inhabitants. The Metis did not think that McDougall had any right to enter the Red River Settlement as lieutenant-governor until December first, when the official transfer of Rupert's Land to Canada was to take place. In fact, Prime Minister Macdonald had instructed McDougall not to officially take over Rupert's Land until he was told to do so. McDougall was acting before he received Macdonald's instructions.*

The next step for the National Committee was to seize Fort Garry, which was the headquarters of the Hudson's Bay Company in Red River. They did this without firing a shot. The Metis now had control of the settlement. Riel invited both

Riel and the National Committee of Metis, 1869. Riel is third from the left, in the centre row.

*Many historians believe McDougall used poor judgement in attempting to enter the North-West before it had officially become part of Canada. His reputation in Ontario suffered as a result of his actions.

French-speaking and English-speaking Metis to an assembly at Fort Garry. He thought it was important to present a united front to the Canadian government. At this meeting the Metis wrote a **List of Rights**, the conditions by which they would join Canada.

Macdonald did not want the Red River Settlement to become part of Canada until calm had been restored. The Hudson's Bay Company officials did not want to step in because their authority was almost over. As a result, there was no official government in the North-West. At this time Louis Riel was offered a great deal of money to have the Red River Colony join the United States, but he refused because of his loyalty to Britain. McDougall waited until December 1, 1869, which was the day that Rupert's Land would be officially transferred to the Canadian government. On that day he crossed the border and claimed Rupert's Land for Canada.

A week later, on December 8, 1869, Riel helped set up a **provisional government**. This government replaced the National Committee. The leader was Louis Riel.

An Exercise in Decision-Making

1. While in groups, write a list of the rights and responsibilities you think teenagers attending school should have. Record your list on chart paper and have one student in each group read your list to the rest of the class. As a class make a list of the ten most important rights. You may want to send a delegation to discuss the list with your school's principal. He or she may be able to point out implications that you may not have considered.
2. In groups, list the rights you think the Metis would have listed regarding their conditions for joining with Canada.
3. Were the Metis justified in seizing Fort Garry? Write a paragraph defending this action from the Metis point of view, and a paragraph describing it from the Canadian government's point of view.

C-18082, National Archives of Canada, Ottawa (detail).

Louis Riel (1844–1885)

Louis David Riel was born at Red River on October 22, 1844. He was the eldest of Louis Riel and Julie Lagimodière's 11 children. Louis Riel's father was also a leader of the Metis. He had helped to lead the protest against the monopoly of the Hudson's Bay Company on trade in the 1840s. Riel's mother was the daughter of the first European woman to come from Canada to the North-West.

In 1858, Bishop Taché sent Louis Riel to Montreal to study for the priesthood. By 1865, having decided that the priesthood was not for him, he left school. For a short time he studied in a law office. Then he moved west.

By the summer of 1868 he was back in the Red River Settlement. There, his fluency in both French and English, his education, and his pride in the Metis people made him a natural leader. Riel is known as the Father of Manitoba because of his work to make Manitoba a province of Canada. Approximately 15 years later, Riel again championed Metis Rights, this time in Saskatchewan. For his part in the 1885 Resistance Riel was hanged. His sentence remains controversial to this day.

List of Rights—a list of conditions that the Metis wanted the government to meet and enforce

Provisional Government—a temporary government set up until a more permanent one can be established

The Metis List of Rights

In late December of 1869 Prime Minister Macdonald sent Donald Smith, a senior officer of the Hudson's Bay Company, to speak to the people of Red River. Smith had two jobs to do. One was to explain to the Metis what plans the Canadian government had for the area. The other was to find out what the Metis' concerns were and to report back.

Riel let Smith speak to the people. In spite of the cold winter temperature, over 1000 people, mainly Metis, attended an outdoor meeting at Fort Garry to listen to Smith.

After the meeting Smith worked with the Metis to draw up a revised List of Rights. Three Metis then travelled to Ottawa, taking this List of Rights with them.

The Metis List of Rights

The Metis List of Rights asked for these things:

- the right to elect their own Legislative Assembly, with the power to pass all local laws
- the right to approve or reject any federal government laws affecting the Red River area
- the right to elect local officials such as sheriffs and constables
- the right to have land set aside for schools, roads, and public buildings
- that the territories of Rupert's Land and the North-West enter the Dominion of Canada as a province
- the right to have Winnipeg connected by rail to the nearest railway line
- that the federal government pay all the expenses involved in governing the new province for the first four years
- that any military forces to be stationed in the Red River area be made up of Red River residents
- that treaties be signed between the federal government and Native people in the area
- that both French and English be used in the provincial legislature and courts, and all provincial government documents and acts
- that every male householder aged 21 or over be entitled to vote
- that all existing customs, rights, and privileges remain after joining Canada

An Exercise in Decision-Making

Exercise 1:

(a) Divide into small groups. Each group will take three or four different items from the Metis' List of Rights shown to the left. Analyse each item from the point of view of the Canadian government and accept or discard it. Discuss each item until consensus is reached as to whether it should be accepted or discarded.*

(b) Compile a class list from the items each group has not used. Compare the class list to the Metis list. Discuss why the Metis and the Canadian government would have different ideas about the rights of the people of Assiniboia. Explain to the rest of the class your reason for accepting or discarding items.

Exercise 2:

(a) The Metis have requested, in their List of Rights, that the territories of Rupert's Land and the North-West enter the Dominion of Canada as a province. Use a decision-making frame-work to chart the issue, "Should Assiniboia be made into a province of Canada?" Present the issue from the point of view of the government of Canada.

For Your Notebook

1. Explain why the Canadian government wanted to gain control of Rupert's Land.
2. What was the Rupert's Land Act? What change did it bring to Assiniboia?
3. What should Prime Minister Macdonald do about the situation in Red River?

*Check back to Chapter 1, pages 2 and 3, for ideas on how to reach a consensus.

Thomas Scott

Thomas Scott was a surveyor and had been a member of the Canada Party, the group of English-speaking Protestants in Red River that was working to make the North-West part of Canada. This group believed that English Protestants should control the North-West. They were not interested in the rights of the Metis. Some of them, including Thomas Scott, had been given permission to try to drive the Metis away.

When the Metis took over Fort Garry on November 2, 1869, they put some members of the Canada Party, including Thomas Scott, in jail. While in jail Scott insulted and attacked the guards. He also threatened to escape and kill Riel.

Scott was brought before a traditional Metis military council similar to the ones that dealt with crimes during the Metis buffalo hunts. This council found Scott guilty of insubordination. Insubordination is disobedience to a lawful authority. According to the rules of a buffalo hunt, this was a serious crime. Even though Louis Riel recom-mended mercy, Scott was sentenced to death and was shot by a Metis firing squad on March 4, 1870.

Many people in Quebec and Ontario reacted strongly to the execution of Thomas Scott. Many French-speaking Roman Catholics in Quebec saw Riel as a man who stood up for French rights. Riel had stated that Scott was shot to make the government in Ottawa respect the Metis. Many English-speaking Ontario Protestants called Riel a murderer. They demanded that Prime Minister Macdonald send an army to the Red River Settlement to capture Riel and bring him to Canada for punishment. They also thought the army might be needed to protect English Canadians in the Red River area.

The reaction over the execution of Thomas Scott put the Conservative government of Sir John A. Macdonald in Ottawa in a difficult position. The Conservative government did not want to lose the support of either Quebec or Ontario, but it was very difficult to keep the majority of people in both provinces happy.

The Manitoba Act, 1870

After several months of consideration, the Canadian government agreed that the areas surrounding the Red River Settlement should join Canada as a province. The government had originally planned to leave it as a territory. The Metis wanted the area to become a province, because a province had much greater control over its own affairs than did a territory.

Dominion of Canada, 1870

Canada
Britain
United States of America
France (St. Pierre and Miquelon)

0   500 km

NORTH-WEST TERRITORIES

MANITOBA

QUEBEC
ONTARIO
NOVA SCOTIA
NEW BRUNSWICK

On July 15, 1870, the Manitoba Act went into effect. Through this act Canada's fifth province, Manitoba, came into being. Manitoba was known as the "postage stamp" province. It was much smaller than it is today, being only 224 kilometres wide and 176 kilometres long. The rest of Rupert's Land continued to be part of the North-West Territories.

Many of the points from the Metis List of Rights became part of the Manitoba Act. For instance, French and English were both to be official languages and there would be two publicly funded school systems—Roman Catholic and Protestant. However, the federal government retained control of Crown lands.

Left: In 1870, Manitoba became the fifth province to join Confederation.

Riel Leaves

 Because of the unrest in the area and in order to satisfy people in Ontario, Macdonald decided to send troops to Manitoba. When an expedition under Colonel Wolseley arrived in Red River on August 23, 1870, they were unable to find Riel.

Angered at not finding Riel, some of Wolseley's troops broke loose and attacked two of Riel's friends, Elzear Goulet and Andre Nault.

Fearing for his life, Riel fled to the United States. Riel did not return to Canada until 1884 because he feared he would be tried for the death of Thomas Scott. You will read about what happened in 1885 in Chapter 11.

C-2775/C-134840, National Archives of Canada (detail).

The Red River Expedition, 1870. Colonel Garnet Wolseley led 1200 men on the difficult journey from Toronto to Fort Garry.

An Exercise in Critical Thinking

A Rebellion or Not a Rebellion?

 Some historians have called the events in Red River in 1869 and 1870 the Red River Rebellion or the First Riel Rebellion. The term rebellion is used when people attempt to overthrow a government that is legally in power. However, some historians raise the question as to whether there was a government in power in Red River.

Red River was not going to belong to the government of Canada until December 1, 1869. When Prime Minister Macdonald heard about the troubles there he told Lieutenant-Governor McDougall not to enter the area until the problems were resolved. The Hudson's Bay Company considered that its rule was over, since the agreement to transfer Rupert's Land had already been signed.

Therefore, can it be said that the Metis overthrew the government in power? Rather, they set up a provisional or temporary government in order to negotiate the best terms possible for the entry of the area into Confederation. The Metis were asking for the right to enter Confederation with provincial status rather than enter as a territory.

In your opinion should the events in the Red River in 1869 and 1870 be classified as a rebellion? Give reasons for your answer.

Exploring Further

1. Use the information from this chapter to develop a game on the events leading to Manitoba entering Confederation.
2. Prime Minister Macdonald decided to send troops to Manitoba. What could he have done instead? What might have happened in the North-West if he had not sent troops? (Use a decision-making model to arrive at your decision.)

British Columbia Joins Confederation

Before 1867 (Confederation)

In 1867, when the colonies of Nova Scotia, New Brunswick, Ontario, and Quebec united as provinces of the new Dominion of Canada, the only British **Crown colony** to their west was the colony of British Columbia.*

The British had claimed the Pacific Coast of North America following exploration by such men as James Cook, Captain George Vancouver, Alexander Mackenzie, David Thompson, and Simon Fraser during the late 1700s and early 1800s. During these years both the Hudson's Bay Company and the North West Company were actively searching for furs in the West.

In 1849 Vancouver Island became a British colony. There were fewer than 1000 settlers living on the island at the time. The mainland area, which was known as New Caledonia, consisted of only a few fur forts. Since there were so few non-Native people in the area, it was considered unnecessary to declare it a colony.

In 1858 a gold rush on the lower Fraser River brought over 30 000 miners to New Caledonia. Many of these miners came from the United States. The British were afraid that the Americans would try to annex Vancouver Island and New Caledonia. James Douglas, the Chief Factor of the Hudson's Bay Company post of Fort Victoria, became the new governor of the British colony of Vancouver Island. He had heard about the lawlessness in California during the gold rush there, and did not want the same thing to happen on British territory. Therefore, he convinced the British government to make New Caledonia into another colony. In 1858, New Caledonia became a colony and was renamed British Columbia. The formation of a colony on the mainland gave the governor authority to punish lawbreakers and to maintain control, in spite of all the new people who were moving into the area.

By 1862 there was a second gold rush in the Cariboo region, bringing more people into the colony of British Columbia. By 1865 the gold boom was nearing its end and the colony of Vancouver Island and the colony of British Columbia were in a financial crisis. By 1866 Britain decided to unite the two colonies of Vancouver Island and British Columbia under the name of British Columbia. The capital was at Victoria. Frederick Seymour became the new governor.

The united colony had a representative government. The people elected nine members of a 22 member Legislative Council. The Legislative Council and the Executive Council answered to the appointed British governor. The governor, although he held a great deal of power, answered to the British colonial secretary, who was a member of the British Cabinet. The monarch, who at this time was Queen Victoria, had the final authority.

By 1868 the colony of British Columbia was heavily in debt because roads and other expensive services had been needed during the gold rush. With the gold rush over, there was no money left to pay for these services. Also, the colony spent more money importing goods than they made exporting goods. During the gold rush, gold had been exported; but by the late 1860s the main industries left were farming, coal mining, and lumbering. These industries could not make up for the lack of gold. People in the colony of British Columbia began to consider the economic advantages that could be gained by joining Canada.

There were some people in the area who favoured ties with Britain. There was also growing pressure for annexation to the United States. Britain concluded that British Columbia should be joined to Canada in order to preserve its link with Britain.

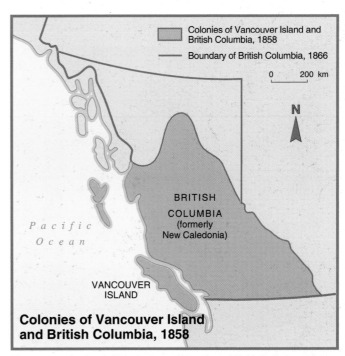

Colonies of Vancouver Island and British Columbia, 1858

The two colonies of Vancouver Island and British Columbia united in 1866 under the name of British Columbia.

Crown colony—a colony under the direct control of Britain
* Assiniboia was not a Crown colony since it was owned by the Hudson's Bay Company.

Focus On: Gold Rush

The early part of the 1800s found the Native people of present-day British Columbia bringing furs to the trading posts of the Hudson's Bay Company. In exchange, the fur traders gave them such trade goods as guns, metal pots, beads, tea, and sugar.

In the summer of 1856 the Natives along the Thompson River noticed "shiny stones" in the shallow gravel beds. After collecting some, they took them to the traders at Fort Kamloops. Word soon spread that the traders at Fort Victoria were interested in the yellow stones. By 1858 the Hudson's Bay Company men had collected about 800 ounces of these yellow stones (gold).

These gold lumps were taken by the purser of the Hudson's Bay Company boat *The Otter* to the United States mint in San Francisco to be analysed, weighed, and made into coins.

The first big strike in the British territory was made at a place known today as Hill's Bar. The discovery was made by a small group who had come up from California after the gold rush ended down there. They had heard the rumours of gold found in the Thompson River. Word about the gold in the Hill's Bar area soon spread. This gold mining area became known as the Lower Fraser.

Soon there were 10 000 miners in the Lower Fraser. With all these people arriving, the Lower Fraser changed. The river banks were soon covered with miners as far as the eye could see. Some of them were digging in the sand, others were working at their **rockers**, others were at their **sluice-boxes** taking out anywhere from five dollars to 100 dollars worth of gold a day. Thirty dollars was about average.

Eventually the Lower Fraser had all been claimed and the miners searched northward into unclaimed areas. By the end of the year many an unsuccessful miner had turned homeward, convinced that the tales about gold in the Fraser River were a hoax. Luckily for the miners, the gamblers, the businesspeople, and the merchants, the Cariboo soon became the next big gold area.

Some of the hardier, more hopeful prospectors ventured northward up

Above: This miner is separating gold from sand and dirt.

Left: The town of Douglas was a typical gold rush settlement in the Cariboo.

Rocker—a cradle used in mining, whereby the material being mined can be sorted and washed

Sluice-box—a long box-like container in which gold is separated from gravel and mud

convinced his partners to ignore the jeers of the other miners, and to continue digging in order to prove them wrong. At 17 metres they struck the richest **pay dirt** to be found in the Cariboo—pay dirt that yielded Barker and his partners a $600 000 fortune.

A town soon grew up around Barker's mine. The miners named it Barkerville in honour of Billy Barker. It was a typical gold rush town with blacksmith shops, laundries, butcher shops, banks, **assay offices,** log shanties, churches, saloons, and hotels. The buildings were built on stilts along a long, narrow, and usually very muddy street.

Just like all great gold rushes throughout history, the Cariboo rush came to an end. With the end of the gold rush, the Pacific Coast experienced great financial difficulties. Because of these financial problems, the issue of whether to join the new Confederation (Canada), or to remain as a British colony, or to join the United States were the options open to the colony of British Columbia.

Above: These miners are bringing gold out of a tunnel mined by the Neversweat Company in the Cariboo, 1868.

Right: Billy Barker.

the Fraser to the Quesnel River in 1859. From there they branched out into Keithley Creek, Antler Creek, Lightning Creek, and Williams Creek, finding many rich bars that they worked with good results.

In the celebrated Williams Creek in 1861, the richest diggings ever discovered in the Cariboo were found by a man known as "Dutch Bill." Many more claims were taken up on this creek. Several of them paid dividends from $20 000 to $60 000 a year. One man, Cameron, left the country after a year's work with $150 000 in gold dust.

One miner who came to the Williams Creek area was Billy Barker.

Barker arrived during the summer of 1862 to find the area humming with activity. Thousands of miners were working furiously at their claims and all seemed to be striking it rich.

Barker selected a spot set back from the river and away from all the other successful claims. Here he and his partners dug a simple vertical mine.

The other miners disagreed with Barker because they believed gold was always found by the creek, not where Barker was digging. Barker

Pay dirt—earth or ore containing valuable minerals such as gold

Assay office—a place that examines gold or other minerals for its quality

An Exercise in Decision-Making

The following is an imaginary conversation between Dr. John Helmcken and Amor de Cosmos about whether British Columbia should join Confederation. The date is 1868. Dr. Helmcken was a doctor in Victoria. He was the first president of the British Columbia Medical Society. Dr. Helmcken was strongly in favour of British Columbia remaining a colony of Britain. Amor de Cosmos was a newspaper editor and a strong advocate of Confederation. Dr Helmcken ran against de Cosmos for a seat in the legislative council in 1868 and won. Start by reading what Dr. Helmcken says. Then read what Amor de Cosmos says directly across the page. The exercise continues on the next page.

Dr. John Helmcken

Mr. de Cosmos, you are wrong to try to convince the people of the colony of British Columbia that we should join the Dominion of Canada. Confederation is only an experiment so far. Why should we ally ourselves with something that has not yet been proved to be workable?

Rupert's Land, with its vast area, is between us and the Dominion of Canada. There is no road or railway to join us. If we unite with Canada, the other four provinces that are near to one another geographically will make decisions for their own benefit. They are not going to worry about British Columbians who are 2000 kilometres away.

The American trading centre of San Francisco is much nearer to us than the Canadian trading centres of Montreal and Toronto. California would be a good market for British Columbian goods. What's more, the people of this colony care little for the difference between the form of government in Canada and that in the United States. Eventually, we may become part of the United States.

My loyalty cannot be bought. I won't agree to join the Dominion of Canada just so our debts will be paid. As for your point about government, the British government will probably grant us a government where the voters have more influence. There is no reason to join Canada just to get better government.

Amor de Cosmos

My dear Dr. Helmcken, the people of Ontario, Quebec, Nova Scotia, and New Brunswick put a lot of thought into their decision to join together to form the Dominion of Canada. Confederation has been successful so far and will continue to be successful.

If British Columbia becomes part of Canada, the other provinces will have to consider what we want, because they will not want us to leave Confederation. Besides, eventually Canada will be one nation that stretches from the Atlantic Ocean to the Pacific Ocean. There will be a railway to join the provinces and transport goods from one province to another.

You must remember, Dr. Helmcken, that our colony is in debt. We are importing more goods than we are exporting. If we join the Dominion of Canada, the Canadian government will pay our debts and we will be off to a fresh start. Also the government may grant us the type of government we want where the decision-makers are responsible to the voter's representatives.

I hope that one day you will come to see the advantages for British Columbia of joining the Dominion of Canada.

The main street of Barkerville in the 1860s

Three Choices

The people of the colony of British Columbia had three choices:

Choice One: They could remain a British colony and hope to gain a government where they had more influence in the future. A small but powerful British group of Hudson's Bay Company and government officials supported this position.

Choice Two: They could become part of the United States. This appealed to the Americans in the colony who had arrived during the gold rush. The United States was south of British Columbia and, since the **annexation** of Alaska in 1867, to the north as well. California would be a good market for British Columbian goods, and the American trading centre of San Francisco was much nearer than the Canadian trading centres of Toronto and Montreal.

Choice Three: They could join Canada. The British government favoured this choice. Some people in the colony of British Columbia felt threatened by the United States that was both north and south of them. They thought they might be forced to become part of the United States if they did not have the protection of being part of Canada. Also, they could ask the Canadian government to pay the colony's debts if they joined Confederation.

Note: The decision-makers in Ottawa did not ask the minority peoples of British Columbia their opinions. The 25 000 Native people and the 1500 Chinese were not consulted.

In groups, decide which choice you would have made had you lived in the colony of British Columbia in the 1860s. Would you have considered the wishes of all the people living there? Why or why not? Use a decision-making model to chart the decision facing British Columbians. You could use a model from this textbook as an example, or design your own.

Annexation—joining of one territory to a larger political entity

The British Columbia Act, 1871

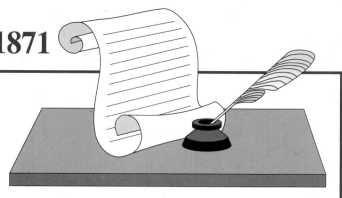

Confederation Negotiations

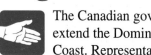 The Canadian government was anxious to extend the Dominion of Canada to the Pacific Coast. Representatives from British Columbia, including Amor de Cosmos and Dr. Helmcken, who had gradually changed his anti-Confederation position, went to Ottawa in 1870 to discuss becoming a province of Canada.

In return for joining Confederation, the Canadian government promised the following:

- a railway joining British Columbia to Canada, to be begun within two years of the date of union (July 20, 1871) and to be finished within 10 years

- payment of the colony's debt of over $1 000 000

- an annual subsidy to the province of $35 000 and a yearly grant of 80¢ per person until the population reached 400 000

- British Columbia would have control of government-owned public land (Crown lands), like the other provinces.*

	Canada
	Britain
	United States of America
	France (St. Pierre and Miquelon)

0   500 km

NORTH-WEST TERRITORIES

BRITISH COLUMBIA

MANITOBA

QUEBEC

ONTARIO

NOVA SCOTIA

NEW BRUNSWICK

Dominion of Canada, 1871

In 1871, British Columbia became the sixth province to join Confederation.

James Douglas (1803–1877)

James Douglas came to Canada from Scotland in 1819 to work for the North West Company. He moved west to work for the Hudson's Bay Company after it and the North West Company united in 1821. In 1842 Douglas was asked to select the site for a new Hudson's Bay Company headquarters on Vancouver Island. He found a suitable location and built Fort Victoria, where he was the Chief Factor.

James Douglas is known as "The Father of British Columbia." He was the first governor of the colony of Vancouver Island. He became governor of the mainland as well when that region became the colony of British Columbia in 1858. He established a Legislative Assembly in each colony and managed to keep law and order, even during the influx of thousands of gold seekers.

When the two colonies joined together in 1866, Douglas continued as governor.

*Crown lands are lands belonging to the government. When the BNA Act was passed, Crown lands were transferred to the provinces. British Columbia was to receive ownership of the Crown lands also; Manitoba did not control its Crown lands.

The Colony of Newfoundland

Newfoundland was not invited to the Charlottetown Conference in 1864 because no one thought Newfoundland supported the union. Two important sections of the population were strongly anti-Confederation — the business community and the Roman Catholics. The merchants had few dealings with Canadians. They exported salt fish to Europe, the West Indies, and Brazil, and imported food and manufactured goods from the United States. They were against political changes that might increase their taxes or restrict their freedom to choose their own trading partners.

The Irish Catholics had several reasons for opposing Confederation. They were afraid of losing their government-funded separate schools. Also, they were pleased that Newfoundland had been granted responsible government by Great Britain in 1855 and felt it was far too soon to abandon it. They saw it as a means to future prosperity, particularly since many people thought Newfoundland had many resources that had not yet been found.

There was another reason for the lack of support for Confederation among Irish Catholics. It reminded some of them of the Act of Union of 1801, by which Britain and Ireland had joined together. They saw that event as a tragedy for Ireland and did not want to see it repeated in North America.

In 1874, the Conservatives returned to power. Even though members of this party tended to favour union, they made it clear to the voters that there would be no attempts to force Confederation on them. They proceeded with a program of railway building, which they hoped would help to develop the rich resources that they believed were in the interior of the colony and on the west coast. They saw a railway as a way to bring investment dollars into the colony and to develop the industries of mining, forestry, and agriculture.

Many members of the business community were against the railway. They were afraid that if building a railway led Newfoundland to the verge of bankruptcy, as it did in Prince Edward Island, it would be difficult to remain independent. By 1894, the colony was in fact facing bankruptcy. But this was not due to the cost of building a railway. Prices for fish and seal oil had dropped, plunging the business community into debt and despair.

A delegation was sent to Ottawa to negotiate the terms by which Newfoundland would enter Confederation. However, the terms could not be worked out.

Newfoundland did not join Confederation until 1949.

Anti-Confederation Song

Hurrah for our own native Isle, Newfoundland,
Not a stranger shall hold one inch of its strand,
Her face turns to Britain, her back to the Gulf,
Come near at your peril, Canadian Wolf.
Ye brave Newfoundlanders who plough the salt sea,
With hearts like the eagle so bold and so free,
The time is at hand when you'll all have to say
If Confederation will carry the day.
Cheap tea and molasses they say they will give,
All taxes take off that the poor man may live:
Cheap rails and cheap lumber our coffins to make,
And homespun to mend our old clothes when they break.
If they take off the taxes how then will they meet
The heavy expense on the country's up-keep?
Just give them the chance to get us in the scrape
And they'll chain you as slaves with pen, ink, and red tape.
Would you barter the right that your fathers have won,
Your freedom transmitted from father to son?
For a few thousand dollars of Canadian gold,
Don't let it be said that your birthright was sold.

For Your Notebook

1. Why did the people of Newfoundland not join Confederation during the late 1800s?

Exploring Further

1. What argument is used in the anti-Confederation song to convince Newfoundlanders to vote against Confederation? What image is used for Canada? How does the song picture Newfoundlanders who would be willing to join Confederation?

Prince Edward Island Joins Confederation

Before 1867 (Confederation)

Prince Edward Island rejected the idea of joining Confederation in 1867. This may seem surprising since the process that led to Confederation began in Prince Edward Island, at the Charlottetown Conference in 1864. Many of the people did not see the need for Confederation at this time.

Prince Edward Island was prosperous in the 1860s. Island shipyards were building over 100 ships a year. Excellent harvests were being sent to markets on both sides of the Atlantic Ocean. People could see no financial benefits to becoming part of Canada.

However, many Prince Edward Island farmers did not own their land, but rented it from absentee landlords who lived in Britain. Most of the colony's revenue was being spent in an effort to buy the land from the absentee landlords, but Prince Edward Island could afford to buy only a few of the estates from the landlords.

Islanders had achieved responsible government in 1851. They were happy as a self-governing British colony, with its own Legislative Assembly. It was the opinion of the majority that they had more independence as a colony of Britain than they would have as a very small province of Canada. After all, if they joined Confederation they would have only five representatives in the 200-member Canadian House of Commons—not enough to have any say in how their area would be governed.*

However, in 1873 Prince Edward Island joined Confederation. What had happened to change Islanders' minds?

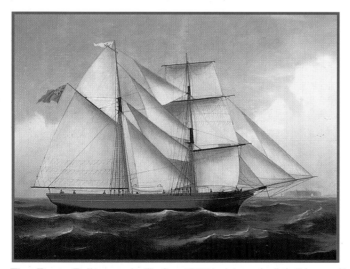

The *Fanny Bailey* was built after 1856, when wooden ships were still in demand and the shipyards of Prince Edward Island were still prosperous.

Reasons for Joining Confederation

 The most important situation that changed people's minds regarding Confederation was the issue of absentee landlords. Many Prince Edward Island farmers did not own their own land, but rented it from landlords who lived in Britain. The farmers wanted the British government to grant them the right to own the land themselves. Islanders who were for Confederation pointed out that, if Prince Edward Island became a part of Confederation, then perhaps the British government would pay more attention to their demands to own their own land.

The government of the colony of Prince Edward Island was deeply in debt, owing a sum equal to about $41 for each of the 80 000 people who lived on the island. The island economy had been declining in the six years since Confederation. The wooden sailing ships built on the island were no longer needed. Steam engines and iron hulls were taking their place. Exports declined more every year.

But the major reason for the large debt was the cost of building an island railway. Islanders had thought that a railway would employ thousands of people, help farmers get their produce to markets, and promote industry. People also hoped that the railway would attract tourists. They thought the railway would definitely improve the ability of the island to continue to remain independent of Confederation.

Unfortunately, costs, which had been estimated at approximately $4000 per kilometre, went to $14 000 per kilometre. By 1873 railway construction had stopped because the builders feared they would never be paid. Prince Edward Island was on the verge of bankruptcy. It began to look as though the only way of getting out of debt would be to join Confederation and get the help of the federal government.

For Your Notebook

1. List the points for and against Prince Edward Island joining Confederation in 1867.
2. Why did Prince Edward Island join Confederation in 1873?

---

*Representation to the House of Commons was determined by "representation by population" and Prince Edward Island had a small population in 1867.

Prince Edward Island Act, 1873

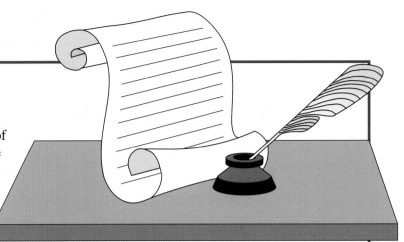

On July 1, 1873, Prince Edward Island joined the Canadian Confederation. There was not a great deal of celebration or even interest in the event at the time. Islanders considered the decision to be more a matter of necessity than choice. A local newspaper described the interest shown in the reading of the Union Proclamation on July 1, 1873 as follows: "The audience within hearing consisted of three persons, and even they did not appear to be very attentive."

In return for joining Confederation, the Canadian government gave Prince Edward Island an $800 000 loan, which was to be used to buy the land back from the absentee landlords. The government agreed to pay all the railway debts, as well as agreeing to provide a $50 grant for every person living on the island. Ferry and telegraph service would be provided between Prince Edward Island and the mainland.

Prince Edward Island was the seventh province to join Confederation. The first four provinces—Ontario, Quebec, Nova Scotia, and New Brunswick—had joined in 1867. Manitoba had joined in 1870 and British Columbia in 1871. In 1873, when Prince Edward Island joined Confederation, the future provinces of Alberta and Saskatchewan were still known as the North-West Territories and the future province of Newfoundland was still a British colony.

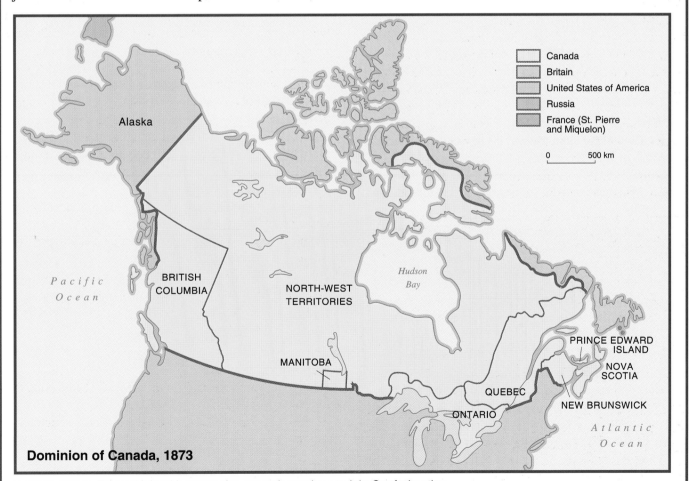

Dominion of Canada, 1873

In 1873, Prince Edward Island became the seventh province to join Confederation.

Review ●

Summarizing the Chapter

- The Canadian government was interested in Rupert's Land because it wanted to expand from "sea to sea" and needed more farmland. It did not want the area to be taken over by the United States.

- Prime Minister Macdonald wanted Rupert's Land to join Canada, but saw no reason to grant it provincial status. Following the Red River Resistance (also called the Riel Resistance), Manitoba became Canada's fifth province on July 15, 1870. The rest of Rupert's Land was renamed the North-West Territories.

- The British had claimed the Pacific Coast following exploration during the late 1700s and early 1800s. Vancouver Island became a British colony in 1849. The mainland became a separate colony in 1858, following two gold rushes, which brought thousands of new people into the area. The British government needed to assert its authority over the area to prevent lawlessness and a possible takeover by the United States. In 1866 the two colonies formed the united colony of British Columbia with James Douglas as its governor.

- On July 20, 1871, British Columbia became the sixth province to join Confederation. Among other promises, the Canadian government made a commitment to build a railway across the country to join the new province to the rest of Canada.

- Newfoundland had little interest in Confederation in 1867. In 1894 the colony tried to negotiate its entry into Confederation, but the terms could not be worked out. Newfoundland did not become part of Canada until 1949.

- The people of Prince Edward Island decided not to join Confederation in 1867 because they could see no advantages. There were no financial benefits to joining Canada, because the province was very prosperous. They thought they would lose some of their independence by joining Canada, since their small population would mean they would have only five representatives in the 200-member House of Commons.

- Prince Edward Island became the seventh province to join Confederation on July 1, 1873. The main reason for joining was financial. The Canadian government promised Prince Edward Island financial assistance, including an $800 000 loan to be used to buy land from absentee landlords. The colony was heavily in debt at this time due to costs of railway construction.

Checking Predictions

1. At the beginning of this chapter you made some predictions based on the Overview and what you already knew. Now use what you found out by reading the chapter to fill in the third column of the Prediction Chart that you began earlier.

2. Refer to the "Questions to Talk About" on page 177. Discuss the questions based on what you have learned about Confederation in Chapter 9, and about Manitoba, British Columbia, and Prince Edward Island joining Confederation in Chapter 10.

Working with Information

1. Here are some of the main ideas from this chapter:
   - westward expansion (nation building)
   - Red River Settlement
   - Metis lifestyle
   - resistance
   - List of Rights
   - Confederation negotiations
   - gold rush
   - railway building

   Use a web to make a permanent record to show the relationships among the main ideas.

2. Review all of the examples of co-operation and conflict that are found in this chapter. Work with a partner to draw a mind map that organizes all of these examples on one sheet of paper. Use simple line drawings and at least three colours. Show how conflict and co-operation were used in bringing about a nation that stretched from sea to sea.

3. Which person from this chapter would you have liked to have met? Tell why you found this person interesting.

4. Louis Riel has been called a Father of Confederation. Explain. Do you agree with this label? Discuss why or why not. Use a decision-making model to arrive at your decision, or hold a debate.

Building Thinking Strategies

Conceptualizing

1. Settlement is a major concept in this textbook. Follow the steps in concept formation as found on page 39. Make a bulletin board display of your triad's idea of settlement. Use the Red River Settlement as your example.

Communicating Ideas

Reading

1. Read "LaLouise Letendre" by Alice Lee Setka and "Alex MacBeth" by Ted Stone in *Ordinary People in Canada's Past,* by Nancy Sellars Marcotte. Make a list of points about the Red River Settlement found in these stories that you did not read in Chapter 10.

Writing

1. Take the point of view of a Metis farmer living in the Red River area in 1869. Describe your thoughts as you see the surveyors walking over your land.
2. Conduct research on a famous British Columbian of this time. Some possibilities are Amor de Cosmos, John Robson, James Douglas, Amelia Douglas, Billy Barker, Sir Matthew Baillie Begbie, or Dr. J. S. Helmcken.

Speaking

1. Check to see if there is a Metis organization in your area. Arrange for a speaker to come in and discuss the events of 1869 and 1870 in Red River with your class. The speaker might also discuss the goals of the Metis today and the ways in which they are working toward these goals.
2. In this chapter there is an imaginary discussion between Amor de Cosmos and Dr. J. S. Helmcken about whether British Columbia should join Confederation. With a partner, pretend you are both Prince Edward Islanders in 1873 discussing whether the colony should join Confederation. List the points both of you make. One person should be for Confederation and the other should be against Confederation. Improvise a discussion in front of the class based on the points you listed.
3. Debate the following statement: British Columbia would be better off today if it had joined the United States rather than Canada.

Listening

1. Work with a partner and carry out an imaginary interview between a newspaper reporter and John A. Macdonald regarding Macdonald's reasons for dealing with the Red River Resistance as he did.

Creating

1. Create an article that might have been written by Dr. Schultz in his newspaper, *The Nor'Wester,* promoting the union of the Red River Settlement with the rest of Canada.

Canada Revisited

This modern-day diorama of Billy Barker striking it rich is found in Barkerville, British Columbia.

Chapter 11

The Nation Has Growing Pains (1873–1911)

Overview
Use this Overview to predict the events of this chapter.

1871–1877
Seven treaties were drafted with the Aborigines of the North-West. The Aborigines were moved onto reserves.

1873
The North-West Mounted Police were formed.

1873–1878
Alexander Mackenzie and the Liberals governed Canada.

1878–1896
Macdonald won over the voters with his National Policy, which dealt with protective tariffs, a national railway, and settlement of the West. Canada was governed by a Conservative government.

1885
The Canadian Pacific Railway, a national railway, was completed.

The North-West Territories Act

1875
The North-West Territories Act was passed.

1885
The North-West Resistance occurred and was led by Riel.

1900–1914
There was a flood of immigrants into the Canadian West.

1896–1911
Sir Wilfrid Laurier and the Liberals governed Canada.

1905
The provinces of Saskatchewan and Alberta were created.

CONFEDERATION

Alberta

Saskatchewan

Farming was the most important economic activity in the Canadian West.

Chapter Focus

Chapter 11 studies the period from 1873–1911, during which time Canada's regions were joined. Canada's two new provinces, Alberta and Saskatchewan, were created and joined to the nation of Canada. Chapter 11 looks in detail at the National Policy of the Conservative government and the major events that helped shape our nation's foundation. The concepts of power, co-operation, decision-making, and conflict underlie the events of Chapter 11. The focus will be on the concepts of co-operation, decision-making, and conflict.

Power

Co-operation

Decision-making

Conflict

Between 1870 and 1910, nearly three million people immigrated to Canada.

Overview/Prediction Chart

Examine the Overview found on the previous two pages. In pairs or small groups use the Overview and what you already know to predict answers to the questions in the Prediction Chart. Put your predictions in the "My Predictions" column. Once you have finished the chapter, complete the "What I Found Out" column to help you review and summarize what you have learned. Your teacher will provide you with a full-sized working copy of the Prediction Chart.

Prediction Chart—What Do You Think?		
Questions	My Predictions (fill out now)	What I Found Out (fill out at end of chapter)
1. What might be the major events?		
2. Who might be some of the important people or groups?	SAMPLE	
3. Who might hold power?		
4.		

Liberal Administration (1873–1878)

In order to reach his goal of *"A Mari usque ad Mare"* (from sea to sea), Prime Minister Macdonald had promised a railway for British Columbia if it joined Confederation. Macdonald's Conservative government had awarded the contract to build the Canadian Pacific Railway to Sir Hugh Allan. It soon became public knowledge that Allan had donated $325 000 to the Conservative Party during the 1872 election campaign. Macdonald's Conservative government was accused of accepting a **bribe** in exchange for giving the railway contract to Allan. The resulting scandal was called the Pacific Scandal. Macdonald resigned and the Liberals were asked to form the government. They called an election in early 1874 and Alexander Mackenzie returned as Liberal leader.

C-10460, National Archives of Canada, Ottawa (detail).

2nd Prime Minister

Personal Summary

Alexander Mackenzie was born in Scotland in January 1822. In 1842, when he was 20, he followed his sweetheart, Helen Neil, to Canada. She had settled on a farm near Kingston, Ontario, with her family. They were married in 1845. Helen died seven years later and two of their three children also died when they were very young. Mackenzie later married Jane Sym, who also came from his home county in Scotland.

Political Summary

In the early 1850s Mackenzie edited a Reform* newspaper called the *Lambton Register*. He was elected to the Legislative Assembly of Canada in 1861. In 1867 he won a seat in the first Canadian House of Commons. In 1872 he was chosen as Liberal leader. In 1873, when Macdonald's government fell as a result of the Pacific Scandal, Alexander Mackenzie became Canada's second prime minister.

Canadians called Alexander Mackenzie "Plain Sandy." This was a good name for a man who refused a knighthood and described himself as "Clear Grit—pure sand without a particle of dirt in it." He was known for his honesty and fair dealings with people.

Alexander Mackenzie (1822–1892)
Dates as Prime Minister—1873–1878
Party—Liberal

During the time the Liberals were in office under Mackenzie, they established several lasting, important institutions. The Supreme Court of Canada, the Royal Military College at Kingston, and the practice of voting by secret ballot were all begun by Mackenzie's Liberals.

Alexander Mackenzie and his Liberal Party had a difficult time governing Canada. The country's economy was hurt by a world-wide depression and did not prosper while the Liberals were in office. There were crop failures because of plagues of insects. These factors brought economic hardships for many of the people. Canadians were buying goods made in the United States because they were cheaper than many of the goods that were made in Canada. The lack of sales caused many Canadian workers to be laid off from their jobs and some companies went bankrupt. The many economic problems made it difficult for the Liberals to win the upcoming 1878 election.

---

*Before Confederation (1867) the Liberals were called the Grits or Reformers. After Confederation they were called the Liberals, but the nickname Grits was still used.

Bribe—a gift, usually money, that is given to people in order to get them to do something wrong or against their wishes

North-West Territories Act, 1875*

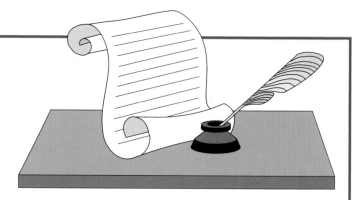

Initially the North-West Territories was governed from Ottawa. It had no government of its own. Then it was placed under the control of the lieutenant-governor of Manitoba. He and his 11-member appointed council ruled it. This was not a very satisfactory arrangement. Since all bills that were passed by the council had to be approved by the federal government, there were long delays before decisions could be carried out.

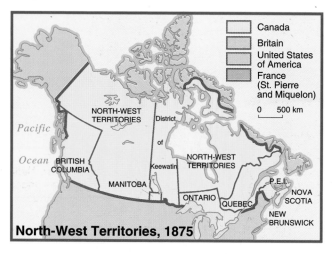

Canada
Britain
United States of America
France (St. Pierre and Miquelon)

0   500 km

NORTH-WEST TERRITORIES   District

Pacific

Ocean   BRITISH COLUMBIA   of   Keewatin   NORTH-WEST TERRITORIES

MANITOBA   P.E.I.
    ONTARIO   NOVA SCOTIA
    QUEBEC   NEW BRUNSWICK

North-West Territories, 1875

As more people came into the North-West, changes were made concerning the way in which it was to be governed. The North-West Territories Act of 1875 provided for the gradual implementation of representative government. It gave the territories its own lieutenant-governor and an appointed council of five members. The Act said that as soon as a district of 2590 square kilometres had 1000 inhabitants, it would become an electoral district and would have the right to elect a member to the council. When the district's population reached 2000, it could elect two members. When the council had 21 members, it could have a fully-elected Legislative Assembly.

Indian Act, 1876**

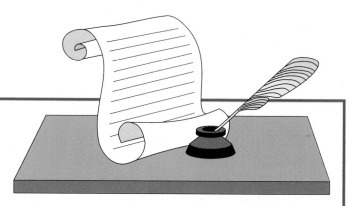

Introduction
In 1876 the government of Canada passed the Indian Act. This Act governs the First People and their lands.

Aim: to move the First People onto reserves and use the remaining lands for settlement

- The first Indian Act assumed the First People would change and become like Europeans. (This process is called assimilation.)

- The Canadian government also introduced isolation policies, whereby the First People were put onto reserves. Once on the reserves they were educated, Christianized, and protected until they were assimilated into the dominant Canadian culture and society.

---

*An amendment to the North-West Territories Act was passed in 1877. It provided guarantees for the French language and for separate schools. French and English were given equal status in the council and in the courts. Documents were to be printed in both languages.

**The Indian Act of 1876 has been revised many times. The most recent Indian Act was passed in 1988.

Conservative Administration (1878–1896)

The Liberals, under the leadership of Alexander Mackenzie, had been governing Canada since 1873. During this time the country was experiencing economic problems. In an attempt to win the election of 1878 both the Liberal Party and the Conservative Party members were trying to convince the people of Canada to vote for them.

The Conservative Party under Sir John A. Macdonald proposed a new policy called the National Policy. The National Policy had three parts: protective tariffs, a national railway, and settlement of the West. A description of Macdonald's National Policy follows.

Sir John A. Macdonald's National Policy brought important changes to Canada.

National Policy Overview

1. **Protective Tariffs**: To encourage the development of Canadian industries, raw materials such as cotton, wool, and unrefined sugar were to be allowed into the country cheaply. High import duties or taxes, called tariffs, were to be put on goods that Canadian industries could manufacture, such as woollen cloth, refined sugar, nails, and steam engines. Tariffs would make goods from other countries more expensive than Canadian goods, so Canadian industries would sell more of their own manufactured goods. Tariffs would also generate the revenues necessary to build the national railway.

2. **National Railway**: The railway would take settlers to the West and bring their crops to the East.

3. **Settlement of the West**: Macdonald planned to help immigrants from other countries settle on the Canadian Prairies. These settlers would buy the products of Canadian industries and would grow wheat to be sold in Canadian cities.

The Canadian voters responded favourably to the ideas of Macdonald and his Conservative Party regarding the National Policy. In 1878 Sir John A. Macdonald became prime minister of Canada once again, after a landslide victory at the polls. The Conservative Party was returned to power.

This painting shows a slice of life during Macdonald's administration. Canadians were developing a social life that suited their climate. These people are skating on the St. Lawrence River at Quebec City in 1894.

NA-1375-1, Glenbow Museum (detail).

Macdonald Puts the National Policy into Effect

This part of the chapter will look at the results of the National Policy in three areas: protective tariffs, a national railway, and settlement of the West.

1. Protective Tariffs

Macdonald and the Conservatives announced that, as soon as they returned to power, higher tariff rates on goods coming into the country would be put into effect. The Conservatives had promised the tariffs as part of their National Policy. The new tariffs were almost double what the previous ones had been. These new tariffs were placed on imported items that threatened to prevent Canadian industry and agriculture from making a profit.

Fortunately for the Conservatives, a world-wide period of prosperity began soon after they returned to power. Ontario, which was Canada's centre of manufacturing, enjoyed an increase in business. It appeared that the National Policy had worked a miracle. However, the prosperity was mainly due to the world-wide business boom, a series of excellent grain crops, and the renewal of the timber trade with the United States.

2. A National Railway

Macdonald began work on a national railway immediately after being elected in 1878. In 1880 the Canadian Pacific Railway Company (CPR) was formed. The company was given the task of building a transcontinental railway that would go from Montreal to the west coast of British Columbia. The railway was to travel along the tracks that were already in existence from Montreal east to the Maritimes.

The building of a transcontinental railway in Canada was a tremendous accomplishment. Canada, with a population of only 4 000 000, managed to complete its railway only a few years after the United States, a nation with ten times the population of Canada.

3. Settlement of the West

Even though settlement of the West was part of Sir John A. Macdonald's National Policy, population growth was still disappointing in the years following the election of 1878. In fact, during the 1890s more people were leaving Canada than were coming in from other countries.

The Dominion Lands Act had been passed back in 1872. This Act gave settlers about 64 hectares (then referred to as a quarter section) of land in return for a 10-dollar registration fee with the condition that one must live on the land and work it for three years. In spite of the Dominion Lands Act the West still had few settlers.

Prairie Homesteads

Many settlers chose to live in the western United States rather than in western Canada. There was a railway in the United States, as well as free land. These features made the United States look inviting. Also, there had been some droughts in the Canadian West in the 1870s and grasshopper plagues in 1874 and 1875. As a result of these conditions, people did not view the Canadian West as a good place to farm. The next part of the chapter will look at what the Canadian government did to get the Canadian West prepared for settlement.

In preparation for the anticipated influx of settlers to the West, the government first had to have the land surveyed. The western lands were divided into squares called townships. Each township contained 36 sections of land, with each section containing 260 hectares (640 acres). The sections were divided into quarter sections of 64 hectares (160 acres) each. A prairie homestead was a quarter section in size. Land was also reserved for the Crown (government lands), schools, the Hudson's Bay Company, and the Canadian Pacific Railway.

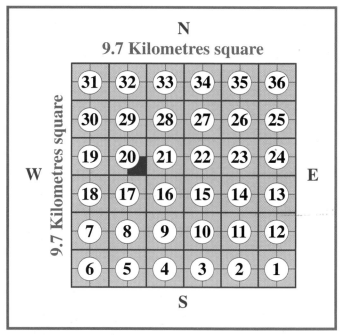

Prairie farmlands were surveyed into townships 9.7 kilometres square. The shaded portion is the southeast quarter of section 20. The legal description for this homestead was SE 20 4725, the 47 standing for township and the 25 for range.

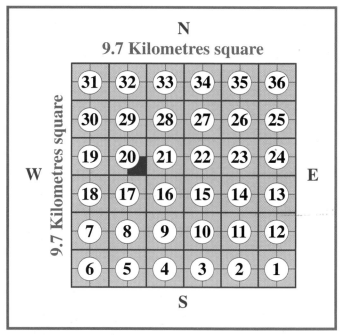

The Canadian Pacific Railway

The Canadian Pacific Railway (CPR) was completed in 1885 under the leadership of William Cornelius Van Horne. The building of the railway was part of Macdonald's dream of binding the country together from "sea to sea." It fulfilled the Canadian government's promise to bring British Columbia into Confederation. With the completion of the Canadian Pacific Railway thousands of settlers chose to settle in the Canadian West.

An Expensive Project

The CPR was extremely expensive to construct. Even though it was a private company (not government owned), it needed the financial help of the government. The government promised the CPR the following:

- $25 000 000
- 10 000 000 hectares of western land
- 1100 kilometres of railway lines that had already been built
- that tax would not be applied to railway material.

The $25 000 000 that was given to the CPR when it was formed proved to be too little. The company went back to the government twice to get more money to continue the building of the railway.

In 1885, when officials from the CPR approached the government to ask for more money, many people said that a transcontinental railway was a crazy dream that the country could not afford. These people were against giving money to the CPR. When a Native resistance took place in the West that year, Van Horne transported soldiers to the West on the railway, even though it was unfinished in some places. The Canadian public were very impressed by the speed with which the railway transported the soldiers to the area of conflict. As a result, the Canadian government gave the CPR some money for further construction, without hesitation.

William Cornelius Van Horne

C-8549, National Archives of Canada, Ottawa (detail).

William Cornelius Van Horne was responsible for completing the construction of the CPR.

In 1882 William Cornelius Van Horne, an American, was hired to be the general manager of the CPR. Van Horne was determined to get the Canadian Pacific Railway completed according to the time schedule that was promised by Macdonald. The Canadian government had built only 480 kilometres of track in the previous 10 years. Van Horne declared that he would build 800 kilometres of track in one year, but by the end of the first year he had built 830 kilometres of track. Under his leadership, the railway was completed by 1885, six years before the estimated date of 1891. Because of his drive and commitment, Van Horne was a man who achieved what he set out to do. With the completion of the CPR in 1885, the West was ready for large numbers of settlers.

Exploring Further

1. How was the building of the CPR a benefit to Canada?
2. Conduct research on one of the people involved in the building of the CPR. Some possibilities of people to study are: Donald Smith, Andrew Onderdonk, William Cornelius Van Horne, James Hill, and Sir Sanford Fleming.
3. Write a week's entries in the journal of a navvy—an unskilled labourer who works on canals, roads, or railways.

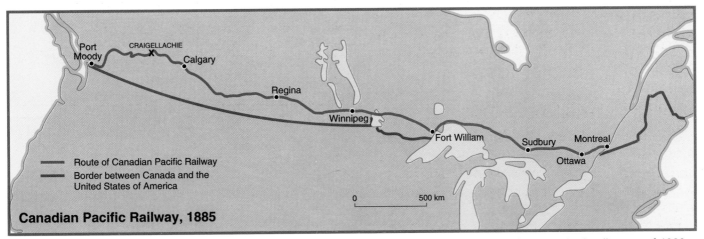

- Route of Canadian Pacific Railway
- Border between Canada and the United States of America

Port Moody CRAIGELLACHIE Calgary Regina Winnipeg Fort William Sudbury Montreal Ottawa

0   500 km

Canadian Pacific Railway, 1885

This map shows the route of the main line of the Canadian Pacific Railway. The complete railway line stretched a distance of 4660 kilometres from Port Moody, British Columbia, east to Montreal. The first train from Montreal arrived at the Pacific Coast in July 1886.

The Last Spike

by Brenda Bellingham

Edward Mallandaine was only 17 when he pushed his way into Canada's most famous railway photograph.

The photograph, taken on November 7, 1885, shows one of the richest and most powerful men in Canada, Donald Smith (soon to be named Lord Strathcona), pounding in the last spike on the new Canadian Pacific Railway. In the photograph young Mallandaine stands in front of a group of bearded men, his right foot planted on the rail as he peers around Smith. He seems determined to get into the picture. The young man is not related to anyone in this historic photograph, nor was he a railway worker. So who was he and how did he appear here, in this photograph?

He was born in Victoria, British Columbia, a place described at the time as a city "of tents, gullies and swamps, and the inhabitants were mostly miners." His father was an engineer and architect. His mother was a housewife.

It seems likely that the boy's childhood was comfortable. When the 1885 North-West Resistance broke out, he eagerly followed its progress in the newspapers. Patriotically, he decided to join up and fight against the rebels. This was easier said than done. To get off Vancouver Island, he had to take a ship to New Westminster, British Columbia. Then he made his way to Port Moody to catch a local train that connected with the new Canadian Pacific Railway line.

Donald Smith driving the symbolic Last Spike. Behind him is Edward Mallandaine.

By the time he reached Golden, the North-West Resistance had been quashed at Batoche, Saskatchewan, and most of the government troops had already been shipped out. Edward's soldiering days were over before they had begun.

Disappointed and dejected, the boy turned around and headed back towards the coast. At Revelstoke, then called Farwell, he stopped to look around. Victoria was small, but Farwell just had one street with wooden shacks and a few log houses. The largest building was the Columbia Hotel, which was named for the nearby river.

It was not much to look at but it was a busy place. Between the mining at Big Bend and the railway construction with the CPR, Farwell's storekeepers were smiling.

There was talk of a new post office. In conversation, somebody suggested that maybe Edward would be interested in a delivery route. No wages were to be paid for the job; of course it was up to Edward to decide how to make things pay.

Each week he would make a mail run from Farwell to Eagle Pass. On the way he picked up orders for papers or supplies. Then the following week, he'd make the deliveries, charging a service fee. At first he found the life of a business-person very hard.

His life on the road was never dull. Work on the new railway line was going full steam ahead. Some days, he would see as many as 50 men suspended over the cliffs at Summit Lake, drilling holes in the rock face to take the dynamite charges. Twice daily the huge blasts would roar through the pass, echoing like deep thunder off the mountain walls. Thousands of metres of material were moved by an army of labourers, most of them arriving on crowded ships through the port of Hong Kong. This mighty railway machine, with its moving parts of human beings, could build a 100-metre truss bridge in one day.

The towns and work camps were lively too. Even after long hours of backbreaking work, workers found energy for fights and brawls. Gambling and drinking were the chief entertainments, both in towns and in the camps. Medical people were kept busy attending to work accidents, accidents as a result of drinking, and injuries from fights. There was always something happening to satisfy the curiosity and thirst for excitement of a 17-year-old boy.

As the rails originating in the East and West drew daily closer together, so the towns that grew up almost overnight began to shrink. Contractors, their projects over, let their workers go. Some of those who were unemployed moved on. A few went into business as "road agents" preying on their former work-mates, stealing their hard-earned wages. Some workers fought back, adding blood to the sweat on their Canadian railway dollars.

By the fall of 1885, deliveryman Edward Mallandaine found his route was taking him through deserted camps and ghost towns. Gone were the brawling crowds of men, the lights of the saloons, and the eager, smiling storekeepers.

The silent pass began to oppress Edward now. Once in awhile he would hear the eery shriek of a construction locomotive hauling flatcars loaded with rails. The weather started to turn colder. It was time to close down the delivery business.

There was still one last moment of railway glory for Edward, one last, cold ride to Craigellachie and a place in Canada's history. In a *Victoria Colonist* interview in 1899 he described the trip:

On the afternoon of November 6 several of us left Farwell on a train consisting of an engine and tender and three flat cars loaded with rails—the last train to load rails for Craigellachie. A cold cheerless rough ride we had. Shortly after leaving Farwell, it began to snow. This made the rails slippery and when we reached the big gumbo slide or grade, we were unable to get over it, and after three attempts, in each of which the train would run back on itself, we were obliged to cut off one car. Then we managed to make it over the grade.

Far into the darkness of the night we travelled . . . Finally it came to an end. It was pitch dark and we were able to get off and after a great deal of difficulty we managed to snatch a short sleep in a vacant box car. All through the night the rails were laid from both East and West and early the following morning, November 7, we were astir watching the rails gradually approaching each other.

Soon there remained but a single rail to be laid. The distance was measured: it was discovered that the rail was about three feet too long and while this was being shortened, Sir Donald Smith and his party came on the scene. They watched the proceedings in readiness to drive the last spike.

Then the rail was laid. The spectators numbering probably 50 outside of the workmen intently watched each spike as it was driven. Finally, there remained but one more spike to be driven. It was partly driven in and a hammer was given to Sir Donald Smith to drive it home.

Before doing so three photographs were taken by a photographer named Ross, of Ross Best & Co., Winnipeg; one when Sir Donald had the hammer over his shoulder, preparatory to striking; one with the hammer over his head, and one with the hammer on the nail head. Then he quickly and in a most workmanlike manner, drove the spike home. Everybody cheered; the locomotives whistled and shrieked; several short speeches were made; hands were shaken, and Major Rogers, the discoverer of the pass named after him, became so gleeful that he up-ended a huge tie and tried to mark the spot by the side of the track by sticking it in the ground.

Thus was the Dominion of Canada bound together by bands of steel reaching from the Atlantic to the Pacific . . .

As soon as the ceremony was over the last spike was extracted and hammered to bits, and the last piece of rail that was cut off was chipped, and the last tie was splintered and everyone who wanted it secured a memento of this memorable occasion. ■

The North West Mounted Police

Reasons for Formation

In August of 1873 Parliament created a special police force for the West called the North West Mounted Police (NWMP). Officials in the North-West, especially Alexander Morris, lieutenant-governor of Manitoba and the North-West Territories, had been asking for such a force. Since the Hudson's Bay Company had transferred its control to the Canadian government in 1869, it was not easy to enforce the laws of the western lands. There was no one to arrest and punish people who robbed and murdered. There was no one to stop the American traders who were selling whiskey to the Native peoples and others living in Canada. The Canadian government wanted to make it clear that the North-West was part of Canada and that law and order were going to be enforced. The government was also concerned about American settlers coming north and perhaps trying to make the North-West part of the United States.

An incident in the Cypress Hills, which are in Alberta and Saskatchewan, demonstrated the great need for a police force. In June of 1873 a group of American traders and trappers had shot and killed 30 Assiniboine people. News of this incident reached the Canadian government in the summer of 1873. The Cypress Hills incident became a symbol of the lawlessness that occurred in the West. Something had to be done about it.

Lieutenant Colonel George A. French, Commissioner of the North West Mounted Police

The March West

The first group of men that was sent west to patrol numbered only 300. This was an amazingly small group to be given the task of patrolling the whole North-West, but they were successful. By the early 1880s they were well respected by both Canadians and Americans for their ability to keep law and order in the Canadian West.

1874

1888

The scarlet jackets worn by the police were distinctive. They reminded people of the jackets worn by soldiers in the British army.

Fort Macleod, 1880. The first NWMP post in present-day Alberta later grew into a town.

Jerry Potts (1837–1898)

Jerry Potts worked as a guide and translator for the NWMP for 25 years. He was a Metis whose mother was from the Blood tribe. His father was a clerk for the American Fur Company.

On the famous March West, when the NWMP first came West, Potts led the NWMP to Fort Whoop-Up, where American whiskey traders were selling liquor to the Natives. He also found the spot on the Oldman River where Fort Macleod was to be built.

Potts once had a dream that cat skin would protect him, so he wore a cat's skin under his shirt from then on. After that he was never injured in battle.

Translations by Potts were often very short. A 90-minute speech by a Native chief to the governor general was translated to: "He wants grub."

Accomplishments

One of the first tasks of the North West Mounted Police, after their arrival in the North–West, was to force the whiskey smugglers who had been selling American liquor to leave. By December of 1874 they were able to report the "complete stoppage of the whiskey trade throughout the whole section of this country."

The NWMP fearlessly tracked down lawbreakers. They also gave friendly advice to new settlers, carried mail, fought fires, and prevented open conflict among Native peoples, between Natives and non-Natives, and amongst settlers.

They made a special effort to win the trust of Native leaders and assisted the Canadian government in the treaty negotiations with western tribes. These are the words of Chief Crowfoot of the Blackfoot, when signing the Blackfoot Treaty in 1877: "The Police have protected us as the feathers protect the bird. I wish them all good, and trust that our hearts will increase in goodness from this time. I will sign."

For Your Notebook

1. Why did the Canadian government establish the North West Mounted Police?
2. What duties did the North West Mounted Police perform in the West?

Exploring Further

1. Conduct research on one of the people involved in the early days of the North West Mounted Police. Some possibilities are: Inspector James Walsh, Jerry Potts, Lieutenant-Colonel James Farquharson Macleod, Lieutenant-Colonel George Arthur French, Lieutenant-Colonel A.G. Irvine.

Seven Treaties

In the early years of contact there was considerable interdependence between the First People and the Europeans. Each group voluntarily traded its goods with the other. Gradually over the years the First People became more dependent on European trade goods. Many preferred European goods. Gradually their lifestyle changed.

When the Loyalists came to British North America they wanted land, and quite often the land they wanted was occupied by the First People. While not everyone would have agreed to the following, the general Caucasian thinking at the time was to move the First People out of the way of European settlement, to Christianize and Europeanize them, and to try to make them into farmers rather than hunters.

Often non-Native settlers (squatters) moved into an area set aside for the First People, began to clear the lands, and then petitioned the government for the deed to the land. While many in the government felt this was wrong, the mood of the times was such that Caucasians considered expansion and individual land ownership more important than the rights of the First People.

Prime Minister John A. Macdonald believed that the First People should be assimilated or absorbed into Canadian culture. Macdonald's National Policy favoured building a railway to cross the country and using this railway to bring in hundreds of thousands of settlers to build a new nation. In order to do this the Canadian government needed to isolate the First People on reserves—lands set aside exclusively for their use. But before this could be done the government had to make some decisions about Rupert's Land, the land between the Great Lakes and the Rockies.

In 1869, the Canadian government bought the Hudson's Bay Company's claims to Rupert's Land. The next step for the Canadian government was to resolve all the land claims made by the First People before settlers could move into an area. This was done through a series of treaties that came to be known as the numbered treaties. From 1871 to 1877, seven treaties were signed between the Canadian government and the First People living between Lake Superior and the Rockies.* Four more treaties were signed between 1889 and 1921. Once the treaties were signed, great numbers of settlers began to move across Canada.

Generally, in exchange for their **aboriginal** rights to the land, the First People received the following: reserve lands, a lump-sum payment, yearly payments, and a school on each of the reserves that requested one.

The First People often received promises from the Canadian government that they would be given farm implements, tools, seeds, and the right to hunt, fish, and trap on Crown land located throughout the treaty area.**

Many questioned whether the First People had a choice as to whether they moved onto the reserves or not. Over time their bargaining position had been eroded. Towards the end of the eighteenth century and the beginning of the nineteenth century, epidemics of smallpox, tuberculosis,

Blackfoot Chief Crowfoot addresses the Native people and Canadian government representatives present at the signing of Treaty No. 7.

and measles spread throughout the land. Tens of thousands of people lost their lives. These epidemics combined with the influx of the American whiskey traders put them in a weakened bargaining position. By the 1870s the buffalo were well on their way to extinction. With their main source of food gone, the First People were forced to accept the terms and help from the Canadian government. (*See* page 238.)

In 1876 the first Indian Act was passed. In the years ahead, the Canadian government exercised increasing control over the lives of the First People. The people who belonged to groups that signed treaties and the descendents of these people are legally known as "status Indians." Those who did not sign treaties and their descendents are legally known as "non-status Indians."

---

*Treaties 1, 2, and 3 were signed on behalf of the Conservatives while Treaties 4, 5, 6, and 7 were signed on behalf of the Liberals.
Aboriginal—being the first in a region
**Note: Crown land—the land held by the government of Canada, was not intended to be used for settlement by non-Natives.

An Exercise in Critical Thinking

Critical thinkers realize there is more than one point of view on every issue. Read the following points of view as presented by various modern-day Native people,* and identify the issues being discussed. Prepare arguments both for and against each issue. You may wish to do additional library research.

• The land wasn't ours to give away. We did not surrender all our rights to the land. We gave some powers to the Canadian government in exchange for certain rights and privileges. As nations we retained use of the land and its resources. The land is ours to take care of—for all to use. We did not know that thousands of non-Native settlers would come here expecting to claim the lands as their exclusive private property. Our chiefs did not know they were giving up possession of our people's traditional lands.

• We thought the treaties were intended to guarantee us our rights over lands that we traditionally occupied and used for thousands of years. When we signed the treaties we agreed to share the land with the newcomers. When the Canadian government signed, they recognized our aboriginal rights and our claim to these lands. As nations we entered into formal and political agreements with your country. We formed a confederation, a political agreement with you.

• The treaties are not fair! They are one-sided. They do not look after our interests. The treaties say the government will take care of us, teach us how to make a living like the Europeans. They haven't done this! Sure we signed our treaty and got reserve land to live on. But according to the Indian Act, the Minister has control over the reserve lands. He decides what to do on the reserve—not us! We were told we could hunt on our reserves and get food from the Crown lands. And now they won't let us! There are even some non-Native settlers farming on reserve lands!

---

*These are not actual quotes, but have been written after interviewing a large number of Native people.

• Both the Native people and the representatives of the Canadian government acted in good faith. Both intended to follow the terms of the treaties. We just interpret the treaties differently. To Caucasians they mean one thing. To Native people they mean something different. It is unfortunate there are misunderstandings.

• When we signed the treaties we did not give up our rights to govern ourselves. They took our hereditary chief, whose ancestry went back 20 generations, and replaced him with an elected chief and council. The age-old rules for law and order were replaced by foreign laws of Canada and the police courts. Often the Native people did not understand these Canadian laws.

• We had no other choice. Our ancestors had to sign the treaties. At first we had enough land for our people, assistance from the government, and promises of help and protection. Without that we would have become extinct. The buffalo were gone. Our people were starving. Many had died from smallpox. Before long we would all be gone. We're safe on the reserves. We would have lost our land anyway to the settlers who would have taken it from us. At least by signing the treaties we have a place to live on the reserves.

• They said we were a bunch of pagans and so they outlawed our beliefs, our ceremonies, and our songs. We wanted to preserve our stories and legends, our arts, crafts and handiwork, and our dances. The teachers in your schools told our children that our ways were wrong and not to be followed. When we spoke our Indian language we were punished. We had to speak English.

• Why did you take away our children from ages seven to 15 for 10 months of the year and take them to residential schools? Why were non-Native children not treated the same way? When you took away our language and our culture, our children didn't survive. In your school books you called us "savages." Our children lost pride in themselves and our culture when they read these books. They started to think the ways of the non-Native people were better than the ways of their own people.

Some people in the North-West were not pleased with the Conservative government in the early 1880s, as you can see from the following accounts.

Settlers

The settlers were impatient with the government's delay in completing the land survey and the registering of land claims. Until these were done, they could not take possession of their land.

They were anxious because the price of their grain was falling and because it was very expensive to ship their grain to eastern markets along the CPR route.

The settlers were angry because they had to pay high prices for farm machinery that was manufactured in Eastern Canada, instead of being able to buy the cheaper American machinery. As part of his National Policy, Prime Minister Macdonald put tariffs (taxes) on American farm machinery in order to make it more expensive, so that people would buy the Canadian products.

The fact that the government had set aside so much land for the Hudson's Bay Company and the CPR also angered the settlers.

Furthermore, they were disappointed with the decision made by the CPR in 1881 to reroute the railway farther south than had been originally planned. This meant that it would not run near the northern communities of Battleford, Prince Albert, and Batoche. As a result of this decision, the capital of the North-West Territories was moved from Battleford to Pile of Bones (later renamed Regina) in 1883. Many people had bought land in the northern area hoping to make money on it when the railway came through. Their hopes were dashed when the railway was rerouted to the south.

First People

Many of the First People had signed treaties with the government and had settled on reserves. Not having the settlers' concept of land ownership, they considered land as something to be shared just as the air and the sunshine are shared. They were only now, as they saw the settlers trickling into the North-West, beginning to realize how their lives were changing.

Many deeply missed their old way of life as buffalo hunters. Buffalo had always been the main source of food for the Plains people. Because of more people hunting buffalo using more efficient killing techniques, there were fewer and fewer buffalo left. Many Native people believed buffalo hunters from the United States were hired to kill off the buffalo in order to starve them into negotiation. As a result of the dwindling supply of buffalo, some tribes were facing starvation. The Canadian government was slow to come to their help. Many of the federal agents in charge of Native affairs did nothing to let the government know what needed to be done.

Metis

The Metis were also affected by the fact that there were fewer and fewer buffalo. They did not have reserve land on which to live. They were afraid of losing their long, narrow river-lot farms, because the lots had not been officially surveyed and registered. They did not have representation in the Canadian federal government in Ottawa, so they had to resort to letters and petitions. The federal government under John A. Macdonald was very slow to respond to their concerns. The Metis found this extremely frustrating. It seemed that no one in power cared what happened to them as a people.

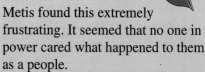

The North-West Resistance, 1885

Causes

The Manitoba Act of 1870 set aside about 500 000 hectares exclusively for use by the Metis. When the Metis had first settled on their lots in the 1870s, the area had not yet been surveyed. But the government's policy elsewhere on the prairies had been to recognize claims to land made before the official survey took place, even if the lots did not fit into the plan of square lots usually created by government surveyors. When the government surveyors first reached the Metis area on the South Saskatchewan in 1878, the river lots were recognized. However, when the surveyors began work again in the summer of 1879, they surveyed the remaining lots using the square system. The Metis could not understand why some river lots were officially recognized while others were not. Some Metis settled on river lots in the area after 1878, and ignored the square lots altogether. The Canadian government under John A. Macdonald was slow in distributing the promised land grants to the Metis.

In the meantime, more and more settlers were coming into Manitoba and the Metis were soon outnumbered. Many of the Metis decided the only answer was to move farther west. There was a community of Metis who were already farming along the banks of the North Saskatchewan River. Some of these Metis from Manitoba chose to join them. There they hoped to continue their old way of life of farming and hunting buffalo.

By 1885 the community on the North Saskatchewan River numbered about 500 people. At this time Sir John A. Macdonald's National Policy was in place. One aspect of the National Policy encouraged the settlement of the West. Even though the expected rush of settlers after the completion of the CPR did not take place, 25 000 new settlers did arrive between 1871 and 1881. The West was changing; the buffalo were disappearing and with them went the lifestyle of the Native people. The Metis lifestyle on the farms was also being threatened. It became increasingly difficult for the Metis to continue their old way of life, since there were large numbers of settlers moving into the area.

As you read on page 248, the Metis were very concerned over the government surveys, which ignored their long, narrow river-lot farms. Without a proper government survey they could not get official title to their land. They were becoming very frustrated at the lack of response to their concerns by the government of John A. Macdonald.

Louis Riel

Louis Riel played an important role in the North-West Resistance of 1885.

Following the events of 1869 and 1870 in the Red River area,* Louis Riel had fled to the United States. He was elected to Canadian Parliament twice, but was prevented from taking his seat. He suffered an emotional breakdown and spent nearly two years in asylums in Quebec. In 1875 he was granted **amnesty** if he stayed out of Canada for five years. He ended up in Montana, where he married and had two children.

On June 4, 1884, a four-man delegation, including Gabriel Dumont, arrived in Montana. Riel agreed to accompany them back to Saskatchewan so that he could help them.

Events Leading to the Resistance

After arriving back in Canada in the summer of 1884, Riel met with various groups living along the Saskatchewan River. It was decided that a petition should be sent to Ottawa. This petition was sent to the federal government in December 1884. It included the concerns of the Metis, the First People, and the settlers. It also asked for responsible government for the North-West, with control over its natural resources and representation in the federal Cabinet and Parliament, as well as provincial status for the District of Saskatchewan.

*Refer to page 222.

Amnesty—a general pardon for past offences against a government

The government had made considerable cutbacks in their treaty promises to the First People. This resulted in increased distress and problems for them.

Other letters were sent to Ottawa. These were from local North-West government officials, the North West Mounted Police, missionaries, and others. These letters warned the federal government that there could be trouble if they did not respond to the complaints that had been outlined in the petition.

Prime Minister Macdonald did respond. A commission was formed to draw up a list of all the Metis who were eligible for scrip and land grants. Scrip is a certificate or coupon that was given to Metis people as compensation for land, entitling the holder to a choice between cash or land.

The Metis were disappointed at Macdonald's response to their petition, since they had expected more assistance. They asked Riel to stay in Canada to help them.

On March 19, 1885, Riel set up a provisional or temporary government, like the provisional government he had set up in Manitoba. Gabriel Dumont was appointed to be the military leader.

The Caucasian settlers along the Saskatchewan River were not interested in joining the Metis in an armed resistance against the Canadian government. They were very angry at the federal government, but they refused to follow Riel once he decided to take action in such a violent manner. Most of the First People decided not to take up arms against the federal government. Two exceptions were the bands led by Poundmaker and Big Bear.

An Armed Uprising

 The North-West Resistance began on March 26, 1885, with a battle at the small town of Duck Lake. Gabriel Dumont and a group of Metis attacked Superintendent Crozier of the North West Mounted Police and some of his men as they were on their way to rescue arms and ammunition from a store in Duck Lake. Twelve of Crozier's men were killed and 11 wounded after a half-hour battle. Five Metis were killed. After the Battle of Duck Lake the Metis destroyed Fort Carlton. The non-Native inhabitants there had fled to Prince Albert.

Chief Poundmaker travelled at the end of March to Battleford to meet with the government agent to discuss getting more food for his people. When the townspeople heard that the First People were coming, they fled to the safety of the fort. The town was deserted when Poundmaker arrived and the government agent refused to come out of the fort to talk with him. Poundmaker's companions became frustrated and angry. They broke windows and took supplies.

The most serious incident involving the First People occurred on April 2 at Frog Lake. Chief Big Bear's men killed nine people, including the government agent, Thomas Quinn.

Prime Minister Macdonald, having heard news of armed rebellion, ordered 8000 soldiers and volunteers to travel west on the unfinished Canadian Pacific Railway. The trip took them only nine days.

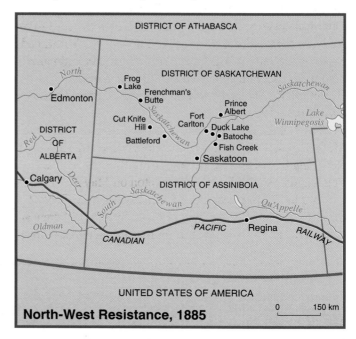

North-West Resistance, 1885

*Major-General Middleton, the commander of the Canadian Militia, was in charge of battle operations. He divided his troops into three groups. He and his column set out for the Metis headquarters at Batoche. A column led by Colonel Otter set out for Battleford, where he hoped to find Poundmaker. The third column, led by Major-General Strange, set out after Big Bear and his men.

Throughout the North-West Resistance of 1885, Riel was guided by his religious convictions. Dumont wanted to use hit-and-run guerrilla tactics to defend Batoche, but Riel insisted that he had been ordered by visions from God to wait until Batoche was attacked and then defend it.

On April 24, at Fish Creek, Gabriel Dumont's men attacked Middleton's column, using the hit-and-run and then hit again tactics that Dumont found so effective. Dumont was able to slow down Middleton's progress, but he did not stop him from reaching Batoche. Middleton arrived there on May 9.

The battle at Batoche lasted for four days, from May 9 to May 12. The 300 Metis and First People had dug rifle pits from which they fired at their attackers. By the last day the defenders were out of ammunition and were firing stones and nails from their rifles. Finally Middleton's troops stormed the rifle pits and the battle was over. There were over 25 dead from both sides.

---

*You read on page 241 about how Prime Minister Macdonald was able to get the money he needed to finish the railway after transporting soldiers so quickly to the trouble spot.

Both Riel and Dumont managed to escape. Riel gave himself up after a few days, but Dumont fled to the United States.

Colonel Otter located Poundmaker and about 200 followers at Cut Knife Hill, near Poundmaker's reserve. Otter had hoped to make a surprise attack, but the Cree were ready for them and drove them off. Poundmaker's men had every opportunity to kill Otter's soldiers, but Poundmaker held them back and allowed the soldiers to return to Battleford. He saw no honour in killing an enemy who had already been defeated.

Poundmaker then decided to go to Batoche to help the Metis. On their way they heard the news of the Metis defeat. Realizing that there was no point in further resistance, Poundmaker surrendered to Middleton on May 26.

On May 28 Big Bear and his men clashed with General Strange's soldiers at Frenchman's Butte. Strange withdrew at the end of the day, planning to fight again on the next. Big Bear and his men, being low on ammunition, took advantage of the lull in the action to escape while they could.

Both General Strange and General Middleton followed Big Bear for the next few weeks. They never did find him, but on July 2 he surrendered, accompanied only by his young son. His followers had either surrendered or simply gone elsewhere. Big Bear's surrender marked the end of the 99-day North-West Resistance.

Exploring Further

1. List the groups of people in the North-West and the concerns that each had regarding the federal government prior to the North-West Resistance.
2. Are uprisings like the North-West Resistance ever justified? Explain your answer.
3. What other methods might the Metis and the First People have used to solve their problems? How might Prime Minister Macdonald have avoided the resistance?

Canadian government troops met the Metis at the Battle of Batoche, May 9 to 12, 1885.

On Trial

 Riel was put on trial in Regina for **treason**. He was found guilty by a jury of six English-speaking Canadian men. The jury asked the judge for mercy, but the judge chose the maximum penalty of hanging.

The decision to hang Riel caused a great reaction. Petitions were sent to Prime Minister Macdonald asking that Riel be pardoned. Queen Victoria ordered the governor general to ask that Riel not be hanged. The newspapers were full of articles on the subject. The debate was carried on in the House of Commons and in the Cabinet in Ottawa.

Prime Minister Sir John A. Macdonald took two months to make up his mind. He had the power to step in and stop the hanging, but he refused to do so. He knew that by not stopping it he would make French Canadians very angry and his Conservative Party would lose many votes in Quebec, but he and his Cabinet decided that the hanging should go ahead. Riel was hanged on November 16, 1885.

Louis Riel addresses the court at his trial, Regina, 1885.

Results for Canada of the North-West Resistance

 One immediate result of the Metis resistance was the completion of the CPR. At the time of the North-West Resistance, the CPR had run out of funds. People were beginning to wonder if it would ever be finished. Once it was shown how quickly troops could be transported to the North-West on the railway, the government granted the CPR the money needed to complete the laying of track.*

Another result of the resistance was the feeling that was aroused by Riel's hanging. These feelings caused a rift between English and French Canada. Riel's hanging caused great bitterness on the part of many French Canadians. They felt that it was wrong of Riel to lead a resistance against the lawful government of Canada. However, they did not think Riel should have been hanged for it. Some believed that he was insane. Others felt that he was hanged because he was French Canadian. They saw it as a direct insult to all French Canadians.

The English Canadian reply was that if Riel had been English Canadian, or anything other than French Canadian for that matter, not a word of protest would have been heard from French Canadians. They said that French Canadians had no right to demand special treatment. Most English Canadians felt that Riel was sane and that he had committed treason by fighting against the government.

Therefore, the only choice was to punish him according to the law.

The country was in an uproar. Newspapers across the country were full of the issue day after day. Petitions were sent to the government. Speeches were made both in and out of the House of Commons. Many French Canadians, and even some English Canadians, blamed John A. Macdonald's Conservative government for ignoring the concerns of the North-West for so long.

Far-Reaching Effects

 In his own time many English Canadians viewed Riel as a lawless rebel. In recent years Riel has become a Canadian hero. Many people see Riel as a symbol of Western Canada's ability to stand up to what they see as Central Canada's unfair treatment, and as a defender of French Canadian minority rights in the West.

Many French Canadians have always viewed Riel as a hero because he stood up for the rights of the French-speaking Metis in the North-West against an uncaring federal government dominated by English-speaking Canadians.

In 1992, over 100 years after the North-West Resistance, the Canadian Parliament passed a resolution recognizing the contributions that Louis Riel made to Canada's growth as a nation.

Treason—the crime of betraying one's country
*Refer to page 241 for more information on the funding of the CPR.

Military Leaders

Gabriel Dumont

R-A6277, Saskatchewan Archives Board (detail).

Gabriel Dumont was one of the most respected men in the North-West. He was an excellent rider and marksman. He had come to the North-West in 1872 from Manitoba because he was unhappy with conditions there.

Dumont spoke French and six Native languages. He was a natural leader. He proved to be a skillful military strategist. He often argued with Riel about military plans. Dumont wanted to use guerrilla hit-and-run tactics on the Canadian troops, knowing that this was the only way their small number of men could have any success against the far larger Canadian force. Riel insisted they meet the troops in an eye-to-eye battle at Batoche. Following the resistance, Dumont fled to the United States, where he joined "Buffalo Bill" Cody's travelling Wild West Show. He returned to Batoche after an official pardon (an amnesty) was granted to those who had taken part in the Resistance.

Major-General Frederick Middleton

ACC6876#23, Archives of Ontario.

Major-General Frederick Middleton was a British infantry officer who had served in Africa, India, and New Zealand. He came to Canada in 1884 and was placed in charge of the Canadian Militia. Middleton led his soldiers in the battles of Fish Creek and Batoche. It is thought that the storming of the Metis rifle pits by his troops on the fourth day at Batoche was not done under his orders. For his part in the Resistance, Middleton received a medal and $20 000.

Poundmaker

PA-28853, National Archives of Canada, Ottawa (detail).

Poundmaker was a Cree chief and adopted son of Crowfoot. Crowfoot adopted him in an effort to keep peace between their peoples. Poundmaker got his name from his skill at driving buffalo into "pounds" or enclosures where they were trapped and then killed.

Poundmaker's people were having trouble adjusting to a farming life from the hunting life they had known. They missed the freedom of following the buffalo and were confined to a reserve with sandy soil that was not good for growing crops. They did not have enough to eat and grew more and more frustrated because the government would not listen to them.

It was this frustration which found its expression in Battleford after the government agent refused to speak with the Cree delegation. Poundmaker then withdrew to Cut Knife Hill, where he awaited Colonel Otter and his soldiers. After about six hours of fighting, the First People were gradually surrounding the troops, when Colonel Otter withdrew. Poundmaker stopped his men from following the soldiers and attacking them.

After the rebellion Poundmaker was sentenced to three years in prison, but was released after several months. He died while visiting Chief Crowfoot shortly after his release, and was buried in Crowfoot's camp. In 1967, his body was returned to his reserve and buried on the hill where the battle of Cut Knife took place.

Big Bear

C-17430, National Archives of Canada, Ottawa (detail).

Big Bear was very unhappy with the federal government's treatment of the First People and hoped that threats of a resistance would make the government take notice. He did not want to take part in a confrontation; he wanted to resist peacefully. But when his followers took up arms, as their leader he took responsibility for their actions. He was sentenced to three years for his part in the resistance. Like Poundmaker, he died shortly after his release.

Liberal Administration (1896–1911)

From Confederation until 1896, the Conservatives were in power, except during the years 1873–1878, when Alexander Mackenzie was prime minister. When Wilfrid Laurier became prime minister in 1896, it was an astounding victory for the Liberals. Laurier led Canada from 1896 to 1911.

C-688, National Archives of Canada, Ottawa (detail).

7th Prime Minister

Personal Summary

Laurier was born into a French-speaking Roman Catholic family at St. Lin, Quebec. He had a bicultural childhood. At the age of 10 he went to live with an Anglo-Protestant family, where he learned English and about the Protestant faith. Laurier obtained his law degree from McGill University in 1864. In 1868 Laurier married Zoe Lafontaine. They did not have any children.

Political Summary

Laurier practised law before winning a seat in the Legislative Assembly in Quebec. He first became a Member of Parliament in 1873, when Alexander Mackenzie's Liberals took over from John A. Macdonald's Conservatives. In 1896 Laurier became Canada's seventh prime minister and the first Francophone one. (Francophone means that he spoke French.) He was sympathetic to French Canada's needs. He was prime minister for 15 years, the longest uninterrupted term of any prime minister before or since.

Throughout his career, Laurier practised what he called his "sunny ways" approach. He always searched for a compromise, a middle path between French and English interests in order to try to please everyone. He once said:

Canada has been the inspiration of my life. I have had before me, as a pillar of fire by night, and a pillar of cloud by day, a policy of true Canadianism, of moderation, of conciliation.

He stressed that there was no single Canadian identity, but rather two identities, French and English, both of which had to be respected. He urged Canadians to be tolerant of **diversity**.

Sir Wilfrid Laurier (1841–1919)
Dates as Prime Minister—1896–1911
Party—Liberal

Laurier was fortunate enough to be prime minister during a period of economic growth. European cities were demanding Canadian wheat. The development of hardy new strains made it possible to meet that demand. He encouraged large numbers of immigrants to settle in the West. The population increase caused a huge demand for new goods and services. Canadian businesspeople produced and marketed such products as steel, bread, paint, and cement, partly with the help of the British and American investment capital that was pouring into the country. Canada's new-found wealth inspired Laurier with such confidence that he said:

. . . the twentieth century shall be the century of Canada and of Canadian development. For the next seventy-five years, nay for the next hundred years, Canada shall be the star towards which all men who love progress and freedom shall come.

Laurier had the difficult task of trying to please both French-Canadian and English-Canadian interests. One of the issues he dealt with was the Manitoba Schools Question: whether there should be two school systems in the Province of Manitoba.

Laurier lost the election of 1911 to Robert Borden and his Conservative Party. After Laurier lost, he worked to rebuild the Liberal Party. He continued to believe that Canada needed a Liberal government to maintain prosperity and unity.

Diversity—differences

French Canadian Nationalism

A new sense of French Canadian nationalism* in Quebec was becoming a challenge to Confederation. French Canadians viewed Confederation as an agreement that guaranteed the equality of French and English across Canada. Francophones (French-speaking Canadians) were becoming more and more concerned as they saw ever greater numbers of English-speaking immigrants arriving.

It seemed that the idea of biculturalism, or two cultures living side by side, was being rejected in English Canada. For instance, in 1871, the provincial government of New Brunswick decided to stop supporting Roman Catholic schools. French Acadian people objected, but their objections were ignored. In 1890, the provincial government of Manitoba voted to replace its dual school system (of French Roman Catholic and English Protestant schools), with one system that would just have English schools.

The French-speaking Roman Catholics were afraid that the English Canadian culture would overwhelm the French Canadian culture and that it would slowly disappear.

Henri Bourassa

Henri Bourassa, in his roles as journalist, Liberal, and then independent Member of Parliament, became a champion of the rights of Canada's French-speaking minority. He wanted to see a bicultural nation in which the French and English cultures were of equal strengths. He said that "we do not have the right to make Canada an exclusively French country, any more than the Anglo-Canadians have the right to make it an English country." He argued that the French language and the Roman Catholic religion must be protected. He was against the immigration policy of the Liberals. He said, "I want selective immigration, so that we will not be swamped by the waves of European socialists . . . causing a decrease in the percentage of people of French origin . . ." He was also against the national railway because it brought too many English-speaking settlers. Bourassa and the French Canadian nationalists wanted to see a strong, independent Canada, free of ties with Britain. They did not want to see increased trade with Britain and they definitely did not want to assist Britain should a war occur.

Manitoba Schools Question

The first major controversy involving biculturalism was the Manitoba Schools Question. In 1870, when Manitoba joined Confederation, about half the population was French-speaking. Schools were Roman Catholic supported with a subsidy from the HBC. Over the next 20 years English immigration greatly outnumbered that of French-speaking people. In 1890 the Manitoba legislature voted to set up a single English public school system. This was a very controversial move. The following comments from imaginary people illustrate the points of view of the French Roman Catholics and the English Protestants:

English person: It will save a great deal of money to have one school system instead of two. We will have lower taxes!

French person: It doesn't matter if money is saved. The BNA Act states that no provincial government can interfere with the rights of **denominational** schools. It is against the law for Manitoba to set up a single school system.

English person: More people in this country speak English than French. How can immigrants learn to speak English if they attend French-speaking schools?

French person: It is important for French Roman Catholic children to attend school with children who are brought up the same way.

---

*French Canadian nationalism refers to patriotic feelings or desires by the French Canadians to preserve their own language, traditions, and religion.
Denominational — under the control of a religious group

The French Catholics appealed to Prime Minister Macdonald. He tried not to become involved. The Supreme Court ruled that the federal government had the power to disallow the legislation. Politically, it was a no-win situation for the Canadian government. If it supported the French Catholics it would be seen as interfering in provincial affairs. If it did not support the Catholics, it would lose votes in Quebec. The difficulty of the situation was increased by Prime Minister Macdonald's death three months after the election of 1891. In the next five years there were four Conservative prime ministers. Finally, in 1895, the Conservatives did prepare a bill that proposed giving back the rights of the French-speaking Catholics in Manitoba.

But before the bill could become law an election was called.

Wilfrid Laurier and his Liberal party won the election of 1896. As a result of Laurier's **compromises** with provincial leaders, the provincially funded, non-denominational public school system remained in effect, but when there were enough students, religious teaching could take place in the last half-hour of the school day. Also, when there were 10 or more students who spoke a language other than English, they could be taught in that language.

Canadians are still struggling to establish a balance between the rights of French-speaking and English-speaking Canadians—to work out an approach that is fair to everyone.

Prime Minister Laurier could not guarantee equality between French and English in the North-West. Schools were seen as a means to assimilate minorities.

Compromise—a settlement in which each side gives up some demands

The Last Best West

Land Rush at the Prince Albert Court House, 1907

From 1900 to 1914 (the start of World War I) there was a flood of **immigrants** into western Canada. Most of these people came from Ontario, Britain, and the United States. Others came from Europe. There were several reasons why these people chose western Canada as the place to settle. Six reasons are outlined below.

1. Good farmland near transportation routes was becoming scarce in Ontario. Many people believed that the same was true in the western United States. Canada took advantage of this and promoted its available western lands as "the Last, Best West."

Immigrants 1890–1914			
Years	**Numbers**	**Years**	**Numbers**
1890	75 067	1903	138 660
1891	82 165	1904	131 252
1892	30 996	1905	141 465
1893	29 633	1906	211 653
1894	20 829	1907	272 409
1895	18 790	1908	143 326
1896	16 835	1909	173 694
1897	21 716	1910	286 839
1898	31 900	1911	331 288
1899	44 543	1912	375 756
1900	41 681	1913	400 870
1901	55 747	1914	150 484
1902	89 102		

Immigrant—person who comes to live in a new country

2. In 1885 the Canadian Pacific Railway had been completed. This meant that it was much easier and faster for settlers to travel to the West. Crops from the West could now be transported by railway to the markets of eastern Canada.
3. Changes to the Dominion Lands Act encouraged immigration. The settlers still had to pay a 10-dollar fee, and now only had to reside on the homestead for three years before it was considered to be their land.
4. The general opinion of the quality of the farm-land in Canada's West had improved. Canada had developed a reputation as a major grain producer. Western farmers had learned how to make the most of their farms. Their costs were lower and they were getting higher prices for their crops. Red Fife, a hardy spring wheat that ripened 10 to 12 days earlier than any other variety, was developed. Western farmers no longer needed to fear early autumn frosts.
5. The Canadian government had signed treaties with the First People settling them on reserves. This freed vast amounts of western lands for settlement.
6. The North West Mounted Police had established law and order in the West, making it safe for settlers to move there.

In spite of everything the Canadian government had done to encourage western settlement, new settlers were slow to come to the Canadian West. It was not until the good land in the United States was filled up that Canada became settled. It was Clifford Sifton who was largely responsible for bringing the settlers to the Canadian West through advertising and other means.

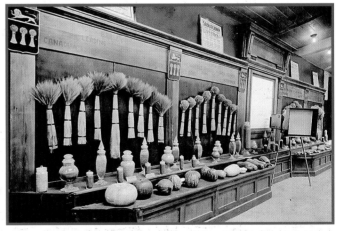

Elaborate displays show the quality of Canadian farm products.

Clifford Sifton

Clifford Sifton enthusiastically promoted immigrant settlement in the West. Wilfrid Laurier, the Liberal prime minister who came to power in 1896, decided to do all he could to encourage settlement of the West. Laurier appointed Clifford Sifton to be the minister in charge of immigration.

Advertising for Settlers

Sifton placed advertisements in 6000 newspapers in the United States. He gave American newspaper editors free trips to the Canadian Prairies so that they could see the inexpensive, fertile land for themselves. This advertising campaign was very successful. Between 1897 and 1912, of the 2 381 061 settlers who immigrated to Canada, 785 137 were from the United States. The chart on page 257 shows Canadian immigration from the years 1890 to 1914.

Sifton also sent agents to the British Isles to promote settlement in the Canadian West. Then he decided to advertise heavily in Central and Eastern Europe. Exhibition vans travelled the countryside displaying Canadian products.

There were many people in these parts of Europe who would never have the chance to have a large farm of their own if they did not move. They either owned very small farms that were often highly taxed, or they worked on the large farms of powerful landowners for very little pay. Many of these people sold most of what they owned in order to buy steamship tickets for their families and the supplies they would need once they had their homesteads.

Clifford Sifton (1861–1929)

Clifford Sifton was a Manitoba lawyer, businessman, and provincial Cabinet minister before becoming a Liberal Member of Parliament in 1896. That same year, Prime Minister Laurier appointed him to the Cabinet post of minister of the interior, a position he was to hold for nine years. As minister of the interior, Sifton was responsible for immigration and overseeing the vast western lands.

The area for which he was responsible included all the land between the Ontario–Manitoba border and the Rocky Mountains, and north from the United States border to the Arctic Ocean. He looked after Native peoples, immigration, homesteads, railways, schools, forests, minerals, grazing lands, and national parks policy.

At the age of 35 Sifton was an energetic young government minister. His major interest seemed to be immigration and he was thoroughly committed to encouraging rapid settlement of the West. Instead of waiting for immigrants to come to the West, as had been the tendency in the past, he went out to get them. In the United States there were newspaper advertisements, pamphlets about the Canadian West, and free guided tours for American journalists and prospective settlers. Europe was also bombarded with advertisements.

It was largely due to Sifton's advertising campaign that thousands of people came to settle in Western Canada, as the chart on page 257 indicates.

Left: This cover is typical of the many booklets sent to Europe by the Canadian government and the CPR to encourage immigration to the Canadian West.

The **primary source** material on page 259 is taken from Barry Broadfoot's book *The Pioneer Years, 1895–1914*.

The Greatest Country in the World

I got to Lashburn and located my quarter section. My boy and I lined up stakes along the edge of the quarter and I hitched up a horse I had that was about 1,400 pounds and a mare about 1,000 pounds. I sunk the blade of my hand plow in and I got them going up that stake line and I went a half mile without a quiver. Then I stopped and looked back and there was my furrow, stretching away for half a mile, straight as a gun barrel. The land was black and rich and beautiful and I knew I was in the greatest country in the world.

Oatmeal, Tea, and Rabbits

The first winter I don't know how we did it. All we had to live on was oatmeal and tea and rabbits. Oatmeal without milk. Tea without sugar. My mother used to make scones, like bannock, with only water, and that is what we lived on.

Rabbits. White rabbits. Trap them. You don't see them around anymore, but there would be a dozen at a time in them days in a little patch of bush as big as this room. Or shoot the rabbits. You'd see the two black eyes and you'd shoot between them.

Oatmeal, tea, and rabbits. They kept us alive. Sure. I don't know how we did it. I honestly don't.

This woman is cutting oats with a team and mower.

Not a Penny in the World

We come to Calgary in 1898 and then we moved out of there about 10 miles and then my father died, so my mother she took a homestead. Oh yes, a woman could take up land then but not many did. Not many.

. . . At first she'd hire to get a little bit of plowing done when she could get a dollar or two. She'd sell eggs in High River, and sometimes women in the town would hire her for a day. She'd walk into town, work all day, walk back. For just a few cents. Wages wasn't nothing in those days. Not too many people had money and those that had it were awfully close with it.

First she got an acre plowed and that became a garden. That's an awful lot of garden, but all of us worked in it. We didn't go to school much but we sure worked around the place. In that garden. Then the next year she got another acre plowed and so forth, and after that I was big enough to drive a team around and I plowed up the rest.

A Prairie Woman Remembers

. . . After many miles Mother grew weary of asking how much further, and on the fourth day crossing that huge prairie, on the 18th of March, Dad said that if she looked in the distance she would see a building. Mother said later it looked like a lone toilet on nothing but prairie, and Dad said that was their new home. Mother made sure no one saw her and then she turned her head and cried.

. . . and Mother had to walk a good mile to another neighbor's place to get two buckets of water—it was as scarce on our place as if we had been in the Sahara Desert. Every day she made the trip.

One day when the men were away and Mother had just returned to the shack she saw fire and smoke in the distance and she had the pails of water. She dipped gunny sacks in the water and ran to meet it. It was a prairie fire and they were terrible thing those days. As the fire got close to the house Mother fought it, beating at the high flames with the two wet potato sacks, and she fought it and fought it until she was exhausted. But she managed to protect a little bit of land right around our shack and a bit of the thick grass where our horse could graze. When Dad and Paul Carr came back and saw where the fire had been they ran to the house and there they found Mother, very dirty, very smoky, very tired, but she had saved the children's prairie home and enough grass for their horse.

Primary source—a first-hand account of a historical event by someone who witnessed it or lived during the time of the event; the main source of information

Focus On: Photo Essay—Life in the North-West Territories

At the beginning of the 1900s, farming was the most important economic activity in the North-West Territories. Other industries included ranching and coal mining.

Left: When there were trees nearby, prairie settlers built log cabins.

Below: These wheatfields were near Wetaskiwin.

Left: Milner's Coal Mine, Edmonton, 1902

Above: Pieces of sod from the prairie were cut and made into homes for prairie settlers.

Right: Ranching was suited to the dry prairie lands.

Above: This homestead was near present-day Lloydminster, 1902.

Right: In the fall crops were harvested. Steam supplied the power to drive the threshing machines.

By the beginning of the 1900s, Western Canada had several busy towns and cities.

Above: Edmonton, North-West Territories, 1902

Left: Main Street, Winnipeg, Manitoba, c. 1905

Above: The general store was the source of most goods not grown or made by the settlers.

Left: Main Street, Wetaskiwin, North-West Territories

This section focuses on the development before 1912 of Canada as a multicultural nation. A multicultural nation is one that has people from many different cultural backgrounds. The term cultural backgrounds refers to the language, religion, traditions, music, art, and literature of the person's ancestral homeland.

It is sometimes said that Canada has people from many different ethnocultural groups. Ethno refers to the person's race, or country of origin; ethnocultural background refers to the country and culture of a person or that person's ancestors.

In the earlier chapters of *Canada Revisited*, we studied the origins and culture of three of Canada's ethnocultural groups: the Native peoples, the French, and the British. This study will focus on ethnocultural groups known as Canada's minorities. A group that is a minority forms only a small percentage of a country's population.

In Canada, many of the ethnocultural minorities have kept their cultures. Not only do they practise the religion of their country of origin, but also they teach their children the music, dances, and literature of their people. Some even live in communities where they are able to conduct most of their daily lives using the language of their country of origin.

Most of the ethnocultural minorities came to Canada during three specific time periods that are often called waves of immigration. Many immigrants came to British North America during the Migration of 1815 to 1850, but most of these people were from Great Britain. With the introduction of Macdonald's National Policy, including the plan to settle the Canadian West, in the 1870s, many immigrants from eastern and central Europe came to Canada. This first wave of ethnocultural minority immigration was halted by World War I (1914–1918).

There was a brief second wave of immigration after World War I, but it ended during the Depression of the 1930s.

After World War II (1939–1945), there was a third wave of immigration, including people from all over the world.

Germans

Germans have been coming to Canada since the 1750s, but large numbers of Germans came to the Prairies during the 1870s and later, especially during the 1890s and the early years of the twentieth century. William Hespeler, a German immigrant, recruited German settlers from Europe and Russia to immigrate to Manitoba. Large numbers of Mennonites came to Canada as a result of Hespeler's offers. In 1911, 403 417 German immigrants came to Canada.

These Canadians are wearing traditional Ukrainian clothing.

Ukrainians

A Ukrainian community was not established until large numbers of immigrants came to Canada near the end of the 1800s. Many Ukrainians left their homelands to start a new life elsewhere as a result of shortages of land and required military service, combined with religious persecution. The Prairies were a popular choice, since they were similar to the steppe lands of the Ukraine. Once the new Canadians were established in their homes, they often encouraged and sometimes paid for family members and friends to come to Canada. Enticed by the golden opportunities in Canada, especially the "free land" (the 64 hectares offered by Sifton's homestead system), the Ukrainians prospered in Canada and made many contributions to their new country.

Wasyl Eleniak and Ivan Pylypiw were among the first immigrants from the Ukraine to be documented. Their arrival started the first wave of Ukrainian immigration to Canada. Arriving by ship from Europe, they set out from Montreal in late 1891 on the free Canadian Pacific Railway tickets that were supplied by the Canadian government. They travelled westward

into the North-West Territories. At Calgary, the end of the railway, they set out for Edmonton. Travelling by wagon or on foot, they finally reached the land they wished to settle. In the years to follow, family members, relatives, and villagers from their native Ukraine followed. They settled in several locations in the North-West Territories. Some came on their own, others came in small groups, or they came in large groups such as the Oleskiw group, numbering 107. In 1896, under Sifton's direction, the Canadian government advertised for settlers to come from the Ukraine.

They first settled in what is now the province of Alberta, then in Manitoba, and later in what became Saskatchewan. They chose large areas of land close to their families and friends. From 1896 to 1914 bloc settlements were established along railway lines east of Edmonton; north and east of Saskatoon; northwest, north, and southeast of Winnipeg. From 1000 Ukrainian settlers in 1896, numbers rapidly increased to 27 000 in 1900, and about 200 000 in 1914.

Italians

Many of the early Italians came to Quebec as mercenary soldiers to fight with the French army before 1759. Later, others fought with the American army during the War of 1812 and then decided to remain in British North America. By the 1880s, a few craftsmen, artists, and musicians had come as well.

Many Italian immigrants came to British North America to assist in the building of the CPR in 1885. Others came to homesteads in the West. However, the largest numbers of Italians came to Canada after World War II.

This cowboy came to Canada from Italy in the early 1890s.

PA-66890, National Archives of Canada, Ottawa (detail).

Most of Canada's Japanese are descended from people who arrived in Canada in the early 1900s.

Japanese

In 1858 Japanese workers came to British Columbia to work in the gold fields. Their exact names and numbers were not documented. Manzo Nagano was the first recorded Japanese person to come to British North America. In 1877 he arrived and settled in Victoria. Settlement on the West Coast was gradual. By 1894 there were approximately 1000 Japanese immigrants and by 1904 there were close to 7000. Most of them settled on the west coast of British Columbia.

Jews

The first Jewish family to arrive in Canada was the Hart family, who came to Quebec with General Wolfe in 1759. The small numbers of Jews who came to British North America were often wealthy merchant families who settled in Montreal. During the late 1800s many Jews left eastern Europe (particularly Russia) to settle in Canada. They settled mostly in Montreal, Toronto, and Winnipeg. (Since they were denied the right to own land in most European countries, they were not used to farming.) The 1901 census reported that there were 16 000 Jews in Canada. By 1911 the Jewish population in Canada had climbed to 76 000.

Blacks

When the Canadian government offered "free land" for settlers in the West, black settlers from Ontario and the United States moved west to become farmers and ranchers in present-day Alberta. Some moved as far west as Vancouver Island. In 1902 there were roughly 10 000 and in 1912 there were approximately 15 000 blacks in Canada.

Of the 300 000 blacks in Canada today, approximately one quarter have emigrated from the West Indies since the 1960s.

NA-263-1, Glenbow Archives, Calgary (detail).

John and Mildred Ware. A former slave from the southern United States, Ware came to the area that is now southern Alberta in 1882. He worked as a cowboy, then bought a ranch.

Chinese

Large numbers of Chinese people (about 14 000) worked as labourers on the construction of the CPR. Upon the completion of the railway in 1885, the Canadian government tried to force them to leave Canada. In 1886 restrictions were put on Chinese immigrants coming into Canada by imposing a 50-dollar "head tax" on all new Chinese immigrants. This tax was increased to $100 in 1900 and to $500 in 1904.

At the beginning of the 1900s, many Chinese were working as household servants or in the service industries, running restaurants, laundries, or small shops. In 1907 they were subjected to racial riots and many of their homes and businesses were destroyed by English Canadians. Large numbers of Chinese families left British Columbia and moved to other parts of Canada.

Today, there are nearly half a million Canadians of Chinese ancestry.

Immigrants from Other Parts of Europe

- Scandinavians arrived in approximately AD 1000 and then again in the late 1800s. They settled primarily in the western provinces.

- Portugal sent early explorers and fishermen in the late 1400s; but few Portuguese settlers stayed in Canada prior to 1912.

- In the late 1400s early explorers and fishermen came from Spain. In the 1700s Spanish explorers went to the Pacific Coast. Few Spanish settlers stayed in Canada prior to 1912.

- French-speaking Swiss immigrants settled in New France beginning in the 1600s. Later they located on the Prairies and in British Columbia.

- Czechoslovakians started immigrating to Canada in the 1770s to set up missions for the Native peoples of Newfoundland and Ontario. Most came in the 1890s and set up homes on the Prairies.

- Dutch people started coming to Canada in the 1800s, at which time they lived mostly on the Prairies and in Ontario.

- Polish immigrants came largely at the turn of the century and set up homes primarily on the Prairies.

- A small number of Greek immigrants came around 1900 and settled largely in the cities in Ontario and Quebec.

- Austrians came around 1900 and settled mostly on the Prairies.

- Belgians started coming to Canada in the 1900s and settled primarily in Manitoba, British Columbia, Quebec, Ontario, and Nova Scotia.

- Immigrants from Luxembourg have been immigrating to Canada since the early 1900s. They inhabited areas around Manitoba, British Columbia, Quebec, Ontario, and Nova Scotia.

Major Cultural Groups in Canada
Up to 1912

BRITISH	3 999 081
FRENCH	2 061 719
GERMAN	403 417
UKRAINIANS	75 432
ITALIANS	45 963

An Exercise in Creative Thinking

Choose one of these projects as a way of revisiting one of the many times in Canadian history when ordinary people made major contributions to the growth of our country. It is important that you reread pages 257 to 265 before starting the projects that follow. Either work individually, in triads, or in small groups. Your school library and local public library have excellent books from which to obtain additional information. Books that contain primary source materials are very useful for going back into the lives of the people who settled the Canadian West.

Activity 1

You work in Clifford Sifton's department of the interior. You have been given the job of designing some promotional materials on the Canadian West. Choose one of the following tasks:

(a) Create posters that will encourage people living in Europe, Russia, and/or the United States to immigrate to the Canadian West.

(b) Design a travel brochure that will entice people in Europe, Russia, and the United States to come to the Canadian West. Readers will want to know about the landforms, rivers and bodies of water, climate, vegetation, and soil types.

(c) Research and prepare a speech to present to the citizens of Europe, Russia, and the United States. Tell them about the many wonderful opportunities that will exist for them should they chose to immigrate.

Present your materials to the publicity department (your class). Since this is to be a promotional presentation, make it as interesting as you can.

Activity 2

You are to take on the role of a reporter from Europe visiting the West in 1902. You have just completed a tour and are very impressed by what you have seen. Write an article for the newspaper describing one of the following: the rich farmlands, one of the Prairie towns, one of the reserves, one of the North West Mounted Police forts, one of the fur-trading forts you visited, or your ride westward on the Canadian Pacific Railway.

Activity 3

Imagine you are a reporter from Ottawa attending the Confederation celebration on the day that Alberta (or Saskatchewan) became a province. Describe the day's events. Compare your description to primary source materials describing what actually happened.

Activity 4

Using charts and/or bulletin boards, plan and construct a display illustrating one of the events from this chapter. Use maps, simple drawings, fancy letters, and bright colours to make your display informative and interesting.

Activity 5

Use drawings, fancy letters, and bright colours to create an informative timeline of the major events of Confederation (*see* Chapters 9, 10, and 11).

Activity 6

Make large wall maps showing what Canada looked like from 1867 until 1905 as the various regions joined Confederation. Include dates. Use basic drawings and bright colours to make the maps look interesting.

Activity 7

Imagine you are a young adult from Europe visiting the Canadian West in 1904. You have just arrived at your relative's home and are very excited. Write a letter to your family or to a friend describing the fertile farmlands or one of the Prairie towns, reserves, North West Mounted Police forts, or fur-trading forts you visited, your ride westward on the Canadian Pacific Railway, or any other event or situation you found especially fascinating.

Activity 8

Create a wall mural illustrating something you read in this chapter.

Activity 9

Draw examples of the clothing that was worn at the turn of the twentieth century. Dress a doll in one of the costumes or make a costume and wear it to social studies class.

Activity 10

Design and build a model of a typical log cabin, soddie, or part of a western town.

Alberta and Saskatchewan Become Provinces, 1905

An important issue that faced the federal government and the North-West Territories concerned whether the territories should be granted provincial status. As leader of the Executive Council, Frederick Haultain urged the federal government to make the North-West Territories a province. The government argued that there were too few people living there. It also said that, since people in the North-West Territories could not agree on whether it should be one province or two, it was best not to do anything, at least for the time being.

Finally, in 1905, the disagreement was over. On September 1, 1905, the two new provinces of Alberta and Saskatchewan were created. The new provinces were promised the following by the federal government:

- more than $1 000 000

- money for public works and government expenses to be sent each year by the federal government

- taxes could be used to support separate Protestant and Roman Catholic schools.

The period after 1900 saw several developments that limited the rights of French-Canadian minorities. In 1905, the French language and the publicly supported **denominational schools** in Alberta and Saskatchewan did not have official status.

The federal government kept control of public lands and natural resources.* You read earlier in this chapter about how the federal government used free homestead land to encourage settlement in the Prairie provinces.

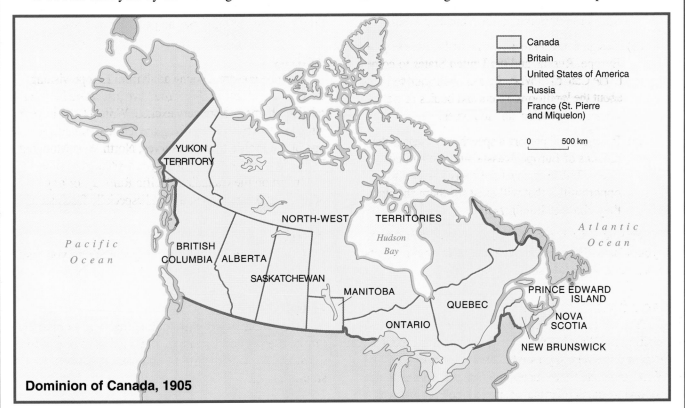

Dominion of Canada, 1905

In 1905 Alberta and Saskatchewan become the eighth and ninth provinces to join Confederation.

Denominational school— school run by a religious group
*Control of public lands was turned over to the Prairie Provinces in 1930, after most of the land that was suitable for farming had been settled.

Alberta

Calgary or Edmonton?

Several urban centres wanted their town or city to be Alberta's new capital. Major contenders were Edmonton and Calgary. In 1905 Edmonton and Calgary each had a population of about 12 000. The people of each had reasons why their city would be a more suitable capital of Alberta.

Edmonton was the geographic centre of the new province, so Edmontonians believed theirs should be the capital city. Edmonton had been the centre of activities in the northern part of the province for many years. It had also been an early fur-trading post. Calgary, on the other hand, was located on the main line of the Canadian Pacific Railway, and so Calgarians believed theirs should be the capital city. Calgary also was the centre for the cattle industry, and Calgarians felt this qualified their city for becoming the capital.

In the end, Frank Oliver, member of parliament for Edmonton and minister of the interior in 1905, was asked to make the decision. He chose Edmonton to be the capital of Alberta.

Prime Minister Sir Wilfrid Laurier spoke at the Alberta Inaugural Day ceremonies in Edmonton on September 1, 1905.

Middle right: When Alberta became a province, people celebrated in the streets.

Below: The Alberta Legislative Buildings, showing the old Fort Edmonton, 1912.

Above: Alexander Cameron Rutherford was the first premier of Alberta.

Prime Minister Sir Wilfrid Laurier (seated left) and Governor General Earl Grey (seated centre) attended inauguration ceremonies for the Province of Saskatchewan at Regina, 1905.

Saskatchewan

Prime Minister Sir Wilfrid Laurier and Governor General Earl Grey and their wives attended the Saskatchewan inauguration day ceremonies on September 4, 1905.* There were crowds, bands, **bunting**, parades, speeches, the swearing in of the lieutenant-governor of the new province, the musical ride of the Mounties, and a grand inaugural ball—all to celebrate the occasion.

As in the new province of Alberta, different cities wanted to become the provincial capital. However, in the case of Saskatchewan, there were six cities—Regina, Moose Jaw, Saskatoon, Prince Albert, Fort Qu'Appelle, and Battleford—vying for the honour, rather than the two major contenders of Alberta. Regina already had the distinction of having been appointed the capital of the North-West Territories in 1883. It was the headquarters of the NWMP and the most important city on that part of the CPR line. Of the other cities, Saskatoon, in particular, seemed to be anxious to win this status. Members of boards of trade, newspaper editors, members of the Legislative Assembly, and other important people were invited to a lavish banquet, where the hosts informed them of the benefits of Saskatoon as capital. Alas for Saskatoon—in the end its efforts were to no avail. The Legislature voted 21 to two for Regina to become the capital of Saskatchewan.

For Your Notebook

1. How did the new provinces of Alberta and Saskatchewan benefit from becoming provinces?
2. Reread page 231, which describes the day Prince Edward Island joined Confederation. Briefly describe and compare each situation. Why do you think they were so different?

Left: Walter Scott was the first premier of Saskatchewan.

Elaborate decorations were made to celebrate Saskatchewan's inauguration ceremonies in Regina on September 4 and 5, 1905.

---

*The province actually came into being on September 1, 1905.
bunting — strips of cloth used as holiday decorations

Review ●●●●●●●●●●●●●●●●●●●●●●●●

Summarizing the Chapter

- As a result of the Pacific Scandal, Prime Minister John A. Macdonald and his Conservative Party were forced to resign in 1873. The Conservatives had received a contribution of $325 000 from Sir Hugh Allan during the 1872 election campaign. The government was accused of accepting a bribe in return for granting the contract for the building of the CPR to Allan.

- The Liberal Party, led by Alexander Mackenzie, took over the government in 1873. While in power the Liberals established the Supreme Court of Canada, introduced voting by secret ballot, established the Royal Military College in Kingston, Ontario, and passed the North-West Territories Act of 1875.

- Macdonald won the election of 1878 on the strength of his proposed National Policy. It had three parts:

  1. Protective tariffs: High import duties were to be paid on imported goods in order to encourage Canadians to buy Canadian-made products.

  2. A national railway: This would bind the country together.

  3. Settlement of the West: Immigrants would be encouraged to settle on the Prairies. They would buy the products of Canadian industries and would grow food for city dwellers to eat.

- The Canadian Pacific Railway was completed by 1885 under the leadership of William Cornelius Van Horne.

- In 1873 the Canadian government created a police force for the Canadian West called the North West Mounted Police. The American whiskey smugglers left when the NWMP established law and order. With the establishment of the NWMP, the Canadian West was safe for settlers to make their homes. The North West Mounted Police were also a help in treaty negotiations with the First People.

- Between 1871 and 1877, seven treaties were signed between the Canadian government and the First People living between Lake Superior and the Rockies. They were given reserve lands on which to live, money payments, and often the right to hunt, fish, and trap on Crown land found throughout the treaty area.

- In 1885 the Metis and some of the First People in the North-West Territories resisted the Canadian government actions there. Louis Riel, the Metis leader, was convicted of treason and hanged. Many of the people of Quebec were outraged because they viewed Riel's hanging as an insult to all French Canadians. This caused problems between French and English Canadians for years to come.

- Canada's seventh prime minister was Wilfrid Laurier, leader of the Liberal Party. Laurier had the difficult task of trying to please both French-Canadian and English-Canadian interests. One of the issues that called upon Laurier's abilities to arrive at a compromise was the Manitoba Schools Question. It had to do with whether there should be two school systems in the province of Manitoba.

- The completion of the Canadian Pacific Railway allowed for increasing numbers of immigrants to travel to Canada's West. The greatest number of immigrants arrived between 1897 and 1914. This influx was during the time of the Liberal Prime Minister, Sir Wilfrid Laurier. Other reasons for the increase in settlers moving West include the aggressive advertising campaign that the Canadian Pacific Railway Company and the Canadian government waged in Great Britain and central and eastern Europe, and changes to the homesteading laws.

- The North-West Territories Act of 1875 gave the territories their own lieutenant-governor and an appointed council of five members. In 1888 a Legislative Assembly with limited powers was established. In 1897 responsible government was granted.

- On September 1, 1905, the two new provinces of Alberta and Saskatchewan were created.

Checking Predictions

1. At the beginning of this chapter you made some predictions based on the Overview and what you already knew. Now use what you have learned by reading the chapter to fill in the third column of the chart that you began earlier.

2. Discuss the following questions by referring to the Section V story on pages 176 and 177. Answer these questions in light of the information you have gained from Chapters 9, 10, and 11.

   (a) In what ways was the mega-council the same as Canada's government under Confederation? In what ways was it different?

   (b) Who participated in the Student's Council at Fairmont School? Who participated in the government of the new Dominion of Canada?

   (c) How were decisions to be made under the mega-council? How are decisions made in the government of Canada?

   (d) Who would hold the power in the mega-council? Who holds the power in the government of Canada?

   (e) Break into triads. Explain to each other whether the section story on pages 176 and 177 illustrates federalism or not. (*See* page 196.)

Working with Information

1. Here are some of the main ideas that were covered in this chapter:

   - national railway
   - western settlement
   - North West Mounted Police
   - treaties
   - North-West Resistance
   - the new provinces of Alberta and Saskatchewan

   Design a pictorial image for each area of focus. Write a brief explanation for each, telling why you designed that particular image. Make a poster collage showing the images you chose. The posters could be displayed on a bulletin board labelled Nation Building.

2. How was the growing French Canadian nationalism a challenge to Confederation?

3. Read a newspaper every day for a week. Record problems that are occurring today as: a) a result of Canada's multicultural nature, or, b) on some aboriginal issue. Choose one and explain the situation to someone who is unfamiliar with it.

4. Relate what you found in this chapter on treaties to the section titled "Alternatives Open to the British" on page 80.

5. Use the information in Chapters 10 and 11 to prepare a game to illustrate the entrance into Confederation of Manitoba, British Columbia, Prince Edward Island, Alberta, and Saskatchewan.

Building Thinking Strategies

Point of View

1. One important thinking strategy is the ability to take the perspective of another. The building of the CPR has been described in this chapter from the perspective of the settlers. Describe the building of the CPR from the viewpoint of a Native person living at the time in an area directly affected by the construction of the CPR. Think in terms of the assistance that was provided by Native peoples and the ways in which their lifestyle was disrupted. You will need to do additional research in order to complete this task.

Conceptualizing

1. Colonization, settlement, and nationhood are major concepts in this book. Using examples from this textbook create some form of assessment for your classmates.

Communicating Ideas

Reading

1. Read one of the following stories: "Treaties" by Laura Okemaw, "Dong Yee" by Nancy Sellars Marcotte, "Angelique Dumas" by Jeanne Laboucane, "Josef Cherniak" by Josephine E. Hancheruk, or "Polly Enkin" by Abraham J. Arnold in *Ordinary People in Canada's Past* by Nancy Sellars Marcotte.

Creating

1. If you made a mobile as suggested on page 80, regarding the alternatives open to the British, use information from this chapter to add to your mobile.

Canada Revisited

1. With a partner conduct a survey of your neighbourhood, school, and parents about how they think the Canadian nation will change in the future. Share your findings with your classmates.

Glossary

Aboriginal—being the first in a region

Absentee landlord—a landowner who takes an income from his land but does not live there

Absolute Monarchy—a leader who has unlimited power over the subjects; one who is not limited or restricted by a set of rules, parliament, or any form of government

Acculturation—effect that two cultures have on each other when they meet; also called cultural exchange

Act—a legislative decision; law

Adze—tool similar to an axe, used for shaping wood

Alliance—union formed between nations or groups of people based on an agreement that benefits both groups

Amnesty—a general pardon for past offences against a government

Annex—to join together

Annexation—joining of one territory to a larger political entity

Anthropologist—a scientist who studies and compares the customs, beliefs, and ways of life of different groups of people

Apprentice—a person who works with a skilled craftsperson in order to learn that craft

Artisan—worker very skilled in his or her craft

Assay office—a place that examines gold or other minerals for its quality

Assembly—an elected group that made laws. The Assembly had little power as the governor or his council could veto its decisions.

Assimilate—the process through which one culture is absorbed into another

Bias—an unfair way of looking at a situation; slanting or distorting something

Bicultural—having two cultures (British and French) existing side by side in the same country or province

Biculturalism—a policy that favours having two cultures. In Canada, biculturalism refers to the British and the French as the two cultures.

Bill—a proposed law that is presented to the Legislative Assembly to be debated and voted on. When it becomes law it is called an Act.

Blockade—closed off; usually done to a harbour or port in wartime to prevent supplies from reaching their destination

Block system of holding land—subdividing land into blocks or squares; also called the square system

Boycott—refusal to trade with a country or company or to buy its products

Bribe—gift, usually money, that is given to people in order to get them to do something wrong or against their wishes

Brigade—group of canoes, carts, or dogsleds carrying trade goods and supplies to and from inland posts

Bunting—strips of cloth used as holiday decorations

Canada East—former name for Quebec; also called Lower Canada

Canada West—former name for Ontario; also called Upper Canada

Canadiens—French-speaking people born in New France (Quebec); the name shows that the *Canadiens* were distinct from the French in Europe

Caucasian—member of the white race

Caste System—social system with distinct classes based on differences of birth, rank, position, or wealth

Census—an official count of the people of a country or district to find out the number of people living there

Charter—written permission given by someone in authority who grants privileges

Civil law—having to do with private rights of citizens, especially property disputes; as opposed to criminal law, which has to do with public wrongs

Clan—a group of related families that claim to be descended from common ancestors

Clergy Reserves—one-seventh of all public lands was set aside for Protestant schools and churches by the Constitutional Act of 1791

Coalition Government—temporary joining of political parties

Colonial Government—a form of representative government, but many decisions were still made in Britian and the colonists were still subject to British laws

Colonization—settling and controlling new lands

Community government—a form of local government that was also called a town meeting. All free adult males could take part in the decision-making process.

Compromise—an agreement in which each side gives up some of its demands

Compulsory—required

Concept—a general idea or thought (e.g., colonization, nationhood)

Concession—giving in

Concilliation—gaining good will

Concord—agreement between two groups of people

Confederation—the federal union of British North American colonies. The members would retain some power over their own affairs and turn some powers over to a central government

Confiscate—property taken away by someone in authority, usually a government

Conjugal—pertaining to a married couple

Consensus—general agreement among all people consulted

Conservative traditions—customs, opinions, and habits that are cautious and opposed to change

Controversial—having several sides or differences; open for dispute or debate

Corvée—free labour that the habitants owed their seigneurs. In France, this often meant weeks of repairing roads in the spring time just when the habitants should have been farming for themselves. In New France, the habitants spent little time on corvée as the St. Lawrence River served as the colony's main road.

Crofter—a person who cultivates a small farm

Crown colony—a colony under the direct control of Britain

Crown land—land held by the government of Canada and not intended to be used for settlement by non-Natives

Crown reserves—one-seventh of all public land was set aside for the British government by the Constitutional Act of 1791. By 1825, these lands were finally sold because they prevented road building.

Cultural background—the language, religion, traditions, music, art, and literature of a person's ancestral homeland

Cultural exchange—objects or ideas passed from one culture to another

Culture—the way of life of specific groups of people

Denominational—under the control of a religious group

Denominational school—school run by a religious group

Deport—to remove, or move away; to force people away from their homes and country by order of authority

Diversity—differences

Dominant Canadian culture—the group in Canada that has the control or that is the most powerful, influential; often this group controls the government

Dowry—money or property that a woman brings with her into marriage, usually supplied by her father

Economic—having to do with the production, distribution, and consumption of wealth; money, taxes, wages, selling price, etc.

Effigy—an imitation, made of cloth, of a person who is disliked

Elite—special group, usually more educated and rich

Emigrate—leave one's country or region to settle in another

English Freehold System—land held for life or with the right to pass it on to one's heirs

Ethnocentrism—believing one's own culture is better than everyone else's

Ethnocultural—refers to the country and culture of a person or that person's ancestors

Exile—to officially order someone to leave the country

Exploration—seeking new lands

Extended family—includes cousins and grandparents and great-grandparents, not just parents and brothers and sisters

Fatally—to death

Federal union—a political union in which the members have certain powers over their own affairs, and certain powers are turned over to a central government

Figurehead—a person who is head of a country in name or title only and has no real power or responsibility

First Nations—includes Native people, the Inuit, and the Metis

First People—includes Native people, the Inuit, and the Metis. In this book, the terms First People and First Nations will also be used in reference to Indian people.

Francophone—being able to speak and/or write the French language

Freehold—a piece of land held for life or with the right to pass it on to one's heirs

Free trade—trade between countries where taxes or tariffs are not involved

Gen—membership in a gen (or band) is inherited through the mother

Gimlet—a small hand tool used for boring holes in wood

Guerrilla tactics—surprise attacks

Guerrilla warfare—fighting in small bands, making sudden attacks and ambushes on the enemy

Habitant—farmer in New France, and later in Quebec

Heterogenous—made up of different parts

Homogenous—similar; like everyone else

Icon—a picture

Illiterate—unable to read or write or only at a very low level

Immigrant—person who comes to live in a new country

Immigrate—move to another country to live

Imperial—referring to the monarchy; the crown

Indian—a descendent of the First People of North America

Institution—an organization or society established for some public or social purpose. An organized way of doing things. Examples include: government, education, church, and finance.

Intercolonial railway—a railway that joins the various colonies

Investment capital—lending money or buying shares so that Canadian businesses have money to fund their day-to-day operations

La Survivance—cultural survival, especially the French language and culture, and the Roman Catholic religion

Legislative Assembly—the group of representatives elected to the Legislature who represent the people of each province; a law-making body

Libel—a printed statement or picture that unjustly injures a person's reputation

List of Rights—a list of conditions that the Metis wanted the government to meet and ensure would be followed

Literate—educated; having the ability to read and write

Lobby—represent a special interest to the government. A lobbyist tries to get lawmakers to introduce or vote for measures favourable to the lobbyist's special interest

Lower Canada—the southern portion of Quebec in 1791 ("down" the St. Lawrence River)

Majority government—party that receives the most seats in the House of Commons governs the country

Manifesto—a public declaration of intentions by an important group of people

Matrilineal—tracing descent through the mother's side of the family

Mercantilism—an economic theory for the accumulation of wealth in gold and silver

Mercenary—doing something where money is the main reason for doing it; e.g., a soldier serving for pay in a foreign army

Metis—people of mixed North American Indian and European ancestry

Migratory—moving from place to place, usually according to the season

Militia—a part of an army made up of citizens who are not regular soldiers but who undergo training for emergency duty or national defense

Minority Government—one that does not have a majority of Members of Parliament in its caucus

Minutemen—armed men ready to fight at a moment's notice

Mire—wet, soggy ground

Moderate—a person who does not hold extreme opinions

Moderator—the person who directs a formal debate

Monopoly—a right granted for one person or group to control buying and selling

Mother country—the country where one was born; a country in relation to its colonies

Multicultural nation—one that has people from many different cultural backgrounds

Nation—a nation is a group of people who live in a certain area, generally speak the same language, have the same way of life, have the same system of decision-making (government), and are usually made up of a number of tribes or groups that are the same

Native—refers to the Indians (status and non-status), the Inuit, and the Metis. In this book, the terms First People and First Nations will also be used in reference to Indian people

Native Peoples—includes the eight Inuit nations, the Indian nations, and the Metis

Nobility—a person with special rank and authority by virtue of birth or title. A duke, count, earl, or marquis are examples of nobility.

Nutrient—food for plants or animals; minerals in the soil that provide food and nourishment for plants

Occupation—the control of an area by foreign military force

Opportunist—a person who takes an advantage of a situation for his or her own benefit

Oppression—to lose one's freedom; having little power

Oratory—the art of public speaking

Paraphrase—to express the meaning of a book, a passage, or a set of words in different words

Parish—district that is the responsibility of a particular church

Parish System—the system of districts having their own churches

Patrilineal—tracing descent through the father's side of the family

Patriots—colonists who rebelled against British rule

Pay dirt—earth or ore containing a valuable mineral such as gold

Pemmican—a food made of buffalo meat, buffalo fat, and berries. One kilogram of pemmican was considered equal to four kilograms of ordinary meat and it would last for years. It was an ideal food for long journeys

Peoples—when more than one group or nation is involved

Petition—a document containing a request directed to the government containing statements describing what the petitioners want changed and has space for the petitioners to sign their names

Platform—the principles and policies of a political party, what the political party feels is important, and what they believe in

Political Party—a group of people with similar beliefs about government, who work together to get their candidates elected as representatives

Political reform—changes to make the government better

Poll—voting; results of voting

Potash—grey ash left after trees have been burned and the ash boiled in a pot until no water is left. The "potash" was sold for making soap and cosmetics.

Primary source — a first-hand account of a historical event by someone who witnessed it or lived during the time of the event; the main source of information

Privateer — privately owned and staffed armed ship

Provisional government — a temporary government set up until a more permanent one can be established

Provincial rights — the powers maintained by the provincial governments, usually involving cultural, social, and local issues

Puppet — a leader who is not independent, who waits for orders, or does what somebody else says

Purser — the officer in charge of money matters on board a ship

Radical — holding extreme opinions; wants fundamental social, economic, and political changes

Radical policy — plan for extreme changes

Rank — position based on importance

Re-annex — to unite with a country or province again

Red River cart — a strong two-wheeled cart pulled by horses or oxen

Refugee — person who leaves home or country to seek safety elsewhere

Relic — the body or parts of the body of a saint, or a sacred memento associated with a saint

Rep by pop — The number of elected members of a Legislative Assembly (the representatives) is based on the number of voters (based on the population). "Rep by pop" is an abbreviation for representation by population.

Representative Government — citizens elect people who represent them in their Legislative Assembly (decision-making body). Every individual has a voice in government, but only a small group actually makes the decisions.

Resolution — something formally decided on as a group with the idea of holding firmly to the choice

Resolutions — a list of guidelines or rules that are to be followed as a basis for ruling a group of people

Responsible Government — Members of the executive council (today known as the Cabinet) are chosen from the group with the most elected members in the Legislative Assembly (rather than by the governor). The government is the Cabinet. The Cabinet is thus responsible to the representatives of the voters for its conduct of public business. If the Cabinet loses the confidence of the majority of the Legislative Assembly, it must resign. The government can function only if it has the support of the legislature—it is responsible to the legislature.

Revenue — income; money coming in

Rocker — a cradle used in mining, whereby the material being mined can be sorted and washed

Royal colony — a colony governed directly by a king or queen in another country

Sachem — the appointed respresentatives of an individual clan

Scrip — a certificate or coupon that was given to Metis people as compensation for land, entitling the holder to a choice between cash or land

Scurvy — disease caused by lack of vitamin C

Seminary — special school for the training of priests

Serge — a strong woolen cloth

Slate — thin slice of bluish-grey rock on which children wrote

Sluice-box — a long box-like container in which gold is separated from gravel and mud

Social problems — problems concerning life in a community, problems between people that arise in day to day living

Speculation — the act of buying or selling land, at some risk, with the hope of making large profits from future price changes

Squatter — a person who settles on public land in order to obtain ownership; a person who settles on another's land without obtaining permission

Subsidy — a grant or contribution of money

Subsistence farmers — only grew enough food for their families; none was left to sell for much-needed cash to buy other products and supplies

Sympathetic — in agreement with

Taboos — customs or traditions that set things apart as sacred, unclean, or cursed

Tariff — a tax on money paid to the government of a country when products are brought into a country

Taxation Without Representation — being taxed without benefit of elected representatives to speak on your behalf

Technology — the knowledge and application of developments in science, manufacturing, business, and the arts

Tithe — a tax of one-tenth of the produce of one's land or the amount in money, paid to support the church

Tory — today called Conservatives. A member of the Conservative Party in Great Britain is also called a Tory.

Traditional Natives — believers of the old ways: the old customs and traditions

Transcontinental — extending across a continent

Treason — betrayal of one's country

Tributaries — streams feeding larger streams, or lakes

Universal — for everybody

Upper Canada — Quebec was divided into two colonies in 1791. Upper Canada was "up" the St. Lawrence River and is part of present-day Ontario.

Value — a long-established idea on which one's life is modelled

Veto — the right or power to forbid or reject

Winnow — to separate grain from chaff

Picture Credits

The publisher gratefully acknowledges the assistance of the various public institutions, private firms and individuals who provided material for use in this book. Every effort has been made to identify and credit all sources. The publisher would appreciate notification of any omissions or errors so that they may be corrected.

BCARS — British Columbia Archives and Records Service
CLG — The Confederation Life Gallery of Canadian History
GM — Glenbow Museum, Calgary, Alberta
MMCH — McCord Museum of Canadian History
MTRL — Metropolitan Toronto Reference Library
NAC — National Archives of Canada, Ottawa
NGC — National Gallery of Canada
PAA — Provincial Archives of Alberta
PAM — Provincial Archives of Manitoba
PANB — Provincial Archives of New Brunswick

Front Cover Map, *"Map of Canada and the north part of Louisiana," by Thomas Jefferys (1760)* (detail), William C. Wonders Map Collection, Department of Geography, University of Alberta. **7,** *Jules (Ojibwa and Cree),* by Carl D. Fontaine. **17,** *Girl in native costume at a Prince Charles School Powwow,* Ian Scott, The Edmonton Journal. **20,** *The First British Flag,* CLG. **26,** *The Discovery of Canada,* by J. D. Kelly, CLG. **28,** *In the Trading Room,* by C.W. Jefferys (detail), Courtesy: Environment Canada – Parks Service, Atlantic Region. **29,** *Oeuvres de Champlain (Samuel de Champlain),* by C.H. Laverdiere, MTRL. **30,** *The Fur Traders of Montreal,* by Reid, C–11013, NAC. **31,** *Beaver hats of the 1770's to the 1820's,* C-17338, NAC. **32,** *Marguerite Bourgeoys* (Stamp), Reproduced courtesy of Canada Post Corporation. **33,** *Fortifications at Ste. Marie Among the Hurons, In Huronia,* Kathleen Vanderlinden, 1985. **33,** *Chapel at Ste. Marie Among the Hurons, In Huronia,* Kathleen Vanderlinden, 1985. **34,** *An Acadian House, Belleisle, Nova Scotia, c. 1720.* **34,** *Inside an Acadian House, Belleisle, Nova Scotia, c. 1720.* **35,** *Trading, Belleisle, Nova Scotia, c. 1720.* **35,** *Repairing a Saltmarsh Dyke, Belleisle, Nova Scotia, c. 1720.* **35,** *Acadians Cutting Saltmarsh Hay, Belleisle, Nova Scotia, c. 1720.* Each is an artist's concept, based on archaeological and historical research by the Nova Scotia Museum. Artist: Azor Vienneau, of the Nova Scotia Museum staff. Nova Scotia Museum. **35,** *Micmac Indians,* #6663, NGC. **36,** *Morning Services,* Phyllis Arnold. **36,** *Collecting Hay,* Phyllis Arnold. **37,** *Hudson's Bay Company Coat-of-Arms,* H.B.C.A. Photograph Collection 1987/363-C-43. **44,** *King Louis XIV,* by Hyacinthe Rigaud, C-5400, NAC. **45,** *Meeting of the Sovereign Council,* by Charles Huot, photographed by Kedl, 72-266-26, Assemblée Nationale, Québec. **46,** *Jean Baptiste Colbert, late 18th Century,* by Philippe de Champaigne, C-9628, NAC. **46,** *French Girls Arriving at Quebec,* by C.W. Jefferys, C-10688, NAC. **48,** *Portrait of Mgr François de Laval,* by Pierre Soulard, École Canadienne (detail), Pc 84.1, Musée de Séminaire de Québec. **49,** *Portrait of Jean Talon* (detail), by Theophile Hamel (attr.), Pc 984-22, Musée de Séminaire de Québec. A**49,** *Canada's First Trade Treaty,* by J.D. Kelly, CLG. **49,** *Canada's First Shipyard,* by Rex Woods, CLG. **50,** *A View of the Château Richer,* by Davies, #6275, NGC. **53,** *Intendant Talon Visiting the Habitants,* by Lawrence R. Batchelor, G-11925 76-I-3, NAC. **54,** *Harvest Festival by Berczy,* #16648, NGC. **55,** *First Ursuline Nuns With Children,* by Lawrence R. Batchelor, C-10520, NAC. **57,** *Saint Marguerite de Youville,* Sisters of Charity of Montreal, "Grey Nuns." **60,** *French Fusilier,* Reproduced from Montcalm's Army, published by Osprey Ltd. in 1973, Copyright 1973 Osprey Publishing Company, London. **60,** *British Grenadier,* Reproduced from Wolfe's Army, published by Osprey Ltd. in 1974, Copyright 1974 Osprey Publishing Company, London. **62,** *Hudsons Bay Company Trade Goods from the Hudsons Bay Company Museum Collection,* H.B.C.A. 1987 / 363-T-37/13, H.B.C.A. PAM. **63,** *Kelsey on the Plains,* by Rex Woods, CLG. **64,** *Fleur-de-lis,* Michael Burgess. **64,** *Louisbourg Citadel,* Phyllis Arnold. **65,** *Local Inn, French soldiers, A Local Micmac, Drying Fish,* Phyllis Arnold. **66,** *Halifax and the Environs,* by T. Jeffreys, PAC (H12/240), NAC. **68,** *Deportation of the Acadians from the Isle of St. Jean,* by Lewis Parker, Courtesy: Environment Canada – Parks Service, Atlantic Region. **71,** *Plains of Abraham,* Phyllis Arnold. **73,** *A View of the Taking of Quebec, September 13th, 1759,* C-1078, NAC. **73,** *Surrender of Montreal ,* C-11043, NAC. **74,** *Louis Joseph, Marquis de Montcalm* (detail), C-27665, NAC. **74,** *General James Wolfe* (detail), M245, MMCH. **78,** *A View of the Cathedral,* by Richard Short, C-361, NAC. **80,** *A view of the church of Notre Dame de la Victoire,* by Richard Short, C-357, NAC. **83,** *General James Murray* (detail), C-26065, NAC. **87,** *Quebec City Wall,* Phyllis Arnold. **92,** *House of Burgesses,* Phyllis Arnold. **95,** *Stamp Acts Paper,* Michael Burgess. **96,** *George Washington,* by Gilbert Stuart (detail), Dover Publications Inc. New York. **97,** *Americans Invading Canada at Québec city,* by Alan Daniel, c.1978, The Readers Digest Association, Heritage of Canada. **101,** *Loyalists Drawing Lots For Their Lands, 1784,* by C.W. Jefferys, C-96362, NAC. **102,** *Tory Refugees on their way to Canada,* by H. Pyle, Delaware Art Museum. **105,** *The Coming of the Loyalists, 1783,* by Henry Sandham, C-168, NAC. **106,** *The Church of St. Paul, and the Parade at Halifax in Nova Scotia,* by R. Short (detail), C-4293, NAC. **108,** *Cape Breton Council,* by Charles Walter Simpson, Copyright: Estate of Charles Walter Simpson, C-13954, NAC. **109,** *Duhamel Du Monceau's 1769 View of Newfoundland,* C-105230, NAC. **112,** *Sir Guy Carleton* (Lord Dorchester), copied by Mabel B. Messer, 1923 (detail), C-2833, NAC. **113,** *Joseph Brant,* by Berczy (detail), #5777, NGC. **116,** *Circular Dance of the Canadians,* by George Heriot (detail), C-251, NAC. **122,** *Laura Secord (Ingersoll),* (detail), C-10717, NAC. **123,** *The Battle of Queenston Heights, October 13th, 1812,* by Major Dennis, C-276, NAC. **124,** *Samual Hearne at Cumberland House on the Saskatchewan River, 1774,* P-416, HBCA Picture Collection. **125,** *Captain Cook on Vancouver Island,* E-10, CLG. **126,** *Simon Fraser Clinging to Ropes of the Black Canyon,* by John Innes (detail), Native Sons of British Columbia, Post #2, Vancouver, B.C. (painting on long-term loan to Art Gallery, Simon Fraser University, B.C. **127,** *Old Fort William,* John de Visser, Photographer Ltd, Cobourg, Ontario. **134,** *Bush Farm near Chatham, c.1838,* by Philip John Bainbrigge, C-11811, NAC. **136,** *Emigrants Arrival at Cork—A Scene on the Quay, c.1830* (detail), IUV 10/5/1851, P. 386, The Illustrated London News Picture Library. **137,** *Emigation Vessel – Between Decks, circa 1830* (detail), IUV 10/5/1851, P.387, The Illustrated London News Picture Library. **138,** *Breaking a Log Jam,* P4/3/3, PANB. **139,** *Spring Brigade Goes West,* by Franklin Arbuckle (detail), HBCA Picture Collection, P–412 (N8907), Hudson's Bay Company Archives, Provincial Archives of Manitoba. **139,** *Shooting the Rapids,* by Francis Ann Hopkins, C-2774, NAC. **140,** *Louis Joseph Papineau, by Alfred Ferland* (detail), P600-6/GH 871-25, Quebec Archives. **143,** *Attack of St. Charles,* by Beauclerk, C-393, NAC. **143,** *Back view of the Church of St. Eustache and Dispersion of the Insurgents,* by Lord Charles Beauclerk, M4777.6, MMCH. **144,** *Behind Bonsecours Market,* by Raphael, #6673, NGC. **147,** *Process of Clearing the Town Plot of Stanley* (detail), C–17, NAC. **148,** *Road Between Kingston and York, Upper Canada, c.1830,* C-12632, NAC. **148,** *First Home,* Phyllis Arnold. **148,** *Pioneer Homestead,* Phyllis Arnold. **148,** *The Old Homestead,* Phyllis Arnold.

149, *Threshing with Flail*, by C.W. Jefferys, C-73395, NAC. 149, *Winnowing Grain*, by C.W. Jefferys, C-73396, NAC. 150, *View of King Street (looking eastward), city of Toronto, Upper Canada*, by T. Young (detail), C-1669, NAC. 151, *The Sawmill, Weaving Spools, Livery Stable, The Schoolhouse, The Church, City Hall*, Phyllis Arnold. 152, *The Royal Mail*, by C.W. Jefferys, C-69849, NAC. 154, *Robert Gourlay* (detail), T16969, MTRL. 154, *William Lyon Mackenzie* (detail), C-1993, NAC. 155, *Detail of a print by Charles Turner after a painting by Nelson Cook of Sir Francis Bond Head, Lieutenant Governor of Upper Canada 1793-1875, dated 1837*, C-18789, NAC. 156, *Rebels of 1837 drilling in North York*, by C.W. Jefferys, 1898, T-1316 #1, Art Gallery of Ontario, Toronto. 157, *Death of Colonel Moodie, T 13350 (1086)*, MTRL. 157, *Captured Rebels, 1837*, by Hayes, C-3653, NAC. 157, *Executions, 1837-1838*, by Julien, C-13493, NAC. 159, *Mackenzie's Press*, Phyllis Arnold. 163, *Lord Durham*, C–5456, NAC. 165, *Lord Elgin*, by Cornelius Krieghoff (detail), M22464, MMCH. 171, *The Burning of the Parliament Buildings, Montreal*, by Joseph Legaré, M11588, MMCH. 172, *Egerton Ryerson*, S-623 (detail), Ontario Archives, Toronto. 173, *Joseph Howe* (detail), C–22002, NAC. 173, *Joseph Howe Being Hoisted above the Crowd*, by C.W. Jefferys, C-73708, NAC. 175, *Rideau Canal*, Phyllis Arnold. 180, *Handbill, "By the Queen, A Proclamation for uniting ...Canada"* (detail), Collection of the New Brunswick Museum. 183, *Great Western Railway, Canadian Railway Museum, "Gilson Homan" Globe, 1853. Rebuilt Great Western Railway, 1870*, Canadian Railway Museum. 183, *Old Great Western Railway Station, London, C.W., 1858*, JRR. 1456TIB, MTRL. 184, *Battle of Ridgeway c.w. Desperate Charge of the Fenians, under Col. O'Neill near Ridgeway Station, June 2, 1866* (detail). C-18737, NAC. 186, *St. John, New Brunswick, 1864*, P4-3-52, PANB. 186, *Charlottetown Harbour in 1864, as it appeared in Picturesque Canada, 1882*, 2755/26, Prince Edward Island Public Archives and Records Office. 186, *City of Halifax, Nova Scotia as seen from the cupola of the Mount Hope Asylum, by F. Day*, 948 140 17, Courtesy of the Royal Ontario Museum. 189, *Province House Ball, 1864*, by Dusan Kadlec, Environment Canada, Canadian Parks Service. 189, *The Fathers of Confederation, 1864*, C-6, CLG. 190, *The Old Parliament Buildings, burnt in 1883 in Montmorency-Laval Park, Québec (Montreal)*, P6006-6/N1073-85, National Archives of Quebec. 190, *Delegates at the Quebec Conference*, C-6350, NAC. 192, *Sir Samuel Leonard Tilley* (detail), P37-40, PANB. 192, *All in The Family, Le Perroquet, January 7th, 1865* (cartoon), Canadian Microfilming Company Limited. 193, *The Governor's House and St. Mother's Meeting House in Holles Street, also looking up George Street, Halifax, Nova Scotia* (detail), *c.1759 to 1761*, by Richard Short, C-2482, NAC. 193, *Sir Charles Tupper, 1871* (detail), C-6168, NAC. 194, *London Conference On Confederation*, by J.D. Kelly (detail), C-4, CLG. 195, *Sir John A. Macdonald* (detail), C-4154, NAC. 200, *Large Queen Issue, Scott #24, 1868-1876* (stamp), POS 1434, NAC. 200, *Viscount Monck* (detail), C-10813, NAC. 200, *First Dominion*, Pg-K142-1, Queens University Archives. 200, *Canada Confederation Medal, 1867*, National Medal Collection #5001, C-14989, NAC. 201, *Queen Victoria*, C-18292, NAC. 201, *Canada's First Postage Stamp, Five Cent Beaver, 1859*, designed by Sanford Fleming, C-1670, NAC. 201, *Sir John A. Macdonald*, NA-1375-1, GM. 201, *Rear View of the Parliament Buildings*, by Samuel Mclaughin, #C-18371, NAC. 205, *Prime Minister Trudeau and Queen Elizabeth II signing the Constitution*, Canapress Photo Service. 210, *Lord Selkirk* (detail), C-1346, NAC. 212, *Mrs. James Green Stewart; Sinclair, Caroline (Pruden) 1, 1860s* (detail), N8433, PAM. 213, *Metis Hunting Buffalo by C.W. Jefferys*, C-73392, NAC. 214, *Metis hunters and traders on the plains, 1869*, Manitoba Archives and Records Service, Boundry Commission Collection. 214, Metis Hunter, C-79643, NAC. 214, *Transportation Boat-Dakota 1, Fort Garry, 1873* (detail), N3440, PAM. 215, *The Situation, January 29, 1870, Canadian Illustrated News*, C48653, NAC. 215, *Interior of Fort Garry, 1872 (sic), Fort Garry 24*, by Ernest J. Hutchins, 1912, N12764, PAM. 217, *Hudson's Bay Company Coat-of-Arms*, H.B.C.A.

Photograph Collection 1987/363-C-43. 218, *Riel and his Council, 1869*, NA1039-1, GM. 219, *Louis Riel* (detail), C-18082, NAC. 222, *The Red River Expedition at Kakabeka Falls, Ontario, 1877*, by Frances Anne Hopkins (detail), C-2775 / C-134840, NAC. 224, *Town of Douglas*, PDP1889, BCARS. 224, *Billy Phinney*, HP767, A-353, BCA. 225, *Miners at the Neversweat Company Mine in the Cariboo, 1868*, A-937, #761, BCARS. 225, *Billy Barker* (detail), #914, Vancouver Public Library. 226, *J.S. Helmcken* (detail), HP3044, #A-1350, BCARS. 226, *Amor de Cosmos* (detail), HP2624, #A-1222, BCARS. 227, *Main Street, Barkerville*, HP10109, #A-3786, BCARS. 228, *James Douglas, 1863* (detail), HP2652/A-1228, BCARS. 230, *The Fanny Bailey, built in 1856*, by J. Hunter (detail), Collection of the Confederation Art Gallery and Museum. Purchased with the assistance of the government of Canada through terms of the cultural property export and import act, 1980. 233, *Striking it Rich*, Phyllis Arnold. 236, N7934, PAM. 237 *Hon. Alexander Mackenzie* (detail), C-10460, NAC. 239, *Sir John A, Macdonald* (detail), NA-1375-1, GM. 239, *Skating on the St. Lawrence* (detail), *1894*, P6005, Quebec Archives. 241, *William Cornelius Van Horne* (detail), C-8549, NAC. 242, *The Last Spike*, NA 3012-4, GM. 244, *Lieutenant Colonel George A. French, Commissioner* (detail), NA-23-1, GM. 245, *Main Street of Fort McLeod on the island, 1880*, by George Anderton (photographer), Medicine Hat (detail), NA-1071-1, GM. 245, *Jerry Potts–Famous Guide and Interpreter of the NWMP (detail)*, Negative 756, photo credit: RCMP-GRC/756. 246, *The Blackfoot Treaty, 1877, Crowfoot Speaking*, by Bruce Stapleton, NA-40-1, GM. 249, *Louis Riel (in his heavy coat)* (detail), NA-504-3, GM. 251, *Battle of Batoche*, B.1730, PAA, E. Brown Collection. 252, *Trial of Louis Riel, Regina*, by A. Bonneau, 1885 (detail), NA-1081-3, GM. 253, *Gabriel Dumont* (detail), R-A6277, Saskatchewan Archives Board. 253, *Big Bear* (detail), C-17430, NAC. 253, *Poundmaker* (detail), PA-28853, NAC. 253, *General Middleton* (detail), ACC6876#23, Archives of Ontario. 254, *Sir Wilfrid Laurier* (detail), C-688, NAC. 256, *Horse Hills School, Horse Hills, Alberta*, B.3955, PAA, E. Brown Collection. 257, *Land Rush at the Prince Albert Court House*, ca. 1907, R-A4557-2, Saskatchewan Archives Board. 257, *Saskatchewan and Alberta Exhibits, Chicago (International Grain and Hay Show), 1921*, by Dr. John Lucas, NA-1619-4, GM. 258, *Cover of Dutch emigration booklet on western Canada, 1884*, NA-1083-1, GM. 258, *Clifford Sifton* (detail), PAM. 259, *Woman cutting oats, with team and mower, Beynon, Alberta, c.1909*, NC-43-13, Glenbow Archives, Calgary, Alberta. 260, *Pioneer Log Shack*, B.9945, PAA, E. Brown Collection. 260, *Wheatfield Near Wetaskiwin*, NA-303-158 GM. 260, *Milner's Coal Mine, Edmonton, 1902*, B.1539, PAA, E. Brown Collection. 261, *Pioneers outside sod shack*, Haneyville area, NA474-7, GM. 261, *Cowan Ranch near Calgary, Dog Pound Creek, 1905*, P.226, H. Pollard Collection, PAA. 261, *Homesteaders Shack near Lloydminster, c.1902*, P457, PAA, H. Pollard Collection. 261, *Wheat farming, cutting and bundling*, NA-2420-4, GM. 262, *Edmonton from the top of Queen's Hotel, 1902*, B.5050, PAA, E. Brown Collection. 262, *Winnipeg Streets, Munc. 1905, North from Portage*, W10338, PAM. 262, *General Store, c.1900*, NA-559-12, GM. 262, *Wetaskiwin, 1906*, NA-559-10, GM. 263, *New Canadians in native costume* (detail), B.7235, PAA, E. Brown Collection. 264, NA-695-1, GM. 264, *Japanese Family, Vancouver* (detail), PA 66890, NAC. 265, *John Ware and family, negro rancher, c.1896*, NA-263-1, Glenbow Archives, Calgary, Alberta. 268, *Sir Wilfrid Laurier's Inauguration Ceremony, September 1st, 1905* (detail), B.6661, PAA, E. Brown Collection. 268, *Confederation Celebrations in Edmonton, September 1905*, NA-1043-1, GM. 268, *A.C. Rutherford, September 1909* (detail), A.439, PAA. 268, *General View of Old Fort Edmonton, Legislative Building, and the High Level Bridge, 1912* (detail), B. 6608, PAA, E. Brown Collection. 269, *Inauguration Ceremonies, Regina, 1905* (detail), R-B-1095, Saskatchewan Archives Board. 269, *Walter Scott* (detail), R-A2470, Saskatchewan Archives Board. 269, *Arches on South Railway Street*, R-13930, Saskatchewan Archives Board.

Index

D

E

W

XYZ

43092